John C Mitchell

LOGIC AND COMPUTATION

Cambridge Tracts in Theoretical Computer Science

Titles in the series

LOGIC AND COMPUTATION

Interactive Proof with Cambridge LCF

LAWRENCE C. PAULSON

Computer Laboratory, University of Cambridge

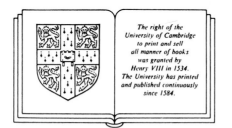

The right of the
University of Cambridge
to print and sell
all manner of books
was granted by
Henry VIII in 1534.
The University has printed
and published continuously
since 1584.

CAMBRIDGE UNIVERSITY PRESS

Cambridge

New York   Port Chester

Melbourne   Sydney

Published by the Press Syndicate of the University of Cambridge
The Pitt Building, Trumpington Street, Cambridge CB2 1RP
40 West 20th Street, New York, NY 10011, USA
10 Stamford Road, Oakleigh, Melbourne 3166, Australia

© Cambridge University Press 1987

First published 1987
First paperback edition 1990

Printed in Great Britain at the University Press, Cambridge

British Library cataloguing in publication data
Paulson, Lawrence C.
Logic and computation: interactive proof with Cambridge LCF — (Cambridge tracts in theoretical computer science).
1. Cambridge LCF (Computer system)
2. Computable functions – Data processing
I. Title
004.1'25   QA9.59
Library of Congress cataloguing in publication data available

ISBN 0 521 34632 0 hardback
ISBN 0 521 39560 7 paperback

To Sue
and to my parents

Contents

Preface

Growing numbers of computer scientists recognise the importance of formal methods of system design [48]. LCF and ML are often mentioned, seldom understood. There is a wide literature, as the bibliography attests. Gordon, Milner, and Wadsworth [41] describe Edinburgh LCF, with a few remarkable examples. The present book aims to make Cambridge LCF accessible to a wide audience.

Serious students of LCF are of several kinds. Some would like an introduction to formal reasoning about computable functions. Others are interested in the principles of the machine implementation. And a few want to perform large proofs in Cambridge LCF, and require a comprehensive description.

Cambridge LCF is not the answer to all problems in formal methods. Like Edinburgh LCF its concern is denotational semantics, domain theory, and functional programming. Related systems support other formal methods, but none supports Z, VDM, CSP, CCS, or Hoare-style verification. Some 'formal' methods lack a precise meaning, making machine implementation impossible. However the goal of formal methods — introducing rigor into computer system design — can be achieved in LCF.

How to read this book

People find LCF difficult to approach because it requires familiarity with a mass of background material. The book consists of two parts. Part I outlines the mathematical preliminaries: elementary logic and domain theory. Many advocates of formal methods have a lamentably weak grasp of this fundamental material. Part II describes Cambridge LCF in enough detail to serve as a reference manual, though operating instructions should be supplied with the software.

Chapter 1 is an informal survey of the LCF family: the many systems descended from Edinburgh LCF. Their common features are the fundamental principles of LCF. A historical survey gives an impression of what can be done with LCF. Next comes the mathematical background required for an informed use of Cambridge LCF. Chapter 2 describes inference rules and first order logic, while Chapter 3 describes the lambda calculus and domain theory. Chapter 4 considers the representation of data structures in domain theory, and the derivation of structural induction. Ideas, motivations, and methods are stressed above technique. Space does not permit complete rigor. You should have some familiarity with mathematics: sets, ordered pairs, relations, and functions. Elementary computability theory would be helpful.

Chapters 5 through 9 describe each facet of Cambridge LCF: syntax, inference rules, theories, tactics and tacticals, and rewriting. The principles of implementation are explained by dissecting examples of the code. After these chapters you should be able to build your own theorem prover. Each chapter progresses from ideas to basic operations to advanced ones. Unless you intend to use Cambridge LCF, you may want to skip sections towards the end of a chapter. You should be familiar with Standard ML. Chapter 10 presents several sample sessions, including proofs about the natural numbers and infinite sequences.

You can read just Part I if your interest is mainly in the underlying mathematics. On the other hand, if you are familiar with domain theory then you might begin with Part II and refer to Part I only when needed. Within each part, read the chapters in order. Most chapters end with discussion and further reading. The examples and exercises extend the material: they should not be ignored. An exercise often depends on previous ones. The symbol □ terminates proofs.

The book can be used for self study or as a text in a graduate or advanced undergraduate course. It can be used to study Cambridge LCF in particular or machine assisted proof in general. It may be helpful for understanding related theorem provers like Nuprl and HOL.

While writing this book I noticed many deficiencies in Cambridge LCF. After the systematic overview of logic in Chapter 2, LCF's tactics look like a bag of tricks. The worst problems have been corrected, but the real never quite attains the ideal.

How to obtain Cambridge LCF

For information on getting Cambridge LCF, write to

> The Software Engineering Group
> Rutherford Appleton Laboratory
> Chilton, Didcot OX11 0QX
> United Kingdom

Acknowledgements

The most important concepts of ML and LCF are due to Robin Milner. He and Michael Gordon, Lockwood Morris, Malcolm Newey, and Chris Wadsworth implemented Edinburgh LCF. My work involved frequent discussions with Gordon. Gérard Huet, Guy Cousineau, and their colleagues at INRIA (Roquencourt, France) improved the ML compiler. Mikael Hedlund of the Rutherford Appleton Laboratory converted Cambridge LCF to Standard ML. The British Science and Engineering Research Council provided funding over many years. Thanks also to

Rod Burstall, Avra Cohn, Carl Gunter, Brian Monahan, Richard Waldinger, and Glynn Winskel; I apologize to anyone who has been omitted.

The editors Ernest Kirkwood and Keith van Rijsbergen gave advice on writing the book. Thierry Coquand, Francisco Corella, Jeff Joyce, Thomas Melham, and anonymous referees commented on the text. Gordon and Milner provided some of the bibliographic references.

Of the Computer Laboratory staff I am particularly grateful to Piete Brooks, Martyn Johnson, and Graham Titmus for keeping the machines running, and to Professor Roger Needham for keeping the Department running.

Part I

Preliminaries

Chapter 1

Survey and History of LCF

Cambridge LCF is an interactive theorem prover for reasoning about computable functions. The terms of its logic, PPλ, constitute a tiny functional programming language. Cambridge LCF can be used for experimenting with first order proof; studying abstract constructions in domain theory; comparing the denotational semantics of programming languages; and verifying functional programs. It can reason about both strict and lazy evaluation.

There are many theorem provers in the LCF family. Each is descended from Edinburgh LCF and retains its fundamental ideas:

- The user interacts with the prover through a programmable meta language, ML.

- Logical formulae, theorems, rules, and proof strategies are ML data.

- The prover guarantees soundness: it checks each inference and records each assumption.

Edinburgh LCF was developed in order to experiment with Scott's Logic of Computable Functions [41]. It performed many proofs involving denotational semantics and functional programming.

Cambridge LCF extended the logic of Edinburgh LCF with ∨, ∃, ⟺, and predicates, improved the efficiency, and added several inference mechanisms. It has been used in proofs about functional programming and several other theorem provers have been built from it.

LCF_LSM was developed for reasoning about digital circuits in a formalism related to CCS [32]. It verified some realistic devices [39], but is now obsolete.

HOL supports Church's Higher Order Logic [37], a general mathematical formalism. It is mainly used to prove digital circuits correct.

Another system supports a higher order *Calculus of Constructions* that can represent many other calculi. Coquand and Huet's examples include definitions of logical connectives and data types [27]. Proofs include Tarski's fixed point theorem and Newman's lemma about confluence of Noetherian relations.

The *Gothenburg Type Theory* system [81] supports Martin-Löf's Constructive Type Theory [65,74], a logic and specification language for computation.

Nuprl supports a similar constructive type theory [26]. It is the most sophisticated of all these systems. Proofs are edited using windows and mouse. From a proof of 'for all x there exists some y' it can extract a program to compute this function.

1.1   The structure of LCF

A typical version of LCF includes the meta language ML, a logic such as PPλ, subgoaling functions (tactics and tacticals), a simplifier, and commands for maintaining logical theories.

1.1.1   The meta language ML

LCF has a *programmable* meta language, ML. Every command is an ML function. Writing ML code adds commands and functions to LCF. ML and a few critical functions are implemented in Lisp. The standard rules and tactics consist of 5000 lines of ML.

ML is an important spin-off from LCF. Designed specifically for theorem proving, it applies to the whole area of symbolic computation. Its data structures allow tree and list processing rather like Lisp. ML supports functional programming; it includes higher order functions. ML supports imperative programming; it includes references and assignments. Exceptions (or *failures*) can be raised and handled. Exceptions allow a function to signal that it cannot compute a result, so that an alternative function can be tried.

ML was the first language to use Milner's polymorphic type system [67]. It prevents run-time type errors while retaining much of the flexibility of untyped languages. The programmer may state type restrictions or omit them. A *polymorphic* type contains type variables; a value of that type has also every instance of that type, obtained by substituting types for type variables. For instance, the function *length*, for taking the length of a list, has type $(\alpha\ list) \rightarrow int$. This function can be applied to a list of elements of any type, and returns the type *int*.

After many dialects started to appear, Milner convened the ML community to develop a Standard [45]. Standard ML is larger and more powerful than its predecessor. The main extensions are recursive data structures, function definitions by patterns, exceptions of arbitrary type, reference types, and modules. Cambridge LCF was converted to Standard ML in 1987. Although all interaction with LCF takes place via ML, only advanced users need to write serious programs.

1.1.2 Inference in the logic, PPλ

Most LCF proofs are conducted in PPλ, a first order logic for domain theory. Theorems are proved with respect to assumptions, the *natural deduction* formalization. If $A_1, \ldots, A_n, B$ are formulae, then $A_1, \ldots, A_n \vdash B$ means B is true if the assumptions $A_1, \cdots, A_n$ are all true.

The logic is embedded in ML as an ML data type *form* of formulae, with axioms and rules for proving theorems. Logical formulae are ML values: functions can take them apart and put them together. Theorems are values of the abstract data type *thm*. Type-checking guarantees that a theorem is constructed by axioms and inference rules, not by manipulation of its representation. Axioms are predeclared ML identifiers; rules are functions from theorems to theorems.

1.1.3 Tactics and tacticals

Applying inference rules to theorems produces other theorems. This is *forwards* proof. Most people work in the *backwards* direction. Start with a *goal*, the theorem to be proved. Reduce goals to simpler subgoals until all have been solved. Functions called *tactics* reduce goals to subgoals. A complete tactical proof may be imagined as a tree whose nodes are goals and whose leaves are known theorems.

The tactic *CONJ_TAC* reduces any goal of the form $A_1, \ldots, A_n \vdash A \wedge B$ to the two goals $A_1, \ldots, A_n \vdash A$ and $A_1, \ldots, A_n \vdash B$. It *fails* (raises an exception) if the goal is not a conjunction.

The tactic *DISCH_TAC* reduces the goal $A_1, \ldots, A_n \vdash A \Longrightarrow B$ to the subgoal $A_1, \ldots, A_n, A \vdash B$, which is the goal of proving B assuming A plus the previous assumptions.

The tactic *ACCEPT_ASM_TAC* reduces the goal $A_1, \ldots, A_n \vdash A$ to an empty subgoal list if A is A_i for some i, and otherwise fails. A goal is solved when it is reduced to an empty subgoal list.

These three tactics can prove any goal of the form $\vdash A \Longrightarrow (B \Longrightarrow A \wedge B)$. Calling *DISCH_TAC* gives the goal $A \vdash B \Longrightarrow A \wedge B$. Calling *DISCH_TAC* again gives $A, B \vdash A \wedge B$. Calling *CONJ_TAC* gives the two goals $A, B \vdash A$ and $A, B \vdash B$. Both are solved by *ACCEPT_ASM_TAC*.

Operators called *tacticals* combine tactics into larger ones. *THEN* combines two tactics *sequentially*; *ORELSE* combines two *alternative* tactics; *REPEAT* makes a tactic *repetitive*. Tacticals can express the above proof in many ways. A literal rendering of the four steps is

DISCH_TAC THEN DISCH_TAC THEN CONJ_TAC THEN ACCEPT_ASM_TAC

A tactic that can perform many similar proofs is

REPEAT(DISCH_TAC ORELSE CONJ_TAC ORELSE ACCEPT_ASM_TAC)

Tactics and tacticals form a level of abstraction, in ML, above theorems and
rules. A tactic that reduces the goal $\vdash A$ to the subgoals $\vdash B_1, \cdots, \vdash B_n$ also
returns a function that takes the list of theorems $\vdash B_1, \cdots, \vdash B_n$ to the theorem
$\vdash A$. Once every subgoal has been solved, these functions are put together to
produce the desired theorem as value of type *thm*. Tacticals and interactive proof
commands do this bookkeeping.

1.1.4 Theories

An LCF *theory* contains a signature: the names of constants, types, and predicates.
It also contains a set of axioms. A logical theory contains all consequences of its
axioms; an LCF theory contains a finite number of theorems, proved and stored
by user command. An LCF theory is stored on a *theory file*, which can be loaded
in a later session for proving additional theorems.

A new theory can be built above other theories, its *parents*. It can itself become
the parent of later ones, forming a hierarchy of theories. Consider a theory *nat* of
the natural numbers, and a theory *list* of lists. A theory defining the length of a
list would have parents *nat* and *list*. A long proof involves months of interactive
sessions and dozens of theories.

1.1.5 Rewriting

Most proofs rely heavily on the *simplifier*, which applies rewrite rules and eliminates tautologies in terms, formulae, or theorems. It is most commonly used, via
a standard tactic, to simplify goals.

A theorem like[1]

$$\vdash f(x,y) \equiv g(x, h(y))$$

is a *rewrite rule*. The simplifier instantiates the variables x and y by pattern matching. Searching in the goal, it replaces every occurrence of $f(t,u)$ by $g(t, h(u))$. A
theorem like

$$\vdash P(x,y) \Longrightarrow f(h(x), y) \equiv h(y)$$

is an *implicative* rewrite rule. The simplifier replaces $f(h(t), u)$ by $h(u)$ whenever
it can prove $P(t, u)$ by recursively invoking simplification.

The simplifier makes use of local assumptions. When simplifying a formula
like $f(x,y) \equiv g(x, h(y)) \Longrightarrow B$, the simplifier assumes the rewrite rule $f(x,y) \equiv
g(x, h(y))$ while simplifying B.

Simplification is not arbitrary symbol crunching. Every step is justified by a
theorem.

---

[1]In LCF, $f(x,y) \equiv g(x, h(y))$ means $f(x,y)$ equals $g(x, h(y))$ for all x and y.

1.2 A brief history

In 1969 Dana Scott developed a Logic for Computable Functions, formalizing a new mathematical model of computability. Through its careful treatment of nontermination the model could handle not only numbers and lists, but also unbounded lists and similar infinite structures. Functions were also data: a function could operate on other functions.

Robin Milner, to perform proofs in this logic, developed the theorem prover Stanford LCF [66]. Stanford LCF performed interesting proofs but required tedious repetition of commands. Milner decided to provide a meta language in which a theorem prover could be programmed; the result was Edinburgh LCF. Edinburgh LCF performed many proofs and was adopted as the basis of several other theorem provers. Many of these take radical new directions; Cambridge LCF closely follows Edinburgh LCF.

The following history is incomplete. It concentrates on proofs performed by my colleagues at Edinburgh and Cambridge. Much other work is in progress, and I apologize to everyone whose work is neglected.

1.2.1 Proofs involving denotational semantics

For her dissertation [20], A. J. Cohn verified three program schemes for recursion removal; a compiler from an **if-while** language into a **goto** language; and a compiler for an abstract language with recursive procedures.

The compiler proofs involve denotational definitions of direct and continuation semantics, and also operational definitions. The second compiler involves four semantic definitions, descending from an abstract to a machine orientation. For the source language Cohn gives a standard denotational semantics, a closure semantics, and a stack semantics. The target machine has an operational semantics. The equivalence between the highest and the lowest level is proved as three equivalences between adjacent levels. Due to the proof's size and complexity, Cohn performed it only on paper. She later proved in LCF that the standard and closure semantics are equivalent [22].

Sokołowski has studied a simple programming language, expressing the **while** command as an infinite nest of **if** commands. He proves the equivalence of a denotational semantics and a Hoare-style axiomatic semantics [95]. The proof that a Hoare rule is sound requires routine but tedious processing: expanding definitions and following chains of implications. Sokołowski gives a search tactic that verifies every rule except the **while** rule, which requires fixed point induction.

Mulmuley has developed theories and tactics for proving the existence of inclusive (recursively defined) predicates [72]. These occur in compiler proofs as the *simulation relation* $x \sim y$ between the denotational semantics of the source

language and the operational semantics of the target machine. Although domain
theory handles recursively defined *functions*, recursive *predicates* may cause inconsistency. Justifying an inclusive predicate involves a morass of technical detail.

Inclusive predicates were a major concern in Cohn's compiler proof. Her simple
language and machine, and intermediate semantic levels, allow simulation relations
of the form $x \sim y$ if and only if $f(x) \equiv g(y)$, for functions f and g. Such relations
need no justification but are rarely useful. Mulmuley's techniques pave the way
for more ambitious compiler proofs.

Mulmuley has LCF theories of the universal domain **U** and the domain **V** of
finitary projections of **U**. The correspondence between domains and elements of
V gives quantification over domains in PPλ. Asked to prove the existence of a
predicate, Mulmuley's system generates goals and submits them to appropriate
tactics, based on rewriting and resolution. The system, which totals sixty pages
of ML, handles several predicates in the literature. It verifies Stoy's predicate
automatically [96]; in another example, only one goal out of sixteen requires human
assistance. Mulmuley relies on a machine-verified predicate in his construction of
fully abstract models of the lambda-calculus [73].

1.2.2   Verification of functional programs

Leszczyłowski verified the 'algebraic laws' of Backus's functional language FP by
defining the FP operations [60]. He also proved [59] the termination of the function NORM, which puts conditional expressions into normal form by repeatedly
replacing

$$\text{IF}(\text{IF}(u, v, w), y, z) \qquad \text{by} \qquad \text{IF}(u, \text{IF}(v, y, z), \text{IF}(w, y, z)) \ .$$

That NORM always terminates is far from obvious. Leszczyłowski proved by struc-
tural induction on x that $\text{NORM}(\text{IF}(x, y, z))$ terminates for all x, y, z such that x is
defined and $\text{NORM}(y)$ and $\text{NORM}(z)$ both terminate. The termination of $\text{NORM}(x)$
for all defined x follows by induction.

Boyer and Moore devised this termination example [12]. Their theorem-prover
only accepts recursive functions that it can prove total.[2] They prove that NORM
is total by considering two numerical measures on conditional expressions. I have
found a proof, with the same structure as the LCF one, in a logic of total functions.
Termination is expressed via well-founded relations instead of partial functions.
My paper includes a termination proof in Cambridge LCF [79].

Cohn and Milner proved the correctness of a parser for expressions composed
of atoms, unary operators, and binary operators within parentheses [25,68]. The
proof is by structural induction on expressions, followed by rewriting and simple

---

[2]The function f is *total* if $f(x)$ is defined for all values of x; otherwise f is *partial*. A nonter-
minating program gives rise to a partial function.

resolution. A more interesting parser uses information about operator precedence [21]. Both parsers are verified against a function for printing an expression. Correctness is stated thus: printing an expression then parsing it yields the original expression. Chisholm has derived a similar parsing algorithm with the help of the Gothenburg Type Theory system [18].

S. Holmström verified several sorting algorithms in Edinburgh LCF. His paper compares LCF with the Boyer/Moore and Affirm theorem provers [49].

I recently verified a function for unification [76]. As an example, the paper presents the proof of a theorem about substitution, describing the workings of Cambridge LCF in detail. Manna and Waldinger developed a theory of unification in order to study the synthesis of a unification algorithm [63]. The theory concerns lists, finite sets, expressions, substitutions, and unifiers, comprising two dozen propositions. Its translation into PPλ is straightforward: quantifiers must be restricted to defined values, and every function proved total. The LCF proof contains nearly three hundred stored theorems, mostly trivial termination proofs and basic properties of lists, sets, truth values, and numbers. Manna and Waldinger prove the final theorem by well-founded induction. PPλ does not provide this general induction principle; correctness is proved by structural induction on the natural numbers followed by structural induction on expressions.

The termination of the unification function relies on the correctness of the results of the nested recursive calls it makes, so termination and correctness must be proved simultaneously [79]. PPλ has the flexibility required for difficult termination proofs. The price is that termination must be explicitly considered at all times.

My first experiments with the unification proof used Edinburgh LCF. That experience influenced the design of Cambridge LCF.

1.2.3 Verification of digital circuits

M. J. C. Gordon's LCF_LSM is a theorem prover, built from Cambridge LCF, for verifying hardware [32]. His Logic for Sequential Machines includes terms that denote synchronous devices, with a binding mechanism to indicate their connections. The next state of a device depends on its current state and inputs. Gordon used LCF_LSM to verify a simple sixteen-bit computer [33]. Its eight instructions were implemented using an ALU, memory, various registers, a thirty-bit microcode controller, and ROM holding twenty-six microinstructions. Gordon defined bit vector operations such as field extraction and addition. Concise axioms specified each component and the circuitry implementing the computer (host machine), and also the intended behavior of the computer (target machine).

J. M. J. Herbert used LCF_LSM to verify an ECL chip designed for the Cambridge Fast Ring [39]. The chip, an interface between the Ring and the slower logic, consisted of NOR gates, inverters, and flipflops, equivalent to about 360 gates. It was developed using the Cambridge Design Automation system for gate arrays, which Herbert modified to produce a file of LCF_LSM axioms describing the chip. Herbert verified the chip with respect to its functional specification. Error messages from LCF_LSM helped to locate flaws in the specification and wiring.

Verification does not guarantee perfection. When fabricated and put into service, the ECL chip displayed minor problems! The error was traced to a discrepancy between the specification of the chip and the way it was actually used. A system is never correct: at best, it is consistent with its specification.

Melham verified an associative memory unit in LCF_LSM, uncovering errors in the gating and microcode [7]. The unit was not designed as a verification example but for an application: to store message identifiers in a network interface device. It contains an AM2910 microprogram controller, memories, counters, busses, and drivers: a total of 37 TTL chips. Correctness of the initialized device was proved; correctness of the initialization sequence was not attempted. The proof, developed over thirty months of part time effort, comprises 4800 lines of ML and requires ten and a half hours of computer time.

As a successor to LCF_LSM, Gordon has implemented a *higher order logic* (HOL) on top of Cambridge LCF [34,35,37,38]. He uses it to represent hardware: each device is a predicate, time is an integer, and each wire is a function over time. A circuit is a conjunction of the predicates representing its component devices; the arguments of a predicate represent the wires connected to the device. To illustrate the power of higher order logic, Gordon specifies devices from a CMOS inverter to a sequential multiplier [36]. Herbert compares LCF_LSM with HOL in specifying the Cambridge Fast Ring chip [46]. Another example is the counter verification by Cohn and Gordon [24].

Recent work includes Cohn's verification of the Viper microprocessor [23]. This microprocessor, designed at the Royal Signals and Radar Establishment (RSRE) for safety-critical applications, may become the first real computer to be formally verified. In the notation of LCF_LSM, RSRE staff wrote Viper's functional specification and informally proved the correctness of its implementation in a state-transition machine. Cohn formalized this work in HOL, uncovering minor errors that fortunately were not reflected in the hardware. Typical of hardware verification are gigantic formulae and proofs: the Viper proof involves more than a million primitive inferences. The next stage of Cohn's work will be to verify the implementation at a level closer to that of circuits.

1.3   Further reading

Other books describing particular theorem provers include Boyer and Moore [12] and Constable et al. [26]. Bledsoe and Loveland's survey [9] is interesting but hardly mentions LCF or other European work.

Several new theorem provers borrow ideas from LCF. Hanna and Daeche's *Veritas* [43] uses a purely functional meta language, Miranda.[3] My *Isabelle* uses Standard ML, represents a rule as a construction instead of a function, and emphasizes unification during inference [80].

You will not get far in this book unless you know Standard ML. The definition [45] is not easy to read; Harper [44] and Wikström [100] have written gentle introductions.

Milner gives a readable introduction to rules, tactics, and induction in Edinburgh LCF [68]. Gordon demonstrates how to implement a simple logic in ML [31]. The Nuprl book by Constable et al. gives a sometimes different interpretation of these ideas [26].

Of the proofs mentioned above, several are described in easily available papers. These include Cohn's proof of semantic equivalence [22], my proof of a unification algorithm [76], and Melham's hardware proof [7]. The earlier theorem provers are still of historical interest. Milner and Weyhrauch describe a simple compiler correctness proof in Stanford LCF [70]. Gordon and Herbert's article [39] includes a readable introduction to LCF_LSM.

---

[3]'Miranda' is a trademark of Research Software Ltd.

Chapter 2

Formal Proof in First Order Logic

Cambridge LCF proofs are conducted in PPλ, a logic of domain theory. Leaving aside domains — discussed in later chapters — PPλ is a typical natural deduction formulation of first order logic. This chapter introduces formal proof, first order logic, natural deduction, and sequent calculi. The discussion of semantics is brief and informal; the emphasis is how to construct formal proofs. See a logic textbook for a proper account of model theory.

If you seriously intend to construct proofs, memorizing the inference rules is not enough. You must learn the individual characteristics and usage of each rule. Many sample proofs are given; study every line. Work the exercises.

2.1 Fundamentals of formal logic

A *formal logic* or *calculus* is a game for producing symbolic objects according to given rules. Sometimes the motivation of the rules is vague; with the lambda calculus there ensued a protracted enquiry into the meaning of lambda expressions. But usually the rules are devised with respect to a well-understood meaning or *semantics*. Too many of us perform plausible derivations using notations that have no precise meaning. Most mathematical theories are interpreted in set theory: each term corresponds to a set; each rule corresponds to a fact about sets. Set theory is taken to be the foundation of everything else. Its axioms are justified by informal but widely accepted intuitions that sets exist, the union of two sets is a set, and so forth. When relying on intuition we must be extremely careful: Russell's Paradox demolished the prevailing notion of set, together with years of Frege's work.

Imagine that arithmetic was invented for counting sheep. In ancient times there were many systems of numerals, each with its particular calculation methods; any system that did not conform to the actual numbers of sheep was soon abandoned. Just as arithmetic is simpler and more precise than moving sheep around, formal logic frees logicians from the slippery ambiguities of human language.

A formal logic comprises *assertions* and *inference rules*. The assertions A, B, C, ... express meaningful statements. Each inference rule has the form 'from A_1

and ... and A_n conclude B', for $n \geq 0$:

$$\frac{A_1 \ldots A_n}{B}$$

The assertions $A_1 \ldots A_n$ are the *premises* of the rule, and B is the *conclusion*. The *theorems* are those assertions that can be proved by applying inference rules to other theorems. In order to have any theorems there must be at least one *axiom*, a rule with no premises. A proof can be written as a tree whose root is the theorem, whose branches are rules, and whose leaves are axioms. Natural deduction complicates this structure: leaves can be assumptions, and assumptions can be discharged.

Inference rules allow formal proofs to be constructed without thinking about the meaning of each formula: dumb machines can prove theorems. But we must remain aware of the difference between *provability* and *truth*. Ideally, an assertion should be provable in the logic if and only if it is true in the semantics. Every theorem should be true and every truth a theorem. An inference rule is *sound* provided that if every premise is true, then so is the conclusion. If every inference rule is sound then every theorem of the logic is true; if not, that logic serves little purpose. A logic is *complete* if every true assertion is a theorem (has a formal proof). Completeness is usually unattainable: Gödel demonstrated that no logic allowing nontrivial reasoning about arithmetic can be complete.

The 'differential calculus' is indeed a formal calculus. It has expressions like $\frac{du}{dx}$ and rules like $(\frac{d}{dx})(uv) = u\frac{dv}{dx} + v\frac{du}{dx}$. Each expression and rule has a complicated mathematical justification. The rules are used long after their justification has been forgotten.

2.2   Introduction to first order logic

First order logic is the most familiar formal language for mathematics.

2.2.1   Syntax

In an arbitrary logic the set of assertions can be completely abstract. But typically it is described by a grammar: each assertion is constructed from atomic symbols using logical connectives.

Terms denote mathematical values such as sets, functions, or numbers. Let there be an infinite set of *variables* and, for each $n \geq 0$, a set of n-place *function symbols*.[1] A *term* is a variable or a function application $f(t_1, \ldots, t_n)$, where f is an n-place function symbol and $t_1, \ldots, t_n$ are terms. A 0-place function symbol is a *constant symbol*; the term $c()$ is invariably written c.

---

[1] An n-place function symbol is one that requires n arguments.

The assertions of first order logic, called *formulae*, are built up from terms. Let there be a set of n-place *predicate symbols* for each $n \geq 0$. An *atomic formula* has the form $P(t_1, \ldots, t_n)$, where P is an n-place predicate symbol and $t_1, \ldots, t_n$ are terms. Every formula either is an atomic formula or is one of $A \wedge B$, $A \vee B$, $A \implies B$, $\neg A$, $\forall x.A$, $\exists x.A$, or (A), where A and B are formulae and x is a variable. Observe that every formula contains at least one predicate symbol.

Here are some conventions for writing formulae.

The *bi-implication* $A \iff B$ abbreviates $(A \implies B) \wedge (B \implies A)$. It can alternatively be taken as a connective in its own right.

Precedence conventions lessen the need for parentheses in formulae. The symbol $\neg$ binds most tightly, followed by $\wedge$, $\vee$, $\implies$, and $\iff$ in decreasing order.

The scope of a quantifier extends as far to the right as possible. One quantifier can bind several variables at once.

Examples:

$$
\begin{array}{rcl}
\forall x.\, A \wedge B \vee A \wedge C & \text{abbreviates} & \forall x.\, ((A \wedge B) \vee (A \wedge C)) \\
A \implies B \iff \exists z.\, B \implies C & \text{abbreviates} & (A \implies B) \iff \exists z.\, (B \implies C) \\
\forall xy.A & \text{abbreviates} & \forall x.\forall y.A \\
\exists xyz.\, P(x) \wedge Q(y, z) & \text{abbreviates} & \exists x.\exists y.\exists z.\, (P(x) \wedge Q(y, z))
\end{array}
$$

2.2.2 Semantics

The semantics of first order logic is usually expressed in set theory. An *interpretation* or *model* assigns a mathematical value to each symbol. The variables, functions, and predicates are all defined with respect to a fixed set (or *universe*). Each variable is assigned an element of the universe; each n-place function symbol is assigned a function on the universe; each n-place predicate symbol is assigned an n-place relation over the universe. Under an interpretation, each term has a value and each atomic formula is either true or false. The truth of the other formulae is determined as follows:

The *conjunction* $A \wedge B$ is true if both A and B are.

The *disjunction* $A \vee B$ is true if either A or B is.

The *implication* $A \implies B$ is true provided that if A is true then so is B.

The *negation* $\neg A$ is true if A is false.

The *universal quantification* $\forall x.A$ is true if A is true for every x.

The *existential quantification* $\exists x.A$ is true if A is true for some x.

Propositional logic is the logic of the connectives, $\wedge$, $\vee$, $\implies$, and $\neg$. Adding quantifiers gives *first order* logic, sometimes called the *predicate calculus*. Adding quantifiers over formula variables gives *higher order* logic.

2.2.3   Meta and object languages

Consider statements we might make about formulae. 'The negation of a formula is also a formula.' Clear enough. 'The conjunction of a formula with the conjunction of two other formulae implies the conjunction of the conjunction of the first and second formulae with the third.' Eh? Readable statements must use symbols from the logic itself: 'if A is a formula then $\neg A$ is also a formula' or 'the formula $A \wedge (B \wedge C)$ implies $(A \wedge B) \wedge C$'. Clearly this does not mean that the symbol 'A' is itself a formula. We have the classic confusion between an object and its name. The object is a formula; its name is A.

To clear up the confusion we must distinguish the *meta language* from the *object language*. The formal language of terms and formulae is the object language. We make statements about the object language in the meta language. Here the meta language is English augmented with mathematical notation: symbols from the object language, proof trees, and names for object language expressions. Those names are called *syntactic meta variables*:

- names of formulae include A, B, C

- names of terms include r, s, t, u

- names of predicate symbols include P, Q, R

- names of function symbols include f, g, h

- names of object variables include x, y, z

To get additional names, add subscripts and primes: A' and C_3 are names of formulae. But A must never be a predicate symbol: then it would be both a formula and the name of one.

Inference rules are described using syntactic meta variables:

$$\frac{A \qquad B}{A \wedge B}$$

This stands for the infinite set of inferences obtained by replacing A and B by actual formulae.

The programming language ML is the meta language of LCF, providing all manipulation of terms, formulae, theorems, and rules. ML's *quotations* facilitate the construction of object language expressions (Chapter 5). It may be contrasted with Lisp's `QUOTE`, which raises as many problems as it solves. The confusion between an object and its name occurs in programming languages. The assembly language or Lisp programmer has direct access to internal objects, not necessarily through their names.

2.2.4   Natural deduction

Natural deduction is an approach to proof using rules that are designed to mirror human patterns of reasoning. For each logical connective, say ∨, there are two kinds of rules:

- Each *introduction* rule answers the question, 'under what conditions can $A \vee B$ be concluded?'

- Each *elimination* rule answers the question, 'what follows from $A \vee B$?'

Full answers to these questions precisely characterize $A \vee B$. The elimination rules are generally inverses of the introduction rules: introducing $A \vee B$ then immediately eliminating it neither gains nor loses information. Often one connective can be defined in terms of others. In classical logic all the connectives can be defined in terms of ∧, ∨, and ¬. But the natural deduction rule for a connective mentions no others; in a proof, each inference involves only one connective.

There is a complete search procedure for first order logic: if a proof exists, it will be found [30]. In propositional logic the search always terminates, even if no proof exists. The general method for searching for a proof is 'break down' then 'build up'. Elimination rules break down assumptions into smaller assumptions; introduction rules build up conclusions from smaller conclusions.

In natural deduction, certain rules *discharge* an assumption of a premise. The set of assumptions changes during the proof: 'to prove $A \implies B$, assume A and prove B'. The premise of a rule is not a formula but a proof tree with a formula at the root and assumptions in the leaves. The examples ought to show that such proofs are indeed natural.

Intuitionism is a school of the philosophy of mathematics that questions certain tenets of classical logic. Intuitionism demands a *constructive* interpretation of the quantifiers: if $\exists x.A$ is true then the value of x satisfying A should be effectively computable. In certain constructive logics, like Intuitionistic Type Theory [65], proving $\exists x.A$ constructs a function to compute x. The potential applications to the specification and synthesis of programs are attracting attention [26,74]. A proper discussion of intuitionism does not belong here: PPλ is a classical logic. But note: *natural deduction has an intuitionistic orientation*. Classical deduction requires an additional rule and much additional thought.

2.3   Conjunction

The conjunction $A \wedge B$ is true if and only if both A and B are true. The introduction rule states when $A \wedge B$ can be concluded:

$$\frac{A \quad B}{A \wedge B} \qquad (\wedge\text{-intro})$$

The two elimination rules state the consequences of $A \wedge B$:

$$\frac{A \wedge B}{A} \qquad (\wedge\text{-elim-1})$$

$$\frac{A \wedge B}{B} \qquad (\wedge\text{-elim-2})$$

It is not hard to see that these rules capture informal reasoning about conjunction.

Putting the rules together yields proof trees such as

$$\frac{\dfrac{A \wedge B}{B} \qquad \dfrac{A \wedge B}{A}}{B \wedge A}$$

which is a proof of

$$\frac{A \wedge B}{B \wedge A}.$$

This is a *derived rule*; the formula $B \wedge A$ has been proved *under the assumption* $A \wedge B$. In general a proof may depend upon many assumptions:

$$\frac{A \qquad \dfrac{B \qquad C}{B \wedge C}}{A \wedge (B \wedge C)}$$

is a proof of $A \wedge (B \wedge C)$ from the assumptions A, B, and C.

An alternative rule for conjunction elimination discharges assumptions. If $A \wedge B$ is true, then so are A and B; it is sound to assume them when proving something else:

$$\frac{A \wedge B \qquad \dfrac{[A, B]}{C}}{C} \qquad (\wedge\text{-elim 3})$$

The square brackets around A and B indicate that these assumptions are discharged from the proof of C when the rule is applied. Given a proof of $A \wedge B$, and a proof of C from A and B, the rule concludes C.

Example 2.1 Here is a proof of $B \wedge A$ from $A \wedge B$ using the new rule:

$$\frac{A \wedge B \qquad \dfrac{[B] \qquad [A]}{B \wedge A}}{B \wedge A}$$

The assumptions B and A, enclosed in square brackets, are discharged from the proof of $B \wedge A$. It does not matter that B appears to the left of A; the order of assumptions does not matter. Indeed the assumptions need not be used:

$$\frac{A \wedge B \qquad [A]}{A}$$

This is a perfectly sound use of $\wedge$-elim-3, and derives the rule $\wedge$-elim-1. The assumption A is discharged from the trivial proof of itself.

The rule ∧-elim-3 is an inverse of the introduction rule: the proof

$$\frac{\dfrac{A \quad B}{A \wedge B} \qquad \begin{array}{c} [A, B] \\ C \end{array}}{C}$$

is a complicated version of the proof of C from A and B. Those assumptions are discharged from the second premise, but appear also in the first premise. Therefore the conclusion depends upon A and B.

This version of ∧-elimination anticipates the sequent calculus rules for conjunction, and works nicely with the elimination rules for ∨ and ∃.

Exercise 2.1 Derive the rule

$$\frac{A}{A}$$

Exercise 2.2 Derive the rule

$$\frac{(A \wedge B) \wedge C}{A \wedge (B \wedge C)}$$

Exercise 2.3 Show how to transform every proof that uses ∧-elim-3 into one that uses only ∧-elim-1 and ∧-elim-2, and conversely.

2.4 Disjunction

The two introduction rules state that $A \vee B$ can be concluded from either A or B:

$$\frac{A}{A \vee B} \qquad \frac{B}{A \vee B}$$

The elimination rule is

$$\frac{A \vee B \qquad \begin{array}{c} [A] \\ C \end{array} \qquad \begin{array}{c} [B] \\ C \end{array}}{C} \qquad \text{(∨-elim)}$$

The elimination rule is understood by case analysis on $A \vee B$ because C follows from A and also follows from B. Either A or B is true. If A is true then the second premise proves C; if B is true then the third premise proves C.

We now have enough logic to consider interesting examples.

Example 2.2 Here is proof of $B \vee A$ from $A \vee B$:

$$\frac{A \vee B \qquad \begin{array}{c} [A] \\ B \vee A \end{array} \qquad \begin{array}{c} [B] \\ B \vee A \end{array}}{B \vee A}$$

The two ∨-introduction rules are used; ∨-elimination discharges their premises.

Example 2.3 The distributive laws are a good source of examples. A proof of

$$(A \vee C) \wedge (B \vee C) \iff (A \wedge B) \vee C$$

would be excessive, but here is a proof that $A \vee C$ follows from $(A \wedge B) \vee C$:

$$\cfrac{(A \wedge B) \vee C \qquad \cfrac{\cfrac{[A \wedge B]}{A}}{A \vee C} \qquad \cfrac{[C]}{A \vee C}}{A \vee C}$$

Here $\wedge$-elim-1 is used, as well as the disjunction rules. As the number of rules at our disposal grows, the proofs become harder to follow. There is no space for labels on the rules; you must learn to recognize them.

Exercise 2.4 Derive the rule

$$\cfrac{(A \wedge B) \vee C}{(A \vee C) \wedge (B \vee C)}$$

Exercise 2.5 Derive the rule

$$\cfrac{(A \vee C) \wedge (B \vee C)}{(A \wedge B) \vee C}$$

Exercise 2.6 Derive the rule

$$\cfrac{(A \vee B) \wedge C}{(A \wedge C) \vee (B \wedge C)}$$

Exercise 2.7 Derive the rule

$$\cfrac{(A \wedge C) \vee (B \wedge C)}{(A \vee B) \wedge C}$$

2.5 Implication

The introduction rule states that if B follows from A, then conclude $A \implies B$. It is called the *discharge rule* because it discharges the assumption A:

$$\cfrac{\begin{array}{c}[A]\\B\end{array}}{A \implies B}$$

The elimination rule is *Modus Ponens*:

$$\cfrac{A \implies B \qquad A}{B}$$

Example 2.4 An important logical identity is

$$((A \wedge B) \Longrightarrow C) \iff (A \Longrightarrow (B \Longrightarrow C)).$$

Here is the proof in the left to right direction:

$$
\dfrac{
(A \wedge B) \Longrightarrow C \qquad
\dfrac{[A] \qquad [B]}{A \wedge B}
}{
\dfrac{\dfrac{C}{B \Longrightarrow C}}{A \Longrightarrow (B \Longrightarrow C)}
}
$$

The assumptions A and B are discharged at different times: first B, then A. Some authors use numeric labels to keep track of which instance of a rule discharges each assumption. Soon we will have ample motivation for learning a *sequent calculus*, where the assumptions are explicitly listed at every step.

Example 2.5 Here is a proof where every assumption is discharged:

$$
\dfrac{
\dfrac{
\dfrac{[A \Longrightarrow (B \wedge C)] \qquad [A]}{B \wedge C}
}{
\dfrac{B}{A \Longrightarrow B}
}
}{
(A \Longrightarrow (B \wedge C)) \Longrightarrow (A \Longrightarrow B)
}
$$

The proof contains a proof of $A \Longrightarrow B$ from $A \Longrightarrow (B \wedge C)$. This example comes from the identity

$$(A \Longrightarrow (B \wedge C)) \iff (A \Longrightarrow B) \wedge (A \Longrightarrow C)$$

Example 2.6 A generalization of a de Morgan law is

$$((A \vee B) \Longrightarrow C) \iff (A \Longrightarrow C) \wedge (B \Longrightarrow C)$$

As a consequence, $(A \vee B) \Longrightarrow C$ implies $A \Longrightarrow C$. The proof tree:

$$
\dfrac{
(A \vee B) \Longrightarrow C \qquad
\dfrac{[A]}{A \vee B}
}{
\dfrac{C}{A \Longrightarrow C}
}
$$

Exercise 2.8 Explain why the introduction and elimination rules for $\Longrightarrow$ are sound.

Exercise 2.9 Derive the rule

$$\frac{A \implies (B \implies C)}{(A \wedge B) \implies C}$$

Exercise 2.10 Derive the rule

$$\frac{(A \implies B) \wedge (A \implies C)}{A \implies (B \wedge C)}$$

Exercise 2.11 Prove both directions of the identity

$$((A \vee B) \implies C) \iff (A \implies C) \wedge (B \implies C)$$

2.6   Negation

Negation: what could be simpler or more problematical? Cambridge LCF uses Prawitz's [83] formulation of first order logic, where Λ stands for *contradiction* and $\neg B$ abbreviates $B \implies \Lambda$. This view of negation is popular among intuitionists, but is also sound for classical logic.

Since $\neg B$ abbreviates $B \implies \Lambda$, rules about implication encompass negation as special cases. The introduction rule is a special case of $\implies$-introduction; if assuming B leads to contradiction then conclude $\neg B$:

$$\frac{\begin{array}{c}[B]\\ \Lambda\end{array}}{\neg B} \qquad\qquad (\neg\text{-intro})$$

By $\implies$-elimination, $\neg B$ and B lead to contradiction:

$$\frac{\neg B \quad B}{\Lambda} \qquad\qquad (\neg\text{-elim})$$

2.6.1   Contradiction rules

The rules given so far yield *minimal logic*, where Λ is just another symbol. We must make Λ behave like contradiction. The laws of arithmetic illustrate the essential property of contradiction: $0 = 1$ implies every numeric equation. A contradiction rule makes Λ imply every formula.

The classical contradiction rule is, if $\neg B$ leads to contradiction then conclude B:

$$\frac{\begin{array}{c}[\neg B]\\ \Lambda\end{array}}{B} \qquad\qquad (\Lambda C\text{-elim})$$

The name ΛC-elim is short for Λ-elimination in Classical logic. Observe the similarity to $\neg$-introduction with B replaced by $\neg B$. Both rules discharge the assumption $\neg B$, but $\neg$-introduction concludes $\neg\neg B$ instead of B.

A weaker contradiction rule gives intuitionistic logic.

$$\frac{\Lambda}{B} \qquad\qquad (\Lambda I\text{-elim})$$

This is the elimination rule for Λ. It fits the same pattern as the elimination rules for conjunction ($\land$-elim-3), disjunction, and existential quantifier. There is no introduction rule: no set of premises (not involving Λ) imply Λ.

The contradiction rule is the *only* difference between the classical and intuitionistic natural deduction logics. LCF provides both forms of the rule to allow experimentation.

2.6.2 Derived rules for classical reasoning

Classical reasoning in natural deduction is not really natural unless several derived rules are used along with the primitive rules. To prove A it may be necessary to assume $\neg A$ and derive a contradiction. Breaking down $\neg A$ requires derived rules involving negated formulae.

The *double negation law* is

$$\frac{\neg\neg A}{A} \qquad\qquad (\neg\neg\text{-elim})$$

The proof follows directly from the classical contradiction rule, ΛC-elim:

$$\frac{\neg\neg A \qquad [\neg A]}{\dfrac{\Lambda}{A}}$$

The de Morgan law mentioned in Example 2.6 is $\neg(A \lor B) \iff \neg A \land \neg B$.

It suggests two derived rules for negated disjunction:

$$\frac{\neg(A \lor B)}{\neg A} \qquad\qquad (\neg \lor\text{-elim-1})$$

$$\frac{\neg(A \lor B)}{\neg B} \qquad\qquad (\neg \lor\text{-elim-2})$$

These hold in intuitionistic logic: their proofs require only implication and disjunction rules. Here is a proof of $\neg\lor$-elim-1:

$$\frac{\neg(A \lor B) \qquad \dfrac{[A]}{A \lor B}}{\dfrac{\Lambda}{\neg A}}$$

Example 2.7 The *excluded middle*, namely $A \lor \neg A$, is a theorem of classical logic but not of intuitionistic logic. The proof uses the derived rules $\neg\lor$-elim-1 and $\neg\lor$-elim-2, together with classical contradiction (of course):

$$
\cfrac{
\cfrac{[\neg(A \lor \neg A)]}{\neg\neg A} \qquad \cfrac{[\neg(A \lor \neg A)]}{\neg A}
}{
\cfrac{\Lambda}{A \lor \neg A}
}
$$

Example 2.8 The other de Morgan law is $\neg(A \land B) \iff \neg A \lor \neg B$. The left to right direction requires classical logic:

$$
\cfrac{
\neg(A \land B) \qquad \cfrac{\cfrac{\cfrac{[\neg(\neg A \lor \neg B)]}{\neg\neg A}}{A} \qquad \cfrac{\cfrac{[\neg(\neg A \lor \neg B)]}{\neg\neg B}}{B}}{A \land B}
}{
\cfrac{\Lambda}{\neg A \lor \neg B}
}
$$

The bottom inference is classical contradiction; also $\neg\lor$-elim-1, $\neg\lor$-elim-2, and the double negation law appear.

Exercise 2.12 Explain why 'A implies contradiction' means the same as 'not A'.

Exercise 2.13 Prove $\neg\neg(A \lor \neg A)$ without using the classical contradiction rule. (In fact every propositional formula A can be proved in classical logic if and only if $\neg\neg A$ can be proved in intuitionistic logic [29].)

Exercise 2.14 Once we have a symbol for *contradiction*, we can define a symbol for *truth*: give three examples of formal theorems containing no meta variables and depending upon no assumptions.

Exercise 2.15 Derive the rule

$$
\cfrac{(A \implies C) \lor (B \implies C)}{(A \land B) \implies C}
$$

What rule concerning negation is a special case of this?

Exercise 2.16 Derive the rule

$$
\cfrac{\neg(A \implies B)}{A} \qquad\qquad (\neg \implies \text{-elim-1})
$$

Hint: use the classical contradiction rule.

2.7 Understanding quantifiers

Analysis — the field of mathematics underlying the differential calculus — offers many examples of quantification. 'If ϵ is arbitrary such that $P(\epsilon)$, then there exists δ such that $Q(\epsilon, \delta)$.' Quantifiers are obviously indispensable but require great care. The semantics becomes more complicated: what is an arbitrary value? New syntactic issues arise: substitution, free and bound variables. Propositional logic is decidable but first order logic is not: there is no algorithm for determining whether a given formula is a theorem.

Let P be a 1-place predicate symbol. In the semantics, $\forall x.P(x)$ is true whenever P is interpreted as the predicate that holds for all values. In the formal logic, if $\forall x.P(x)$ is a theorem and t is a term then $P(t)$ is a theorem. The correspondence between '$\forall x.P(x)$ holds' and '$P(t)$ holds for every term t' is imperfect because the model may contain values that are not expressed by any term. If the universe is the set of all real numbers, and the function symbols are the ordinary decimal numerals and arithmetic operators, then there are only countably many terms and uncountably many real numbers.

2.7.1 Substitution

Generally A is a formula containing a variable x. The formula $\forall x.A$ asserts that A is true for every assignment of a value to x. Each theorem that follows from $\forall x.A$ is obtained by *substituting* a term t for x in A. We will need to be precise about what substitution means, but for now let us just define a bit of notation: if A is a formula, t is a term, and x is a variable, then $A[t/x]$ is the formula that results from substituting t for x in A. Read $A[t/x]$ as 'A putting t for x'.

Simultaneous substitution for n variables ($n \geq 0$) is useful: $A[t_1/x_1, \ldots, t_n/x_n]$ is the formula that results from simultaneously substituting t_1 for x_1 and $\cdots$ and t_n for x_n in A. Observe that the simultaneous substitution $Q(x, y)[x/y, y/x]$ yields $Q(y, x)$, while the iterated substitution $Q(x, y)[x/y][y/x]$ yields $Q(x, x)[y/x]$ which is $Q(y, y)$.

Substitution is also defined on terms: $u[t_1/x_1, \ldots, t_n/x_n]$ is the term that results from simultaneously substituting t_1 for x_1 and $\cdots$ and t_n for x_n in the term u.

The substitution notation belongs to the meta language, not the object language. The formula $A[t/x]$ does not literally contain the symbols [, /,], or A. Rather it is the result of substitution in the formula denoted by A. The situation in LCF is analogous: substitution is not part of the logic PPλ; instead, substitution functions are available in ML.

2.7.2   Free and bound variables

Let A stand for a formula. In $\forall x.A$, the variable x is said to be *bound*. The name x is not significant: the bound variable can be renamed provided that all its occurrences in A are correspondingly renamed. For example, '$P(x)$ holds for arbitrary x' means the same as '$P(y)$ holds for arbitrary y'. The formula $\forall x.A$ is logically equivalent to $\forall y.A[y/x]$; we can even regard them as syntactically identical. LCF takes a middle course: the formulae $\forall x.A$ and $\forall y.A[y/x]$ are different but can be used interchangably in proofs.

A bound variable must sometimes be renamed prior to substitution. If x and y range over the natural numbers then $\forall x.\, \exists y.\, x \not\equiv y$ is a true formula.[2] Substituting y for x, it is wrong to conclude $\exists y.\, y \not\equiv y$. The problem is the *capture* of a free variable: the free variable y comes into the scope of $\forall y$ and turns into a bound variable. The cure is to define what it means for a variable to occur *free* or *bound* in a term, and to restrict substitution accordingly.

A variable x occurs *bound* in a formula if $\forall x$ or $\exists x$ is part of the formula. More precisely, here are the cases in which x occurs bound in a formula:

- x occurs bound in $\forall y.A$ or $\exists y.A$ if x and y are the same variable or x occurs bound in A

- x occurs bound in $\neg A$ if x occurs bound in A

- x occurs bound in $A \wedge B$, $A \vee B$, or $A \Longrightarrow B$ if x occurs bound in A or x occurs bound in B

A variable x occurs *free* in a formula if it occurs outside the scope of every subformula of the form $\forall y.A$ or $\exists y.A$. More precisely, here are the cases in which x occurs free in a formula:

- x occurs free in $\forall y.A$ or $\exists y.A$ if x and y are different variables and x occurs free in A

- x occurs free in $\neg A$ if x occurs free in A

- x occurs free in $A \wedge B$, $A \vee B$, or $A \Longrightarrow B$ if x occurs free in A or x occurs free in B

- x occurs free in $P(t_1, \ldots, t_n)$ if x occurs in one of $t_1, \ldots, t_n$.

In the substitution $A[t/x]$, the free variables of t stand in danger of becoming bound in A. Substitution requires special care if a free variable of t occurs bound in A. Only free occurrences of x are replaced by t.

In LCF, substitution renames bound variables of A if necessary to avoid the capture of a free variable. Substitution can be precisely defined by induction on the structure of a formula:

---

[2]In domain theory, 'x equals y' is written $x \equiv y$. See next chapter.

- in $\forall y.A$, if x equals y then the result of the substitution is $\forall y.A$. Otherwise, if y is not free in t then the result is $\forall y. A[t/x]$. Otherwise, let z be a variable different from x and every variable occurring in A or t; the result is $\forall z. A[z/y][t/x]$.

- in $\exists y.A$, substitution is similar to the previous case.

- in $\neg A$, the result is $\neg(A[t/x])$

- in $A \wedge B$ the result is $A[t/x] \wedge B[t/x]$

- in $A \vee B$ the result is $A[t/x] \vee B[t/x]$

- in $A \Longrightarrow B$ the result is $A[t/x] \Longrightarrow B[t/x]$

- in $P(u_1, \ldots, u_m)$ the result is $P(u_1[t/x], \ldots, u_m[t/x])$, by substitution in the terms $u_1, \ldots, u_m$.

Example 2.9 In $\forall x.R(x, y, f(z, y))$ there is a bound occurrence of x, a free occurrence of z, and two free occurrences of y. In $P(x) \wedge (\forall x. Q(x, y))$ there is a free occurrence of y, and x occurs both free *and* bound. In order to put y for x in $\forall x. \exists y. x \not\equiv y$, the bound variable y is first renamed to z. From the equivalent formula $\forall x. \exists z. x \not\equiv z$ the conclusion $\exists z. y \not\equiv z$ is valid. LCF invents new variable names by adding primes. It would automatically rename the bound variable y to y' before substituting the free variable y.

The lambda calculus, described in Chapter 3, has similar notions of free and bound variables. Renaming a bound variable is called α-*conversion*. A term can contain bound variables: $\lambda x.t$ has the bound variable x.

Exercise 2.17 Precisely define substitution on terms: $u[t/x]$.

Exercise 2.18 Precisely define simultaneous substitution: $A[t_1/x_1, \ldots, t_n/x_n]$.

2.7.3 The semantics of quantifiers

In order to understand the rules for a symbol it is essential to know the meaning of that symbol. I have omitted discussing the semantics of the familiar connectives $\wedge$, $\vee$, $\Longrightarrow$. Space does not even allow a detailed discussion of quantifiers. But a brief look at the semantics of quantifiers will make the rules easier to understand. The 'proofs' below are just sketches intended for illustration. For a rigorous treatment, see a logic textbook [30,64].

A formula A is *valid* if it is true in every interpretation and for every assignment of values to its free variables. So A is valid if and only if $\forall x.A$ is valid, regardless of whether x is free in A.

Understanding universal introduction

From the above, a proof of A should also count as a proof of $\forall x.A$. To understand proofs depending upon assumptions requires something stronger:

Theorem 2.1 *If the variable x is not free in B, then $B \implies A$ is valid if and only if $B \implies (\forall x.A)$ is valid.*

Proof: Consider the left to right direction, leaving the converse as an exercise. To simplify matters, suppose that x is the only free variable in $B \implies A$. To show that $B \implies (\forall x.A)$ is valid requires showing it true for every x. Since x is not free in the formula, it suffices to show that $B \implies (\forall x.A)$ is true. Assume that B is true and show $\forall x.A$. Since $B \implies A$ is valid, for every x we have B implies A. Since B is true, A holds for every x. □

   Given assumptions $A_1, \ldots, A_n$, where x is free in no assumption, let B be $A_1 \wedge \cdots \wedge A_n$ in the theorem. If the assumptions $A_1, \ldots, A_n$ imply A then they imply $\forall x.A$.

Understanding existential elimination

To frame a rule of existential elimination, we need to characterize the logical consequences of an existential formula:

Theorem 2.2 *If the variable x is not free in B, then $A \implies B$ is valid if and only if $(\exists x.A) \implies B$ is valid.*

Proof (left to right direction): As before, suppose that x is the only free variable in $A \implies B$. To show that $(\exists x.A) \implies B$ is valid requires showing it true for every x. Since x is not free, it suffices to show that $(\exists x.A) \implies B$ is true. Assume $\exists x.A$ and show B. Choose x such that A is true. Since $A \implies B$ is valid, for every x we have A implies B. So B is true. □

   Given a formula C and assumptions $A_1, \ldots, A_n$, where x is free in no assumption nor C, let B be $(A_1 \wedge \cdots \wedge A_n) \implies C$ in the theorem. If A and the assumptions $A_1, \ldots, A_n$ imply C then $\exists x.A$ and those assumptions imply C.

Exercise 2.19 Show (by semantical reasoning) that if $B \implies (\forall x.A)$ is valid then $B \implies A$ is valid.

Exercise 2.20 Show that $A[t/x] \implies (\exists x.A)$ is valid, justifying the rule of existential introduction.

Exercise 2.21 Show that $(\forall x.A) \implies A[t/x]$ is valid, justifying the rule of universal elimination.

Exercise 2.22 Show that $A \implies (\forall x.A)$ is not valid by exhibiting a formula A and an interpretation that falsifies it.

Exercise 2.23 Explain the difference between '$A \iff B$ is valid' and 'A is valid if and only if B is valid'.

2.8   The universal quantifier

The formula $\forall x.A$ means that A is true for every x. The introduction rule (*generalization*) states that if A is a theorem and x is an arbitrary variable then $\forall x.A$ is a theorem:

$$\frac{A}{\forall x.A} \qquad provided\ x\ is\ not\ free\ in\ the\ assumptions\ of\ A \qquad (\forall\text{-intro})$$

Theorem 2.1 justifies the rule.

The rule is subject to a *proviso*: the conclusion only holds if the proviso is satisfied. The variable x is called the *eigenvariable* or *parameter* of the rule. The introduction rule is often formulated to allow the renaming of the eigenvariable as it is bound:

$$\frac{A[y/x]}{\forall x.A} \qquad provided\ y\ is\ not\ free\ in\ \forall x.A\ or\ the\ assumptions\ of\ A[y/x]$$

The elimination rule (*specialization*) states that if $\forall x.A$ is a theorem and t is a term then $A[t/x]$ is a theorem:

$$\frac{\forall x.A}{A[t/x]} \qquad (\forall\text{-elim})$$

Since $A[x/x]$ is A, an instance of $\forall$-elimination is $\frac{\forall x.A}{A}$.

Example 2.10 If P is a 1-place predicate symbol then $\forall x.\,P(x) \Longrightarrow P(x)$ is a theorem:

$$\frac{\dfrac{[P(x)]}{P(x) \Longrightarrow P(x)}}{\forall x.\,P(x) \Longrightarrow P(x)}$$

The $\forall$-introduction rule can be applied because the assumption $P(x)$ has been discharged: $P(x) \Longrightarrow P(x)$ is true under no assumptions.

In contrast, it would be nonsense to conclude $\forall x.\,P(x)$ from $P(x)$. Suppose that the universe is the natural numbers and $P(x)$ is interpreted to mean 'x equals 0' and x is assigned the value 0. Then $P(x)$ is true but $\forall x.\,P(x)$ is false.

The scope of an assumption is of critical importance. When checking a proof, an illegal generalization over x is easily missed if the assumption $P(x)$ is later discharged. This is another reason for using a sequent calculus.

Example 2.11 The universal quantifier satisfies

$$(\forall x.\ A \wedge B) \iff (\forall x.A) \wedge (\forall x.B)$$

Here is a proof of $\forall x.A$ from $\forall x.\ A \wedge B$:

$$\frac{\dfrac{\dfrac{\forall x.\ A \wedge B}{A \wedge B}}{A}}{\forall x.A}$$

Example 2.12 Here is a proof of $\forall x.\ A \lor B$ from $(\forall x.A) \lor (\forall x.B)$:

$$\dfrac{(\forall x.A) \lor (\forall x.B) \qquad \dfrac{\dfrac{[\forall x.A]}{A}}{\dfrac{A \lor B}{\forall x.\ A \lor B}} \qquad \dfrac{\dfrac{[\forall x.B]}{B}}{\dfrac{A \lor B}{\forall x.\ A \lor B}}}{\forall x.\ A \lor B}$$

Since each connective is defined independently of the others, the proof uses only the rules for $\forall$ and $\lor$.

Example 2.13 An identity for moving quantifiers is

$$(\forall x.\ A \implies B) \iff (A \implies \forall x.B) \qquad \textit{provided } x \textit{ is not free in } A$$

A proof of the left to right direction is

$$\dfrac{\dfrac{\dfrac{\forall x.\ A \implies B}{A \implies B} \qquad [A]}{\dfrac{B}{\forall x.B}}}{A \implies \forall x.B}$$

The assumption A is discharged in the final inference. The use of generalization to prove $\forall x.B$ is allowed because x is not free in that assumption. The converse of the rule also holds.

Exercise 2.24 Use the rule $\land$-elim-3 to prove $\forall x.\ A \land B$ from $(\forall x.A) \land (\forall x.B)$.

Exercise 2.25 Show that $(\forall x.A) \lor (\forall x.B)$ does not follow from $\forall x.\ A \lor B$.

Exercise 2.26 What is wrong with this 'proof' of $(\forall x.A) \lor (\forall x.B)$ from $\forall x.\ A \lor B$?

$$\dfrac{\forall x.\ A \lor B \qquad \dfrac{\dfrac{[A]}{\forall x.A}}{(\forall x.A) \lor (\forall x.B)} \qquad \dfrac{\dfrac{[B]}{\forall x.B}}{(\forall x.A) \lor (\forall x.B)}}{(\forall x.A) \lor (\forall x.B)}$$

2.9   The existential quantifier

The formula $\exists x.A$ means that A is true for some value of x. The existential introduction rule takes this value from a term t:

$$\dfrac{A[t/x]}{\exists x.A}$$

Since $A[x/x]$ is A, an instance of $\exists$-introduction is $\frac{A}{\exists x.A}$.

The elimination rule is

$$\frac{\exists x.A \quad \begin{array}{c} [A] \\ B \end{array}}{B} \qquad \begin{array}{l} \textit{provided } x \textit{ is not free in } B \textit{ nor in} \\ \textit{the assumptions of } B \textit{ apart from } A \end{array}$$

The eigenvariable is x. The elimination rule in LCF allows choice of the eigenvariable:

$$\frac{\exists x.A \quad \begin{array}{c} [\,A[y/x]\,] \\ B \end{array}}{B} \qquad \begin{array}{l} \textit{provided } y \textit{ is not free in } \exists x.A, \ B, \textit{ nor in} \\ \textit{the assumptions of } B \textit{ apart from } A[y/x] \end{array}$$

The existential elimination rule gives a temporary name to the value that supposedly exists. Given the theorem $\exists x.A$, prove B assuming that $A[y/x]$ holds, where y is a new variable. Theorem 2.2 is the semantic justification.

Example 2.14 Existential quantifiers can be permuted: $\exists xy.A$ implies $\exists yx.A$. Proof:

$$\frac{\exists xy.A \quad \dfrac{[\exists y.A] \quad \dfrac{\dfrac{[A]}{\exists x.A}}{\exists yx.A}}{\exists yx.A}}{\exists yx.A}$$

Observe how $\exists$-introduction 'hides' x, then y, by binding those variables. Both instances of $\exists$-elimination are correct because neither x nor y is free in $\exists yx.A$. The rules cannot be applied in a different order; $\exists x.A$ cannot be derived from $\exists y.A$ because y is free in $\exists x.A$.

Example 2.15 The rule

$$\frac{A \Longrightarrow B}{(\exists z.A) \Longrightarrow (\exists z.B)} \qquad \textit{provided } z \textit{ is not free in the assumptions of } A \Longrightarrow B$$

is derived using $\exists$-introduction and $\exists$-elimination:

$$\frac{[\exists z.A] \quad \dfrac{\dfrac{A \Longrightarrow B \quad [A]}{B}}{\exists z.B}}{\dfrac{\exists z.B}{(\exists z.A) \Longrightarrow (\exists z.B)}}$$

The proviso on z is necessary in order to apply $\exists$-elimination on $\exists z.A$.

Example 2.16 An identity good for moving quantifiers is

$$(\exists x.A) \wedge B \iff (\exists x.\, A \wedge B) \qquad \textit{provided } x \textit{ is not free in } B$$

The right to left proof is

$$
\cfrac{\exists x.\, A \wedge B \qquad \cfrac{A \wedge B \qquad \cfrac{\cfrac{[A]}{\exists x.A} \qquad [B]}{(\exists x.A) \wedge B}}{(\exists x.A) \wedge B}}{(\exists x.A) \wedge B}
$$

The bottom inference, $\exists$-elimination, is correct because the assumption A has been discharged and x is not free in the conclusion. The conjunction rule $\wedge$-elim-3 appears.

Example 2.17 An identity of classical logic is

$$(\exists x.\, A \implies B) \iff ((\forall x.A) \implies B) \qquad \textit{provided } x \textit{ is not free in } B$$

The left to right direction, which holds in intuitionistic logic, is a straightforward exercise.

The right to left direction is classical. Recall that classical natural deduction requires derived rules for breaking down negative formulae. This proof uses a derived rule concerning negated existentials:

$$\cfrac{\neg \exists x.A}{\neg A[t/x]} \qquad\qquad (\neg\exists\text{-elim})$$

It also uses the rule $\neg \implies$-elim-1 (Exercise 2.16) and classical contradiction.

$$
\cfrac{\cfrac{[\neg \exists x.\, A \implies B]}{\neg(A \implies B)} \qquad \cfrac{(\forall x.A) \implies B \qquad \cfrac{\cfrac{\cfrac{[\neg \exists x.\, A \implies B]}{\neg(A \implies B)}}{A}}{\forall x.A}}{B}}{\cfrac{\Lambda}{\exists x.\, A \implies B}}
$$

What is going on here? By classical contradiction, assume $\neg \exists x.\, A \implies B$. There follows $\neg(A \implies B)$ and then $\forall x.A$, which implies B. The rule $\implies$-introduction gives $A \implies B$, even though A was not assumed in the proof of B.[3] Deriving $\neg(A \implies B)$ again yields a contradiction.

---

[3]It is not mandatory to use an assumption. If B is true then $A \implies B$ is true regardless of A.

Example 2.18 The relationship between $\exists y.\forall x.A$ and $\forall x.\exists y.A$ illustrates all four primitive quantifier rules. Clearly $\exists y.\forall x.A$ implies $\forall x.\exists y.A$, as in 'if there is a person whom everyone likes, then everyone likes somebody'. A formal proof is

$$
\cfrac{\exists y.\forall x.A \qquad \cfrac{\cfrac{[\forall x.A]}{A}}{\exists y.A}}{\cfrac{\exists y.A}{\forall x.\exists y.A}}
$$

The use of $\exists$-elimination is correct because y is not free in $\exists y.A$.

Exercise 2.27 Show that $\forall x.\exists y.A$ does not imply $\exists y.\forall x.A$.

Exercise 2.28 What is wrong with this 'proof'?

$$
\cfrac{\cfrac{\cfrac{\forall x.\exists y.A}{\exists y.A} \qquad [A]}{A}}{\cfrac{\forall x.A}{\exists y.\forall x.A}}
$$

Exercise 2.29 Derive the rule

$$
\frac{\neg \exists x.A}{\neg A[t/x]}
$$

Exercise 2.30 Derive the rule

$$
\frac{\exists x.\,A \Longrightarrow B}{(\forall x.A) \Longrightarrow B} \qquad provided\ x\ is\ not\ free\ in\ B
$$

2.10 Mathematical induction

An informal statement of mathematical induction is

> *If $P(0)$ is true and if $P(x)$ implies $P(x+1)$ for every natural number x, then $P(x)$ holds for every natural number x.*

To avoid type restrictions, let all terms denote natural numbers. The obvious formal rule involves universal quantifiers:

$$
\frac{A[0/x] \qquad \forall x.\,A \Longrightarrow A[x+1/x]}{\forall x.\,A}
$$

But according to the philosophy of natural deduction, a rule should mention as few connectives as possible. The rule

$$\frac{A[0/x] \qquad \begin{array}{c} [A] \\ A[x+1/x] \end{array}}{A[t/x]} \qquad \textit{provided } x \textit{ is not free in the assumptions of } A[x+1/x] \textit{ apart from } A$$

is as powerful as the previous one and often allows shorter proofs. Its second premise implicitly performs $\forall$-introduction; its conclusion implicitly performs $\forall$-elimination. But the rule can be used in a logic that has no quantifiers, say an equational logic for arithmetic.

Mathematical induction is usually associated with the natural numbers. Recursive data structures such as lists and trees satisfy a similar principle, *structural induction*. The natural numbers can be regarded as the recursive data structure generated by 0 and the successor function, and structural induction on the natural numbers is precisely mathematical induction. Structural induction is described in Chapter 4 and is the main vehicle for reasoning about LCF data structures.

2.11   Equality

LCF makes a subtle but vital distinction between $=$ and $\equiv$. The symbol $=$ is reserved for its use in programming languages, as a *computable* test for the equality of two data. The symbol $\equiv$ denotes the equality between two values; it is not always computable, as in the equality of functions. Syntactically $t = u$ is a *term* while $t \equiv u$ is a *formula*.[4]

So the formula stating 't equals u', conventionally written $t = u$, is here written $t \equiv u$. Whatever symbol we use, the basic properties of equality are the same: the reflexive, symmetric, and transitive laws, and congruence laws for each function and predicate symbol. From these we can derive substitution of equals for equals, as well as term rewriting.

The equality predicate is an *equivalence relation* because it satisfies three fundamental laws. It is *reflexive*:

$$\forall x.\, x \equiv x$$

It is *symmetric*:

$$\forall xy.\, x \equiv y \Longrightarrow y \equiv x$$

It is *transitive*:

$$\forall xyz.\, x \equiv y \wedge y \equiv z \Longrightarrow x \equiv z$$

---

[4]Contrast with the treatment of equality in Higher Order Logic [37], which does not distinguish terms from formulae.

Using the $\forall$-elimination and $\Longrightarrow$-elimination rules it is straightforward to derive the corresponding rules:

$$t \equiv t \qquad \frac{t \equiv u}{u \equiv t} \qquad \frac{s \equiv t \qquad t \equiv u}{s \equiv u}$$

2.11.1 Equality reasoning about terms

The *congruence law* of a function states that equal arguments give equal results. To add equality to a logic requires asserting the congruence law for every function symbol. If f_n is an n-place function symbol then its congruence axiom (or *equality axiom*) is

$$\forall x_1 \ldots x_n. \forall y_1 \ldots y_n. x_1 \equiv y_1 \land \cdots \land x_n \equiv y_n \Longrightarrow f_n(x_1, \ldots, x_n) \equiv f_n(y_1, \ldots, y_n)$$

The corresponding derived rule is

$$\frac{t_1 \equiv u_1 \qquad \cdots \qquad t_n \equiv u_n}{f_n(t_1, \ldots, t_n) \equiv f_n(u_1, \ldots, u_n)}$$

A way of asserting the congruence laws for all functions at once is by adding *substitution rules* for terms. The rule

$$\frac{t \equiv u}{s[t/x] \equiv s[u/x]}$$

states that if t equals u then any term constructed from t equals the term constructed similarly from u. The term s serves as a template for substitution of terms at occurrences of the variable x. A rule for substitution in formulae is presented later.

Example 2.19 Let f be a 2-place function symbol and g a 1-place function symbol. Their congruence laws are expressed by the rules

$$\frac{t_1 \equiv u_1 \qquad t_2 \equiv u_2}{f(t_1, t_2) \equiv f(u_1, u_2)} \qquad \frac{t \equiv u}{g(t) \equiv g(u)}$$

The proof tree

$$\frac{r \equiv r \qquad \dfrac{t \equiv u}{g(t) \equiv g(u)}}{f(r, g(t)) \equiv f(r, g(u))}$$

is obtained using reflexivity and the congruence rules. It derives $f(r, g(t)) \equiv f(r, g(u))$ from $t \equiv u$, an instance of the substitution rule where s is $f(r, g(x))$. But the substitution rule cannot be derived once and for all from the congruence rules, because each template s requires a different proof tree.

The congruence rules can be derived from the substitution rule and transitivity. A derivation of the congruence rule of f is

$$\frac{\dfrac{t_1 \equiv u_1}{f(t_1, t_2) \equiv f(u_1, t_2)} \qquad \dfrac{t_2 \equiv u_2}{f(u_1, t_2) \equiv f(u_1, u_2)}}{f(t_1, t_2) \equiv f(u_1, u_2)}$$

2.11.2 Equality reasoning about formulae

The bi-implication $\Longleftrightarrow$ is an equivalence relation on formulae. It is easy to derive the rules

$$A \Longleftrightarrow A \qquad\qquad \frac{A \Longleftrightarrow B}{B \Longleftrightarrow A} \qquad\qquad \frac{A \Longleftrightarrow B \qquad B \Longleftrightarrow C}{A \Longleftrightarrow C}$$

Bi-implication is also a congruence relation with respect to the logical connectives. For example, the rules

$$\frac{A \Longleftrightarrow B \qquad C \Longleftrightarrow D}{A \wedge C \Longleftrightarrow B \wedge D} \qquad\qquad \frac{A \Longleftrightarrow B \qquad C \Longleftrightarrow D}{A \vee C \Longleftrightarrow B \vee D}$$

assert that conjunction and disjunction yield logically equivalent results if applied to logically equivalent formulae. The rules for the quantifiers are similar, but require eigenvariable provisos:

$$\frac{A \Longleftrightarrow B}{(\exists x.A) \Longleftrightarrow (\exists x.B)} \qquad \textit{provided } x \textit{ is not free in the assumptions}$$

Such rules are not hard to derive. One of the trickiest is implication:

$$\frac{A \Longleftrightarrow B \qquad C \Longleftrightarrow D}{(A \Longrightarrow C) \Longleftrightarrow (B \Longrightarrow D)}$$

Here is half of its derivation, the left to right direction. Observe that it uses the *right to left* direction of $A \Longleftrightarrow B$:

$$\frac{\dfrac{C \Longleftrightarrow D}{C \Longrightarrow D} \qquad \dfrac{[A \Longrightarrow C] \qquad \dfrac{\dfrac{A \Longleftrightarrow B}{B \Longrightarrow A} \quad [B]}{A}}{C}}{\dfrac{\dfrac{D}{B \Longrightarrow D}}{(A \Longrightarrow C) \Longrightarrow (B \Longrightarrow D)}}$$

For predicates as well as functions, equal arguments should yield equal results. We must add a congruence law for every predicate. If P_n is an n-place predicate symbol then the axiom is

$$\forall x_1 \ldots x_n. \forall y_1 \ldots y_n. x_1 \equiv y_1 \wedge \cdots \wedge x_n \equiv y_n \wedge P_n(x_1, \ldots, x_n) \Longrightarrow P_n(y_1, \ldots, y_n)$$

A derived rule involving both equivalence relations is

$$\frac{t_1 \equiv u_1 \quad \cdots \quad t_n \equiv u_n}{P_n(t_1, \ldots, t_n) \Longleftrightarrow P_n(u_1, \ldots, u_n)}$$

Recall that $\equiv$ is itself a predicate. Its congruence axiom can be proved using transitivity and symmetry.

We now can justify a rule for the substitution of terms in formulae. Applying the derived rules to construct logically equivalent formulae gives

$$\frac{t \equiv u}{A[t/x] \Longleftrightarrow A[u/x]}$$

The LCF substitution rule is slightly different:

$$\frac{t \equiv u \qquad A[t/x]}{A[u/x]}$$

Example 2.20 Let f and g be as in the previous example, and let P and Q be 1-place predicate symbols. Then

$$\frac{\dfrac{t \equiv u}{P(t) \Longleftrightarrow P(u)} \qquad \dfrac{t \equiv u}{Q(t) \Longleftrightarrow Q(u)}}{(P(t) \Longrightarrow Q(t)) \Longleftrightarrow (P(u) \Longrightarrow Q(u))}$$

derives an instance of substitution where the formula A is $P(x) \Longrightarrow Q(x)$.

The substitution rules only substitute for terms that are free in a formula. But the (derived) congruence laws for the quantifiers allow substitution for terms that contain bound variables of the formula. This generalized substitution is called *rewriting*. Consider the derivation

$$\frac{\dfrac{\dfrac{\forall x. f(x, x) \equiv x}{f(g(z), g(z)) \equiv g(z)}}{P(f(g(z), g(z))) \Longleftrightarrow P(g(z))}}{(\exists z. P(f(g(z), g(z)))) \Longleftrightarrow (\exists z. P(g(z)))}$$

The inferences are $\forall$-elimination, congruence for P, and congruence for $\exists$. The formula $\exists z. P(f(g(z), g(z)))$ is rewritten to $\exists z. P(g(z))$ using $\forall x. f(x, x) \equiv x$ as a rewrite rule. The term $f(g(z), g(z))$ is replaced by $g(z)$ even though it is not free in the formula.

Exercise 2.31 Derive the transitive law for the relation $\Longleftrightarrow$.

Exercise 2.32 Derive the congruence law for conjunction.

Exercise 2.33 Modify the proof in the previous exercise to derive a congruence law for conjunction that discharges assumptions in the second premise:

$$A \Longleftrightarrow B \qquad \begin{array}{c} [A, B] \\ C \Longleftrightarrow D \end{array}$$
$$\overline{A \wedge C \Longleftrightarrow B \wedge D}$$

This law allows *local assumptions*: it is valid to assume that A and B are true when rewriting C to produce D.

Exercise 2.34 Derive the congruence law for $\forall$, namely

$$\frac{A \Longleftrightarrow B}{(\forall x.A) \Longleftrightarrow (\forall x.B)} \qquad \textit{provided } x \textit{ is not free in the assumptions}$$

2.12   A sequent calculus for natural deduction

PPλ includes essentially the natural deduction rules given above. But we must be precise about assumptions and discharging them. Writing an assumption above a proof and later crossing it off is natural and concise, but it is easy to get confused about which assumptions are still in force.

In a *sequent calculus*, the current set of assumptions is listed at every line of the proof. The sequent $A_1, \ldots, A_n \vdash B$ means that B depends upon the set of assumptions $\{A_1, \ldots, A_n\}$. The sequent $A \vdash A$ represents the assumption of A. The *assertion sign* $\vdash$ is popularly called the turnstile; $A \vdash B$ is read 'A entails B'.

Each of our examples can be reworked using sequents. Example 2.2 becomes

$$A \vee B \qquad \frac{A \vdash A}{A \vdash B \vee A} \qquad \frac{B \vdash B}{B \vdash B \vee A}$$
$$\overline{B \vee A}$$

Sequents require a notation for sets. Let Γ, Δ, and Θ be syntactic meta variables for sets of formulae. The *union* of sets is written with a comma: write Γ, Δ instead of writing $\Gamma \cup \Delta$. Set brackets are omitted: write $A_1, \ldots, A_n$ instead of $\{A_1, \ldots, A_n\}$ and Γ, A instead of $\Gamma \cup \{A\}$. The conjunction introduction rule becomes

$$\frac{\Gamma \vdash A \qquad \Delta \vdash B}{\Gamma, \Delta \vdash A \wedge B}$$

The conclusion depends upon every assumption of A and of B.

How should we express the discharge of assumptions? We could use set subtraction: if $\Delta - A$ is the set containing every member of Δ except A, then

$$\frac{\Gamma \vdash A \vee B \qquad \Delta \vdash C \qquad \Theta \vdash C}{\Gamma, \Delta - A, \Theta - B \vdash C}$$

could express the rule of disjunction elimination. This notation makes clear what the conclusion may assume, but obscures that the second premise may assume A. It is conventional to express discharge using union:

$$\frac{\Gamma \vdash A \vee B \qquad \Delta, A \vdash C \qquad \Theta, B \vdash C}{\Gamma, \Delta, \Theta \vdash C}$$

To discharge A in the premise $\Delta, A \vdash C$, partition the assumptions into A and a set Δ not containing A.

2.12.1 Inference rules

First of all we require an *assumption axiom*

$$A \vdash A$$

for every formula A.

Conjunction

The introduction rule is

$$\frac{\Gamma \vdash A \qquad \Delta \vdash B}{\Gamma, \Delta \vdash A \wedge B}$$

The elimination rules are

$$\frac{\Gamma \vdash A \wedge B}{\Gamma \vdash A} \qquad\qquad \frac{\Gamma \vdash A \wedge B}{\Gamma \vdash B}$$

The alternative elimination rule, $\wedge$-elim-3, becomes

$$\frac{\Gamma \vdash A \wedge B \qquad \Delta, A, B \vdash C}{\Gamma, \Delta \vdash C}$$

Disjunction

The introduction rules are

$$\frac{\Gamma \vdash A}{\Gamma \vdash A \vee B} \qquad\qquad \frac{\Gamma \vdash B}{\Gamma \vdash A \vee B}$$

The elimination rule is

$$\frac{\Gamma \vdash A \vee B \qquad \Delta, A \vdash C \qquad \Theta, B \vdash C}{\Gamma, \Delta, \Theta \vdash C}$$

Implication

The introduction rule is

$$\frac{\Gamma, A \vdash B}{\Gamma \vdash A \Longrightarrow B}$$

The elimination rule is

$$\frac{\Gamma \vdash A \Longrightarrow B \qquad \Delta \vdash A}{\Gamma, \Delta \vdash B}$$

Negation

Recall that negation rules are special cases of implication rules, since $\neg A$ abbreviates $A \Longrightarrow \Lambda$. The introduction rule is

$$\frac{\Gamma, A \vdash \Lambda}{\Gamma \vdash \neg A}$$

The elimination rule is

$$\frac{\Gamma \vdash \neg A \qquad \Delta \vdash A}{\Gamma, \Delta \vdash \Lambda}$$

Contradiction

The classical contradiction rule is

$$\frac{\Gamma, \neg A \vdash \Lambda}{\Gamma \vdash A}$$

The intuitionistic contradiction rule is

$$\frac{\Gamma \vdash \Lambda}{\Gamma \vdash A}$$

Universal quantifier

The introduction rule is

$$\frac{\Gamma \vdash A}{\Gamma \vdash \forall x.A} \qquad \textit{provided } x \textit{ is not free in } \Gamma$$

The elimination rule is

$$\frac{\Gamma \vdash \forall x.A}{\Gamma \vdash A[t/x]}$$

Existential quantifier

The introduction rule is

$$\frac{\Gamma \vdash A[t/x]}{\Gamma \vdash \exists x.A}$$

The elimination rule is

$$\frac{\Gamma \vdash \exists x.A \qquad \Delta, A \vdash B}{\Gamma, \Delta \vdash B} \qquad \textit{provided } x \textit{ is not free in } \Delta \textit{ or } B$$

Observe how easily the provisos on eigenvariables are expressed.

Mathematical induction

Mathematical induction could be stated as follows:

$$\frac{\Gamma \vdash A[0/x] \qquad \Delta, A \vdash A[x+1/x]}{\Gamma, \Delta \vdash A[t/x]} \qquad \text{provided } x \text{ is not free in } \Delta$$

2.12.2 Semantics

We can view the rules above as natural deduction rules expressed in a different notation. There is an obvious correspondence between the natural deduction proof tree with root C and leaves A, B and the sequent proof tree with root $A, B \vdash C$ and leaves $A \vdash A$ and $B \vdash B$. In this view of the sequent calculus, the leaves of a proof tree must be assumption axioms. What if we want to prove $\Theta \vdash C$ from $\Gamma \vdash A$ and $\Delta \vdash B$, or even from $\Gamma, A \vdash B$?

Let us view the rules as constituting a new calculus. A sequent no longer abbreviates a natural deduction proof, but is an assertion in its own right.[5] The new calculus requires a semantics. Let Γ be a set of formulae and A a formula. The sequent $\Gamma \vdash A$ means this: if every member of Γ is true then so is A. When there are no assumptions, $\vdash A$ means that A is true.

Many authors use $\vdash$ in the *meta language* to denote provability: $\Gamma \vdash A$ means that A can be formally proved from Γ, and $\vdash A$ means that A is a formal theorem. They view the sequent calculus as a meta logic about provability. In this book, $\vdash A$ is an *object language* assertion. Like any assertion, $\vdash A$ can be false. It is false if A is false.

The semantic justification of a sequent rule follows that of the corresponding natural deduction rule. Let us justify conjunction introduction. Assume the premises, $\Gamma \vdash A$ and $\Delta \vdash B$; prove the conclusion, $\Gamma, \Delta \vdash A \wedge B$. Assume that every formula in Γ and Δ is true, and show $A \wedge B$. If every formula in Γ is true then A is true, by the first premise. Likewise B is true. Therefore $A \wedge B$ is true. The other rules are similarly justified.

Example 2.21 The *cut rule* allows a proof to be structured into lemmas. When trying to prove B, the lemma A can be added to B's assumptions:

$$\frac{\Gamma \vdash A \qquad \Delta, A \vdash B}{\Gamma, \Delta \vdash B}$$

One derivation of the cut rule involves disjunction introduction and elimination:

$$\frac{\dfrac{\Gamma \vdash A}{\Gamma \vdash A \vee A} \qquad \Delta, A \vdash B \qquad \Delta, A \vdash B}{\Gamma, \Delta \vdash B}$$

---

[5]This means that any sequent can be the premise or conclusion of a proof, *not* that sequents can be combined using connectives into things like $(\Gamma \vdash A) \wedge (\Delta \vdash B)$!

In the conclusion of ∨-elimination, note that Δ, Δ equals Δ. Likewise I do not regard the repetition of the premise $\Delta, A \vdash B$ as significant.

Example 2.22 To see how far we have come from 'natural' reasoning, consider a derivation of $B \wedge A \vdash C$ from $A \wedge B \vdash C$:

$$\cfrac{B \wedge A \vdash B \wedge A \qquad \cfrac{\cfrac{A \wedge B \vdash C}{\vdash A \wedge B \Longrightarrow C} \qquad \cfrac{A \vdash A \qquad B \vdash B}{A, B \vdash A \wedge B}}{A, B \vdash C}}{B \wedge A \vdash C}$$

The rules $\Longrightarrow$-intro, $\wedge$-intro, $\Longrightarrow$-elim, and $\wedge$-elim-3 appear.

Exercise 2.35 Justify the existential elimination rule by appealing to the semantics of the sequent calculus.

Exercise 2.36 Derive the cut rule using conjunction introduction and elimination.

Exercise 2.37 Derive the rule

$$\frac{A \vee B \vdash C}{B \vee A \vdash C}$$

2.13   A sequent calculus for backwards proof

The sequent calculus above is the basis of PPλ, the logic of LCF. Let us consider another calculus, equivalent to its predecessor but more in the traditional sequent style. The form of each rule corresponds closely to the reasoning methods of LCF tactics.

An inference rule first suggests the idea of *forwards proof*: working from theorems to theorems. In normal mathematics we start with a desired conclusion, or *goal*, and work from goals to subgoals. LCF provides *tactics* and *tacticals* for conducting *backwards proof*. These are discussed in later chapters. When studying tactics it is easy to be overwhelmed by the complex mechanisms and the names and types of the ML identifiers, losing sight of the logical aspects of backwards proof.

The conjunction rule

$$\frac{\Gamma \vdash A \qquad \Delta \vdash B}{\Gamma, \Delta \vdash A \wedge B}$$

is designed for forwards proof: given A and B it concludes $A \wedge B$, forming the union of the assumptions. The corresponding backwards inference is this: to prove $A \wedge B$, prove A and B. But what about the assumptions? The rule would force us to write the assumptions for $A \wedge B$ as the union of Γ and Δ, as though we could predict which ones would be needed to prove A, and which to prove B. The difficulty is easily resolved. Set Δ equal to Γ, using the same assumptions for the premises and conclusion:

$$\frac{\Gamma \vdash A \qquad \Gamma \vdash B}{\Gamma \vdash A \wedge B}$$

We can adopt this solution for every rule.

From now on we are concerned with backwards proof exclusively. Proof trees are constructed upwards from the root. A rule takes a goal and produces subgoals, rather than taking premises and producing a conclusion. The logical meaning of 'rule' and 'proof' is the same as before; we are merely changing perspective, emphasizing the *process of constructing* a proof.

If the entire set of assumptions is passed to every subgoal, we may need to get rid of surplus assumptions. A *thinning* (or *weakening*) rule forms a subgoal that takes any subset of the assumptions:

$$\frac{\Gamma \vdash A}{\Delta \vdash A} \qquad provided\ \Gamma \subset \Delta$$

As a first application, thinning allows a more general assumption rule:

$$\Delta \vdash A \qquad provided\ A \in \Delta$$

This derived rule gives access to every assumption in Δ.

A typical sequent calculus has *left* and *right* rules instead of elimination and introduction rules. A right rule is similar to an introduction rule; it operates on the right side of the assertion sign ($\vdash$). A left rule has the logical effect of an elimination rule, but operates on the left side of the assertion sign. The formula being eliminated, say $A \vee B$, is assumed in the conclusion. The left rules illustrate how to handle assumptions: especially, when to *delete* an assumption.

The sequent calculus below is intuitionistic.[6] Adding one rule — classical contradiction — would make it classical. But to be really useful for classical deduction, several derived rules must also be added. This extension is discussed in the following section.

Conjunction

The $\wedge$-right rule is

$$\frac{\Gamma \vdash A \qquad \Gamma \vdash B}{\Gamma \vdash A \wedge B}$$

The $\wedge$-left rule is based on the elimination rule $\wedge$-elim-3. It suggests that when trying to prove C from the assumption $A \wedge B$, delete that assumption and prove C from A and B instead:

$$\frac{\Gamma, A, B \vdash C}{\Gamma, A \wedge B \vdash C}$$

---

[6]It is related to one described in Dummett [29, page 146].

Disjunction

The ∨-right rules are

$$\frac{\Gamma \vdash A}{\Gamma \vdash A \vee B} \qquad \frac{\Gamma \vdash B}{\Gamma \vdash A \vee B}$$

The ∨-left rule suggests that when trying to prove C from $A \vee B$, prove C from A, and also prove C from B. In both subgoals, the assumption $A \vee B$ is redundant and should be deleted:

$$\frac{\Gamma, A \vdash C \qquad \Gamma, B \vdash C}{\Gamma, A \vee B \vdash C}$$

Implication

The $\Longrightarrow$-right rule is

$$\frac{\Gamma, A \vdash B}{\Gamma \vdash A \Longrightarrow B}$$

The $\Longrightarrow$-left rule has little resemblance to Modus Ponens. It suggests that when trying to prove C from $A \Longrightarrow B$, first prove A, then prove C from B. The assumption $A \Longrightarrow B$ is redundant in the second subgoal, but not in the first:

$$\frac{\Gamma, A \Longrightarrow B \vdash A \qquad \Gamma, B \vdash C}{\Gamma, A \Longrightarrow B \vdash C}$$

The rule must be used with care: it only leads to a proof if A can be proved.

Negation

Again, the rules are instances of implication rules. The ¬-right rule is

$$\frac{\Gamma, A \vdash \Lambda}{\Gamma \vdash \neg A}$$

The ¬-left rule is

$$\frac{\Gamma, \neg A \vdash A}{\Gamma, \neg A \vdash C}$$

It is $\Longrightarrow$-left, replacing B by Λ.

Intuitionistic contradiction

The Λ-left rule is

$$\Gamma, \Lambda \vdash B$$

If the assumptions include Λ then the sequent is true. A consequence of Λ-left and ¬-left is that every sequent containing contradictory assumptions is a theorem:

$$\Gamma, A, \neg A \vdash B \qquad\qquad\qquad \Lambda\neg\text{-left}$$

Universal quantifier

The ∀-right rule is

$$\frac{\Gamma \vdash A}{\Gamma \vdash \forall x.A} \qquad provided\ x\ is\ not\ free\ in\ \Gamma$$

The ∀-left rule produces new assumptions from $\forall x.A$:

$$\frac{\Gamma, \forall x.A, A[t/x] \vdash B}{\Gamma, \forall x.A \vdash B}$$

The quantified formula is *retained* in the subgoal: it may be needed again! See Exercise 2.43.

Existential quantifier

The ∃-right rule is

$$\frac{\Gamma \vdash A[t/x]}{\Gamma \vdash \exists x.A}$$

The ∃-left rule suggests that when trying to prove B from $\exists x.A$, prove B from A. The assumption $\exists x.A$ is not required in the subgoal.

$$\frac{\Gamma, A \vdash B}{\Gamma, \exists x.A \vdash B} \qquad provided\ x\ is\ not\ free\ in\ \Gamma\ or\ B$$

Mathematical induction

Mathematical induction is almost the same as in the previous calculus:

$$\frac{\Gamma \vdash A[0/x] \qquad \Gamma, A \vdash A[x+1/x]}{\Gamma \vdash A[t/x]} \qquad provided\ x\ is\ not\ free\ in\ \Gamma$$

We can rework previous examples in the sequent calculus. The proofs should be read from the bottom upwards. Observe how the deduction proceeds. The tree grows by applying rules to the bottom sequent. Each rule removes a connective from a formula on either side of the assertion sign. Each branch of the tree terminates at an axiom.

Example 2.23 This is Example 2.4, a proof of $(A \wedge B) \Longrightarrow C \vdash A \Longrightarrow (B \Longrightarrow C)$:

$$\frac{\dfrac{(A \wedge B) \Longrightarrow C, A, B \vdash A \qquad (A \wedge B) \Longrightarrow C, A, B \vdash B}{(A \wedge B) \Longrightarrow C, A, B \vdash A \wedge B} \qquad C, A, B \vdash C}{\dfrac{(A \wedge B) \Longrightarrow C, A, B \vdash C}{\dfrac{(A \wedge B) \Longrightarrow C, A \vdash B \Longrightarrow C}{(A \wedge B) \Longrightarrow C \vdash A \Longrightarrow (B \Longrightarrow C)}}}$$

Unlike in that example, the set of assumptions in force at every line of the proof is clear. The drawback is that we must write a lot more.

Example 2.24 This is Example 2.14, the permutation of existential quantifiers:

$$\frac{\displaystyle\frac{\displaystyle\frac{\displaystyle\frac{\displaystyle\frac{A \vdash A}{A \vdash \exists x.A}}{A \vdash \exists yx.A}}{\exists y.A \vdash \exists yx.A}}{\exists xy.A \vdash \exists yx.A}}{}$$

The proof has a linear structure; compare with the natural deduction one. Observe how, working upwards, we apply ∃-left before ∃-right.

Some of these exercises are based on previous exercises involving intuitionistic natural deduction.

Exercise 2.38 Prove the sequent $(A \lor B) \land C \vdash (A \land C) \lor (B \land C)$.

Exercise 2.39 Prove the sequent $A \Longrightarrow (B \Longrightarrow C) \vdash (A \land B) \Longrightarrow C$.

Exercise 2.40 Prove the sequent

$$\exists x.\, A \Longrightarrow B \vdash (\forall x.A) \Longrightarrow B \qquad \textit{provided } x \textit{ is not free in } B$$

Exercise 2.41 What is wrong with this 'proof' of $\forall x.\exists y.A \vdash \exists y.\forall x.A$?

$$\frac{\displaystyle\frac{\displaystyle\frac{\displaystyle\frac{\displaystyle\frac{\forall x.\exists y.A, A \vdash A}{\forall x.\exists y.A, \exists y.A \vdash A}}{\forall x.\exists y.A \vdash A}}{\forall x.\exists y.A \vdash \forall x.A}}{\forall x.\exists y.A \vdash \exists y.\forall x.A}}{}$$

Exercise 2.42 Derive the rule $\land\neg$-left.

Exercise 2.43 Prove the sequent $A, \forall x.\, A \Longrightarrow A[f(x)/x] \vdash A[f(f(x))/x]$.

2.14   Classical deduction in a sequent calculus

The most convenient sequent calculus for classical deduction is Gentzen's (see Gallier [30, page 187]). In that calculus a sequent has sets of formulae on both sides of the assertion sign; $\Gamma \vdash \Delta$ means that if *every* formula in Γ holds, then *some* formula in Δ holds. Classical deduction happens automatically.

LCF's sequent calculus is best suited for intuitionistic deduction. Classical deduction requires application of the contradiction rule

$$\frac{\Gamma, \neg B \vdash \Lambda}{\Gamma \vdash B}$$

at appropriate points. What are those points? The rule is applicable to every goal!

This section presents classical rules, like those of Gentzen, for our sequent calculus. They apply classical contradiction at the appropriate points. First we consider each rule and its purpose. Then we work through several proofs. Finally we consider how to derive the rules; most are consequences of classical contradiction.

Gentzen's system is much smoother in classical reasoning. Should LCF have adopted it? But then every sequent would have the form $\Gamma \vdash \Delta$; to apply a rule we would need to specify the formula to use in the right part of each premise. Everything would be more complicated.

2.14.1 Derived rules for classical logic

Like before, each rule is intended for backwards proof. The conclusion is the goal, the premises are the subgoals.

The double negation law

An assumption of the form $\neg\neg A$ can be replaced by A:

$$\frac{\Gamma, A \vdash B}{\Gamma, \neg\neg A \vdash B} \qquad (\neg\neg\text{-left})$$

A classical disjunction-right rule

Classically, the disjunction $A \lor B$ is equivalent to the implication $\neg B \implies A$. To prove $A \lor B$, assume $\neg B$ and prove A:

$$\frac{\Gamma, \neg B \vdash A}{\Gamma \vdash A \lor B} \qquad (\lor C\text{-right})$$

This rule replaces both $\lor$-right rules. Unlike those, it makes no commitment to either disjunct. Proving either A or B satisfies the premise.

In the name, $\lor C$ means 'classical disjunction'.

A classical existential-right rule

To prove $\exists x.A$, assume $\forall x.\neg A$ and prove $A[t/x]$:

$$\frac{\Gamma, \forall x.\neg A \vdash A[t/x]}{\Gamma \vdash \exists x.A} \qquad (\exists C\text{-right})$$

The premise can be satisfied by either proving $A[t/x]$ or by proving $A[u/x]$ for any term u. Unlike its intuitionistic counterpart, the rule makes no commitment to the term t.

A classical implication-left rule

Classically, $A \Longrightarrow B$ is equivalent to $\neg A \vee B$. The implication-left rule follows from the disjunction-left rule:

$$\frac{\Gamma, \neg A \vdash C \qquad \Gamma, B \vdash C}{\Gamma, A \Longrightarrow B \vdash C}$$

In backwards proof the rule is safer than its intuitionistic counterpart: each subgoal is no worse than the goal, even if A cannot be proved (of course there are two of them ...).

Since $\neg A$ abbreviates $A \Longrightarrow \Lambda$ in our calculus, the rule leads nowhere if B is Λ. In Gentzen's system, negation is a connective.

A swap rule

In a classical system where a sequent has sets of formulae on both left and right, a formula on one side can be negated and moved to the other. If a sequent has the negative assumption $\neg A$, then proving A proves the sequent.

Our sequents can have only one formula on the right. If a formula moves from the left to the right, the formula on the right must move to the left. Here is a rule to swap that formula with an assumption:

$$\frac{\Gamma, \neg B \vdash A}{\Gamma, \neg A \vdash B}$$

Typically B is an atomic formula and A is not. In the subgoal we can break down A using introduction (right) rules.

A special case of swap can be derived using $\neg$-left and thinning:

$$\frac{\Gamma \vdash A}{\Gamma, \neg A \vdash \Lambda} \qquad\qquad \neg C\text{-elim}$$

The examples below are theorems of classical logic and not of intuitionistic logic. Their proofs without derived rules would be unpleasant. Read these proofs bottom upwards.

Example 2.25 The excluded middle follows by, from bottom to top, $\vee C$-right, double negation, and assumption:

$$\frac{\dfrac{A \vdash A}{\neg\neg A \vdash A}}{\vdash A \vee \neg A}$$

Example 2.26 Here is the classical direction of a de Morgan law:

$$\frac{\dfrac{\dfrac{A,B \vdash A \qquad A,B \vdash B}{A,B \vdash A \wedge B}}{\dfrac{\neg(A \wedge B), A, B \vdash \Lambda}{\dfrac{\neg(A \wedge B), B \vdash \neg A}{\dfrac{\neg(A \wedge B), \neg\neg B \vdash \neg A}{\neg(A \wedge B) \vdash \neg A \vee \neg B}}}}}{}$$

The sequence of inferences is $\vee C$-right, $\neg\neg$-left, $\neg$-right, $\neg C$-left, and $\wedge$-right.

Example 2.27 *Peirce's law,* namely $((A \implies B) \implies A) \implies A$, is a striking example of the difference between classical and intuitionistic logic. The law looks paradoxical — how can we get A from $(A \implies B) \implies A$? — and intuitionists do not accept it. Under classical semantics, the law is trivially verified by inspection of truth tables. Here is its proof in the sequent calculus:

$$\frac{\dfrac{\dfrac{\dfrac{\neg A, A \vdash B}{\neg A \vdash A \implies B}}{\neg(A \implies B) \vdash A} \qquad A \vdash A}{(A \implies B) \implies A \vdash A}}{\vdash ((A \implies B) \implies A) \implies A}$$

We see the swap rule; the key inference is $\implies C$-left.

Example 2.28 In classical logic the quantifiers satisfy $\exists x.A \iff \neg\forall x.\neg A$. The right to left direction is immediate via $\exists C$-right:

$$\frac{\neg\forall x.\neg A, \forall x.\neg A \vdash A}{\neg\forall x.\neg A \vdash \exists x.A}$$

2.14.2 Derivations of the rules

Why are the classical rules sound? Their proofs are not difficult; indeed parts are left as exercises. Each proof uses a formal theorem, via the cut rule, to add an assumption to the subgoal. The thinning rule is used to remove redundant assumptions.

The double negation law follows from the formal theorem $\neg\neg A \vdash A$ via the cut rule and thinning:

$$\frac{\neg\neg A \vdash A \qquad \dfrac{A \vdash B}{\neg\neg A, A \vdash B}}{\neg\neg A \vdash B}$$

The disjunction rule $\vee C$-right follows from $\neg(A \vee B) \vdash \neg B$ via cut, thinning, $\neg$-left, and classical contradiction:

$$
\cfrac{
  \neg(A \vee B) \vdash \neg B \qquad
  \cfrac{
    \cfrac{
      \cfrac{\neg B \vdash A}{\neg B \vdash A \vee B}
    }{\neg(A \vee B), \neg B \vdash A \vee B}
  }{
  }
}{
  \cfrac{\neg(A \vee B) \vdash A \vee B}{\cfrac{\neg(A \vee B) \vdash \Lambda}{\vdash A \vee B}}
}
$$

The existential rule $\exists C$-right similarly follows from $\neg\exists x.A \vdash \forall x.\neg A$:

$$
\cfrac{
  \neg\exists x.A \vdash \forall x.\neg A \qquad
  \cfrac{
    \cfrac{\forall x.\neg A \vdash A[t/x]}{\forall x.\neg A \vdash \exists x.A}
  }{\neg\exists x.A, \forall x.\neg A \vdash \exists x.A}
}{
  \cfrac{\neg\exists x.A \vdash \exists x.A}{\cfrac{\neg\exists x.A \vdash \Lambda}{\vdash \exists x.A}}
}
$$

Exercise 2.44 Prove the sequent $\neg\neg A \vdash A$.

Exercise 2.45 Prove the sequent $\neg(A \vee B) \vdash \neg B$.

Exercise 2.46 Prove the sequent $\neg\exists x.A \vdash \forall x.\neg A$.

Exercise 2.47 Prove $A \Longrightarrow B \vdash \neg A \vee B$ and derive the rule $\Longrightarrow C$-left.

Exercise 2.48 Derive the swap rule.

Exercise 2.49 Prove the sequent $(\forall x.A) \Longrightarrow B \vdash \exists x.\, A \Longrightarrow B$.

2.15   How to find formal proofs

Here is how to prove the goal $A_1, \ldots, A_n \vdash B$. Work backwards from the goal, building a proof tree upwards. Use left rules to break down formulae on the left; use right rules to break down the formula on the right. Assumption and contradiction rules terminate branches of the tree.

Intuitionistic deduction uses the rules of section 2.13. Classical deduction is awkward but possible. Use the derived classical rules of the previous section to supplement the intuitionistic rules.

If more than one rule can apply, as in $B \wedge A \vdash A \wedge B$, it rarely matters which is applied first. For intuitionistic deduction, avoid using the disjunction-right rules before disjunction-left.[7] Consider the sequent $B \vee A \vdash A \vee B$. If the first backwards step is disjunction-left, then the proof tree can obviously be completed:

$$\frac{B \vdash A \vee B \qquad A \vdash A \vee B}{B \vee A \vdash A \vee B}$$

Starting with either disjunction-right rule produces a false subgoal:

$$\frac{A \vee B \vdash A}{B \vee A \vdash A \vee B}$$

The rules ∃-right and ∀-left should never be used before ∃-left and ∀-right in backwards proof. The former rules may put free variables into the goal, violating the provisos of the latter rules. Consider $\forall x.B \vdash \forall x.\, A \Longrightarrow B$, where x is free in B. Using ∀-right then ∀-left yields the proof

$$\frac{\dfrac{\dfrac{\forall x.B, B, A \vdash B}{\forall x.B, A \vdash B}}{\forall x.B \vdash A \Longrightarrow B}}{\forall x.B \vdash \forall x.\, A \Longrightarrow B}$$

Starting with ∀-left makes x free in the subgoal; ∀-right can only be applied if the bound variable x is renamed:

$$\frac{\dfrac{\forall x.B, B \vdash A[y/x] \Longrightarrow B[y/x]}{\forall x.B, B \vdash \forall x.\, A \Longrightarrow B}}{\forall x.B \vdash \forall x.\, A \Longrightarrow B}$$

The proof can only be completed by a second use of ∀-left, producing the assumption $B[y/x]$. There are more examples in sections 2.8 and 2.9.

When the above constraints leave a choice of rules, choose the rule that produces the fewest subgoals. This minimizes duplication in the proof.

An example of quantifier reasoning is 'prove that computing $f(n)$ takes kn^2 steps for some constant k.' *Resolution* theorem provers can leave k unknown: *unification* determines k during the proof. Most other theorem provers, including LCF, cannot automate such proofs. The rule ∃-right is the culprit: 'to prove $\exists x.A$, prove $A[t/x]$ for some term t.' During the search for a proof, the correct choice of t is seldom obvious. Only by completing the proof can t be determined, yet the proof cannot proceed until a value for t is supplied. So the user must intervene.

The rule ∀-left poses the same problem: 'given the assumption $\forall x.A$, assume $A[t/x]$ for some term t.' The choice of t may even be irrelevant, as in $\forall x.B \vdash B$. LCF lays great emphasis on rewriting: using the assumption in

---

[7]Recall that we are constructing proofs backwards from the final conclusion. Disjunction-right should appear above disjunction-left in the proof tree.

$\forall x. f(x) \equiv g(x, x) \vdash A$ to replace every occurrence of $f(t)$ by $g(t, t)$ in the formula A. Rewriting is one case where $\forall$-left can be applied automatically: t is determined by pattern matching in A.

The use of induction requires real intelligence. An induction rule can be applied to any goal but rarely leads to a proof. The next chapter gives examples where induction must be applied to $\forall x. A$ rather than A. Often the proof of a formula involves induction on a stronger formula: the induction step requires the stronger induction hypothesis.

Exercise 2.50   Prove $\exists x. B \vdash \exists x. A \implies B$ and show a fruitless proof attempt obtained by applying the quantifier rules in the wrong order.

2.16   Further reading

Manna and Waldinger give a gentle introduction to logic, with a particularly careful treatment of interpretations [64]. Gallier introduces several sequent calculi and develops proof theory, including cut-elimination and Herbrand's Theorem, with applications to theorem proving and logic programming [30]. Boolos and Jeffrey discuss logic in the context of computability theory, which is a prerequisite of the following chapter. They include enough model theory to prove fundamental results such as the completeness theorem [11]. Another good introduction is Barwise [4].

Dummett [29] describes the philosophy, inference systems, and semantics of intuitionistic logic.

Natural deduction prefers inference rules to axioms for reasoning about logical connectives. Similarly, the mathematical induction rule should not mention connectives. Schmidt argues that inference rules are also preferable for reasoning about non-logical concepts, such as set operators [86]. Starting from the Gödel-Bernays axioms for set theory, he derives inference rules for union, intersection, etc., and demonstrates their use.

Prawitz has written the classic account of natural deduction [83]. It proves deep results about the transformation of proof trees into normal form; it is not intended for beginners.

Chapter 3

A Logic of Computable Functions

To understand domain theory, first you should become acquainted with the λ-calculus. Its syntax could hardly be simpler, but its semantics could hardly be more complex. The *typed* λ-calculus has a simple semantics: each type denotes a set; each lambda expression denotes a function.

Through a careful analysis of nontermination, Dana Scott developed the typed λ-calculus into a Logic for Computable Functions (LCF). In the semantics of this logic, each data type denotes a set whose values are partially ordered with respect to termination properties. A computable function between partially ordered sets is monotonic and continuous. A recursive definition is understood as a fixed point of a continuous function. For reasoning about recursive definitions, Scott introduced the principle of fixed point induction. The resulting logic is ideal for reasoning about recursion schemes and other aspects of computable functions.

3.1   The lambda calculus

The λ-calculus has a long and many faceted relationship with computer science. Back in the 1930's, Alonzo Church formulated a notion of 'effectively computable function' in terms of functions expressible in the λ-calculus. His notion was shown to give the same set of functions as other models of computation such as the general recursive functions and Turing machines. *Church's thesis* states that these functions and no others are effectively computable. The λ-calculus influenced the design of the programming language Lisp and is closely reflected in the language ML.

The λ-calculus is intended for reasoning about functions as computation rules. It allows functions to be defined and applied to arguments, and the result to be evaluated. Here is an example. If f and g are functions such that $f(x) \equiv x^2$ and $g(x) \equiv x + 1$, then $f(g(a)) \equiv f(a + 1) \equiv (a + 1)^2$. *Proof*: by substituting the arguments into the bodies of the functions.

Arguments and results of functions can be arbitrary expressions, including other functions. A function of two arguments is regarded as a function of one argument whose result is another function. Addition is represented as follows. Consider the family of functions $plus_m$. For $m = 0, 1, \ldots$, let $plus_m(y) \equiv m + y$. So $plus_m$ is the function that adds m to its argument. Define the function P such that $P(x) \equiv plus_x$. So P is a function whose result is another function, and $P(m)(n) \equiv plus_m(n) \equiv m + n$. For a function $h(x, y, z)$ of three arguments it is possible to define H such that $H(x)(y)(z) \equiv h(x, y, z)$, and so on for any number of arguments. This representation is called *currying*, and P is called a *curried function*, though it is due to Schönfinkel and not to Curry.

A function that operates on other functions is called a *functional* or a *higher order* function. Another example is the function *twice*, where *twice*(f) equals f composed with itself. In the λ-calculus not only is *twice* easy to define; it can be applied to itself! We shall see below what *twice*(*twice*) could mean.

3.1.1   Syntax

The syntax of the λ-calculus is extremely simple. Functions can be created or applied to arguments. Suppose we are given constant symbols $A, B, C, \ldots$ and variables $x, y, z, \ldots$. Then there are four kinds of term:[1] constants, variables, abstractions, and combinations. The abstraction $(\lambda x.t)$, where t is a term, expresses the dependence of t upon x as a function. The combination $(t\, u)$, where t and u are terms, denotes the application of the function t to the argument u.

Lambda abstraction allows us to express a function without giving it a name. In the example above, f is $(\lambda x.x^2)$ and g is $(\lambda x.x+1)$. The equation can be written without mentioning f and g by name:

$$((\lambda x.x^2)((\lambda x.x + 1)a)) \equiv ((\lambda x.x^2)(a + 1)) \equiv (a + 1)^2$$

Constant symbols are convenient but not essential. They make it easy to extend the notation. If we would like to have terms like $x + 1$ and x^2, then let the constants include P for plus and E for exponentiation. Let $x + 1$ abbreviate $((Px)1)$ and x^2 abbreviate $((Ex)2)$. Infix operators like $+$ aid clarity. LCF allows any constant to be made infix.

The *conditional* $p \Rightarrow t \mid u$, means, if p is true then t else u. There is a constant *COND*, and $p \Rightarrow t \mid u$ abbreviates $(((CONDp)t)u)$.

Terms in the formal syntax are unambiguous but lengthy. We can omit brackets when the meaning is clear, writing $P\, m\, n$ instead of $((P\, m)n)$. Also we can let a single λ do the work of several, writing $\lambda x\, y.t$ instead of $\lambda x.\lambda y.t$. These conventions are especially convenient for curried functions: write $(\lambda x\, y.x^2 + y^2)m\, n$ instead of $(((\lambda x.\lambda y.x^2 + y^2)m)n)$. Traditionally a variable name is a single letter and the letters all get run together. Most LCF identifiers are longer than one letter. Write *twice f*, better still *twice*(f), instead of *twicef*.

---

[1] The word 'term' is used in LCF, but 'lambda expression' is more common in the literature.

3.1.2 Evaluation

Lambda reductions or *conversions* allow a term to be evaluated. Each reduction, named by a Greek letter, converts a term to an equivalent term. Most important is *β-reduction*, the substitution of a function's argument into its body:

$$((\lambda x.t)u) \equiv t[u/x]$$

The properties of evaluation are formalized in a calculus for proving that terms are equivalent. Each reduction is expressed by an axiom. The rules include a rule for forming combinations,

$$\frac{r \equiv s \qquad t \equiv u}{(rt) \equiv (su)}$$

a rule for forming abstractions,

$$\frac{t \equiv u}{(\lambda x.t) \equiv (\lambda x.u)}$$

and rules to make the relation $\equiv$ reflexive, symmetric, and transitive:

$$t \equiv t \qquad \frac{t \equiv u}{u \equiv t} \qquad \frac{s \equiv t \qquad t \equiv u}{s \equiv u}$$

We saw these in the previous chapter.

Unlike in conventional first order logic, the terms of the λ-calculus can bind variables. And the treatment of function application is completely different. The first order term $f(r, s, t)$ corresponds to the λ-term $((fr)s)t$. To say that f is a 3-place function symbol seems wrong, for f, fs, $(fs)t$, and $(((fr)s)t)u$ are perfectly legitimate λ-terms. Really f is a constant symbol. The λ-calculus has only one function symbol, the 2-place function *APPLY*, where $APPLY(t, u)$ applies the function t to the argument u. It is easy to forget about *APPLY* because it is invisible: instead of $APPLY(t, u)$ we write the combination tu. The rule for forming equivalent combinations is precisely the congruence law for *APPLY*.

Example 3.1 A conversion can be applied to a subterm at any depth in a term, yielding an equivalent term. Applying $\lambda x\, y.\, x^2 + y^2$ to the arguments m and n illustrates β-reduction and currying. An informal derivation is

$$\begin{aligned} ((\lambda x\, y.\, x^2 + y^2)m)n &\equiv (\lambda y.\, m^2 + y^2)n \\ &\equiv m^2 + n^2 \end{aligned}$$

The subterm $(\lambda x\, y.\, x^2 + y^2)m$ is first converted to $\lambda y.\, m^2 + y^2$.

The full proof tree uses the rules for β-reduction, combinations, reflexivity, and transitivity:

$$\frac{\dfrac{(\lambda x\, y.\, x^2 + y^2)m \equiv \lambda y.\, m^2 + y^2 \qquad n \equiv n}{((\lambda x\, y.\, x^2 + y^2)m)n \equiv (\lambda y.\, m^2 + y^2)n} \qquad (\lambda y.\, m^2 + y^2)n \equiv m^2 + n^2}{((\lambda x\, y.\, x^2 + y^2)m)n \equiv m^2 + n^2}$$

Observe the connection between the reduction of a subterm and the use of congruence laws to perform substitution. In the future, substitution of subterms will be taken for granted.

3.1.3   Free and bound variables

In the λ-calculus, like in first order logic, we must distinguish free and bound variables. In $\lambda x.t$, the variable x is bound. Renaming the bound variable is called *α-conversion*:

$$\lambda x.t \equiv \lambda y.t[y/x]$$

So $f(x) \equiv x^2$ means exactly the same as $f(y) \equiv y^2$.

A variable x occurs *bound* in a term if λx is part of the term. A variable x occurs *free* in a term if it occurs outside the scope of every subterm of the form $\lambda x.t$.

Here is an inductive definition of $u[t/x]$, the substitution of t for x in u:

- In $\lambda y.r$, if x equals y then the result of the substitution is $\lambda y.r$. Otherwise, if y is not free in t then the result is $\lambda z.r[t/x]$. Otherwise, let z be a variable different from x and every variable occurring in r or t; the result is $\lambda z.r[z/y][t/x]$.

- In rs the result is $r[t/x](s[t/x])$.

- If u is a constant or variable, then if u equals x then the result is t; otherwise the result is u.

Note that the bound variable may be renamed. Barendregt points out that if substitution did not prevent the capture of variables, every equation $t \equiv u$ would be provable [2, page 25]. The λ-calculus would be formally inconsistent.

Example 3.2 It is wrong to write

$$(\lambda x.\lambda y.x^2 + y^2)y\,n \;\equiv\; (\lambda y.y^2 + y^2)n$$
$$\equiv\; n^2 + n^2$$

since the variable y is captured. Here is an evaluation that renames y to z so that substitution is valid:

$$(\lambda x.\lambda y.x^2 + y^2)y\,n \;\equiv\; (\lambda x.\lambda z.x^2 + z^2)y\,n$$
$$\equiv\; (\lambda z.y^2 + z^2)n$$
$$\equiv\; y^2 + n^2.$$

Exercise 3.1 Give precise definitions of 'x occurs free in t' and 'x occurs bound in t' by case analysis on the term t.

Exercise 3.2 Show that $(\lambda x_1 \cdots x_n.\,t)u_1 \cdots u_n$ is equivalent to the simultaneous substitution $t[u_1/x_1, \ldots, u_n/x_n]$.

3.2 Semantic questions

Since the λ-calculus purports to be about functions, there must be some sense in which the term $\lambda x.t$ can be regarded as a mathematical function. It is not difficult to construct a *term model*: each term t denotes the set $[\![t]\!]$ of terms equivalent to it, and $[\![\lambda x.t]\!]$ is the function that maps $[\![u]\!]$ to $[\![t[u/x]]\!]$. But incest leads nowhere. What is the connection between functions in the λ-calculus and functions in ordinary mathematics?

As we shall see below, the function *twice* can be applied to itself. It therefore is not a function as conventionally understood. In set theory, a function f is the set of all pairs (x, y) such that $f(x) = y$. If *twice* were such a set then $(twice, y)$ would be an element of *twice* for some y, violating the axiom that no set can belong to itself. Interesting models of the λ-calculus were constructed by Dana Scott; see Barendregt [2].

3.2.1 Applying a function to itself

The functional *twice* is defined by $twice \equiv \lambda f\, x.f(f(x))$. It applies its argument f twice to x. By β-conversion, if t and u are terms then $twice\, t\, u \equiv t(t(u))$:

$$(\lambda f\, x.f(f(x)))t\, u \;\equiv\; (\lambda x.t(t(x)))u$$
$$\equiv\; t(t(u)).$$

Using this fact repeatedly evaluates *twice twice t u*:

$$twice\ twice\ t\ u \;\equiv\; twice(twice\ t)u$$
$$\equiv\; twice\ t\,(twice\ t\ u)$$
$$\equiv\; twice\ t\,(t(t(u)))$$
$$\equiv\; t(t(t(t(u))))$$

Self-application makes sense: *twice twice* is a functional that applies its argument four times.

Self application can do stranger things. Define $Y \equiv \lambda f.(\lambda x.f(x\, x))(\lambda x.f(x\, x))$. Now

$$Y(f) \;\equiv\; (\lambda x.f(x\, x))(\lambda x.f(x\, x))$$
$$\equiv\; f((\lambda x.f(x\, x))(\lambda x.f(x\, x))) \qquad \text{(by } \beta\text{-conversion)}$$
$$\equiv\; f(Y(f))$$

The evaluation of lambda terms need not terminate; repeated conversions produce $Y(f)$, $f(Y(f))$, $f(f(Y(f)))$, on to infinity. $Y(f)$ is called a *fixed point* of the function f: a value x such that $f(x) \equiv x$.

3.2.2   Recursive functions

Computer programs contain complex patterns of recursion. In elementary mathematics, recursion is encountered in its simplest form: the recurrence relation. For example, the factorial of an integer k is defined by the equation[2]

$$fact(k) \quad \equiv \quad (k = 0) \Rightarrow 1 \mid k * fact(k - 1)$$

If $k \geq 0$ then this equation specifies a unique value for $fact(k)$, namely $k * \cdots * 2 * 1$. If $k < 0$ then evaluation of $fact(k)$ will *diverge*: run forever.

Through Y the lambda-calculus can express functions that satisfy arbitrary recursion equations, even functions that do not terminate for all arguments. The first step is to turn the equation into a non-recursive definition of a functional. Each recursive call becomes a call to a function argument:

$$F(g)(k) \quad \equiv \quad (k = 0) \Rightarrow 1 \mid k * g(k - 1)$$

Define $fact \equiv Y(F)$. Then

$$fact(k) \equiv Y(F)(k) \equiv F(Y(F))(k) \equiv F(fact)(k) \equiv (k = 0) \Rightarrow 1 \mid k * fact(k - 1)$$

and $fact$ satisfies its recursion equation. Through recursion, the λ-calculus can express all computable functions.

3.2.3   Adding types to the lambda calculus

Until now we have been considering the *untyped* λ-calculus. A type discipline can banish many of the strange constructions. The typed λ-calculus begins with basic types such as the natural numbers and booleans. It has function types: if σ and τ are types then $\sigma \to \tau$ is the type of functions from σ to τ. It imposes type constraints on terms:

- Each constant or variable belongs to one fixed type.

- If x has type σ and t has type τ then $(\lambda x.t)$ has type $\sigma \to \tau$.

- If t has type $\sigma \to \tau$ and u has type σ then $(t\,u)$ has type τ; otherwise $(t\,u)$ is ill typed.

The following conventions of the typed λ-calculus are also used in PPλ and ML. Abbreviate 't has type τ' as $t : \tau$. Writing $\lambda x : \tau.t$ indicates the type of the bound variable. The arrow associates to the right: $\sigma \to (\tau \to v)$ is abbreviated $\sigma \to \tau \to v$. This is the type of a curried function with arguments of type σ and τ.

---

[2] Recall that $t = u$ denotes an equality test on t and u. In contrast $t \equiv u$ is a formula, and $(k \equiv 0) \Rightarrow 1 \mid k * fact(k - 1)$ is syntactically incorrect.

It is easy to construct a model of the typed λ-calculus. Each basic type τ is interpreted as a set $D(\tau)$. Each constant of type τ is interpreted as a member of the set $D(\tau)$. Each function type $\sigma \to \tau$ is interpreted as the set of all functions from $D(\sigma)$ to $D(\tau)$. The type constraints make sure that $(\lambda x.t)$ can be interpreted as a function in the corresponding set. In the function call $(t\, u)$, the argument u is sure to belong to the domain of t. A term can have at most one type.

The typed λ-calculus is much weaker than the untyped. Self application can not occur: if $(t\, t)$ were well typed then t would have two different types, $\sigma \to \tau$ and σ. The definition of Y is ill typed; there is no term t such that $t(f) \equiv f(t(f))$. Many computable functions are not expressible. All evaluation sequences terminate.

The type system of ML is similar to that of the typed λ-calculus, but is *polymorphic*. Besides basic and function types it includes *type variables* α, β, γ, ... The function *twice* is given the type $(\alpha \to \alpha) \to (\alpha \to \alpha)$. We can test it in ML:

```
! fun twice f x = f(f(x));
- val twice = fn   : (('a -> 'a) -> ('a -> 'a))

! fun bang s = s^"!";
- val bang = fn   : (string -> string)

! twice bang "hello";
- it = "hello!!" : string

! twice twice bang "hello";
- it = "hello!!!!" : string

! twice twice twice bang "hello";
- it = "hello!!!!!!!!!!!!!!!!" : string
```

Do not be misled: this is not really self application. Let σ abbreviate the type $string \to string$. In *twice twice*, the second occurrence of *twice* has type $\sigma \to \sigma$, while the first has type $(\sigma \to \sigma) \to (\sigma \to \sigma)$. Since the two occurrences of *twice* have different types, they are different terms.

3.3   Computable functions

Dana Scott developed a Logic for Computable Functions (LCF) in 1969 as an outgrowth of his and C. Strachey's work in the denotational semantics of programming languages. Strachey had shown that most of the constructs of complicated programming languages could be reduced to the λ-calculus. The remaining problem was to find a satisfactory mathematical interpretation of the λ-calculus. No interesting models of the untyped λ-calculus were known, and the set-theoretic model of the typed calculus was not appropriate for computation.

Denotational semantics requires a smooth treatment of several concepts:

Computability is fundamental, yet too much of set theory concerns transfinite sets and functions of no computational significance.

Partial functions are needed to express the semantics of programs that run forever on certain inputs.

Functionals are heavily used in denotational semantics. Many programming languages allow functions to be arguments of functions.

Recursion is indispensable in denotational semantics. Even languages that do not allow recursive procedures contain iterative statements that are described via recursively defined functions. The operator Y cannot be defined in the typed λ-calculus.

Scott developed a computational framework of functions and data, the *theory of domains*. Domain theory is deep mathematics. It relies on topological notions such as continuity; most recent research is conducted within category theory. The remainder of this chapter draws on an early paper [89], developing the ideas using elementary facts about partial orderings and least upper bounds. The paper describes a logic, based on the typed λ-calculus, which Milner implemented as Stanford LCF. To distinguish the implementation from the logic, the logic was renamed PPλ: Polymorphic Predicate λ-calculus.[3] The logic underwent extensions and changes in notation, but the underlying concepts did not change.

The basic types of the logic contain all the individuals of interest: the type *tr* contains the truth values *TT* and *FF* and the type *nat* contains the natural numbers $0, 1, 2$, and so forth. There are function types, of the form $\sigma \to \tau$. The terms are those of the typed λ-calculus.

For reasoning about partial functions there are additional symbols for each type τ. The constant symbol $\perp_\tau$, pronounced 'bottom,' expresses nontermination. The symbol $\equiv_\tau$ expresses the equality of two terms having type τ. The relation symbol $\sqsubseteq_\tau$, pronounced 'approximates,' imposes a partial ordering on the type τ. (The subscript τ is omitted when it is obvious from context.) If f is a partial function then '$f(t)$ is undefined' is expressed as $f(t) \equiv \perp$. If f and g are partial functions then 'f is less defined than or equals g' is expressed as $f \sqsubseteq g$. To handle recursion there is the fixed point operator $FIX_{(\tau \to \tau) \to \tau}$ for each τ.

3.3.1   The semantics of nontermination

As usual we must now specify the meaning of each type, term, and formula of the logic. Each type τ denotes a domain $D(\tau)$. Each constant of type τ denotes an

---

[3]Scott's logic is still called LCF in the theoretical literature.

element of $D(\tau)$. The semantics differs from the usual one for the typed λ-calculus: the domain of $\sigma \rightarrow \tau$ contains only certain functions from $D(\sigma)$ to $D(\tau)$. Also, the domain of each type τ includes the element denoted by $\perp_\tau$.

I sometimes blur the distinction between a type τ and its domain $D(\tau)$, between the symbol $\perp_\tau$ in the logic and the corresponding element of $D(\tau)$, between the symbol $\sqsubseteq_\tau$ and the corresponding relation in the model, etc. Otherwise a whole new family of symbols would be required. Just remember that there is a difference between a formal symbol and the mathematical notation used to give its semantics.

The domain of type *nat* is not just the set $\{0, 1, 2, \ldots\}$; it must contain an additional element for $\perp_{nat}$. Consider the functions from *nat* to *nat*. Using computability theory, it is easy to construct a partial computable function that cannot be extended to a total computable function on the natural numbers. Therefore $\perp_{nat}$ is not a natural number. And common sense tells us that $f(x) \equiv 5$ is fundamentally different from $f(x) \equiv \perp$. A program terminates printing '5': this we can observe. A program runs forever with no output: this we can never observe. We can wait only a finite time and can never be certain whether the program will terminate in the future.[4]

The domains of the basic types are $D(nat) = \{\perp_{nat}, 0, 1, 2, \ldots\}$ and $D(tr) = \{\perp_{tr}, FF, TT\}$. The domains of function types are not so simple. They will be explained below.

The formula $x \sqsubseteq y$ means that x approximates y. The meaning is clearest when x and y are complex data structures such as functions or lazy lists. The partial ordering $\sqsubseteq_\tau$ must be specified for each domain $D(\tau)$. On a basic type the ordering is trivial; its purpose is to impose an ordering on types built from it. On function types the ordering is the usual one on partial functions, explained in the following section.

The element $\perp$ is totally undefined. So every type τ satisfies $\perp \sqsubseteq_\tau x$ for all x.

The type τ is called *flat* or *discrete* if its partial ordering is such that

$$x \sqsubseteq_\tau y \quad \text{if and only if} \quad x \equiv \perp \text{ or } x \equiv y$$

The basic types *tr* and *nat* are flat, as shown in Figure 3.1. In *nat*, the numbers 1 and 2 are distinct and totally defined. Neither $1 \sqsubseteq 2$ nor $2 \sqsubseteq 1$ hold: 1 and 2 are *incomparable*.

What does it mean to compute with infinite objects like functions and lazy lists? The partial ordering makes sense of unbounded computation. The infinite output is expressed as the limit of an ascending chain of finite approximations. A total function is the limit of a chain of partial functions, each extending its predecessor. A recursive function is the limit of the chain of functions obtained

---

[4]We can also observe that a program execution is aborted due to run-time error. Errors are often represented by adding error elements, distinct from $\perp$, to the types.

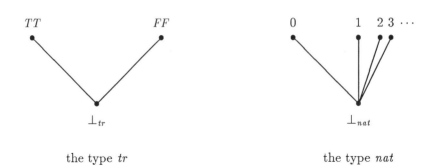

the type tr   the type nat

Figure 3.1: Two flat domains: truth values and natural numbers

by repeatedly unwinding the recursive definition. An infinite lazy list is the limit
of a sequence of partially defined, finite lists.

3.3.2   The semantics of functions: monotonicity

On function types the ordering $\sqsubseteq_{\sigma \to \tau}$ is too complex to be portrayed in a figure. If
$f, g : \sigma \to \tau$, then $f \sqsubseteq_{\sigma \to \tau} g$ holds when $f(x) \sqsubseteq_{\tau} g(x)$ for all $x : \sigma$. If $\sqsubseteq_{\tau}$ is a partial
ordering on $D(\tau)$, with a least element $\perp_{\tau}$, then $\sqsubseteq_{\sigma \to \tau}$ is a partial ordering on
$D(\sigma \to \tau)$. Its least element is the totally undefined function: $\perp_{\sigma \to \tau} \equiv \lambda x : \sigma . \perp_{\tau}$.
For example, suppose f and g are functions in $nat \to nat$. If $f \sqsubseteq g$ then g extends
f: for every number n either $f(n) \equiv \perp$ or else $f(n) \equiv g(n)$.

An important consequence is that equality of functions is *extensional*: if $f(x) \equiv$
$g(x)$ for all x then $f \equiv g$. The proof uses a trivial fact about partial orderings:
$t \equiv u$ if and only if $t \sqsubseteq u$ and $u \sqsubseteq t$. Therefore $f(x) \sqsubseteq g(x)$ for all x; by
the definition of $\sqsubseteq$ on functions, $f \sqsubseteq g$. A symmetric argument proves $g \sqsubseteq f$.
Therefore $f \equiv g$. Extensional equality means that a function is determined by its
input-output graph.

What is the domain of a function type $\sigma \to \tau$? It should contain only 'computable' functions. We cannot take the computable functions of recursion theory,
which only considers functions on the natural numbers. Instead we define a notion
of computable in terms of the partial ordering.

A *monotonic* function $f : \sigma \to \tau$ is one that respects the partial orderings: if
$x \sqsubseteq_{\sigma} y$ then $f(x) \sqsubseteq_{\tau} f(y)$. The domain of a function type contains only monotonic
functions. The idea is this: if a function is computable then making its input more
defined can only make its output more defined. An example of a non-monotonic
function is $HALTS$ such that $HALTS(\perp) \equiv FF$ and $HALTS(n) \equiv TT$ for all numbers
n. Then $HALTS(g(m))$ equals TT if $g(m)$ terminates and FF if $g(m)$ does not,
solving the halting problem for g. Clearly $HALTS$ is not computable.

What functions are monotonic? Say that h is *strict* if $h(\perp) \equiv \perp$. A strict function is monotonic if its type is $\sigma \to \tau$, where σ is a flat domain such as *nat*. Every *constant* function is monotonic: h is constant if $h(x) \equiv h(y)$ for all x and y.

Extending basic functions to domains

The interpretation of symbols like $+$ and $*$ must allow for $\perp$. Normally $+$ denotes the addition function on the natural numbers, but what are $\perp + t$ and $t + \perp$? Since $\perp$ stands for nontermination, and an arithmetic operation can only terminate if both arguments terminate, we can take

$$(\perp + t) \equiv (t + \perp) \equiv \perp_{nat}$$

$$(\perp * t) \equiv (t * \perp) \equiv \perp_{nat}.$$

The functions $+$ and $*$ are strict in both arguments, and hence monotonic, since *nat* is flat. They could have the curried function type $nat \to (nat \to nat)$. Alternatively they could have type $(nat \times nat) \to nat$; the product type is discussed later.

For any type σ, its test for equality, $=_\sigma$, must be strict:

$$(\perp =_\sigma x) \equiv (x =_\sigma \perp) \equiv \perp_{tr}.$$

You might think that a strict equality test is not doing its job. Surely $0 =_{nat} 0$ should be TT and $\perp =_{nat} 0$ should be FF. But then the function $=_{nat}$, like $HALTS$ above, would be neither monotonic nor computable. Because the equality test must be monotonic, it makes sense only for flat types.

The conditional operator satisfies

$$\perp \Rightarrow t \mid u \equiv \perp$$
$$TT \Rightarrow t \mid u \equiv t$$
$$FF \Rightarrow t \mid u \equiv u$$

The conditional is strict in its condition, but *not* in t and u! The conditional must only evaluate one of t or u. If it evaluated both, then it would not terminate in the base case of a recursive function like *fact*.

The boolean operations AND and OR can be defined in various ways. They can be strict functions:

$$(\perp\ OR\ t) \equiv (t\ OR\ \perp) \equiv \perp_{tr}$$

$$(\perp\ AND\ t) \equiv (t\ AND\ \perp) \equiv \perp_{tr}$$

Alternatively, they can be defined within PPλ via the conditional:

$$(t\ OR\ u) \equiv t \Rightarrow TT \mid u$$
$$(t\ AND\ u) \equiv t \Rightarrow u \mid FF$$

In the latter case $TT\ OR\ \perp\equiv TT$ and $FF\ AND\ \perp\equiv FF$: the second operand is only evaluated if necessary, as in ML's operators *andalso* and *orelse*. The operators AND and OR might both have the type $tr\rightarrow(tr\rightarrow tr)$.

A look at recursive functions

The treatment of recursive functions illustrates the properties of the partial ordering $\sqsubseteq_{\sigma\rightarrow\tau}$ on a function type.

Let *fact* be the factorial function of type $nat\rightarrow nat$, with $fact(k)\equiv k!$ for all numbers k in nat, and $fact(\perp)\equiv\perp$. For each natural number n let $fact_n$ be the function such that

$$fact_n(k)\ \equiv\ \begin{cases} k! & \text{if } k \text{ is one of } 0,1,\ldots,n-1 \\ \perp & \text{otherwise.} \end{cases}$$

If $m<n$ then $fact_m\sqsubseteq fact_n$ and $fact_n\sqsubseteq fact$. If $g(k)\not\equiv fact(k)$ for some k in nat, then g is incomparable with *fact* and each of the $fact_n$. The ascending chain $fact_0\sqsubseteq fact_1\sqsubseteq fact_2\ldots$ converges to *fact*: thus *fact* is the *least upper bound* of the $fact_n$ under the partial ordering $\sqsubseteq_{nat\rightarrow nat}$. Using the symbol $\bigsqcup$ for least upper bounds, we can write

$$fact\equiv\bigsqcup_{n=0}^{\infty}fact_n$$

Exercise 3.3 Prove that if the type σ is flat then every strict function of type $\sigma\rightarrow\tau$ is monotonic. Similarly, if $\sigma_1,\ \ldots,\ \sigma_n$ are flat types then every function of type $\sigma_1\rightarrow(\cdots\rightarrow(\sigma_n\rightarrow\tau)\cdots)$ that is strict in its first n arguments is monotonic.

Exercise 3.4 Using extensionality of functions, prove the validity of η-conversion: $\lambda x.f(x)\equiv f$ where x is not free in f.

3.3.3   The semantics of functionals: continuity

To be computable, a function must be *continuous* and not just monotonic. Continuity means

> *The result of an infinite computation is the limit of the results of a sequence of finite computations.*

The need for continuity becomes clear when we consider *functionals*: functions over functions. Suppose that the functional F has type $(nat\rightarrow nat)\rightarrow nat$. A computation of $F(g)$ can call g only a finite number of times. Therefore the value of $F(g)$ can depend on only a finite number of values computed by g, say $g(x_1),\ldots,g(x_k)$. If g is the least upper bound of the chain $g_0\sqsubseteq g_1\sqsubseteq g_2\sqsubseteq\cdots$ then there must be some point at which the values computed for $x_1,\ldots,x_k$ remain unchanged: some finite m such that if $n \geq m$ then g_m, g_n, and g all agree on $x_1, \ldots, x_k$. Since $F(g)$ depends only on those values, $F(g) \equiv F(g_m)$.

Suppose that g is the function *fact*. If $n \geq 1 + \max\{x_1, \ldots, x_k\}$ then *fact*$_n$ agrees with *fact* on $x_1, \ldots, x_k$.

Since F is monotonic, the chain $g_0 \sqsubseteq g_1 \sqsubseteq \cdots$ produces the chain $F(g_0) \sqsubseteq F(g_1) \sqsubseteq \cdots$. The above argument suggests that F must preserve least upper bounds:

$$\text{if} \qquad g_0 \sqsubseteq g_1 \sqsubseteq g_2 \sqsubseteq \cdots \qquad \text{has least upper bound } g$$
$$\text{then} \quad F(g_0) \sqsubseteq F(g_1) \sqsubseteq F(g_2) \sqsubseteq \cdots \quad \text{has least upper bound } F(g).$$

In short, F is *continuous*. Using the symbol $\bigsqcup$, this is

$$\bigsqcup_{n=0}^{\infty} F(g_n) \equiv F(g) \equiv F\left(\bigsqcup_{n=0}^{\infty} g_n\right).$$

This argument for continuity may not be convincing. But we shall soon see the importance of continuity in understanding recursion. It allows an interpretation of the fixed point operator *FIX*, for defining recursive functions. It also allows the rule of *fixed point induction*, for reasoning about recursive definitions.

Rigorous definitions will allow further development of this naive domain theory. Real domain theory imposes stronger requirements — for example, a domain must have a countable basis. During the 1970's, domains were generally required to be lattices.

Definition 3.1 Let the set D be partially ordered by $\sqsubseteq_D$, and E by $\sqsubseteq_E$.

Call x the *least* member of D if $x \in D$ and each y in D satisfies $x \sqsubseteq_D y$.

Call x an *upper bound* of D if each y in D satisfies $y \sqsubseteq_D x$. (A set need not have an upper bound.)

The *least upper bound* (lub) of D, written $\bigsqcup D$, is the least member of the set of upper bounds of D. Conventions: $\bigsqcup\{x, y\}$ is written $x \sqcup y$ and $\bigsqcup\{x_0, x_1, x_2, \ldots\}$ is written $\bigsqcup_{n=0}^{\infty} x_n$. (So $\bigsqcup D$, if it exists, is an upper bound of D and is smaller than every other.)

A *ascending chain* in D is a set $\{x_0, x_1, x_2, \ldots\}$ of members of D such that $x_0 \sqsubseteq_D x_1 \sqsubseteq_D x_2 \sqsubseteq_D \cdots$.

The set D is a *complete partial ordering* (cpo) if it has a least member $\bot_D$ and every ascending chain contained in D has a least upper bound in D.

A function $f : D \to E$ is *monotonic* when $x \sqsubseteq_D y$ implies $f(x) \sqsubseteq_E f(y)$.

A monotonic function $f : D \to E$ is *continuous* provided that if $x_0 \sqsubseteq x_1 \sqsubseteq \cdots$ is a chain in D then $f(\bigsqcup_{n=0}^{\infty} x_n) \equiv \bigsqcup_{n=0}^{\infty} f(x_n)$. $\square$

The domain of each type τ of PPλ is a cpo $D(\tau)$. The domain of the function type $\sigma \to \tau$ is the set of all continuous functions from $D(\sigma)$ to $D(\tau)$. Each function symbol of PPλ denotes a continuous function; therefore so does every term of function type. The proof requires showing that the operations of abstraction and combination are continuous [88]. A special case concerns function composition. The composition of the functions g and h is $\lambda x.g(hx)$, often written $g \circ h$.

Theorem 3.1 *Function composition is continuous: if g and h are continuous then so is $g \circ h$.*
Proof: By continuity, push the $\bigsqcup$ operator to the outside:

$$(g \circ h)(\bigsqcup_{n=0}^{\infty} x_n) \equiv g(h(\bigsqcup_{n=0}^{\infty} x_n)) \equiv g(\bigsqcup_{n=0}^{\infty} h(x_n)) \equiv \bigsqcup_{n=0}^{\infty} g(h(x_n)) \equiv \bigsqcup_{n=0}^{\infty} (g \circ h)(x_n)$$

$\square$

Exercise 3.5 Show that the domain of each basic type is a cpo. Show that if $D(\sigma)$ and $D(\tau)$ are cpos, then so is $D(\sigma \to \tau)$, with $(\bigsqcup_{n=0}^{\infty} f_n)x \equiv \bigsqcup_{n=0}^{\infty} f_n(x)$.

Exercise 3.6 A member of $D(\sigma \to (\tau \to \upsilon))$ is a (curried) continuous function of two arguments. Show that if f, g, and h are continuous then so is $\lambda x\, y.\, f(g(x))(h(y))$. Hint: first show that $\bigsqcup_{m=0}^{\infty} \bigsqcup_{n=0}^{\infty} f(x_m)(y_n) \equiv \bigsqcup_{n=0}^{\infty} f(x_n)(y_n)$.

Exercise 3.7 Show that the application operation $\lambda xy.x(y)$ is a continuous function of type $(\sigma \to \tau) \to (\sigma \to \tau)$.

3.3.4   Recursion and least fixed points

We now come to the point of this entire development. The operator $FIX_{(\tau \to \tau) \to \tau}$ allows PPλ to express recursively defined functions. It must be interpreted by a function such that $FIX(f) \equiv f(FIX(f))$ for all f of type $\tau \to \tau$. At the time of Scott's paper, the interpretation of FIX could not be determined from the definition of Y in the untyped λ-calculus, which had no useful model. Instead Scott appealed to Tarski's Fixed Point Theorem.

Define exponentiation f^n of a function f as $f^0(x) \equiv x$ and $f^{n+1}(x) \equiv f(f^n(x))$. So

$$f^n(x) \equiv \underbrace{f(f(\cdots f(x)\cdots))}_{n\ \text{times}}.$$

For each type τ, the interpretation of $FIX_{(\tau \to \tau) \to \tau}$ is the function that maps f to $\bigsqcup_{n=0}^{\infty} f^n(\bot_\tau)$. Here is the theorem that $FIX(f)$ is a fixed point of f.

Theorem 3.2 *Every continuous function f has a fixed point, the least upper bound $\bigsqcup_{n=0}^{\infty} f^n(\bot_\tau)$ of the ascending chain*

$$\bot \sqsubseteq f(\bot) \sqsubseteq f(f(\bot)) \sqsubseteq f(f(f(\bot))) \cdots$$

Proof:

$$f(FIX(f)) \equiv f(\bigsqcup_{n=0}^{\infty} f^n(\bot))$$

$$\equiv \bigsqcup_{n=0}^{\infty} f(f^n(\bot)) \qquad \text{(by continuity)}$$

$$\equiv \bigsqcup_{n=1}^{\infty} f^n(\bot)$$

$$\equiv \bigsqcup_{n=0}^{\infty} f^n(\bot)$$

$$\equiv FIX(f) \ \square$$

Example 3.3 The λ-calculus definition of *fact* indeed denotes the factorial function. The functional

$$F \equiv \lambda g\, k.\,(k = 0) \Rightarrow 1 \mid k * g(k-1)$$

has type $(nat \rightarrow nat) \rightarrow (nat \rightarrow nat)$. Define $fact \equiv FIX(F)$. Then $fact$ has type $nat \rightarrow nat$ and denotes $\bigsqcup_{n=0}^{\infty} F^n(\bot)$.

Theorem 3.3 *The function $F^n(\bot)$ is equal to $fact_n$.*
Proof: By extensionality, it is enough to show $F^n(\bot)(k) \equiv fact_n(k)$ for all k. Use induction on n.

Base case: $F^0(\bot) \equiv \bot_{nat \rightarrow nat} \equiv fact_0$, the totally undefined function.
Induction step:

$$F^{n+1}(\bot)(k) \equiv F(F^n(\bot))(k)$$

$$\equiv F(fact_n)(k) \qquad \text{(by induction hypothesis)}$$

$$\equiv (k = 0) \Rightarrow 1 \mid k * fact_n(k-1).$$

There are several cases. If $k \equiv \bot$ then because the conditional and equality test $(=)$ are strict, $F^{n+1}(\bot)(\bot) \equiv \bot \equiv fact_{n+1}(\bot)$.

Otherwise $k \not\equiv \bot$. If $k < n+1$ then $fact_n(k-1)$ equals $(k-1)!$, so $F^{n+1}(\bot)(k) \equiv k * (k-1)! \equiv k! \equiv fact_{n+1}(k)$. If $k \geq n+1$ then $fact_n(k-1) \equiv \bot$ and so $F^{n+1}(\bot)(k) \equiv k * \bot \equiv \bot \equiv fact_{n+1}(k)$. $\square$

The equality $fact \equiv \bigsqcup_{n=0}^{\infty} fact_n$ can be seen as the application of the Fixed Point Theorem to the recursive definition of the factorial. Note that $fact$ is used in two senses here: as a symbol of PPλ having type $nat \rightarrow nat$, and as the interpretation of this symbol, a continous function in the domain $D(nat \rightarrow nat)$.

Example 3.4 A function may have many fixed points. Consider the recursive definition

$$loop(x) \equiv loop(x)$$

The interpretation of *loop* is $FIX(\lambda Lx.L(x))$. The argument of FIX is the identity functional: it takes a function L and returns $\lambda x.L(x)$. By extensionality, these functions are the same. So every function L is a fixed point of $\lambda Lx.L(x)$. The *least* fixed point is the totally undefined function, $\lambda x.\bot$, and so the function *loop* diverges on all arguments. Example 3.6 proves that $FIX(f)$ is the least fixed point of f, approximating every other fixed point:

$$f(z) \equiv z \quad \text{implies} \quad FIX(f) \sqsubseteq z$$

So FIX is called the least fixed point operator.

The least fixed point gives the minimum information: a recursive function does not terminate unless it must. Why favor the least fixed point over the others? The least fixed point always exists and is unique. Especially, it is computable: the function FIX is continuous.

Exercise 3.8 Prove that $FIX_{(\tau \to \tau) \to \tau}$ indeed belongs to $D((\tau \to \tau) \to \tau)$ by proving that $\bigsqcup_{n=0}^{\infty} f^n(\bot)$ is a continuous function in f.

3.4 Axioms and rules of the logic

The semantics given above, particularly the treatment of functions, justifies the axioms and inference rules of PPλ. A full listing appears in Chapter 7.

The partial ordering is reflexive, antisymmetric, and transitive:

$$t \sqsubseteq t \qquad \frac{t \sqsubseteq u \qquad u \sqsubseteq t}{t \equiv u} \qquad \frac{s \sqsubseteq t \qquad t \sqsubseteq u}{s \sqsubseteq u}$$

Scott took $t \equiv u$ as an abbreviation for $t \sqsubseteq u \wedge u \sqsubseteq t$. Alternatively, use the rules

$$\frac{t \equiv u}{t \sqsubseteq u} \qquad \frac{t \equiv u}{u \sqsubseteq t}$$

The value $\bot$ is minimal in the partial ordering:

$$\bot \sqsubseteq t$$

Function application is monotonic:

$$\frac{f \sqsubseteq g \qquad t \sqsubseteq u}{f(t) \sqsubseteq g(u)}$$

Functions are extensional:

$$\frac{f(x) \sqsubseteq g(x)}{f \sqsubseteq g} \qquad \textit{provided x is not free in the assumptions}$$

The premise could be stated more simply using a universal quantifier. But Scott's original logic had no logical connectives apart from conjunction.

The function *FIX* returns a fixed point of its argument:

$$f(\textit{FIX } f) \equiv \textit{FIX } f.$$

That this is the least fixed point follows by fixed point induction, as we shall see below.

Scott had infinite families of constants indexed by types. For each type τ there were symbols $\perp_\tau$, $\textit{FIX}_{(\tau\to\tau)\to\tau}$, and so on. PP$\lambda$ uses a *polymorphic* type system with type variables. The symbol $\perp$ has the generic type α, and *FIX* has type $(\alpha \to \alpha) \to \alpha$. A type checking algorithm similar to ML's finds the appropriate type instance for the context in which these symbols appear. Polymorphic type inference means treating type variables as schematic variables of the inference rules. The minimality axiom is really $\perp_\alpha \sqsubseteq t$, and is schematic in the type α as well as in the term t.

Example 3.5 The bottom element of type $\sigma \to \tau$ is the totally undefined function: $\perp_{\sigma\to\tau} \equiv \lambda x : \sigma.\perp_\tau$. The proof tree uses the minimality of $\perp$, β-reduction, the rules for $\equiv$, transitivity, and extensionality:

$$\cfrac{\perp \sqsubseteq_{\sigma\to\tau} \lambda x.\perp \qquad \cfrac{\cfrac{(\lambda x.\perp)(x) \equiv_\tau \perp}{(\lambda x.\perp)(x) \sqsubseteq_\tau \perp} \qquad \perp \sqsubseteq_\tau \perp(x)}{\cfrac{(\lambda x.\perp)(x) \sqsubseteq_\tau \perp(x)}{\lambda x.\perp \sqsubseteq_{\sigma\to\tau} \perp}}}{\perp \equiv_{\sigma\to\tau} \lambda x.\perp}$$

3.5 Fixed point induction

Proving the correctness of programs, program transformations, or compilers requires the ability to prove statements about recursively defined functions. A program transformation is verified by proving that $f \equiv g$, where g is a more efficient program than f.

We must distinguish formal proofs from proofs in the semantics. PPλ is a *formal logic* of computation. Recursive functions are expressed via the symbol *FIX*. In the semantics, *FIX*(f) is interpreted as $\bigsqcup_{n=0}^{\infty} f^n(\perp)$. Statements about *FIX* can be verified by proving facts about its semantic interpretation, but this is a proof *about* PPλ rather than *in* PPλ. To reason formally about $\bigsqcup_{n=0}^{\infty} f^n(\perp)$ would require extending PPλ with the operator $\bigsqcup$, the natural numbers, and mathematical induction. A simpler alternative is Scott's rule of *fixed point induction*:

$$\cfrac{A \text{ chain-complete in } x \qquad A[\perp/x] \qquad \cfrac{[A]}{A[f(x)/x]}}{A[\textit{FIX}(f)/x]}$$

provided x is not free in the assumptions of $A[f(x)/x]$ apart from A.

Using quantifiers and implication, the rule is

$$\frac{A \text{ chain-complete in } x \qquad A[\perp/x] \qquad \forall x.\, A \Longrightarrow A[f(x)/x]}{A[FIX(f)/x]}$$

The first premise requires an explanation. Suppose x has type τ. Let $[\![A]\!]_x$ denote the set of all x such that A holds:

$$[\![A]\!]_x = \{x \in D(\tau) \mid A\}$$

A set E is *chain-complete* provided for every chain $y_0 \sqsubseteq y_1 \sqsubseteq y_2 \sqsubseteq \cdots$ contained in E, the least upper bound $\bigsqcup_{n=0}^{\infty} y_n$ is also in E. The formula A is *chain-complete* (or *admissible*) in x if $[\![A]\!]_x$ is chain-complete.[5]

Fixed point induction is difficult to formalize. An inference rule operates on the syntactic structure of its premises, but chain-completeness refers to semantics. No simple test is known for determining that a formula is chain-complete. PPλ's complicated test rejects many chain-complete formulae. Below we will examine ways of constructing such formulae.

It is easy to see why fixed point induction is sound. The second and third premises imply the series of theorems $A[\perp/x]$, $A[f(\perp)/x]$, $A[f(f(\perp))/x]$, $\ldots$, and so $\perp$, $f(\perp)$, $f(f(\perp))$, $\ldots$ belong to $[\![A]\!]_x$. By chain-completeness, $\bigsqcup_{n=0}^{\infty} f^n(\perp)$ is in $[\![A]\!]_x$, so $A[FIX(f)/x]$ is true. Fixed point induction is the only rule that depends upon the continuity of functions in PPλ: if f were not continuous then $FIX(f)$ would not be a fixed point.

The following examples compare fixed point induction with proof using the semantics of FIX. For now just assume that the induction formulae of fixed point induction are chain-complete; a proof follows.

Example 3.6 David Park's version of fixed point induction is a basic fact about FIX. It implies that $FIX(f)$ is the least fixed point of f. Manna [62, page 406] uses Park's rule to study McCarthy's 91-function. The rule is

$$\frac{f(z) \sqsubseteq z}{FIX(f) \sqsubseteq z}$$

Let us verify the rule using both approaches.

Proof in the semantics: Assume $f(z) \sqsubseteq z$ and prove $\bigsqcup_{n=0}^{\infty} f^n(\perp) \sqsubseteq z$. The monotonicity of f gives a sequence of approximations:

$$\perp \sqsubseteq z$$
$$f(\perp) \sqsubseteq f(z) \sqsubseteq z$$
$$f(f(\perp)) \sqsubseteq f(f(z)) \sqsubseteq f(z) \sqsubseteq z$$
$$\vdots$$

---

[5]Since a chain-complete set need not have a least element, it is not necessarily a cpo.

and $f^n(\bot) \sqsubseteq z$ for all n. So z is an upper bound of the chain $\bot \sqsubseteq f(\bot) \sqsubseteq f(f(\bot)) \cdots$. Since $\bigsqcup_{n=0}^{\infty} f^n(\bot)$ is the *least* upper bound of that chain, the conclusion follows. $\square$

Proof via fixed point induction: Assume $f(z) \sqsubseteq z$ and prove $FIX(f) \sqsubseteq z$ using $x \sqsubseteq z$ as the induction formula. In fixed point induction, the base case is the trivial $\bot \sqsubseteq z$. The inductive step is to prove that $x \sqsubseteq z$ implies $f(x) \sqsubseteq z$, which holds by monotonicity: $f(x) \sqsubseteq f(z) \sqsubseteq z$. $\square$

This informal argument corresponds to the proof tree

$$\dfrac{\bot \sqsubseteq z \qquad \dfrac{\dfrac{f \sqsubseteq f \qquad [x \sqsubseteq z]}{f(x) \sqsubseteq f(z)} \qquad f(z) \sqsubseteq z}{f(x) \sqsubseteq z}}{FIX(f) \sqsubseteq z}$$

The proof trees for the other examples are too large to present.

Example 3.7 (Manna [62, page 394]) Let $G : \sigma \to \sigma$ be an arbitrary function, and $P : \sigma \to tr$ a strict function: $P(\bot) \equiv \bot$. Define the function $H : \sigma \to \sigma$ as $H \equiv FIX(K)$, where $K \equiv \lambda h\, x.\, P(x) \Rightarrow x \mid h(h(Gx))$. We can now prove $H(Hx) \equiv H(x)$ for all x.

First, let us prove in PPλ that H is strict. Since $FIX(K) \equiv K(FIX(K))$, clearly $H(x) \equiv P(x) \Rightarrow x \mid H(H(Gx))$. Now

$$H(\bot) \equiv P(\bot) \Rightarrow \bot \mid H(H(G\bot)) \equiv \bot \Rightarrow \bot \mid H(H(G\bot)) \equiv \bot$$

by strictness of P and the conditional. $\square$

Proof in the semantics: The proof of $H(Hx) \equiv H(x)$ proceeds by unfolding only two of the three occurrences of H: prove $H(FIX(K)x) \equiv FIX(K)(x)$. By the interpretation of FIX it suffices to prove

$$H(\bigsqcup_{n=0}^{\infty} K^n(\bot)x) \equiv \bigsqcup_{n=0}^{\infty} K^n(\bot)(x).$$

By continuity, the left side equals $\bigsqcup_{n=0}^{\infty} H(K^n(\bot)x)$. Considering the chains element by element, it suffices to prove

$$\forall x.\, H(K^n(\bot)x) \equiv K^n(\bot)(x).$$

Use mathematical induction on n. The base case holds:

$$H(K^0(\bot)x) \equiv H(\bot x) \equiv H(\bot) \equiv \bot \equiv K^0(\bot)x.$$

To prove the inductive step, assume $\forall x.\, H(K^n(\bot)x) \equiv K^n(\bot)(x)$ and prove $\forall x.\, H(K^{n+1}(\bot)x) \equiv K^{n+1}(\bot)(x)$. This reduces to

$$H(K(K^n(\bot))x) \equiv K(K^n(\bot))(x)$$

and then, unfolding K on both sides, to

$$H(P(x) \Rightarrow x \mid K^n(\bot)(K^n(\bot)(Gx))) \equiv P(x) \Rightarrow x \mid K^n(\bot)(K^n(\bot)(Gx))$$

Consider the three cases: $P(x)$ is either $\bot$, TT, or FF. The case for $P(x) \equiv \bot$ follows by strictness of H and the conditional:

$$H(\bot \Rightarrow x \mid K^n\bot(K^n\bot(Gx))) \equiv H(\bot) \equiv \bot \equiv (\bot \Rightarrow x \mid K^n\bot(K^n\bot(Gx))).$$

Observe that if $P(x) \equiv TT$ then

$$H(x) \equiv TT \Rightarrow x \mid H(H(Gx)) \equiv x$$

and this case follows:

$$H(TT \Rightarrow x \mid K^n\bot(K^n\bot(Gx))) \equiv H(x) \equiv x \equiv (TT \Rightarrow x \mid K^n\bot(K^n\bot(Gx))).$$

The case for $P(x) \equiv FF$ holds:

$$\begin{aligned}
H(FF \Rightarrow x \mid K^n\bot(K^n\bot(Gx))) &\equiv H(K^n\bot(K^n\bot(Gx))) \\
&\equiv K^n\bot(K^n\bot(Gx)) \\
&\equiv FF \Rightarrow x \mid K^n\bot(K^n\bot(Gx)).\square
\end{aligned}$$

The second step depends on the universal quantifier in the induction hypothesis. An alternative: the induction formula could be stated $H \circ FIX(K) \equiv FIX(K)$.

Proof via fixed point induction: Again prove $\forall x.\, H(FIX(K)x) \equiv FIX(K)(x)$, using fixed point induction on h in $\forall x.\, H(hx) \equiv h(x)$. The base case holds:

$$H(\bot x) \equiv H(\bot) \equiv \bot \equiv \bot x.$$

The induction step is proved by assuming $\forall x.\, H(hx) \equiv h(x)$ and proving

$$\forall x.\, H(Khx) \equiv Khx.$$

The rest of the proof is identical to the previous version, with h taking the place of $K^n\bot$. Show

$$H(P(x) \Rightarrow x \mid h(h(Gx))) \equiv P(x) \Rightarrow x \mid h(h(Gx))$$

by case analysis on $P(x)$. If $P(x) \equiv \bot$ then

$$H(\bot \Rightarrow x \mid h(h(Gx))) \equiv H(\bot) \equiv \bot \equiv \bot \Rightarrow x \mid h(h(Gx)).$$

If $P(x) \equiv TT$ then

$$H(TT \Rightarrow x \mid h(h(Gx))) \equiv H(x) \equiv x \equiv TT \Rightarrow x \mid h(h(Gx)).$$

If $P(x) \equiv FF$ then

$$H(FF \Rightarrow x \mid h(h(Gx))) \equiv H(h(h(Gx))) \equiv h(h(Gx)) \equiv FF \Rightarrow x \mid h(h(Gx)).\square$$

As before, the universal quantifier in the induction hypothesis allows the proof to go through.

Fixed point induction allows a more abstract proof. Continuity and fixed points are taken care of automatically: they are built into the rule. In principle, reasoning directly about the least fixed point can prove more theorems than fixed point induction. In practice, fixed point induction is adequate.

Example 3.8 (Manna [62, page 397]) Let $G : \sigma \to \sigma$ and $P : \sigma \to tr$ be arbitrary functions, and $F : \tau \to \tau$ a strict function. Define the function $H : \sigma \to (\tau \to \sigma)$ as $H \equiv FIX(K)$, where

$$K \equiv \lambda hxy. \, P(x) \Rightarrow y \mid F(h(Gx)(y))$$

Then $F(Hxy) \equiv H(x)(Fy)$ for all x and y.

Proof via fixed point induction: Prove $\forall x \, y. \, F(FIX(K)xy) \equiv FIX(K)(x)(Fy)$ using fixed point induction on h in $\forall x \, y. \, F(hxy) \equiv h(x)(Fy)$. The base case, $F(\perp xy) \equiv \perp(x)(Fy)$, holds because F is strict.

The induction step requires assuming $\forall x \, y. \, F(hxy) \equiv h(x)(Fy)$ and proving

$$F((Kh)xy) \equiv (Kh)(x)(Fy).$$

Unfolding K, it suffices to show

$$F(P(x) \Rightarrow y \mid F(h(Gx)(y))) \equiv P(x) \Rightarrow Fy \mid F(h(Gx)(Fy))$$

Case analysis on $P(x)$ gives three subgoals: If $P(x) \equiv \perp$ then

$$F(\perp \Rightarrow y \mid F(h(Gx)(y))) \equiv F(\perp) \equiv \perp \equiv \perp \Rightarrow Fy \mid F(h(Gx)(Fy)) \, .$$

If $P(x) \equiv TT$ then

$$F(TT \Rightarrow y \mid F(h(Gx)(y))) \equiv Fy \equiv TT \Rightarrow Fy \mid F(h(Gx)(Fy)) \, .$$

If $P(x) \equiv FF$ then, using the induction hypothesis,

$$
\begin{aligned}
F(FF \Rightarrow y \mid F(h(Gx)(y))) &\equiv F(F(h(Gx)(y))) \\
&\equiv F(h(Gx)(Fy)) \\
&\equiv FF \Rightarrow Fy \mid F(h(Gx)(Fy)) \, . \square
\end{aligned}
$$

The quantification over x is essential; that over y is not.

Exercise 3.9 Work the final example by reasoning about $\bigsqcup_{n=0}^{\infty} K^n \perp$.

Exercise 3.10 (Scott [89].) Let f, g, and h be functions of type $\tau \to \tau$ such that $f \circ g \equiv g \circ f$ and $f \circ h \equiv h \circ f$. Prove that $g \perp \sqsubseteq h \perp$ implies $g(FIX \, f) \sqsubseteq h(FIX \, f)$ using fixed point induction.

Exercise 3.11 Let f and g be functions of type $\tau \to \tau$ such that $f \circ g \equiv g \circ f$. Prove that $f \perp \equiv g \perp$ implies $FIX \, f \equiv FIX \, g$ by fixed point induction. Hint: prove $g(FIX \, f) \sqsubseteq f(FIX \, f)$, then $FIX \, g \sqsubseteq FIX \, f$.

Exercise 3.12 Let f and g be as in the previous exercise. Prove $\bigsqcup_{n=0}^{\infty} f^n(\perp) \equiv \bigsqcup_{n=0}^{\infty} g^n(\perp)$. The theorem considered in these two exercises is useful for proving the equivalence of two recursive function definitions.

3.6   Admissibility of fixed point induction

The problem with fixed point induction is determining whether the induction formula is admissible. In Scott's original logic all formulae are conjunctions of inequivalences, which are all chain-complete: see Manna [62, page 393]. Extending fixed point induction to first order logic requires a study of the structure of chain-complete formulae [52].

Clearly the formula A is chain-complete in x if x is not free in A, since its truth does not depend upon x. For discussing other classes of chain-complete formulae, let $y_0 \sqsubseteq y_1 \sqsubseteq y_2 \cdots$ be an ascending chain.

Theorem 3.4 *Every PPλ formula of the form $t \sqsubseteq u$ is chain-complete in x.*
Proof: In the semantics, the dependence of a term upon x is a continuous function. It suffices to consider $f(x) \sqsubseteq g(x)$, where f and g are continuous functions. Assume that $f(y_n) \sqsubseteq g(y_n)$ for all n. Therefore $\bigsqcup_{n=0}^{\infty} f(y_n) \sqsubseteq \bigsqcup_{n=0}^{\infty} g(y_n)$ (exercise: justify in detail). By continuity, $f(\bigsqcup_{n=0}^{\infty} y_n) \sqsubseteq g(\bigsqcup_{n=0}^{\infty} y_n)$. $\square$

Theorem 3.5 *The negated formula $t \not\sqsubseteq u$ is chain-complete in x provided that x is not free in u.*
Proof: Working in the semantics, it suffices to consider $f(x) \not\sqsubseteq c$, where f is a continuous function and c is constant. If $f(y_n) \not\sqsubseteq c$ then $\bigsqcup_{n=0}^{\infty} f(y_n) \not\sqsubseteq c$, because $f(y_n) \sqsubseteq \bigsqcup_{n=0}^{\infty} f(y_n)$. $\square$

Certain connectives preserve chain-completeness.

Theorem 3.6 *If A is chain-complete in x then so is $\forall z.A$.*
Proof: To show that $[\![\forall z.A]\!]_x$ is chain-complete, assume that $y_0, y_1, y_2, \ldots$ belong to it and show that $\bigsqcup_{n=0}^{\infty} y_n$ does. By the meaning of the universal quantifier, it is enough to show that $\bigsqcup_{n=0}^{\infty} y_n$ is in $[\![A]\!]_x$ for all z. Since A is chain-complete, it is enough to show that $y_0, y_1, y_2, \ldots$ belong to $[\![A]\!]_x$. This follows because they belong to $[\![\forall z.A]\!]_x$. $\square$

The concept of chain-completeness can be extended to several variables, justifying *simultaneous* fixed point induction in n variables. For two variables the rule is

$$\frac{A \text{ chain-complete in } x \text{ and } y \qquad A[\bot/x, \bot/y] \qquad \forall xy.\, A \implies A[f(x)/x, g(y)/y]}{A[FIX(f)/x, FIX(g)/y]}$$

Structural induction can be derived from fixed point induction. Induction over finite lists and trees is most familiar, but PPλ allows inductive proofs about unbounded computations over lazy lists. Induction over lazy data types is sound for chain-complete formulae; induction on flat types (like the natural numbers) is sound for all formulae. To handle all these possibilities, Cambridge LCF's admissibility test is extremely complicated. Perhaps chain-completeness should be formalized: each use of induction would require a formal proof of admissibility.

Exercise 3.13 Show that if A and B are chain-complete in x, then so is $A \wedge B$.

Exercise 3.14 Show that if A and B are chain-complete in x, then so is $A \vee B$.

Exercise 3.15 Show that if $\neg A$ and B are chain-complete in x, then so is $A \implies B$.

Exercise 3.16 Show that $t \equiv u$ is chain-complete in x.

Exercise 3.17 Show that $t \not\equiv \bot$ is chain-complete in x.

Exercise 3.18 Show that 'f is not total,' in symbols $\exists x.\ f(x) \equiv \bot$, is *not* chain-complete in f. (Hint: consider the chain of functions $fact_n$.)

3.7 Further reading

Hindley and Seldin is a good introduction to the λ-calculus [47], while Barendregt has written the comprehensive reference [2].

Reynolds has written a readable introduction to denotational semantics, including aspects of the λ-calculus. He explains why functions must be continuous [84]. More advanced books on denotational semantics, by Schmidt [88] and Stoy [96], develop the theory.

Manna's chapter on the fixed point theory of programs, while slightly out of date, contains a readable account of fixed point induction and related rules [62].

Must nontermination be represented by an undefined element? An alternative to $\bot$ is to allow only total functions, as in the Boyer/Moore theorem prover [12] and in Martin-Löf's Type Theory [65].

The next chapter shows how data structures and their structural induction principles are constructed in PPλ.

Chapter 4

Structural Induction

Reasoning about functional programs requires the ability to define interesting data structures in PPλ. In Scott's original calculus the only type constructor is function space: if σ and τ are types then so is the function type $\sigma \to \tau$. A fundamental data structure is the Cartesian product, the type $\sigma \times \tau$. Other data type constructors are the strict product, various sums, and lifting. Starting from atomic types, many data structures can be expressed. Each type constructor has *constructor functions* for creating elements of the type. For taking elements apart it may have *destructor functions* or else an *eliminator functional*.

Furthermore *recursive* type constructors are definable. Domain theory allows the solution of recursive domain equations involving sum, product, function space, and several other type constructors. Cambridge LCF provides a mechanism for defining PPλ types in a style similar to Standard ML datatype definitions: LCF can generate axioms to define a PPλ type recursively as the sum of products of types, with one constructor function for each summand of the type.

The constructor functions determine whether a type is strict or lazy. If a constructor function is not strict in all arguments then it can construct *partial objects*: objects that have undefined parts. The resulting type, if recursive, also contains infinite objects. An example is the type of lazy lists, which contains partially defined and infinite lists. If every constructor is strict in every argument, then the resulting *strict* type contains only finite objects. Examples are ML lists and the natural numbers. Sometimes *mixed* types are useful, where constructors are strict in certain arguments but not in all. PPλ is best suited for reasoning about lazy data types. Cambridge LCF provides structural induction, via fixed point induction, for both strict and lazy types.

Domain theory is often developed within *category theory*, an abstract framework of mappings (called *morphisms*) between types (called *objects*). Morphisms can be composed; every type has an identity morphism. Type constructors correspond to *functors*, which map objects to objects and morphisms to morphisms. The product and sum of types correspond to functors satisfying particular abstract properties. Sets and functions form a category; the Cartesian product of sets is a functor.

Category theory is concerned with mappings that preserve structure. For example, a functor is not an arbitrary map: it must respect the identity morphisms and the compositions of morphisms. Groups and group homomorphisms form a category; the direct product of groups is a functor. The morphisms and functors preserve algebraic structure. Similarly, rings, fields, and topological spaces give rise to categories. Domains and continuous functions also form a category; the functors are domain constructors.

We do not have space for a proper account of category theory. The categorical notions of sum and product are expressed through isomorphisms between domains. The solution of recursive domain equations involves the *inverse limit*, a categorical construction that is sketched below.

Type constructors in PPλ obey the same postfix syntax as in ML. For example, if *list* is a 1-place type constructor and σ is a type then $(\sigma)\,list$ is a type, also written without parentheses: $\sigma\,list$. If *tcon* is an n-place type constructor and σ_1, ..., σ_n are types then $(\sigma_1, \ldots, \sigma_n)tcon$ is a type.

The description of each type constructor includes a discussion of its purpose, the names and types of its constructor and destructor functions, and the axioms they satisfy. A type's constructors and destructors determine its partial ordering. We shall consider alternative formalizations, relationships with other types, and a semantics in set theory. Of course, this is not how to go about inventing a new type constructor. The inventor would begin with a vague idea of the operations that the type should satisfy, construct a model, verify that it is a cpo, and only then consider the precise properties of operations in the model.

The interesting mathematics takes place at the level of domains. A type is just a symbol denoting a domain. So we may confuse syntax with semantics, regard type constructors as domain constructors, and speak of the domains $D \times E$ or $D \oplus E$ instead of the types $\sigma \times \tau$ or $\sigma \oplus \tau$.

4.1   The Cartesian product of two types

The ordered pair is a basic concept in mathematics. In set theory the Cartesian product of two sets A and B is the set of all pairs $\langle x, y \rangle$ with x in A and y in B. A function $f(x, y)$ is interpreted as a function whose argument is the pair $\langle x, y \rangle$, not as a curried function. Domain theory has various notions of pair, differing in the treatment of $\bot$.

The Cartesian product is provided in Cambridge LCF. The other type constructors are not provided but are easily constructed.

4.1.1   Syntax and axioms

If σ and τ are types then so is the *Cartesian product* type $\sigma \times \tau$. The type $\sigma \times \tau$ comes with three constant symbols:

$$PAIR : \sigma \to \tau \to (\sigma \times \tau)$$
$$FST : (\sigma \times \tau) \to \sigma$$
$$SND : (\sigma \times \tau) \to \tau$$

The ordered pair (t, u) is an abbreviation for $PAIR(t)(u)$. For $x : \sigma$ and $y : \tau$, the pair (x, y) has type $\sigma \times \tau$.

The axioms are

$$FST(x, y) \equiv x$$
$$SND(x, y) \equiv y$$
$$(FST\ z, SND\ z) \equiv z$$

The third axiom, sometimes called *surjective pairing*, asserts that every member of $\sigma \times \tau$ has the form (x, y) for unique $x : \sigma$ and $y : \tau$. Equivalent is the *exhaustion axiom*

$$\forall z : \sigma \times \tau . \exists xy . z \equiv (x, y)$$

The surjective pairing axiom implies the exhaustion axiom, putting $FST(z)$ for x and $SND(z)$ for y. Exhaustion implies surjective pairing: it lets us replace z by (x, y), reducing the goal $(FST\ z, SND\ z) \equiv z$ to

$$(FST(x, y), SND(x, y)) \equiv (x, y)$$

What is the partial ordering $\sqsubseteq_{\sigma \times \tau}$ on the product type? Recall from the previous chapter that all functions in PPλ must be monotonic and continuous; the monotonicity of *PAIR*, *FST*, and *SND* determines the partial ordering. If $u \sqsubseteq x$ and $v \sqsubseteq y$ then $(u, v) \sqsubseteq (x, y)$ because *PAIR* must be monotonic. If $(u, v) \sqsubseteq (x, y)$ then $u \sqsubseteq x$ and $v \sqsubseteq y$ because *FST* and *SND* must be monotonic. To summarize:

$$(u, v) \sqsubseteq_{\sigma \times \tau} (x, y) \iff u \sqsubseteq_\sigma x \wedge v \sqsubseteq_\tau y$$

We also have to prove that the Cartesian product is a domain.

Theorem 4.1 *The relation $\sqsubseteq_{\sigma \times \tau}$ is a complete partial ordering.*
Proof: It is reflexive, antisymmetric, and transitive because $\sqsubseteq_\sigma$ and $\sqsubseteq_\tau$ are. There is a least element, namely $(\bot_\sigma, \bot_\tau)$. Chains have least upper bounds, for if $(x_0, y_0) \sqsubseteq (x_1, y_1) \sqsubseteq \ldots$ is a chain then so are $x_0 \sqsubseteq x_1 \sqsubseteq \ldots$ and $y_0 \sqsubseteq y_1 \sqsubseteq \ldots$, by monotonicity of *FST* and *SND*. Continuity of *FST* gives

$$FST(\bigsqcup_{n=0}^{\infty} (x_n, y_n)) \equiv \bigsqcup_{n=0}^{\infty} FST(x_n, y_n) \equiv \bigsqcup_{n=0}^{\infty} x_n$$

and similarly for *SND*. So the least upper bound is

$$\bigsqcup_{n=0}^{\infty} (x_n, y_n) \equiv (\bigsqcup_{n=0}^{\infty} x_n, \bigsqcup_{n=0}^{\infty} y_n)$$

□

4.1.2   Semantics

The type $\sigma \times \tau$ is interpreted in set theory via $D(\sigma \times \tau) = D(\sigma) \times D(\tau)$. Careful! The left occurrence of $\times$ is a type symbol of PPλ; the right refers to the Cartesian product of set theory. It is the set of pairs taking the first component from $D(\sigma)$ and the second from $D(\tau)$:

$$D(\sigma \times \tau) = \{\langle x, y \rangle \mid x \in D(\sigma) \wedge y \in D(\tau)\}$$

To minimize confusion, a PPλ pair is written (x, y) while a set theory pair is written $\langle x, y \rangle$. The set is partially ordered so that $\sqsubseteq_{\sigma \times \tau}$ has the properties given above.

The symbols *FST* and *SND* denote the projection functions of set theory, while *PAIR* denotes the pairing function. This interpretation clearly satisfies the axioms for *FST*, *SND*, and *PAIR*.

4.1.3   Isomorphisms between types

We have several ways of constructing types; when are two types equal? Presumably $\sigma = \tau$ means $D(\sigma) = D(\tau)$: the underlying sets are equal. Equality is too strong; there are few equalities apart from the trivial $\sigma = \sigma$. The weaker notion of isomorphism is indispensable for understanding data structures in domain theory.

The types σ and τ are *isomorphic*, written $\sigma \cong \tau$, if there exist continuous functions $\phi : \sigma \to \tau$ and $\psi : \tau \to \sigma$ such that $\phi(\psi(x)) \equiv x$ for all x in τ and $\psi(\phi(y)) \equiv y$ for all y in σ. To be more concise, let ID_σ be the identity function on type σ, namely $\lambda x : \sigma.x$, and let ID_τ be the identity function on τ. Then ϕ and ψ must satisfy

$$\phi \circ \psi \equiv ID_\tau \qquad\qquad \psi \circ \phi \equiv ID_\sigma$$

The *isomorphism functions* ϕ and ψ give a one-to-one correspondence between elements of σ and elements of τ. Clearly $\cong$ is an *equivalence relation*, namely it satisfies the reflexive, symmetric, and transitive laws:

$$\sigma \cong \sigma$$

$$\sigma \cong \tau \Longrightarrow \tau \cong \sigma$$

$$\sigma \cong \tau \wedge \tau \cong \upsilon \Longrightarrow \sigma \cong \upsilon$$

Because the isomorphism functions are monotonic and continuous, the correspondence preserves the structure of the types. If $u \sqsubseteq x$ in σ then $\phi(u) \sqsubseteq \phi(x)$ in τ, and likewise limits are preserved. It should be no surprise that the functions are strict and total.

Theorem 4.2 *Isomorphism functions are strict,* $\phi(\perp_\sigma) \equiv \perp_\tau$ *and* $\psi(\perp_\tau) \equiv \perp_\sigma$.
Proof: The minimality of bottom implies $\perp_\tau \sqsubseteq \phi(\perp_\sigma)$ and $\perp_\sigma \sqsubseteq \psi(\perp_\tau)$. Monotonicity implies $\phi(\perp_\sigma) \sqsubseteq \phi(\psi(\perp_\tau)) \equiv \perp_\tau$. So $\phi(\perp_\sigma) \equiv \perp_\tau$; the case for ψ is symmetric. $\square$

Theorem 4.3 *Isomorphism functions are total, namely* $x \not\equiv \perp_\sigma \Longrightarrow \phi(x) \not\equiv \perp_\tau$
and $y \not\equiv \perp_\tau \Longrightarrow \psi(y) \not\equiv \perp_\sigma$.
Proof: If $\phi(x) \equiv \perp_\tau$ then

$$x \equiv \psi(\phi(x)) \equiv \psi(\perp_\tau) \equiv \perp_\sigma$$

The case for ψ is symmetric. $\square$

Example 4.1 The type constructor $\times$ is commutative and associative under the relation $\cong$. To see that $\sigma \times \tau$ is isomorphic to $\tau \times \sigma$ for all types σ and τ, define isomorphism functions ϕ and ψ such that ϕ maps $(x : \sigma, y : \tau)$ to $(y : \tau, x : \sigma)$ and ψ maps $(y : \tau, x : \sigma)$ to $(x : \sigma, y : \tau)$. A diagram:

$$\sigma \times \tau \quad \cong \quad \tau \times \sigma$$

$$(x, y) \quad \longleftrightarrow \quad (y, x)$$

The functions are written using *FST* and *SND*:

$$\phi \equiv \lambda u : \sigma \times \tau . (SND\, u, FST\, u)$$
$$\psi \equiv \lambda u : \tau \times \sigma . (SND\, u, FST\, u)$$

The correspondence between elements of $(\sigma \times \tau) \times \upsilon$ and $\sigma \times (\tau \times \upsilon)$ is

$$(\sigma \times \tau) \times \upsilon \quad \cong \quad \sigma \times (\tau \times \upsilon)$$

$$((x, y), z) \quad \longleftrightarrow \quad (x, (y, z))$$

The isomorphism functions are

$$\phi \equiv \lambda u : (\sigma \times \tau) \times \upsilon . (FST(FST\, u), (SND(FST\, u), SND\, u))$$
$$\psi \equiv \lambda u : \sigma \times (\tau \times \upsilon) . ((FST\, u, FST(SND\, u)), SND(SND\, u))$$

In PPλ the n-place product of the types $\sigma_1, \cdots, \sigma_{n-1}, \sigma_n$ is expressed via the 2-place product: (x, y, z) abbreviates $(x, (y, z))$, which represents an ordered triple. Iterated pairing gives rise to n-tuples. Suppose we have the terms $t_1 : \sigma_1, \ldots,$

$t_{n-1} : \sigma_{n-1}$, and $t_n : \sigma_n$. Then $(t_1, \ldots, t_{n-1}, t_n)$ abbreviates $(t_1, (\ldots, (t_{n-1}, t_n) \ldots))$. Its type is $\sigma_1 \times \cdots \times \sigma_{n-1} \times \sigma_n$, which abbreviates $\sigma_1 \times (\cdots \times (\sigma_{n-1} \times \sigma_n) \cdots)$. The n-place product is expressed by association to the right; the associative law tells us that association to the left would yield essentially the same type.

Example 4.2 The Cartesian product of domains corresponds to the notion of product in category theory. This is reflected in the isomorphism

$$\sigma \to (\tau \times \upsilon) \;\cong\; (\sigma \to \tau) \times (\sigma \to \upsilon)$$

To every pair of functions (h, k), with h in $\sigma \to \tau$ and k in $\sigma \to \upsilon$, corresponds the function $\lambda x.(h(x), k(x))$ in $\sigma \to (\tau \times \upsilon)$. Conversely, to j in $\sigma \to (\tau \times \upsilon)$ corresponds the pair of functions $FST \circ j$ and $SND \circ j$. The details are left as an exercise.

Example 4.3 What is the domain of functions of two arguments? As it happens, the two most likely domains are isomorphic. Consider a continuous function with arguments of types σ and τ and result of type υ. Pairs provide the usual representation, $h : (\sigma \times \tau) \to \upsilon$, while currying provides the other, $h' : \sigma \to (\tau \to \upsilon)$. If x has type σ and y has type τ then both $h(x, y)$ and $h'(x)(y)$ have type υ. There is a one-to-one correspondence between curried and paired functions,

$$(\sigma \times \tau) \to \upsilon \;\cong\; \sigma \to (\tau \to \upsilon)$$

which is the categorical property of Cartesian closure. One of the isomorphism functions is $CURRY$ of type $((\sigma \times \tau) \to \upsilon) \to \sigma \to \tau \to \upsilon$; it satisfies

$$CURRY(f)(x)(y) \equiv f(x, y)$$

The other isomorphism function is $SPLIT$, discussed below in the exercises.

A function of n arguments can have one of several different types, such as

$(\sigma_1 \times \sigma_2 \times \cdots \times \sigma_n) \to \tau$	using products only
$\sigma_1 \to \sigma_2 \to \cdots \to \sigma_n \to \tau$	using currying only
$\sigma_1 \to (\sigma_2 \times \cdots \times \sigma_n) \to \tau$	using a mixture of products and currying

Exercise 4.1 Draw a diagram of the partial ordering structure of $tr \times tr$: write all the elements of $tr \times tr$, smaller elements below larger ones, drawing a line from u to v if $u \sqsubseteq_{tr \times tr} v$. Omit lines that follow by transitivity.

Exercise 4.2 Prove that $\sigma \times \tau$ is a cpo with $\perp_{\sigma \times \tau} \equiv (\perp_\sigma, \perp_\tau)$.

Exercise 4.3 Consider the functional $SPLIT$ of type $(\sigma \to \tau \to \upsilon) \to (\sigma \times \tau) \to \upsilon$, satisfying the axioms

$$
\begin{aligned}
SPLIT(f)(x, y) &\equiv f(x)(y) \\
SPLIT(PAIR)\, z &\equiv z
\end{aligned}
$$

(The variable z has type $\sigma \times \tau$.) Prove that *SPLIT* can be expressed in terms of *FST* and *SND*, and conversely.

Exercise 4.4 In the isomorphism between $\sigma \to (\tau \times \upsilon)$ and $(\sigma \to \tau) \times (\sigma \to \upsilon)$, show that the isomorphism functions are continuous and form a one-to-one correspondence.

Exercise 4.5 Prove that $(\sigma \times \tau) \to \upsilon$ is isomorphic to $\sigma \to (\tau \to \upsilon)$ for all types σ, τ, and υ, writing down the isomorphism functions.

4.2 The strict product of two types

The Cartesian product in PPλ is not quite the same as the product type in ML. The pairing function of ML is strict: (x, y) is undefined unless both x and y are defined. For example, the computation of $(f(t), g(u))$ runs forever if either function call does. Yet the type $nat \times nat$ contains the element $(\bot, 0)$: the pair of a divergent computation with the number zero. Furthermore $SND(\bot, 0) \equiv 0$ is true: the second component can be extracted even though the first component is undefined. Ordered pairs in a lazy programming language may behave like this, but ML uses strict (or eager) evaluation.

The *strict* product is appropriate for ML and other strict languages. The strict product is not provided in Cambridge LCF, but it is easy to build a theory containing the symbols and axioms below.

4.2.1 Syntax and axioms

If σ and τ are types then so is $\sigma \otimes \tau$. The pairing function, *SPAIR*, is strict: it returns $\bot$ if either argument equals $\bot$. (The strict product is also called the *smash* product because $\bot$ in either component 'smashes' the entire pair to $\bot$.) Instead of projection functions, the functional *SSPLIT* gives access to the components of a pair, if the pair is defined. The advantages of this formulation are discussed below.

The symbols are

$$SPAIR : \sigma \to \tau \to (\sigma \otimes \tau)$$
$$SSPLIT : (\sigma \to \tau \to \upsilon) \to (\sigma \otimes \tau) \to \upsilon$$

There are several kinds of axioms.

The *strictness* axioms are

$$SPAIR(\bot_\sigma)(y) \equiv \bot_{\sigma \otimes \tau}$$
$$SPAIR(x)(\bot_\tau) \equiv \bot_{\sigma \otimes \tau}$$

The axioms for *SSPLIT* are

$$SSPLIT(f)(\bot_{\sigma \otimes \tau}) \equiv \bot_\upsilon$$
$$x \not\equiv \bot_\sigma \wedge y \not\equiv \bot_\tau \implies SSPLIT(f)(SPAIR(x)(y)) \equiv f(x)(y)$$

These are *reduction* axioms because they allow expressions involving $SSPLIT(f)$ to be reduced.

The *definedness* axiom states that a pair is defined if both components are:

$$x \not\equiv \perp_\sigma \wedge y \not\equiv \perp_\tau \implies SPAIR(x)(y) \not\equiv \perp_{\sigma \otimes \tau}$$

The *exhaustion* axiom states that an element of type $\sigma \otimes \tau$ is either $\perp_{\sigma \otimes \tau}$ or has the form $SPAIR(x)(y)$ for non-bottom $x : \sigma$ and $y : \tau$. In symbols:

$$\forall z : \sigma \otimes \tau . z \equiv \perp \vee (\exists x : \sigma. \exists y : \tau . z \equiv SPAIR(x)(y) \wedge x \not\equiv \perp \wedge y \not\equiv \perp)$$

An interesting consequence of the exhaustion axiom is $SSPLIT(SPAIR)(z) \equiv z$. To prove this, we need only consider two cases, which turn out to be instances of the reduction axioms:

$$SSPLIT(SPAIR)(\perp) \equiv \perp$$
$$x \not\equiv \perp \wedge y \not\equiv \perp \implies SSPLIT(SPAIR)(SPAIR(x)(y)) \equiv SPAIR(x)(y)$$

4.2.2   A formulation using projection functions

The functional $SSPLIT$, the *eliminator*, is seldom seen in descriptions of the strict product. More typical are the projection functions

$$SFST : (\sigma \otimes \tau) \to \sigma$$
$$SSND : (\sigma \otimes \tau) \to \tau$$

satisfying the axioms

$$SFST(\perp_{\sigma \otimes \tau}) \equiv \perp_\sigma$$
$$SSND(\perp_{\sigma \otimes \tau}) \equiv \perp_\tau$$

$$x \not\equiv \perp \wedge y \not\equiv \perp \implies SFST(SPAIR(x)(y)) \equiv x$$
$$x \not\equiv \perp \wedge y \not\equiv \perp \implies SSND(SPAIR(x)(y)) \equiv y$$

However, the functions $SFST$ and $SSND$ are easily expressed via $SSPLIT$, as $SSPLIT(\lambda xy.x)$ and $SSPLIT(\lambda xy.y)$. To verify $SFST$, note that if x and y are defined then

$$SSPLIT(\lambda xy.x)(SPAIR(x)(y)) \equiv (\lambda xy.x)(x)(y) \equiv x$$

Expressing $SSPLIT$ via $SFST$ and $SSND$ is not so easy. Obvious but wrong is

$$SSPLIT \equiv \lambda fz.f(SFST\ z)(SSND\ z)$$

because $SSPLIT(f)\perp$ should be $\perp$ and not $f\perp\perp$.

To patch things up, we can introduce a functional that turns a function into a strict function:

$$STRICT : (\sigma \to \tau) \to \sigma \to \tau$$

The appropriate axioms are

$$STRICT(f)(\bot) \equiv \bot$$
$$x \not\equiv \bot \implies STRICT(f)(x) \equiv f(x)$$

Now *SSPLIT* can be expressed:

$$SSPLIT \equiv \lambda f. \; STRICT(\lambda z. f(SFST\ z)(SSND\ z))$$

This contrivance is further evidence that *SSPLIT* is more natural than *SFST* and *SSND*.

4.2.3   The partial ordering

As we have seen with the Cartesian product, the properties of *SPAIR*, *SFST*, and *SSND* determine the partial ordering $\sqsubseteq_{\sigma\otimes\tau}$. If $u \sqsubseteq x$ and $v \sqsubseteq y$ then $SPAIR(u)(v) \sqsubseteq SPAIR(x)(y)$. The converse can fail since *SPAIR* is strict: we have $SPAIR(2)(\bot) \sqsubseteq SPAIR(\bot)(\bot)$ while $2 \not\sqsubseteq \bot$. But note that $SFST(SPAIR(x)(y)) \sqsubseteq x$ whether or not x and y are defined. So if u and v are defined and $SPAIR(u)(v) \sqsubseteq SPAIR(x)(y)$ then

$$u \sqsubseteq SFST(SPAIR(u)(v)) \sqsubseteq SFST(SPAIR(x)(y)) \sqsubseteq x$$

and similarly $v \sqsubseteq y$.

To summarize, the partial ordering can be described by three cases:

$$\bot \sqsubseteq_{\sigma\otimes\tau} z$$

$$u \not\equiv \bot \wedge v \not\equiv \bot \implies \begin{cases} SPAIR(u)(v) \not\sqsubseteq_{\sigma\otimes\tau} \bot \\ SPAIR(u)(v) \sqsubseteq_{\sigma\otimes\tau} SPAIR(x)(y) \iff u \sqsubseteq_\sigma x \wedge v \sqsubseteq_\tau y \end{cases}$$

4.2.4   Semantics

The strict product can be interpreted in set theory. The domain of $\sigma \otimes \tau$ is

$$D(\sigma \otimes \tau) = \{0\} \cup \{\langle x, y \rangle \mid x \in D(\sigma) \wedge y \in D(\tau) \wedge x \not\equiv \bot_\sigma \wedge y \not\equiv \bot_\tau\}$$

namely the set of pairs in which both components differ from $\bot$, together with 0 to stand for the bottom element. The interpretation of $\bot$ is arbitrary; we can use the pair $\langle \bot_\sigma, \bot_\tau \rangle$ or almost anything else. Under the partial ordering $\sqsubseteq_{\sigma\otimes\tau}$ as above, the domain is a cpo. The axioms for *SSPLIT* and *SPAIR* can clearly be satisfied by functions on the set.

Let us express the n-place product by association to the right: $\sigma_1 \otimes \cdots \otimes \sigma_{n-1} \otimes \sigma_n$ is an abbreviation for $\sigma_1 \otimes (\cdots \otimes (\sigma_{n-1} \otimes \sigma_n) \cdots)$. Actually $\otimes$ is associative under $\cong$, so association to the left would yield an isomorphic type.

Example 4.4 In ML, function application is strict: the argument is evaluated before the function is called. We can model strict evaluation with the type $\sigma \multimap \tau$, the *strict* continuous functions from σ to τ. The isomorphism

$$(\sigma \otimes \tau) \multimap \upsilon \;\cong\; \sigma \multimap (\tau \multimap \upsilon)$$

gives a one-to-one correspondence between currying and pairing for strict functions. Although the ML product type corresponds to $\otimes$, the ML function type does not quite correspond to $\multimap$. We shall consider this further below.

Exercise 4.6 Show that $\sqsubseteq_{\sigma \otimes \tau}$ is a complete partial ordering.

Exercise 4.7 Show that *STRICT* is a continuous functional, and that $\sigma \multimap \tau$ is indeed a domain constructor: the strict, continuous functions form a cpo.

Exercise 4.8 Exhibit the isomorphism functions for $\sigma \otimes \tau \cong \tau \otimes \sigma$ and $(\sigma \otimes \tau) \otimes \upsilon \cong \sigma \otimes (\tau \otimes \upsilon)$, where σ, τ, and υ are arbitrary types.

Exercise 4.9 Disprove, by exhibiting counterexamples, the following:

$$(\sigma \otimes \tau) \to \upsilon \;\cong\; \sigma \to (\tau \to \upsilon)$$
$$\sigma \to (\tau \otimes \upsilon) \;\cong\; (\sigma \to \tau) \otimes (\sigma \to \upsilon)$$

Exercise 4.10 Disprove $\sigma \multimap (\tau \otimes \upsilon) \cong (\sigma \multimap \tau) \otimes (\sigma \multimap \upsilon)$. This indicates that $\otimes$ is not the categorical product in the category of strict, continuous functions on domains.

4.3   The strict sum of two types

Untyped programming languages like Lisp and BCPL allow the form of data to vary dynamically. A variable can hold an integer at one moment, a character the next. But there are two kinds of typelessness. A Lisp program can test whether a value is an integer or a character. In BCPL these are both bit patterns; integers and characters exist only in the mind of the programmer. We might say that Lisp is dynamically typed while BCPL is untyped.

To have similar flexibility, a strongly typed language must allow the *sum* or *union* of several types. Each element of the union is somehow labeled with its type. ML's datatypes incorporate unions; Pascal's variant records reflect the idea untidily. In Lisp every expression belongs to one universal type: the union of integers, strings, lists, and everything else.

In domain theory, the *sum* type $\sigma \oplus \tau$ contains elements of the form $INL(x)$ and $INR(y)$, for $x : \sigma$ and $y : \tau$. The functions INL and INR are the left and right *injections*. The functional $WHEN$ tests the form of an element of $\sigma \oplus \tau$ and gives access to its parts. Consider the evaluation of $WHEN(f)(g)(t)$, where t has type $\sigma \oplus \tau$. If t evaluates to $INL(x)$ then the result is $f(x)$; if t evaluates to $INR(y)$ then the result is $g(y)$; if t runs forever then the result is $\bot$. Compare with pattern matching in Standard ML.

4.3.1 Syntax and axioms

The symbols, with their types, are

$$INL : \sigma \to (\sigma \oplus \tau)$$
$$INR : \tau \to (\sigma \oplus \tau)$$
$$WHEN : (\sigma \to \upsilon) \to (\tau \to \upsilon) \to (\sigma \oplus \tau) \to \upsilon$$

The definedness axioms are

$$x \not\equiv \bot_\sigma \implies INL(x) \not\equiv \bot_{\sigma \oplus \tau}$$
$$y \not\equiv \bot_\tau \implies INR(y) \not\equiv \bot_{\sigma \oplus \tau}$$

The reduction axioms for $WHEN$ are

$$WHEN(f)(g)(\bot_{\sigma \oplus \tau}) \equiv \bot_\upsilon$$
$$x \not\equiv \bot \implies WHEN(f)(g)(INL\,x) \equiv f(x)$$
$$y \not\equiv \bot \implies WHEN(f)(g)(INR\,y) \equiv g(y)$$

The strictness axioms assert that the injections are strict:

$$INL(\bot_\sigma) \equiv \bot_{\sigma \oplus \tau} \equiv INR(\bot_\tau)$$

So $\sigma \oplus \tau$ is the *strict* sum — also called the *coalesced* sum because the bottom elements of σ and τ are coalesced to the same element, namely $\bot_{\sigma \oplus \tau}$.

The exhaustion axiom asserts that an element of type $\sigma \oplus \tau$ is either $\bot_{\sigma \oplus \tau}$ or has the form $INL(x)$ or $INR(y)$ for defined $x : \sigma$ or $y : \tau$. It is

$$\forall z : \sigma \oplus \tau . z \equiv \bot \lor (\exists x : \sigma . z \equiv INL\,x \land x \not\equiv \bot) \lor (\exists y : \tau . z \equiv INR\,y \land y \not\equiv \bot)$$

It implies $WHEN(INL)(INR)(z) \equiv z$.

4.3.2 Discriminator and destructor functions

Edinburgh LCF formulates the strict sum differently. Instead of the eliminator $WHEN$ it provides the discriminator ISL and the destructors $OUTL$ and $OUTR$:

$$ISL : (\sigma \oplus \tau) \to tr$$
$$OUTL : (\sigma \oplus \tau) \to \sigma$$
$$OUTR : (\sigma \oplus \tau) \to \tau$$

The axioms for *ISL* are

$$ISL \perp \equiv \perp$$
$$x \not\equiv \perp \implies ISL(INL\,x) \equiv TT$$
$$y \not\equiv \perp \implies ISL(INR\,y) \equiv FF$$

The axioms for the destructors include

$$OUTL(INL\,x) \equiv x$$
$$OUTR(INR\,y) \equiv y$$
$$OUTL(INR\,y) \equiv \perp$$
$$OUTR(INL\,x) \equiv \perp$$

Observe that these functions can be expressed in terms of *WHEN*:

$$ISL \equiv WHEN(\lambda x.TT)(\lambda y.FF)$$
$$OUTL \equiv WHEN(\lambda x.x)(\lambda y.\perp)$$
$$OUTR \equiv WHEN(\lambda x.\perp)(\lambda y.y)$$

4.3.3   The partial ordering

The properties of *OUTL* and *OUTR* determine the partial ordering $\sqsubseteq_{\sigma\oplus\tau}$. For instance, $u \sqsubseteq x$ implies $INL(u) \sqsubseteq INL(x)$ by monotonicity of *INL*, and the converse holds by monotonicity of *OUTL*. If $INL(u) \sqsubseteq INR(y)$ then applying *OUTL* to both sides gives $u \sqsubseteq \perp$, implying $u \equiv \perp$. We obtain a strong, and vital, property of *distinctness*: if $u \not\equiv \perp$ then $INL(u) \not\sqsubseteq INR(y)$; if $v \not\equiv \perp$ then $INR(v) \not\sqsubseteq INL(x)$. Recall that $INL(u) \not\sqsubseteq INR(y)$ implies $INL(u) \not\equiv INR(y)$.

In summary, there are four cases:

$$INL(u) \sqsubseteq_{\sigma\oplus\tau} INL(x) \iff u \sqsubseteq_\sigma x$$
$$INR(v) \sqsubseteq_{\sigma\oplus\tau} INR(y) \iff v \sqsubseteq_\tau y$$
$$INL(u) \sqsubseteq_{\sigma\oplus\tau} INR(y) \iff u \equiv \perp_\sigma$$
$$INR(v) \sqsubseteq_{\sigma\oplus\tau} INL(x) \iff v \equiv \perp_\tau$$

Theorem 4.4 *The relation $\sqsubseteq_{\sigma\oplus\tau}$ is a complete partial ordering.*

Proof: Observe that least upper bounds exist. Let $z_0 \sqsubseteq z_1 \sqsubseteq \ldots$ be a chain in $\sigma \oplus \tau$. If all the z_n are $\perp$ then so is their lub. Otherwise choose n such that z_n is not $\perp$: it is either $INL(x)$ or $INR(y)$, for defined x or y. In the first case, the chain from z_n has the form $INL(x_0) \sqsubseteq INL(x_1) \sqsubseteq \ldots$, with lub $INL(\bigsqcup_{k=0}^\infty x_k)$, since *INL* is continuous. The second case gives the chain $INR(y_0) \sqsubseteq INR(y_1) \sqsubseteq \ldots$, with lub $INR(\bigsqcup_{k=0}^\infty y_k)$. $\square$

4.3.4 Semantics

The domain $D(\sigma \oplus \tau)$ of the sum type is easy to construct from the domains $D(\sigma)$ and $D(\tau)$. Simply label each non-bottom element $x \in D(\sigma)$ with the number 1, forming the pair $\langle 1, x \rangle$. Likewise, pair each non-bottom element of $y \in D(\tau)$ with the number 2. The bottom element of $D(\sigma \oplus \tau)$ can be 0. In short

$$D(\sigma \oplus \tau) = \{0\} \cup \{\langle 1, x \rangle \mid x \in D(\sigma) \wedge x \not\equiv \bot_\sigma\} \cup \{\langle 2, y \rangle \mid y \in D(\tau) \wedge y \not\equiv \bot_\tau\}$$

Take the partial ordering $\sqsubseteq_{\sigma \oplus \tau}$ as above. The symbols are easily interpreted. For INL take the function that maps $\bot_\sigma$ to 0 and maps non-bottom x to $\langle 1, x \rangle$.

Example 4.5 Although $WHEN$ may seem more complicated than ISL, $OUTL$, and $OUTR$, it is easier to use with iterated sums like $(\sigma \oplus \tau) \oplus v$. The type $(\sigma \oplus \tau) \oplus v$ is isomorphic to $\sigma \oplus (\tau \oplus v)$ under the correspondence

$$(\sigma \oplus \tau) \oplus v \quad \cong \quad \sigma \oplus (\tau \oplus v)$$

$$
\begin{array}{rcl}
INL(INL\, x) & \longleftrightarrow & INL\, x \\
INL(INR\, y) & \longleftrightarrow & INR(INL\, y) \\
INR\, z & \longleftrightarrow & INR(INR\, z)
\end{array}
$$

The isomorphism functions ϕ and ψ are easily expressed using the eliminator $WHEN$:

$$
\begin{array}{rcl}
\phi & \equiv & WHEN(WHEN(\lambda x.\ INL\, x)(\lambda y.\ INR(INL\, y)))(\lambda z.\ INR(INR\, z)) \\
\psi & \equiv & WHEN(\lambda x.\ INL(INL\, x))(WHEN(\lambda y.\ INL(INR\, y))(\lambda z.\ INR\, z))
\end{array}
$$

The isomorphism functions expressed in terms of ISL, $OUTL$, and $OUTR$ are a mess.

Since the type constructor $\oplus$ is associative, we can express the n-place sum $\sigma_1 \oplus \cdots \oplus \sigma_{n-1} \oplus \sigma_n$ as $\sigma_1 \oplus (\cdots \oplus (\sigma_{n-1} \oplus \sigma_n) \cdots)$.

Exercise 4.11 In Standard ML, define the datatype $(\sigma, \tau)sum$ that corresponds to the strict sum.

Exercise 4.12 Show how to define $WHEN$ in terms of ISL, $OUTL$, and $OUTR$.

Exercise 4.13 Demonstrate the isomorphism $\sigma \oplus \tau \cong \tau \oplus \sigma$.

Exercise 4.14 Express the isomorphism functions for $(\sigma \oplus \tau) \oplus v \cong \sigma \oplus (\tau \oplus v)$ using ISL, $OUTL$, and $OUTR$.

Exercise 4.15 Demonstrate that the types $\sigma \otimes (\tau \oplus v)$ and $(\sigma \otimes \tau) \oplus (\sigma \otimes v)$ are isomorphic. Explain why $\sigma \times (\tau \oplus v)$ and $(\sigma \times \tau) \oplus (\sigma \times v)$ are *not* isomorphic for arbitrary σ, τ, and v.

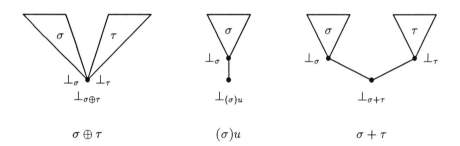

$$\sigma \oplus \tau \qquad\qquad (\sigma)u \qquad\qquad \sigma + \tau$$

Figure 4.1: Domains constructed by strict sum, lifting, and the separated sum

4.4   Lifted types

Under the lazy evaluation of a program, the structure of the answer can be visible before the computation of its parts has terminated. In PPλ, a lazy type is one having values like $(\bot, 0)$, a defined value containing an undefined part.

Lazy types are constructed via the *lifting* constructor u, which attaches a new bottom element to a type. If σ is a type then $(\sigma)u$ is a type that contains elements of the form $UP(x)$ for each x in σ. Most importantly we have $UP(x) \not\equiv \bot$: the bottom element of $(\sigma)u$ sits below the elements of σ. The functional $LIFT$ allows computing with elements of $(\sigma)u$. If the element equals $\bot_{(\sigma)u}$ then it returns $\bot$; if it equals $UP(x)$ then it gives access to x. Operationally, UP is a delay operator: the term $UP(t)$ is not evaluated until it is given to the functional $LIFT$.

Another lazy type is the *separated* sum $\sigma + \tau$, which is sometimes preferred over the strict sum. The separated sum is like the strict sum, but its axioms have no conditions of the form $x \not\equiv \bot$. Its exhaustion axiom is

$$\forall z : \sigma + \tau . z \equiv \bot \ \lor \ (\exists x : \sigma . z \equiv INLUP(x)) \ \lor \ (\exists y : \tau . z \equiv INRUP(y))$$

The injections $INLUP$ and $INRUP$ are not strict: the three values $INLUP(\bot_\sigma)$, $INRUP(\bot_\tau)$, and $\bot_{\sigma+\tau}$ are distinct. The separated sum models lazy evaluation: we can distinguish $INLUP(t)$ from $INRUP(u)$ without waiting for t or u to terminate. The separated sum can be expressed in terms of the coalesed sum and lifting: $\sigma + \tau = (\sigma u) \oplus (\tau u)$. Figure 4.1 illustrates the relationships among these type constructors.

The standard notation for lifting is $\sigma_\bot$, not our $(\sigma)u$. The same notation is used for turning a set into a flat cpo: if $\mathbf{N}$ is the set of natural numbers, then $\mathbf{N}_\bot$ corresponds to our type *nat*. A drawback of this notation is that the bottom element of τ is written $\bot_\tau$, and so the bottom element of $\mathbf{N}_\bot$ would be written $\bot_{\mathbf{N}_\bot}$.

4.4.1　Syntax and axioms

Lifting involves the type $(\sigma)u$ and the symbols

$$UP : \sigma \to (\sigma)u$$
$$LIFT : (\sigma \to \tau) \to (\sigma)u \to \tau$$

The definedness axiom is

$$UP(x) \not\equiv \perp$$

and there are no strictness axioms. The reduction axioms for $LIFT$ are

$$LIFT(f)(\perp_{(\sigma)u}) \;\equiv\; \perp_{\tau}$$
$$LIFT(f)(UP\,x) \;\equiv\; f(x)$$

The exhaustion axiom states that an element of type $(\sigma)u$ is either $\perp_{(\sigma)u}$ or else has the form $UP(x)$:

$$\forall z : (\sigma)u\,.\,z \equiv \perp \;\vee\; (\exists x : \sigma\,.\,z \equiv UP(x))$$

Observe that $LIFT(UP)(z) \equiv z$.

4.4.2　A destructor function

Edinburgh LCF formulates lifting using a destructor:

$$DOWN : (\sigma)u \to \sigma$$

The axioms for $DOWN$ include

$$DOWN\,\perp \;\equiv\; \perp$$
$$DOWN(UP\,x) \;\equiv\; x$$

Note that $DOWN$ is expressible as $LIFT(\lambda x.x)$. Expressing $LIFT$ via $DOWN$ requires the functional $STRICT$.

4.4.3　The partial ordering

As always, the partial ordering is determined by monotonicity of the constructors and destructors:

$$\perp \;\sqsubseteq_{(\sigma)u}\; z$$
$$UP(x) \;\not\sqsubseteq_{(\sigma)u}\; \perp$$

$$(UP(x) \sqsubseteq_{(\sigma)u} UP(y)) \;\Longleftrightarrow\; (x \sqsubseteq_{\sigma} y)$$

4.4.4   Semantics

An interpretation $D((\sigma)u)$ is constructed by pairing each element $x \in D(\sigma)$ with the number 1 and letting the bottom element in $D((\sigma)u)$ be 0. In the language of set theory,

$$D((\sigma)u) = \{0\} \cup \{\langle 1, x \rangle \mid x \in D(\sigma)\}$$

The symbol UP denotes the function that maps x to $\langle 1, x \rangle$. The sets $D((\sigma)u)$ and $D(\sigma \oplus \sigma)$ contain elements like $\langle 1, x \rangle$ in common, which does no harm.

Example 4.6 The type of an ML function is expressed via the strict function space, $\circ\!\!\rightarrow$, and lifting. A key point is to distinguish $\lambda x : \sigma.\bot_\tau$, the function that diverges on all arguments, from $\bot$, the undefined functional value. Under the ML declaration

```
! fun loop(x) = loop(x);
- val loop = fn : ('a -> 'b)
```

the function *loop* diverges on all arguments. Its polymorphic type is $\alpha \rightarrow \beta$, so the expressions *loop* and *loop*(0) can both be constrained to the type $int \rightarrow int$. The value of *loop* : $int \rightarrow int$ is the everywhere undefined function from int to int. The value of *loop*(0) : $int \rightarrow int$ is undefined.

The everywhere undefined function $\lambda x : \sigma.\bot_\tau$ is the bottom element of both $\sigma \rightarrow \tau$ and $\sigma \circ\!\!\rightarrow \tau$. To model ML functions we need an extra bottom element below $\lambda x : \sigma.\bot_\tau$. The ML function space constructor, $\overset{ML}{\longrightarrow}$, is expressed by

$$\sigma \overset{ML}{\longrightarrow} \tau \;\; = \;\; (\sigma \circ\!\!\rightarrow \tau)u$$

ML does not enjoy the isomorphism between curried and paired functions: between $(\sigma \otimes \tau) \overset{ML}{\longrightarrow} v$ and $\sigma \overset{ML}{\longrightarrow} (\tau \overset{ML}{\longrightarrow} v)$. Distinct elements of $\sigma \overset{ML}{\longrightarrow} (\tau \overset{ML}{\longrightarrow} v)$ are

$$\lambda x : \sigma . \lambda y : \tau . \bot_v \qquad\qquad \lambda x : \sigma . \bot_{\tau \overset{ML}{\longrightarrow} v}$$

In the natural conversion to type $(\sigma \otimes \tau) \overset{ML}{\longrightarrow} v$, both correspond to $\lambda z : \sigma \otimes \tau.\bot_v$. This is not a one-to-one correspondence.

Example 4.7 Strict types are constructed via $\otimes$ and $\oplus$ while lazy types are usually constructed via $\times$ and $+$. Strict and lazy types can be put on a common footing because the types $(\sigma \times \tau)u$ and $(\sigma u) \otimes (\tau u)$ are isomorphic.

The desired correspondence is

$$(\sigma \times \tau)u \;\;\; \cong \;\;\; (\sigma u) \otimes (\tau u)$$

$$UP(x, y) \;\;\; \longleftrightarrow \;\;\; SPAIR(UP\, x)(UP\, y)$$

$$\bot \;\; \longleftrightarrow \;\; \bot$$

The isomorphism functions are

$$\phi : (\sigma \times \tau)u \to (\sigma u) \otimes (\tau u) \quad \equiv \quad LIFT(\lambda z.\ SPAIR(\ UP(FST\ z))(\ UP(SND\ z)))$$
$$\psi : (\sigma u) \otimes (\tau u) \to (\sigma \times \tau)u \quad \equiv \quad SSPLIT(LIFT(\lambda x.\ LIFT(\lambda y.\ UP(x,y))))$$

Observe how expressive the eliminators *STRICT* and *LIFT* are. Imagine what ψ would look like if expressed in terms of destructors!

Edinburgh LCF originally implemented the separated sum, which proved unsatisfactory and was replaced by the strict sum. The 2-place separated sum is not associative: $(\sigma + \tau) + v$ is not isomorphic to $\sigma + (\tau + v)$. Neither type is isomorphic to $(\sigma u) \oplus (\tau u) \oplus (vu)$, the separated sum of σ, τ, and v. A general rule about syntactic constructs: if the n-place version cannot be obtained by repeated application of the 2-place version, then it is not convenient for automatic theorem proving.

Exercise 4.16 In the example above, verify that ϕ and ψ are isomorphism functions: $\phi \circ \psi \equiv ID$ and $\psi \circ \phi \equiv ID$.

Exercise 4.17 Express the eliminator *LIFT* in terms of *STRICT* and *DOWN*.

Exercise 4.18 Prove the isomorphism relating the strict and ordinary function spaces: $\sigma u \multimap \tau \cong \sigma \to \tau$.

Exercise 4.19 The strict sum, $\oplus$, is the coproduct in the category of strict, continuous functions on domains. Prove

$$(\sigma \oplus \tau) \multimap v \quad \cong \quad (\sigma \multimap v) \times (\tau \multimap v)$$

for all σ, τ, and v.

Exercise 4.20 Use the previous exercise to prove

$$(\sigma + \tau) \multimap v \quad \cong \quad (\sigma \to v) \times (\tau \to v)$$

for all σ, τ, and v.

4.5 Atomic types

Type constructors are useless without basic types to build upon. The previous chapter introduces two primitive types: the truth values *tr* and the natural numbers *nat*. Both of these will turn out to be definable from the trivial type *void*.

The type *void* contains no elements other than $\perp_{void}$, which is also written (). Its exhaustion axiom is simply $\forall z : void.\, z \equiv ()$. Its interpretation is trivial: $D(void)$ can be any singleton set.

The type *unit* contains one defined element, plus bottom. It can be expressed as $unit = (void)u$. Its exhaustion property is then provable from the axioms for *void* and lifting:

$$\forall z : unit.\, z \equiv \bot \lor z \equiv UP()$$

The type *tr* can be expressed as $tr = unit \oplus unit$, which is equivalent to $void + void$, with $TT \equiv INLUP()$ and $FF \equiv INRUP()$. Its exhaustion property is easily derived from those for $+$ and *void*:

$$\forall z : tr.\, z \equiv \bot \lor z \equiv TT \lor z \equiv FF$$

We can quarrel about the names. The type *void* contains one element, not zero; *unit* contains two elements. Furthermore $void \times \sigma \cong \sigma \cong void \to \sigma$, suggesting that *void* should be called *unit*. But the names make sense since this chapter is primarily concerned with strict type constructors. The type *void* contains no defined (non-bottom) element; *unit* contains one defined element. Note the isomorphisms

$$void \oplus \sigma \;\cong\; \sigma$$

$$void \otimes \sigma \;\cong\; void$$
$$unit \otimes \sigma \;\cong\; \sigma$$
$$tr \otimes \sigma \;\cong\; \sigma \oplus \sigma$$

$$void \multimap \sigma \;\cong\; void$$
$$unit \multimap \sigma \;\cong\; \sigma$$
$$tr \multimap \sigma \;\cong\; \sigma \times \sigma$$

The isomorphisms involving *tr* follow from its equivalence to $unit \oplus unit$ and isomorphisms involving $\oplus$.

Exercise 4.21 Express the conditional operator $p \Rightarrow t \mid u$ via *WHEN*.

Exercise 4.22 Prove $unit \multimap \sigma \cong \sigma$ and $unit \xrightarrow{\text{ML}} \sigma \cong \sigma u$. Lifting can be expressed using ML types, allowing the construction of lazy data structures.

Exercise 4.23 Find types σ, τ, and υ such that $(\sigma + \tau) + \upsilon \not\cong \sigma + (\tau + \upsilon)$.

4.6   Recursive type definitions

Standard ML allows the definition of recursive data types such as lists and trees. Let us consider a simple, non-polymorphic example. A definition of the type of integer lists is

```
datatype intlist = Nil  |  Cons of int * intlist;
```

The type *intlist* has two constructors: the constant *Nil* and the function *Cons*. In ML, constructors are strict, like all other functions. Most ML types are strict, but lazy types can be constructed. In the language Miranda, all types are lazy; Miranda accepts a similar input as defining the type of lazy lists [98]. Both lazy and strict lists are definable in PPλ.

Recursive type definitions are understood in a similar way to recursive function definitions and least fixed points. A recursive function denotes the limit of a chain of function applications; a recursive domain denotes the limit of a chain of applications of domain constructors. For recursively defined sets, the analogy between recursive functions and recursive data structures can be made precise. Domain theory handles a much wider class of recursive definitions, but the analogy breaks down: recursive domains require complex constructions.

4.6.1   Understanding recursive definitions via set theory

We can construct a version of *intlist* in set theory. Its definition can be written using the set operations $\cup$, the union of two sets, and $\times$, the Cartesian product of two sets. (Halmos gives an excellent account of elementary set theory [42].)

Let $\mathbf{N}$ be the set of natural numbers, and let $\mathbf{1}$ be the one-element set $\{0\}$. The set $\mathbf{L}$ of integer lists is specified by the recursion equation

$$\mathbf{L} = \mathbf{1} \cup (\mathbf{N} \times \mathbf{L})$$

As usual the recursive definition can be expressed via a function:

$$F(D) = \mathbf{1} \cup (\mathbf{N} \times D)$$

$$\mathbf{L} = F(\mathbf{L})$$

So the recursion equation states that $\mathbf{L}$ should be a fixed point of the function F.

The Fixed Point Theorem, which we saw in the previous chapter, gives a method of constructing the least fixed point of a continuous function. Continuity is a general concept, not just restricted to domains. We have been concerned with continuous functions over the partial ordering $\sqsubseteq$. But sets are partially ordered by the subset relation $\subseteq$. The least element is then the empty set $\emptyset$, and the least upper bound of sets is their union. A table illustrates the correspondence:

$\bot$	$\emptyset$	bottom element
$\sqsubseteq$	$\subseteq$	partial ordering
$\bigsqcup_{n=0}^{\infty} x_n$	$\bigcup_{n=0}^{\infty} D_n$	least upper bound

Using $\subseteq$ as the partial ordering, a function G is monotonic if $D \subseteq E$ implies $G(D) \subseteq G(E)$. It is easy to show that $\cup$ and $\times$ are monotonic: if $D \subseteq E$ and $D' \subseteq E'$ then $D \cup D' \subseteq E \cup E'$ and $D \times D' \subseteq E \times E'$.

If G is monotonic then it is continuous if $G(\bigcup_{n=0}^{\infty} D_n)$ equals $\bigcup_{n=0}^{\infty} G(D_n)$ for every chain $D_0 \subseteq D_1 \subseteq D_2 \subseteq \cdots$. Continuity also makes sense for functions with more than one argument. It is easy to prove that $\cup$ and $\times$ are continuous in each argument; here is one example.

Theorem 4.5 *The product of sets is continuous in its first argument:*

$$(\bigcup_{m=0}^{\infty} D_m) \times E = \bigcup_{m=0}^{\infty} (D_m \times E)$$

Proof: Each set contains the other.

$$
\begin{aligned}
\langle x, y \rangle \in (\bigcup_{m=0}^{\infty} D_m) \times E \quad &\Longleftrightarrow \quad x \in \bigcup_{m=0}^{\infty} D_m \text{ and } y \in E \\
&\Longleftrightarrow \quad x \in D_m \text{ and } y \in E \text{ for some } m \\
&\Longleftrightarrow \quad \langle x, y \rangle \in D_m \times E \text{ for some } m \\
&\Longleftrightarrow \quad \langle x, y \rangle \in \bigcup_{m=0}^{\infty} (D_m \times E) \quad \square
\end{aligned}
$$

Now F is continuous because $\cup$ and $\times$ are. Because F is monotonic, we have an increasing chain of sets starting from the empty set:

$$\emptyset \subseteq F(\emptyset) \subseteq F(F(\emptyset)) \subseteq F(F(F(\emptyset))) \cdots$$

By the Fixed Point Theorem, the fixed point of F is the union of the chain:

$$L = \bigcup_{n=0}^{\infty} F^n(\emptyset)$$

This set is the solution of the recursion equation for integer lists.

For a closer look at L, let us work out the set $F^n(\emptyset)$ for small n, using elementary properties of union and product:

$$
\begin{aligned}
F^0(\emptyset) &= \emptyset \\
F^1(\emptyset) &= 1 \cup (\mathbf{N} \times \emptyset) = 1 \cup \emptyset = 1 \\
F^2(\emptyset) &= 1 \cup (\mathbf{N} \times 1) \\
F^3(\emptyset) &= 1 \cup (\mathbf{N} \times (1 \cup (\mathbf{N} \times 1))) = 1 \cup (\mathbf{N} \times 1) \cup (\mathbf{N} \times (\mathbf{N} \times 1)) \\
&\vdots
\end{aligned}
$$

A pattern is evident. Clearly

$$L = 1 \cup (\mathbf{N} \times 1) \cup (\mathbf{N} \times (\mathbf{N} \times 1)) \cup \cdots$$

What are the elements of **L**? Let m_0, m_1, and m_2 range over **N**. Then **L** contains 0, which is the empty list; $\langle m_0, 0 \rangle$, the lists of length one; $\langle m_0, \langle m_1, 0 \rangle \rangle$, the lists of length two; $\langle m_0, \langle m_1, \langle m_2, 0 \rangle \rangle \rangle$, the lists of length three, and so on. This representation of lists should be familiar to Lisp programmers, at least!

Exercise 4.24 Verify that $\subseteq$ is reflexive, symmetric, and transitive, with $\emptyset \subseteq D$ for all sets D, and that union gives the least upper bound: if $D_n \subseteq D$ for all n then

$$\bigcup_{n=0}^{\infty} D_n \subseteq D$$

Exercise 4.25 Prove that $\cup$ and $\times$ are monotonic and that $\cup$ is continuous.

4.6.2 Introduction to recursive domains

The solution of a recursive domain equation is often called a *reflexive domain*. Domain theory often considers the recursive type *isomorphism* $\tau \cong F(\tau)$ instead of the equation $\tau = F(\tau)$. It is easier to find a type τ isomorphic to $F(\tau)$ than to find one equal to $F(\tau)$. Solving the equation up to isomorphism suffices for most purposes: the isomorphism functions convert between τ and $F(\tau)$. Regarding these as different types can be an aid to clarity.

The discussion of recursive definitions of sets illustrates the ideas, but only works for simple definitions. Domain theory can solve difficult recursive definitions like

$$D \cong D \to D$$

Such a D is a model of the untyped λ-calculus, where every value can be regarded as a function, and can even be applied to itself.

The obvious set theory construction does not work. No set D is isomorphic to its function space $D \to D$, which is a set of greater cardinality. Restricting $D \to D$ to continuous functions solves the cardinality problem, but something more fundamental is wrong. The operator $\to$ is not monotonic: $D \subseteq E$ and $D' \subseteq E'$ do not imply $D \to D' \subseteq E \to E'$ but something rather like $E \to D' \subseteq D \to E'$. Note that if D is a proper subset of E then a function from D to D' is not a function from E to anything, while a function from E to D' can be seen as one from D to E' by restricting its domain.

As a general rule, the mathematical techniques for recursive definitions require that the operations be continuous, or at least monotonic. In the language of category theory, F must be a *covariant functor* while $\to$ is typically *contravariant*. Scott's construction makes $\to$ a covariant functor in the category of *projection pairs* between domains. Recursive domain equations are solved by constructing an *inverse limit*. A sketch is given below.

If you prefer to skip the details, just accept that recursive type definitions of the form $\tau \cong F(\tau)$ are legitimate in PPλ, where F may involve the built-in type constructors, $\times$ and $\to$, and also those given in this chapter, such as $\otimes$, $\oplus$, u, and $(\alpha)\,llist$. Perhaps PPλ should include a recursive type binding operator rec, such that if F is a function from types to types then $rec\,\alpha.F(\alpha)$ is a type such that

$$rec\,\alpha.F(\alpha) \;\cong\; F(rec\,\alpha.F(\alpha))$$

Then the definition $\tau = rec\,\alpha.F(\alpha)$ would imply $\tau \cong F(\tau)$.

PPλ cannot provide rec because it lacks bound type variables. Instead, assert $\tau \cong F(\tau)$ in PPλ by declaring the isomorphism functions

$$ABS : F(\tau) \to \tau$$
$$REP : \tau \to F(\tau)$$

and asserting the axioms

$$\forall x : \tau.\; ABS(REP\,x) \;\equiv\; x$$
$$\forall y : F(\tau).\; REP(ABS\,y) \;\equiv\; y$$

As the names suggest, these are called the *abstraction* and *representation* functions: $F(\tau)$ is the representation of τ.

4.7   The inverse limit construction for recursive domains

We shall now have a brief look at recursive domain equations. The subset relation, $D \subseteq E$, is replaced by the more general notion of a function embedding D in E. This leads to a related notion of limit. Showing that the domain constructors are continuous — preserve such limits — allows us to repeatedly apply a domain constructor, constructing an increasing chain of domains whose limit is the fixed point. The remainder of this section speaks exclusively of domains, not of types, to be consistent with the literature.[1]

Definition 4.1 If $\langle \epsilon, \pi \rangle$ is a pair of continuous functions $\epsilon : D \to E$ and $\pi : E \to D$ then $\langle \epsilon, \pi \rangle$ is a *projection pair from D to E* provided

$$\pi \circ \epsilon \equiv ID_D \qquad \text{and} \qquad \epsilon \circ \pi \sqsubseteq ID_E$$

Furthermore ϵ is called the *embedding* and π is called the *projection*.

---

[1]This account of inverse limits is largely taken from Gordon Plotkin's notes.

If D can be embedded in E, this means that E has a richer structure, and can represent the structure of D. If elements of D are mapped into E and back again, no information is lost. The mapping in the reverse direction, from E to D and back, may lose information. Observe that every embedding is a one-to-one function, and that every projection is onto. A projection pair is something like a pair of isomorphism functions, but isomorphisms preserve information in both directions. For further insights, let us examine the properties of projection pairs.

Theorem 4.6 *Embedding and projection functions are strict.*
Proof: Similar to that for isomorphisms. □

Theorem 4.7 *If $\langle \epsilon, \pi \rangle$ and $\langle \epsilon', \pi' \rangle$ are projection pairs from D to E then*

$$\epsilon \sqsubseteq \epsilon' \qquad \text{if and only if} \qquad \pi' \sqsubseteq \pi$$

Proof: For the left to right direction, if $\epsilon \sqsubseteq \epsilon'$ then

$$\pi' \sqsubseteq \pi \circ \epsilon \circ \pi' \sqsubseteq \pi \circ \epsilon' \circ \pi' \sqsubseteq \pi$$

The converse is similar. By anti-symmetry we also have

$$\epsilon \equiv \epsilon' \qquad \text{if and only if} \qquad \pi' \equiv \pi$$

□

So if $\langle \epsilon, \pi \rangle$ is a projection pair then the embedding determines the projection, and conversely. We can get away with mentioning the embedding only: if ϵ embeds D in E we can write $\epsilon : D \lhd E$ or $D \overset{\epsilon}{\lhd} E$. The corresponding projection is written ϵ^R.

The function $\lambda x : void. \perp_D$ embeds the domain *void* into the domain D; we can write $(\lambda x. \perp_D) : void \lhd D$. The projection, $\lambda y : D. \perp_{void}$, maps every element of D to $\perp_{void}$. It is trivial to verify that these functions are indeed a projection pair from *void* to D.

The identity map embeds D into itself: $ID_D : D \lhd D$. The projection is also the identity: $ID^R \equiv ID$.

Theorem 4.8 *Projection pairs can be composed. If $\epsilon_1 : D_1 \lhd D_2$ and $\epsilon_2 : D_2 \lhd E$ where the corresponding projections are π_1 and π_2, then $\epsilon_2 \circ \epsilon_1 : D_1 \lhd E$, and the projection is $\pi_1 \circ \pi_2$.*
Proof: The embedding and projection behave as required. One direction is

$$(\epsilon_2 \circ \epsilon_1) \circ (\pi_1 \circ \pi_2) \equiv \epsilon_2 \circ (\epsilon_1 \circ \pi_1) \circ \pi_2 \sqsubseteq \epsilon_2 \circ \pi_2 \sqsubseteq ID_E$$

The other direction is similar. In the R-notation, the projection is expressed in terms of ϵ_1 and ϵ_2 as

$$(\epsilon_2 \circ \epsilon_1)^R \equiv \epsilon_1^R \circ \epsilon_2^R$$

□

4.7.1   The infinite Cartesian product

The limit of a chain of embeddings involves a new domain constructor. The Cartesian product of two domains can be generalized to the product of infinitely many domains $D_0, D_1, \ldots$. Elements are infinite tuples $(x_0, x_1, \ldots, x_n, \ldots)$, with $x_n \in D_n$, partially ordered such that

$$(x_0, x_1, \ldots, x_n, \ldots) \sqsubseteq (y_0, y_1, \ldots, y_n, \ldots) \qquad \text{if and only if } x_n \sqsubseteq y_n \text{ for all } n$$

The bottom element is $(\bot, \bot, \ldots, \bot, \ldots)$.

Least upper bounds of chains are taken by components. To avoid double subscripts, let us write tuples as $(\ldots, x, y, \ldots)$. Then the lub is

$$\bigsqcup_{k=0}^{\infty} (\ldots, x_k, y_k, \ldots) \;\equiv\; (\ldots, \bigsqcup_{k=0}^{\infty} x_k, \bigsqcup_{k=0}^{\infty} y_k, \ldots)$$

The standard notation for the infinite product is $\prod_{n=0}^{\infty} D_n$; instead we can write

$$D_0 \times D_1 \times \cdots \times D_n \times \cdots$$

provided we remember that the infinite product is a new domain constructor. It does not consist of infinitely many applications of $\times$: we are constructing the machinery to deal with such things.

Note that when all the D_n are the same, their infinite product is isomorphic to the strict function space:

$$D \times D \times \cdots \times D \times \cdots \;\cong\; nat \multimap D$$

4.7.2   Inverse limits

Embeddings suggest an analogy to cpo's, with $\stackrel{\epsilon}{\lhd}$ corresponding to $\sqsubseteq$ and *void* as the bottom element. The analogy is rough — the relation $\stackrel{\epsilon}{\lhd}$ is not a partial ordering — and yet it can be helpful. What corresponds to least upper bounds?

Suppose we have the chain of embeddings

$$D_0 \stackrel{\epsilon_0}{\lhd} D_1 \stackrel{\epsilon_1}{\lhd} \cdots \stackrel{\epsilon_{n-1}}{\lhd} D_n \stackrel{\epsilon_n}{\lhd} \cdots$$

For each embedding $\epsilon_n : D_n \to D_{n+1}$ there is a projection $\pi_n : D_{n+1} \to D_n$. The task is to construct a domain, D_∞, that contains all of the D_n. Here 'contains' refers to embeddings: for every n there must be an embedding $\rho_n : D_n \lhd D$. Furthermore the embeddings should identify values that are embedded from D_n into D_{n+1}; if $x \in D_n$ then $\epsilon_n(x)$ is x viewed as a member of D_{n+1}, so we should have the *commuting condition*

$$\rho_{n+1}(\epsilon_n(x)) \;\equiv\; \rho_n(x)$$

Finally, D_∞ must be a cpo: it must include least upper bounds of increasing chains.

If the D_n are finite in number, their limit is the largest one. The embeddings into it are obtained by composing the ϵ_n, and the commuting condition is trivially satisfied.

The limit of infinitely many domains, written D_∞ or $\lim\langle D_m, \epsilon_m \rangle$, is a subdomain of the infinite product $D_0 \times D_1 \times \cdots$. Its elements are tuples $(x_0, x_1, \ldots)$ satisfying an additional condition: that $\pi_n(x_{n+1}) \equiv x_n$ for all n.

Theorem 4.9 *The limit D_∞ is a cpo.*
Proof: Since projections are strict, the tuple $(\bot, \bot, \ldots)$ is in D_∞. To check the existence of least upper bounds, we again suppress subscripts and write the typical element of D_∞ as $(\ldots, x, y, \ldots)$ satisfying $\pi(y) \equiv x$. If $(\ldots, x_k, y_k, \ldots)$ is an increasing chain in D_∞, then the least upper bound $(\ldots, \bigsqcup_{k=0}^\infty x_k, \bigsqcup_{k=0}^\infty y_k, \ldots)$ is also in D_∞, since it satisfies the necessary condition:

$$\pi\left(\bigsqcup_{k=0}^\infty y_k\right) \equiv \bigsqcup_{k=0}^\infty \pi(y_k) \equiv \bigsqcup_{k=0}^\infty x_k$$

□

Consider a typical tuple, $(x_0, x_1, \ldots, x_m, \ldots)$. If x_m is given then $x_n \equiv \pi_n(x_{n+1})$ determines all the x_n for $n < m$, for x_n is obtained from its neighbor x_{n+1} by applying the projection π_n. Putting $x_{n+1} \equiv \epsilon_n(x_n)$ is one way of generating the x_n for $n > m$, but not every tuple need satisfy this: $x_n \equiv \pi_n(x_{n+1})$ implies the *inequivalence* $\epsilon_n(x_n) \sqsubseteq x_{n+1}$.

The embeddings and projections allow us to convert between any two domains D_m and D_n. Define the functions $\epsilon_{mn} : D_m \to D_n$ as the composition of the embeddings from m to n; if $n < m$ then compose the projections instead:

$$\epsilon_{mn} \equiv \begin{cases} \epsilon_{n-1} \circ \cdots \circ \epsilon_m & (m < n) \\ ID_{D_m} & (m = n) \\ \pi_n \circ \cdots \circ \pi_{m-1} & (m > n) \end{cases}$$

For $m \leq n$ this embeds D_m into D_n, as $\epsilon_{mn} : D_m \lhd D_n$. Clearly $\epsilon_{m,m+1}$ is just ϵ_m. It is not hard to show that $\epsilon_{kn} \circ \epsilon_{mk} \sqsubseteq \epsilon_{mn}$. Indeed $\epsilon_{kn} \circ \epsilon_{mk} \equiv \epsilon_{mn}$ if $k \geq \min\{m, n\}$; mapping from D_m to D_n through D_k loses no information provided that D_k is at least as rich as D_m or D_n.

This suggests how to construct a family of embeddings ρ_n from D_n into D_∞, for all n. The function ρ_n maps x in D_n to the tuple

$$(\epsilon_{n0}(x), \epsilon_{n1}(x), \epsilon_{n2}(x), \ldots, x, \ldots)$$

Let us look at this tuple from its nth component:

$$\downarrow$$

$$(\ldots, \pi_{n-2}(\pi_{n-1}(x)), \pi_{n-1}(x), x, \epsilon_n(x), \epsilon_{n+1}(\epsilon_n(x)), \ldots)$$

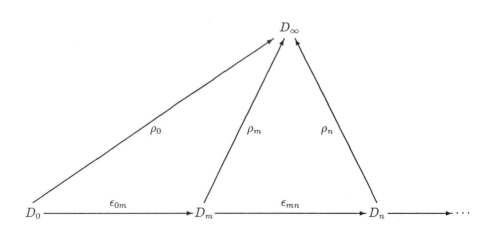

Figure 4.2: Commuting diagram for the inverse limit

The projection ρ_n^R must map this tuple back to x, and in general we have

$$\rho_n^R(x_0, x_1, \ldots, x_n, \ldots) \;\equiv\; x_n$$

Now let us verify that these are embeddings and satisfy the commuting condition $\rho_{n+1}(\epsilon_n(x)) \equiv \rho_n(x)$.

Theorem 4.10 *The function ρ_n embeds D_n into D_∞.*
Proof: Obviously $\rho_n^R \circ \rho_n \equiv ID_{D_n}$. It remains to show $\rho_n \circ \rho_n^R \sqsubseteq ID_{D_\infty}$. Recall that every tuple in D_∞ satisfies $x_m \equiv \pi_m(x_{m+1})$ for all m; therefore $\epsilon_{nm}(x_n) \sqsubseteq x_m$ for all m. Now

$$
\begin{aligned}
\rho_n(\rho_n^R(x_0, x_1, \ldots, x_m, \ldots)) \;&\equiv\; \rho_n(x_n) \\
&\equiv\; (\epsilon_{n0}(x_n), \epsilon_{n1}(x_n), \ldots, \epsilon_{nm}(x_n), \ldots) \\
&\sqsubseteq\; (x_0, x_1, \ldots, x_m, \ldots) \;\square
\end{aligned}
$$

Theorem 4.11 *If $m \le n$ then composing ρ_n with the embedding $\epsilon_{mn} : D_m \lhd D_n$ gives $\rho_n \circ \epsilon_{mn} : D_m \lhd D_\infty$, with $\rho_n \circ \epsilon_{mn} \equiv \rho_m$.*
Proof: We check the equality for an element D_∞ by components. The ith component of $(\rho_n \circ \epsilon_{mn})(x)$ is $\epsilon_{ni}(\epsilon_{mn}(x))$, which equals $\epsilon_{mi}(x)$, which is the ith component of $\rho_m(x)$. $\square$

Figure 4.2 shows the chain of domains and their limit. In category-theoretic terminology, the equality of $\rho_n \circ \epsilon_{mn}$ and ρ_m means that the diagram *commutes*. We now consider $\rho_n \circ \rho_n^R$, the function that projects from D_∞ down to D_n and then back to D_∞. This clearly entails some loss of information, but how much?

Theorem 4.12 *The $\rho_n \circ \rho_n^R$ form an increasing chain of functions in $D_\infty \to D_\infty$:*

$$\rho_0 \circ \rho_0^R \sqsubseteq \rho_1 \circ \rho_1^R \sqsubseteq \rho_2 \circ \rho_2^R \sqsubseteq \cdots$$

Proof: Expand ρ_n using the commuting condition:

$$
\begin{aligned}
\rho_n \circ \rho_n^R &\equiv (\rho_{n+1} \circ \epsilon_n) \circ (\rho_{n+1} \circ \epsilon_n)^R \\
&\equiv \rho_{n+1} \circ \epsilon_n \circ \epsilon_n^R \circ \rho_{n+1}^R \\
&\sqsubseteq \rho_{n+1} \circ ID_{D_{n+1}} \circ \rho_{n+1}^R \\
&\equiv \rho_{n+1} \circ \rho_{n+1}^R \quad \Box
\end{aligned}
$$

Theorem 4.13 *The chain $\rho_n \circ \rho_n^R$ converges to the identity function on D_∞,*

$$\bigsqcup_{n=0}^{\infty} \rho_n \circ \rho_n^R \equiv ID_{D_\infty}$$

Proof: For all n, applying $\rho_n \circ \rho_n^R$ to an element $(x_0, x_1, \ldots, x_n, \ldots)$ of D_∞ yields a tuple with x_n in its nth component. Least upper bounds are taken by components, so $ID_{D_\infty} \sqsubseteq \bigsqcup_{n=0}^{\infty} \rho_n \circ \rho_n^R$. Consider the opposite direction, $\bigsqcup_{n=0}^{\infty} \rho_n \circ \rho_n^R \sqsubseteq ID_{D_\infty}$. For all n, since ρ_n is an embedding, we have $\rho_n \circ \rho_n^R \sqsubseteq ID_{D_\infty}$. $\Box$

The above theorem is fundamental. It means that $\lim\langle D_m, \epsilon_m \rangle$, an infinite structure, contains nothing more than the structure present in the D_n, its finite stages. Such minimality is essential if the domain is to be useful in computation; it also allows induction over the domain.

The minimality of D_∞ and its embeddings ρ_n means it enjoys the *universal property*:[2] if E is a domain with embeddings $\phi_n : D_n \triangleleft E$ that satisfy the commuting condition $\phi_n \circ \epsilon_{mn} \equiv \phi_m$, then there is a unique embedding $\theta : D_\infty \to E$. Furthermore this embedding factors the ϕ_n, via $\phi_n \equiv \theta \circ \rho_n$. The domain $\lim\langle D_m, \epsilon_m \rangle$ has the universal property, as the following theorem shows.

Theorem 4.14 *If $\langle D, \rho_n \rangle$ is a domain with embeddings $\rho_n : D_n \triangleleft D$ that satisfy the commuting diagram, then $\langle D, \rho_n \rangle$ has the universal property if and only if $\bigsqcup_{n=0}^{\infty} \rho_n \circ \rho_n^R \equiv ID_D$.*

Proof: Here is part of the proof in the 'if' direction. Suppose $\bigsqcup_{n=0}^{\infty} \rho_n \circ \rho_n^R \equiv ID_D$. Then $\langle D, \rho_n \rangle$ is universal if, given $\langle E, \phi_n \rangle$ as above, there is an appropriate embedding from D to E. This embedding is

$$\theta \equiv \bigsqcup_{n=0}^{\infty} \phi_n \circ \rho_n^R \qquad\qquad \theta^R \equiv \bigsqcup_{n=0}^{\infty} \rho_n \circ \phi_n^R$$

The equalities among the functions are illustrated in the commuting diagram in Figure 4.3; the dashed arrow indicates that the other functions determine θ.

---

[2] This universal property must not be confused with the notion of universal domain.

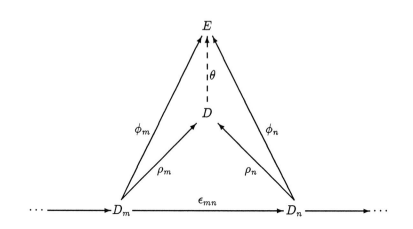

Figure 4.3: The universal property of $\langle D, \rho_n \rangle$

Now θ is an embedding. Here is a proof of $\theta^R \circ \theta \equiv ID_D$, using continuity of composition:

$$\theta^R \circ \theta \equiv (\bigsqcup_{n=0}^{\infty} \rho_n \circ \phi_n^R) \circ (\bigsqcup_{n=0}^{\infty} \phi_n \circ \rho_n^R)$$

$$\equiv \bigsqcup_{n=0}^{\infty} \rho_n \circ \phi_n^R \circ \phi_n \circ \rho_n^R$$

$$\equiv \bigsqcup_{n=0}^{\infty} \rho_n \circ \rho_n^R$$

$$\equiv ID_D$$

The proof that $\phi_n \equiv \theta \circ \rho_n$ relies on the commuting conditions of both the ϕ_n and the ρ_n. Some limits are taken from m, not 0; omitting the first m elements of a chain does not affect the limit.

$$\theta \circ \rho_n \equiv (\bigsqcup_{n=0}^{\infty} \phi_n \circ \rho_n^R) \circ \rho_m$$

$$\equiv \bigsqcup_{n=0}^{\infty} \phi_n \circ \rho_n^R \circ \rho_m$$

$$\equiv \bigsqcup_{n=m}^{\infty} \phi_n \circ \rho_n^R \circ \rho_m$$

$$\equiv \bigsqcup_{n=m}^{\infty} \phi_n \circ \rho_n^R \circ \rho_n \circ \epsilon_{mn}$$

$$\equiv \bigsqcup_{n=m}^{\infty} \phi_n \circ \epsilon_{mn}$$

$$\equiv \phi_m \quad \square$$

4.7.3 Continuity of domain constructors

Recursive domain equations over a domain constructor F can be solved if F satisfies two properties, which are analogous to monotonicity and continuity. The first property is that if ϵ embeds D in E then there is an embedding, written $F(\epsilon)$, of $F(D)$ in $F(E)$. In short:

$$\epsilon : D \lhd E \qquad \text{implies} \qquad F(\epsilon) : F(D) \lhd F(E)$$

As a mapping on embeddings, F should also preserve identities and composition:

$$F(ID_D) = ID_{F(D)}$$
$$F(\epsilon' \circ \epsilon) = F(\epsilon') \circ F(\epsilon)$$

In categorical terms, F is a covariant functor.

Applying such an F to the chain of embeddings

$$D_0 \overset{\epsilon_0}{\lhd} D_1 \overset{\epsilon_1}{\lhd} \cdots \overset{\epsilon_{n-1}}{\lhd} D_n \overset{\epsilon_n}{\lhd} \cdots$$

produces a new chain,

$$F(D_0) \overset{F(\epsilon_0)}{\lhd} F(D_1) \overset{F(\epsilon_1)}{\lhd} \cdots \overset{F(\epsilon_{n-1})}{\lhd} F(D_n) \overset{F(\epsilon_n)}{\lhd} \cdots$$

Continuity of F means that if $\langle D, \rho_n \rangle$ has the universal property, then so does $\langle F(D), F(\rho_n) \rangle$:

$$\bigsqcup_{n=0}^{\infty} \rho_n \circ \rho_n^R \equiv ID_D \qquad \text{implies} \qquad \bigsqcup_{n=0}^{\infty} F(\rho_n) \circ F(\rho_n)^R \equiv ID_{F(D)}$$

This condition may look technical but it is easy to state and easy to prove in each case. It implies that F preserves limits:

$$F(\lim \langle D_n, \epsilon_n \rangle) \equiv \lim \langle F(D_n), F(\epsilon_n) \rangle$$

Let us verify the 'monotonicity' property for the domain constructors $\times$, $\oplus$, u, and $\rightarrow$. These all take two arguments, so suppose we are given $\epsilon : D \lhd E$ and $\epsilon' : D' \lhd E'$, with projections π and π'.

Cartesian product: We have $\epsilon \times \epsilon' : D \times D' \lhd E \times E'$, where $\epsilon \times \epsilon'$ is the embedding that maps (x, x') to $(\epsilon(x), \epsilon'(x))$. The projection maps (y, y') to $(\pi(y), \pi'(y))$.

Strict sum: We have $\epsilon \oplus \epsilon' : D \oplus D' \lhd E \oplus E'$, where $\epsilon \oplus \epsilon'$ is the embedding that maps $INL(x)$ to $INL(\epsilon(x))$ and $INR(x')$ to $INR(\epsilon'(x'))$. The projection maps $INL(y)$ to $INL(\pi(y))$ and $INR(y')$ to $INR(\pi'(y'))$. Recall that embeddings and projections are strict.

Lifting: We have $(\epsilon)u : (D)u \lhd (E)u$, where $(\epsilon)u$ is the embedding that maps $UP(x)$ to $UP(\epsilon(x))$. The projection maps $UP(y)$ to $UP(\pi(y))$.

Function space

The reason for working with projection pairs is to handle function space. We can exhibit an embedding from $f : D \to D'$ to $g : E \to E'$ and prove that $\to$ is a continuous domain constructor.

Theorem 4.15 *There is a continuous way to make an embedding*

$$\epsilon \to \epsilon' : D \to D' \lhd E \to E'$$

from the embeddings $\epsilon : D \lhd E$ and $\epsilon' : D' \lhd E'$.
Proof: Let $\epsilon \to \epsilon'$ be the embedding that maps the function $f : D \to D'$ to $\epsilon' \circ f \circ \pi$, and let the projection map the function $g : E \to E'$ to $\pi' \circ g \circ \epsilon$. In the R-notation, the embedding and projection for function space are

$$\epsilon \to \epsilon' \;\equiv\; \lambda f.\, \epsilon' \circ f \circ \epsilon^R$$
$$(\epsilon \to \epsilon')^R \;\equiv\; \lambda g.\, \epsilon'^R \circ g \circ \epsilon$$

These are a projection pair, for composing the projection with the embedding gives

$$
\begin{aligned}
((\epsilon \to \epsilon')^R \circ (\epsilon \to \epsilon'))(f) &\equiv \pi' \circ (\epsilon' \circ f \circ \pi) \circ \epsilon \\
&\equiv (\pi' \circ \epsilon') \circ f \circ (\pi \circ \epsilon) \\
&\equiv ID_{D'} \circ f \circ ID_D \\
&\equiv f
\end{aligned}
$$

and composing the embedding with the projection gives

$$
\begin{aligned}
((\epsilon \to \epsilon') \circ (\epsilon \to \epsilon')^R)(g) &\equiv \epsilon' \circ (\pi' \circ g \circ \epsilon) \circ \pi \\
&\equiv (\epsilon' \circ \pi') \circ g \circ (\epsilon \circ \pi) \\
&\sqsubseteq ID_{D'} \circ g \circ ID_D \\
&\equiv g
\end{aligned}
$$

The domain constructor $\to$ is continuous, for suppose there are two universal families of embeddings $\langle D, \rho_n \rangle$ and $\langle E, \phi_n \rangle$ with $\rho_n : D_n \lhd D$ and $\phi_n : E_n \lhd E$. Then we need show

$$\bigsqcup_{n=0}^{\infty} ((\rho_n \to \phi_n) \circ (\rho_n \to \phi_n)^R) \equiv ID_{D \to E}$$

or equivalently

$$\left(\bigsqcup_{n=0}^{\infty} ((\rho_n \to \phi_n) \circ (\rho_n \to \phi_n)^R) \right)(g) \equiv g$$

for $g \in D \to E$. A tedious calculation, using continuity of function composition and the universal properties of $\langle D, \rho_n \rangle$ and $\langle E, \phi_n \rangle$, gives

$$(\bigsqcup_{n=0}^{\infty}((\rho_n \to \phi_n) \circ (\rho_n \to \phi_n)^R))(g) \; \equiv \; \bigsqcup_{n=0}^{\infty}(\rho_n \to \phi_n)((\rho_n \to \phi_n)^R(g))$$

$$\equiv \; \bigsqcup_{n=0}^{\infty}(\rho_n \to \phi_n)(\phi_n^R \circ g \circ \rho_n)$$

$$\equiv \; \bigsqcup_{n=0}^{\infty}\phi_n \circ (\phi_n^R \circ g \circ \rho_n) \circ \rho_n^R$$

$$\equiv \; (\bigsqcup_{n=0}^{\infty}\phi_n \circ \phi_n^R) \circ g \circ (\bigsqcup_{n=0}^{\infty}\rho_n \circ \rho_n^R)$$

$$\equiv \; ID_E \circ g \circ ID_D$$

$$\equiv \; g \quad \square$$

There is a general theorem for proving continuity of domain constructors without such a calculation.

Inclusions

A simple kind of embedding, an inclusion, relates the inverse limit construction of recursive domains to naive set theory. If $\phi : D \to E$ is an inclusion then $D \subseteq E$.

Definition 4.2 A function $\phi : D \to E$ is an *inclusion* if $\phi(x) \equiv x$ for all $x \in D$.

Theorem 4.16 *If $\epsilon : D \lhd E$ and $\epsilon' : D' \lhd E'$ are inclusions then so are $\epsilon \times \epsilon' :$ $D \times D' \lhd E \times E'$, $\epsilon \oplus \epsilon' : D \oplus D' \lhd E \oplus E'$, and $(\epsilon)u : (D)u \lhd (E)u$.*
Proof: Obvious. For example,

$$(\epsilon \times \epsilon')(x, x') \; \equiv \; (\epsilon(x), \epsilon'(x)) \; \equiv \; (x, x')$$

The others are equally trivial. $\square$

It is tempting to imagine that the embedding $\lambda x : void. \perp_D$ is an inclusion, but $\perp_{void}$ and $\perp_D$ may differ. We can easily arrange matters such that, for arbitrary D and E,

$$\perp_{void} \; \equiv \; \perp_{D \oplus E} \; \equiv \; \perp_{D+E} \; \equiv \; \perp_{D(u)}$$

by letting the bottom elements of all those domains be 0. But the bottom element of $D \times E$ is the pair $\langle \perp_D, \perp_E \rangle$, and we cannot give *void* and $D \times void$ the same bottom element: this would mean

$$\perp_{void} \; \equiv \; \perp_{D \times void} \; \equiv \; \langle \perp_D, \perp_{void} \rangle$$

and $\perp_{void}$ would contain itself.

Practically all of the domain constructors, apart from function space, map inclusions to inclusions. When $\lambda x : void. \perp_D$ is also an inclusion, we nearly return to the easy problem of solving recursion equations over sets.

4.7.4   Solving recursive domain equations

If F is a continuous domain constructor then the isomorphism $D \cong F(D)$ can be solved by a construction resembling the Fixed Point Theorem. Start with the 'bottom' element *void*, with the embedding $(\lambda x.\bot) : void \lhd F(void)$. Then we have $F(\lambda x.\bot) : F(void) \lhd F(F(void))$, and so on, forming the chain

$$void \overset{\lambda x.\bot}{\lhd} F(void) \overset{F(\lambda x.\bot)}{\lhd} F^2(void) \overset{F(F(\lambda x.\bot))}{\lhd} \cdots$$

with limit D_∞. By continuity, $F(D_\infty)$ is the limit of the chain

$$F(void) \overset{F(\lambda x.\bot)}{\lhd} F^2(void) \overset{F(F(\lambda x.\bot))}{\lhd} \cdots$$

This is the previous chain minus its first element. Each element of the limit is an element of the previous limit, minus its first component, which is always $\bot_{void}$. So the two limit domains are isomorphic.

Furthermore D_∞ is *minimal*: for every E such that $\phi : F(E) \lhd E$ there is an embedding $\theta : D \to E$. The proof involves constructing a family of embeddings $\phi_n : F^n(void) \lhd E$, and then appealing to the universality of $\langle D_\infty, \rho_n \rangle$.

Example 4.8 Let us return to the list example that begins this section, and construct a domain **L** satisfying the isomorphism

$$\mathbf{L} \cong void + (nat \times \mathbf{L})$$

by finding the fixed point of the domain construction

$$F(D) = void + (nat \times D)$$

We get the following sequence of domains:

$$
\begin{aligned}
F^0(void) &= void \\
F^1(void) &= void + nat \times void \\
F^2(void) &= void + nat \times (void + nat \times void) \\
F^3(void) &= void + nat \times (void + nat \times (void + nat \times void)) \\
&\vdots
\end{aligned}
$$

The embeddings are all inclusions, so the $F^n(void)$ are an increasing chain of sets. Let $m_0, m_1, \ldots$ be elements of nat. Then $F^0(void)$ contains $\bot$.

The set $F^1(void)$ contains as well $INLUP(\bot)$ and $INRUP(m_0, \bot)$: the empty list and a partial list whose head is m_0.

The set $F^2(void)$ contains as well

$$INRUP(m_0, INLUP(\bot)) \qquad \text{and} \qquad INRUP(m_0, INRUP(m_1, \bot)):$$

the one-element list $[m_0]$ and the partial list beginning with m_0 and m_1.

We are working not with sets but with domains; the limit of the $F^n(void)$ is not just the union, but also contains infinite lists. So $\mathbf{L}$ is the domain of *lazy lists*, which the following section considers in detail.

Example 4.9 A variation on lazy lists: we can now solve the domain isomorphism

$$D \cong nat \times D$$

namely the infinite iteration of the two-place Cartesian product. The domains are

$$
\begin{aligned}
F^0(void) &= void \\
F^1(void) &= nat \times void \\
F^2(void) &= nat \times (nat \times void) \\
F^3(void) &= nat \times (nat \times (nat \times void))
\end{aligned}
$$

$$\vdots$$

The elements of $F^1(void)$ have the form $\langle m_0, \bot \rangle$, those of $F^2(void)$ have the form $\langle m_0, \langle m_1, \bot \rangle \rangle$, those of $F^3(void)$ have the form $\langle m_0, \langle m_1, \langle m_2, \bot \rangle \rangle \rangle$, and so on.

The embeddings are not quite inclusions:

$$
\begin{aligned}
\epsilon_0(\bot) &= \langle \bot, \bot \rangle \\
\epsilon_1(\langle m_0, \bot \rangle) &= \langle m_0, \langle \bot, \bot \rangle \rangle \\
\epsilon_2(\langle m_0, \langle m_1, \bot \rangle \rangle) &= \langle m_0, \langle m_1, \langle \bot, \bot \rangle \rangle \rangle \\
\epsilon_3(\langle m_0, \langle m_1, \langle m_2, \bot \rangle \rangle \rangle) &= \langle m_0, \langle m_1, \langle m_2, \langle \bot, \bot \rangle \rangle \rangle \rangle
\end{aligned}
$$

$$\vdots$$

The elements of limit of the $F^n(void)$ are infinite tuples $(x_0, x_1, x_2, \ldots)$, with $x_n \in F^n(void)$. The infinite nest of pairs $\langle m_0, \langle m_1, \langle m_2, \ldots \rangle \rangle \rangle$ is represented by the tuple

$$(\bot, \langle m_0, \bot \rangle, \langle m_0, \langle m_1, \bot \rangle \rangle, \langle m_0, \langle m_1, \langle m_2, \bot \rangle \rangle \rangle, \ldots)$$

In set theory, the solution of $D = \mathbf{N} \times D$ is rather boring: the empty set, for $\emptyset = \mathbf{N} \times \emptyset$. By the axiom of foundation, there are no other solutions.

Exercise 4.26 Prove the theorem $\epsilon_{kn} \circ \epsilon_{mk} \sqsubseteq \epsilon_{mn}$. Refine your proof to obtain

$$k \geq \min\{m, n\} \qquad \text{implies} \qquad \epsilon_{kn} \circ \epsilon_{mk} \equiv \epsilon_{mn}$$

Exercise 4.27 Given $\epsilon : D \triangleleft E$ and $\epsilon' : D' \triangleleft E'$, show that $\epsilon \times \epsilon' : D \times D' \triangleleft E \times E'$ is indeed an embedding, and that the Cartesian product is a continuous domain constructor.

Exercise 4.28 For a chain $D_0 \overset{\epsilon_0}{\triangleleft} D_1 \overset{\epsilon_1}{\triangleleft} \cdots$, show that $\lim \langle D_m, \epsilon_m \rangle$ is isomorphic to the limit $\lim \langle D_{m+n}, \epsilon_{m+n} \rangle$ of the chain minus its first n elements. (Hint: recall that the nth component of a tuple determines the components to its left.)

4.8   The type of lazy lists

Suppose we have a type σ, with elements $x_1, \ldots, x_n$. Then $(\sigma)\,llist$ is the type of lazy lists over σ. A lazy list can be $LNIL$, the empty list; it can also have the form $LCONS(x)(l)$, the list with head x and tail l. The ML list $[x_1, x_2 \ldots, x_n]$ is represented by

$$LCONS(x_1)(LCONS(x_2) \cdots (LCONS(x_n)LNIL) \cdots)$$

Furthermore $LCONS$ is not strict. If $SUCC : nat \rightarrow nat$ is the successor function on natural numbers and $FROM$ satisfies the recursion equation

$$FROM(n) \equiv LCONS(n)(FROM(SUCC\,n))$$

then $FROM(1)$ is the least upper bound an increasing chain in $nat\ llist$:

$$\bot$$
$$LCONS(1)(\bot)$$
$$LCONS(1)(LCONS(2)(\bot))$$
$$LCONS(1)(LCONS(2)(LCONS(3)(\bot)))$$
$$\vdots$$

These lists are distinct and their least upper bound is the infinite list $[1, 2, 3, \ldots]$. Of course, a finite computation uses only a finite prefix of the list. A lazy list can also have $\bot$ as a member. The list $[\bot, 8, \bot, 1]$ has length 4 even though some members are undefined. An entire school of functional programming has developed around the possibilities of computing with lazy data structures [97].

The standard construction of $(\sigma)\,llist$ requires solving the recursive domain isomorphism $\sigma\,llist \cong void + (\sigma \times \sigma\,llist)$. An isomorphic type of lazy lists can be constructed using the strict type constructors $\otimes$ and $\oplus$ instead of $\times$ and $+$, via the isomorphism discussed in Example 4.7. Expressing both lazy and strict types using $\otimes$, $\oplus$, and u gives a smooth transition from lazy to strict, allowing mixed types as well. Here is the recursion isomorphism for lazy lists, showing the representation of the constructors, $LNIL$ and $LCONS$, in $unit \oplus (\sigma u \otimes (\sigma\,llist)u)$:

$$\sigma\,llist \quad \cong \quad unit \oplus (\sigma u \otimes (\sigma\,llist)u)$$
$$LCONS(x)(l) \quad \longmapsto \quad INR(SPAIR(UP\,x)(UP\,l)))$$
$$LNIL \quad \longmapsto \quad INL(UP())$$
$$\bot \quad \longmapsto \quad \bot$$

The eliminator functional $LLIST\_WHEN$ operates on a lazy list. It distinguishes $LNIL$ from $LCONS$; for $LCONS(x)(l)$ it gives access to x and l. The constant symbols are[3]

$$LNIL : \sigma \; llist$$
$$LCONS : \sigma \rightarrow \sigma \; llist \rightarrow \sigma \; llist$$
$$LLIST\_WHEN : \tau \rightarrow (\sigma \rightarrow \sigma \; llist \rightarrow \tau) \rightarrow \tau$$

Previous sections introduce the operations on a new type as new constants, asserting new axioms. But *LNIL*, *LCONS*, and *LLIST_WHEN* can be defined, and their properties proven, in terms of the representation type. Let the isomorphism functions be

$$ABS : unit \oplus (\sigma u \otimes (\sigma \; llist)u) \rightarrow \sigma \; llist$$
$$REP : \sigma \; llist \rightarrow unit \oplus (\sigma u \otimes (\sigma \; llist)u)$$

Now define the constants as follows:

$$\begin{aligned}
LNIL &\equiv ABS(INL(UP())) \\
LCONS &\equiv \lambda x \, l. \, ABS(INR(SPAIR(UP\,x)(UP\,l)))) \\
LLIST\_WHEN &\equiv \lambda z f l. \, WHEN(\lambda u. z)(SSPLIT(LIFT(\lambda x. \, LIFT(\lambda l. f x l))))(REP\,l)
\end{aligned}$$

We can prove that the constructors and eliminator behave properly; the proofs can be formalized in PPλ.

Theorem 4.17 *The constructors LNIL and LCONS satisfy the* definedness *property, namely LNIL $\not\equiv \bot$ and LCONS$(x)(l) \not\equiv \bot$.*

Proof: The function *UP* always yields a defined value, and *INL*, *INR*, *SPAIR*, and *ABS* are total functions. So the function *LCONS* is not strict. □

Theorem 4.18 *Lazy lists satisfy the* exhaustion *property:*

$$\forall l : \sigma \; llist \,. \, l \equiv \bot \; \vee \; l \equiv LNIL \; \vee \; (\exists x \, l' \,. \, l \equiv LCONS(x)(l'))$$

Proof: By cases on the representation type using the exhaustion axioms for $\oplus$, $\otimes$, and u. Let l be an element of type $\sigma \; llist$. Then $l \equiv ABS(REP\,l)$. Since $REP(l)$ has type $unit \oplus (\sigma u \otimes (\sigma \; llist)u)$ there are three cases:

- It equals $\bot$, and then $l \equiv ABS\,\bot \equiv \bot_{\sigma \, llist}$.

- It has the form $INL(u)$, where u is a defined element of type *unit*. The only such is $UP()$. So $l \equiv ABS(INL(UP())) \equiv LNIL$.

- It has the form $INR(u)$, where u is a defined element of type $(\sigma u \otimes (\sigma \; llist)u)$. So u has the form $SPAIR(v)(w)$, where $v : \sigma u$ and $w : (\sigma \; llist)u$ are defined. So v is $UP(x)$ and w is $UP(l')$, and $l \equiv ABS(INR(SPAIR(UP\,x)(UP\,l')))) \equiv LCONS(x)(l')$. □

---

[3]The constructor function *LCONS* is curried: we write *LCONS*$(x)(l)$ and not *LCONS*(x, l). In Standard ML, the argument of a constructor function is a tuple. The choice is arbitrary.

Theorem 4.19 *The eliminator LLIST_WHEN satisfies the reduction equations*

$$
\begin{array}{rcl}
LLIST\_WHEN(z)(f)(\bot) & \equiv & \bot \\
LLIST\_WHEN(z)(f)(LNIL) & \equiv & z \\
LLIST\_WHEN(z)(f)(LCONS(x)(l)) & \equiv & f(x)(l)
\end{array}
$$

Proof: Let us verify these one by one. To save space, introduce the abbreviation

$$
h \equiv SSPLIT(LIFT(\lambda x.\, LIFT(\lambda l.f(x)(l))))
$$

Therefore

$$
LLIST\_WHEN(z)(f)(l) \quad \equiv \quad WHEN(\lambda u.z)(h)(REP\ l)
$$

The $\bot$ equation is

$$
\begin{array}{rcl}
LLIST\_WHEN(z)(f)\bot & \equiv & WHEN(\lambda u.z)(h)(REP\ \bot) \\
& \equiv & WHEN(\lambda u.z)(h)(\bot) \\
& \equiv & \bot
\end{array}
$$

The *LNIL* equation is

$$
\begin{array}{rcl}
LLIST\_WHEN(z)(f)LNIL & \equiv & WHEN(\lambda u.z)(h)(REP\ LNIL) \\
& \equiv & WHEN(\lambda u.z)(h)(INL(UP())) \\
& \equiv & (\lambda u.z)(UP()) \\
& \equiv & z
\end{array}
$$

The *LCONS* equation is

$$
\begin{array}{rcl}
LLIST\_WHEN(z)(f)(LCONS\ x\ l) & & \\
\equiv & WHEN(\lambda u.z)(h)(REP(LCONS\ x\ l)) \\
\equiv & WHEN(\lambda u.z)(h)(INR(SPAIR(UP\ x)(UP\ l))) \\
\equiv & SSPLIT(LIFT(\lambda x.\, LIFT(\lambda l.fx\ l)))(SPAIR(UP\ x)(UP\ l)) \\
\equiv & LIFT(\lambda x.\, LIFT(\lambda l.fx\ l))(UP\ x)(UP\ l) \\
\equiv & (\lambda x.\, LIFT(\lambda l.fx\ l))(x)(UP\ l) \\
\equiv & LIFT(\lambda l.fx\ l)(UP\ l) \\
\equiv & (\lambda l.fx\ l)(l) \\
\equiv & fx\ l
\end{array}
$$

The application of *SSPLIT* can be reduced because *UP x* and *UP l* are defined. □

4.8.1   Discriminator and destructor functions

The traditional approach to lists is to provide the discriminator *LNULL* and the destructors *LHEAD* and *LTAIL*:

$$LNULL : \sigma \; llist \to tr$$
$$LHEAD : \sigma \; llist \to \sigma$$
$$LTAIL : \sigma \; llist \to \sigma \; llist$$

Their properties include

$$LNULL(LNIL) \; \equiv \; TT$$
$$LNULL(LCONS(x)(l))) \; \equiv \; FF$$
$$LHEAD(LCONS(x)(l)) \; \equiv \; x$$
$$LTAIL(LCONS(x)(l)) \; \equiv \; l$$

Here are their definitions via *LLIST_WHEN*:

$$LNULL \; \equiv \; LLIST\_WHEN(TT)(\lambda x \, l.FF)$$
$$LHEAD \; \equiv \; LLIST\_WHEN(\bot)(\lambda x \, l.x)$$
$$LTAIL \; \equiv \; LLIST\_WHEN(\bot)(\lambda x \, l.l)$$

Example 4.10 The *append* function, which concatenates two lists, should be familiar to every ML or Lisp programmer. Let *LAPP* be the infix operator for concatenating two lazy lists. It should satisfy

$$\bot \; LAPP \; b \; \equiv \; \bot$$
$$LNIL \; LAPP \; b \; \equiv \; b$$
$$(LCONS \, x \, l) \; LAPP \; b \; \equiv \; LCONS(x)(l \; LAPP \; b)$$

Concatenation makes sense even for infinite lazy lists. If a is infinite then $a \; LAPP \; b$ equals a.

The traditional coding of *LAPP* uses the conditional expression, discriminator, and destructors:

$$a \; LAPP \; b \equiv (LNULL \Rightarrow b \mid LCONS(LHEAD \; a)((LTAIL \; a) \; LAPP \; b)$$

The functional *LLIST_WHEN* allows the more concise

$$a \; LAPP \; b \equiv LLIST\_WHEN(b)(\lambda x \, l. \; LCONS(x)(l \; LAPP \; b))(a)$$

As we shall see below, the function *LAPP* is associative. The proof is by structural induction over lazy lists.

4.8.2   The partial ordering

The discriminator and destructors determine the partial ordering $\sqsubseteq_{\sigma\, llist}$. Since $FF \not\sqsubseteq TT$, monotonicity of $LNULL$ implies $LCONS(x)(l) \not\sqsubseteq LNIL$ and similarly $LNIL \not\sqsubseteq LCONS(x)(l)$, the *distinctness* property for $LNIL$ and $LCONS$. Monotonicity of $LHEAD$ and $LTAIL$ gives the *invertibility* property: if $LCONS(x')(l') \sqsubseteq_{\sigma\, llist} LCONS(x)(l)$ then $x' \sqsubseteq_{\sigma} x$ and $l' \sqsubseteq_{\sigma\, llist} l$.

Ignoring bottom, there are four cases. Distinctness:

$$LNIL \quad \not\sqsubseteq \quad LCONS(x)(l)$$
$$LCONS(x)(l) \quad \not\sqsubseteq \quad LNIL$$

Invertibility:

$$LNIL \sqsubseteq LNIL$$
$$LCONS(x')(l') \sqsubseteq_{\sigma\, llist} LCONS(x)(l) \quad \Longleftrightarrow \quad x' \sqsubseteq_{\sigma} x \wedge l' \sqsubseteq_{\sigma\, llist} l$$

Exercise 4.29   What lazy list is $FIX(LCONS(1))$?

Exercise 4.30   Construct the type $(\sigma)seq$ of infinite sequences, satisfying

$$(\sigma)seq \;\cong\; \sigma \times (\sigma)seq$$

The type has no element corresponding to $LNIL$.

4.9   The type of strict lists

Lists in ML are strict: every list is finite and its members are all defined (non-bottom). A computation like $FROM(1)$ does not produce an infinite list; instead, it runs forever. A domain of strict lists would allow us to reason in LCF about the ML type *list*.

Apart from ML, why consider strict lists when lazy lists are so much more interesting? Because a lazy type has an extremely complicated structure of partial and infinite objects — objects that are not always wanted. Suppose we would like to prove that reversing a list twice results in the same list:

$$REV(REV\ l) \equiv l$$

This holds for finite lists, but reversing an infinite list results in $\bot$. For similar reasons, lazy data types complicated Cohn and Milner's parser proof [25].

The recursion isomorphism for strict lists is similar to that for lazy lists, but omits the lifting operator:

$$\sigma\ list \quad \cong \quad unit \oplus (\sigma \otimes (\sigma\ list))$$

$$CONS(x)(l) \quad \longmapsto \quad INR(SPAIR(x)(l)))$$
$$NIL \quad \longmapsto \quad INL(UP())$$
$$\bot \quad \longmapsto \quad \bot$$

A strict list can be *NIL* or else *CONS(x)(l)*, the list with non-bottom head x and tail l. The eliminator functional *LIST_WHEN* resembles *LLIST_WHEN* but operates on strict lists. The constant symbols are

$$NIL : \sigma \ list$$
$$CONS : \sigma \rightarrow \sigma \ list \rightarrow \sigma \ list$$
$$LIST\_WHEN : \tau \rightarrow (\sigma \rightarrow \sigma \ list \rightarrow \tau) \rightarrow \tau$$

Let the isomorphism functions be

$$ABS : unit \oplus (\sigma \otimes \sigma \ list) \rightarrow \sigma \ list$$
$$REP : \sigma \ list \rightarrow unit \oplus (\sigma \otimes \sigma \ list)$$

Then the functions for strict lists can be defined:

$$
\begin{aligned}
NIL &\equiv ABS(INL(UP())) \\
CONS &\equiv \lambda x\, l.\ ABS(INR(SPAIR(x)(l)))) \\
LIST\_WHEN &\equiv \lambda z f l.\ WHEN(\lambda u.z)(SSPLIT(\lambda x\, l.f(x)(l)))(REP\, l)
\end{aligned}
$$

The properties of these functions resemble those of their lazy list counterparts, but the function *CONS* is strict because *INR*, *SPAIR*, and *ABS* are:

$$CONS(\perp_\sigma)(l) \equiv \perp_{\sigma\ list} \equiv CONS(x)(\perp_{\sigma\ list})$$

So *CONS(x)(l)* is only considered in contexts where both x and l are defined: the exhaustion property is formulated to avoid overlap between the *CONS* and $\perp$ cases; the *CONS* reduction equation (for *LIST_WHEN*) is subject to definedness conditions. The following are informal sketches of proofs in PPλ.

Theorem 4.20 *Strict lists satisfy the definedness properties* $NIL \not\equiv \perp$ *and*

$$x \not\equiv \perp_\sigma \wedge l \not\equiv \perp_{\sigma\ list} \Longrightarrow CONS(x)(l) \not\equiv \perp_{\sigma\ list}$$

Proof: The functions *INL*, *INR*, *SPAIR*, and *ABS* are all total, and *UP()* is defined. $\square$

Theorem 4.21 *Strict lists satisfy the exhaustion property*

$$\forall l : \sigma\ list\,. l \equiv \perp \vee l \equiv NIL \vee (\exists x\, l'\,. l \equiv CONS(x)(l') \wedge x \not\equiv \perp \wedge l' \not\equiv \perp)$$

Proof: The only difference from lazy lists is in the *CONS* case, where the head and tail of the list must be shown to be defined. The property is proved by case analysis on *REP(l)*, of type $unit \oplus (\sigma \otimes \sigma\ list)$. In the *CONS* case, *REP(l)* is *INR(u)*, where u is a defined element of type $\sigma \otimes \sigma\ list$. So u has the form *SPAIR(x)(l')*, where $x : \sigma$ and $l' : \sigma\ list$ are defined, and $l \equiv ABS(INR(SPAIR\, x\, l')) \equiv CONS(x)(l')$. $\square$

Theorem 4.22 *The eliminator LIST_WHEN satisfies the equations*

$$LIST\_WHEN(z)(f)(\perp_{\sigma\ list}) \quad \equiv \quad \perp_\tau$$
$$LIST\_WHEN(z)(f)(NIL) \quad \equiv \quad z$$
$$x \not\equiv \perp \wedge l \not\equiv \perp \Longrightarrow \quad LIST\_WHEN(z)(f)(CONS(x)(l)) \quad \equiv \quad f(x)(l)$$

Proof: We just verify the *CONS* equation; the others are easy.

$$LIST\_WHEN(z)(f)(CONS\ x\ l)$$
$$\equiv \quad WHEN(\lambda u.z)(SSPLIT(\lambda x\ l.f(x)(l)))(REP(CONS\ x\ l))$$
$$\equiv \quad WHEN(\lambda u.z)(SSPLIT(\lambda x\ l.f(x)(l)))(INR(SPAIR(x)(l)))$$
$$\equiv \quad SSPLIT(\lambda x\ l.f(x)(l))(SPAIR(x)(l))$$
$$\equiv \quad (\lambda x\ l.f(x)(l))(x)(l)$$
$$\equiv \quad f(x)(l)$$

The application of *SSPLIT* can be reduced because of the assumption that x and l are defined. □

4.9.1   Discriminator and destructor functions

The functions *NULL*, *HEAD* and *TAIL* are like their lazy counterparts:

$$NULL : \sigma\ list \rightarrow tr$$
$$HEAD : \sigma\ list \rightarrow \sigma$$
$$TAIL : \sigma\ list \rightarrow \sigma\ list$$

Note, again, how we must have defined values for the head and tail before saying anything about *CONS*:

$$NULL(NIL) \equiv TT$$

$$x \not\equiv \perp \wedge l \not\equiv \perp \Longrightarrow \left\{ \begin{array}{rcl} NULL(CONS\ x\ l) & \equiv & FF \\ HEAD(CONS\ x\ l) & \equiv & x \\ TAIL(CONS\ x\ l) & \equiv & l \end{array} \right.$$

The functions *NULL*, *HEAD* and *TAIL* are easily expressed using *LIST_WHEN*.

Example 4.11 It is so easy to go wrong. What might $NULL\perp$ be? The function *NULL* returns *TT* for some arguments and *FF* for others. Like all functions, it must be monotonic, which implies $NULL\perp \sqsubseteq TT$ and $NULL\perp \sqsubseteq FF$. Therefore *NULL* has got to be strict: $NULL\perp \equiv \perp_{tr}$. If we were foolish enough to assert

$$\forall xl\ .\ NULL(CONS\ x\ l) \equiv FF$$

then we would suffer the contradiction

$$FF \equiv NULL(CONS \perp \perp) \equiv NULL\perp \equiv \perp$$

Functions on lists should be expressed using *LIST_WHEN* to prevent this kind of disaster.

Consider also the append function for strict lists, the infix operator *APP*. It satisfies

$$\bot \; APP \; b \; \equiv \; \bot$$
$$NIL \; APP \; b \; \equiv \; b$$
$$x \not\equiv \bot_\sigma \wedge l \not\equiv \bot_{\sigma \, list} \Longrightarrow (CONS \; x \; l) \; APP \; b \; \equiv \; CONS(x)(l \; APP \; b)$$

Here we can assert

$$\forall x l b . (CONS \; x \; l) \; APP \; b \equiv CONS(x)(l \; APP \; b)$$

since if x or l is undefined then both sides collapse to $\bot$.

4.9.2 The partial ordering

The partial ordering $\sqsubseteq_{\sigma \, list}$ gives distinctness and invertibility of the constructors, like for lazy lists. The differences involve *CONS*: a list's head and tail must be defined.

Ignoring bottom, there are again four cases. Distinctness:

$$x \not\equiv \bot \wedge l \not\equiv \bot \Longrightarrow \left\{ \begin{array}{cc} NIL & \not\sqsubseteq \; CONS(x)(l) \\ CONS(x)(l) & \not\sqsubseteq \; NIL \end{array} \right.$$

Invertibility:

$$NIL \sqsubseteq NIL$$

$$x \not\equiv \bot \wedge a \not\equiv \bot \wedge y \not\equiv \bot \wedge b \not\equiv \bot \Longrightarrow$$
$$(CONS(x)(a) \sqsubseteq_{\sigma \, list} CONS(y)(b) \iff x \sqsubseteq_\sigma y \wedge a \sqsubseteq_{\sigma \, list} b)$$

Recall that σ is *flat* or *discrete* if $x \sqsubseteq_\sigma y$ implies $x \equiv \bot$ or $x \equiv y$ for all x and y in σ. A flat type has a trivial partial ordering: the defined elements are incomparable and $\bot$ lies below them. We shall later prove by structural induction that if σ is flat then $\sigma \, list$ is also flat (Section 4.12.3).

Example 4.12 Consider the type $\sigma \, sequence$ satisfying

$$\sigma \, sequence \; \cong \; unit \oplus (\sigma \otimes (\sigma \, sequence) u)$$

Its constructors are $Nil : \sigma \, sequence$ and $Cons : \sigma \otimes (\sigma \, sequence) u \to \sigma \, sequence$. The elements of $\sigma \, sequence$ include infinite and partial lists, but a sequence cannot contain $\bot$ as a member. The constructor $Cons$ is strict in its first argument but not the second: it is neither lazy nor strict, but *mixed*.

The type $\sigma\,sequence$ can be implemented in ML. Recall from Exercise 4.22 that lifting is expressible in ML via $\sigma u \cong unit \xrightarrow{\text{ML}} \sigma$. Here is the declaration of the type $sequence$ and the computation of the sequence of prime numbers, using the Sieve of Eratosthenes:

```
datatype 'a sequence = Nil
                   |  Cons of 'a  *  (unit -> 'a sequence);


(*the list of the first n members of a sequence*)
fun heads (n, Nil) = []
  | heads (n, Cons(x,xf)) =
        if n<=0 then []  else  x :: heads (n-1, xf());


(*the sequence n, n+1, n+2, ...*)
fun from n = Cons(n, fn()=> from(n+1));


(*the sequence of numbers not divisible by p*)
fun siftout p (Cons(n,nf)) =
     if n mod p <> 0 then  Cons(n, fn()=> siftout p (nf()))
     else  siftout p (nf());


fun sieve(Cons(p,pf)) = Cons(p, fn()=> sieve (siftout p (pf())));


val primes = sieve (from 2);
```

This example may seem strange, but the type $sequence$ has important uses: such as to represent the sequence of solution nodes in an infinite tree. Depth first search in the tree gives a different sequence from breadth first search. Computation on sequences of solutions is easier than computation on search strategies.

Exercise 4.31 The type nat satisfies the isomorphism

$$nat \cong unit \oplus nat$$

Its constructors are $0 : nat$ and $SUCC : nat \to nat$. What is its exhaustion axiom? What is its partial ordering?

Exercise 4.32 Work out the details of the type $\sigma\,sequence$: the constructors, eliminator functional, exhaustion axiom, destructors, and partial ordering.

4.10   Formal reasoning about types

Let us consider how to express and reason about functions over each of the type constructors.

Structural induction proves a property P of every element of a type by considering how the elements are constructed. For example, lists are constructed via *NIL* and *CONS*. When proving $P(CONS\,x\,l)$, it is sound to assume the induction hypothesis $P(l)$.

The idea behind structural induction applies to non-recursive types. If no element is constructed from other elements of the type, induction degenerates to case analysis with no induction hypothesis. A look at non-recursive types will give a gentle introduction to structural induction, allowing more examples of first order proof.

4.10.1 Expressing functions

To be safe, a new function symbol f should be given a definition by an axiom of the form $f \equiv t$. However, more readable axioms can be used, taking advantage of the standard operators. Such axioms look like ML clausal function definitions, and must be written with care to avoid inconsistency.

Recursive definitions via fixed points

Instead of writing $c \equiv FIX(F)$ it is safe to write $c \equiv F(c)$, which says that c is a fixed point of F. The assertion $c \equiv FIX(F)$ is stronger: c is the *least* fixed point. Usually F is a lambda-abstraction; instead of $c \equiv FIX(\lambda x.t)$, it is safe to write $c \equiv t[c/x]$.

Function definitions via abstractions

Instead of writing $h \equiv \lambda x.t$ it is equivalent to write $\forall x.\ h(x) \equiv t$, by extensionality. Indeed h can be a term, so this also works for curried functions: $h \equiv \lambda xy.t$ is equivalent to $\forall x.\ h(x) \equiv \lambda y.t$ and to $\forall xy.\ h(x)(y) \equiv t$. By the usual convention, we can drop outermost quantifiers to write $h(x)(y) \equiv t$.

Functions over the Cartesian product

Instead of writing $h \equiv \lambda z : \sigma \times \tau.t$ it is equivalent to write $h(x,y) \equiv t[(x,y)/z]$, which can usually be simplified using $FST(x,y) \equiv x$ and $SND(x,y) \equiv y$. In fact $h(x,y) \equiv t$ corresponds to $h \equiv \lambda z : \sigma \times \tau.\,[FST(z)/x, SND(z)/y]$. These facts, and similar ones below, follow from the exhaustion property of the type and extensionality of functions.

Functions over the strict product

For the strict product, instead of writing $h \equiv SSPLIT(f)$ it is equivalent to write the two axioms

$$h(\perp_{\sigma \otimes \tau}) \equiv \perp_{\upsilon}$$
$$x \not\equiv \perp_{\sigma} \wedge y \not\equiv \perp_{\tau} \implies h(SPAIR(x)(y)) \equiv f(x)(y)$$

Functions over the strict sum

For the strict sum, instead of writing $h \equiv WHEN(f)(g)$ it is equivalent to write the three axioms

$$h(\perp_{\sigma \oplus \tau}) \equiv \perp_{\upsilon}$$
$$x \not\equiv \perp_{\sigma} \implies h(INL\,x) \equiv f(x)$$
$$y \not\equiv \perp_{\tau} \implies h(INR\,y) \equiv g(y)$$

Functions over a lifted type

For a lifted type, instead of writing $h \equiv LIFT(f)$ it is equivalent to write the two axioms

$$h(\perp_{(\sigma)u}) \equiv \perp_{\tau}$$
$$h(UP\,x) \equiv f(x)$$

Functions over the type of truth values

For the type tr, instead of writing $h(x) \equiv x \Rightarrow t \mid u$ it is equivalent to write the three axioms

$$h(\perp_{tr}) \equiv \perp_{\upsilon}$$
$$h(TT) \equiv t$$
$$h(FF) \equiv u$$

Functions over lazy lists

For lazy lists, instead of writing $h \equiv LLIST\_WHEN(z)(f)$ it is equivalent to write the three axioms

$$h(\perp_{\sigma\,llist}) \equiv \perp_{\tau}$$
$$h(LNIL) \equiv z$$
$$h(LCONS\,x\,l) \equiv f(x)(l)$$

An operator for primitive recursion would be similar to $LLIST\_WHEN$ but would call itself recursively on the tail of the list. A list recursion operator is unnecessary because of FIX.

Functions over strict lists

For strict lists, instead of writing $h \equiv LIST\_WHEN(z)(f)$ it is equivalent to write the three axioms

$$
\begin{aligned}
h(\bot_{\sigma\,list}) &\equiv \bot_\tau \\
h(NIL) &\equiv z \\
x \not\equiv \bot \wedge l \not\equiv \bot \Longrightarrow h(CONS\,x\,l) &\equiv f(x)(l)
\end{aligned}
$$

4.10.2 Exhaustion rules for basic type constructors

For each basic type constructor, the exhaustion axiom implies inference rules for case analysis on elements of the type.

The Cartesian product of two types

The exhaustion axiom of the Cartesian product is

$$\forall z : \sigma \times \tau . \exists x : \sigma . \exists y : \tau . z \equiv (x, y)$$

The corresponding exhaustion rule is (types $x : \sigma$, $y : \tau$, $z : \sigma \times \tau$)

$$\frac{\Gamma \vdash A[(x, y)/z]}{\Gamma \vdash A[t/z]} \qquad provided\ x\ and\ y\ are\ not\ free\ in\ \Gamma$$

It means: to prove $A[t/z]$, where t has type $\sigma \times \tau$, it suffices to prove $A[(x,y)/z]$ for arbitrary $x : \sigma$ and $y : \tau$.

Here is a derivation in the sequent calculus of Section 2.13. The topmost inference is substitution and thinning; the bottom inference should be followed by a use of cut to insert the exhaustion axiom:

$$
\frac{\dfrac{\dfrac{\dfrac{\Gamma \vdash A[(x,y)/z]}{\Gamma, t \equiv (x,y) \vdash A[t/z]}}{\Gamma, \exists y. t \equiv (x,y) \vdash A[t/z]}}{\Gamma, \exists xy. t \equiv (x,y) \vdash A[t/z]}}{\Gamma, \forall z. \exists xy. z \equiv (x,y) \vdash A[t/z]}
$$

The strict product of two types

The exhaustion axiom of the strict product is

$$\forall z : \sigma \otimes \tau . z \equiv \bot \ \vee \ (\exists x : \sigma . \exists y : \tau . z \equiv SPAIR(x)(y) \wedge x \not\equiv \bot \wedge y \not\equiv \bot)$$

Two exhaustion rules can be derived, differing in the treatment of the bottom element. The proof of $A[t/z]$ may require a bottom case: (types $x : \sigma$, $y : \tau$, $z : \sigma \otimes \tau$)

$$\frac{\Gamma \vdash A[\bot/z] \qquad \Gamma, x \not\equiv \bot, y \not\equiv \bot \vdash A[SPAIR(x)(y)/z]}{\Gamma \vdash A[t/z]} \qquad x\ and\ y\ not\ free\ in\ \Gamma$$

Alternatively, we may reason about defined elements of $\sigma \otimes \tau$ through defined elements of σ and τ:

$$\frac{\Gamma, x \not\equiv \bot, y \not\equiv \bot \vdash A[SPAIR(x)(y)/z]}{\Gamma, t \not\equiv \bot \vdash A[t/z]} \qquad provided\ x\ and\ y\ are\ not\ free\ in\ \Gamma$$

The former rule, more in the LCF tradition, follows immediately by the rules ∨-left and ∃-left. The latter rule is convenient for the strict type constructors. Obviously either can be derived from the other. A derivation of the former rule is

$$\frac{\dfrac{\Gamma \vdash A[\bot/z]}{\Gamma, t \equiv \bot \vdash A[\bot/z]} \qquad \dfrac{\dfrac{\dfrac{\dfrac{\Gamma, x \not\equiv \bot, y \not\equiv \bot \vdash A[SPAIR(x)(y)/z]}{\Gamma, t \equiv SPAIR(x)(y), x \not\equiv \bot, y \not\equiv \bot \vdash A[t/z]}}{\Gamma, t \equiv SPAIR(x)(y) \wedge x \not\equiv \bot \wedge y \not\equiv \bot \vdash A[t/z]}}{\Gamma, \exists xy.\, t \equiv SPAIR(x)(y) \wedge x \not\equiv \bot \wedge y \not\equiv \bot \vdash A[t/z]}}{\dfrac{\Gamma, t \equiv \bot \vee \exists xy.\, t \equiv SPAIR(x)(y) \wedge x \not\equiv \bot \wedge y \not\equiv \bot \vdash A[t/z]}{\Gamma, \forall z.\, z \equiv \bot \vee \exists xy.\, z \equiv SPAIR(x)(y) \wedge x \not\equiv \bot \wedge y \not\equiv \bot \vdash A[t/z]}}$$

The strict sum of two types

The exhaustion axiom of the strict sum is

$$\forall z : \sigma \oplus \tau.\, z \equiv \bot \vee (\exists x : \sigma.\, z \equiv INL\, x \wedge x \not\equiv \bot) \vee (\exists y : \tau.\, z \equiv INR\, y \wedge y \not\equiv \bot)$$

The derived exhaustion rules are (types $x : \sigma$, $y : \tau$, $z : \sigma \oplus \tau$)

$$\frac{\Gamma \vdash A[\bot/z] \qquad \Gamma, x \not\equiv \bot \vdash A[INL(x)/z] \qquad \Gamma, y \not\equiv \bot \vdash A[INR(y)/z]}{\Gamma \vdash A[t/z]}$$

provided x and y are not free in Γ

and

$$\frac{\Gamma, x \not\equiv \bot \vdash A[INL(x)/z] \qquad \Gamma, y \not\equiv \bot \vdash A[INR(y)/z]}{\Gamma, t \not\equiv \bot \vdash A[t/z]}$$

provided x and y are not free in Γ.

The lifting construction

The exhaustion axiom for the lifting construction is

$$\forall z : (\sigma)u.\, z \equiv \bot \vee \exists x : \sigma.\, z \equiv UP(x)$$

The derived exhaustion rules are (types $x : \sigma$, $z : (\sigma)u$)

$$\frac{\Gamma \vdash A[\bot/z] \qquad \Gamma \vdash A[UP(x)/z]}{\Gamma \vdash A[t/z]} \qquad provided\ x\ is\ not\ free\ in\ \Gamma$$

and

$$\frac{\Gamma \vdash A[UP(x)/z]}{\Gamma, t \not\equiv \bot \vdash A[t/z]} \qquad provided\ x\ is\ not\ free\ in\ \Gamma$$

Observe how the latter rule, in backwards proof, deletes the definedness assumption $t \not\equiv \bot$ in the goal. Its derivation is

$$
\dfrac{
\dfrac{-}{\Gamma, t \not\equiv \bot, t \equiv \bot \vdash A[t/z]} \quad
\dfrac{
\dfrac{\Gamma \vdash A[UP(x)/z]}{\Gamma, t \equiv UP(x) \vdash A[t/z]}
}{\Gamma, \exists x. t \equiv UP(x) \vdash A[t/z]}
}{
\dfrac{\Gamma, t \not\equiv \bot, t \equiv \bot \vee \exists x. t \equiv UP(x) \vdash A[t/z]}{\Gamma, t \not\equiv \bot, \forall z. z \equiv \bot \vee \exists x. z \equiv UP(x) \vdash A[t/z]}
}
$$

As the rules can be derived from the exhaustion axiom, using disjunction and existential elimination (or 'left') rules, the exhaustion axiom can be derived from either rule using disjunction and existential introduction. In the following proof, the central inference is the two-premise form of the exhaustion rule:

$$
\dfrac{
\dfrac{\bot \equiv \bot}{\bot \equiv \bot \vee \exists x. \bot \equiv UP(x)} \quad
\dfrac{
\dfrac{UP(u) \equiv UP(u)}{\exists x.\ UP(u) \equiv UP(x)}
}{UP(u) \equiv \bot \vee \exists x.\ UP(u) \equiv UP(x)}
}{
\dfrac{z \equiv \bot \vee \exists x. z \equiv UP(x)}{\forall z. z \equiv \bot \vee \exists x. z \equiv UP(x)}
}
$$

Atomic types

The type *void* has the trivial exhaustion axiom $\forall z : void.\, z \equiv ()$, giving the rule (type $z : void$)

$$
\dfrac{\Gamma \vdash A[\bot/z]}{\Gamma \vdash A[t/z]}
$$

Recall that $()$ is $\bot_{void}$.

Exercise 4.33 Derive the second version of the exhaustion rule for the strict product.

Exercise 4.34 Derive one of the exhaustion rules for the strict sum.

4.10.3   Exhaustion rules for constructed types

When a type is constructed from other types, its exhaustion rule can be derived from those for the other types.

The separated sum

One of the exhaustion rules for the separated sum is (types $x : \sigma$, $y : \tau$, $z : \sigma + \tau$)

$$
\dfrac{\Gamma \vdash A[INL\,UP(x)/z] \quad \Gamma \vdash A[INR\,UP(y)/z]}{\Gamma, t \not\equiv \bot \vdash A[t/z]}
$$

provided x and y are not free in Γ.

Its derivation uses similar rules for lifting and strict sum:

$$\frac{\dfrac{\dfrac{\Gamma \vdash A[INLUP(x)/z]}{\Gamma \vdash A[INL(UP(x))/z]}}{\dfrac{\Gamma \vdash A[INL(u)/z][UP(x)/u]}{\Gamma, u \not\equiv \bot \vdash A[INL(u)/z]}} \qquad \dfrac{\dfrac{\Gamma \vdash A[INRUP(y)/z]}{\Gamma \vdash A[INR(UP(y))/z]}}{\dfrac{\Gamma \vdash A[INR(v)/z][UP(y)/v]}{\Gamma, v \not\equiv \bot \vdash A[INR(v)/z]}}}{\Gamma, t \not\equiv \bot \vdash A[t/z]}$$

The first (backwards) inference is the $\oplus$-exhaustion rule, using variables $u : (\sigma)u$ and $v : (\tau)u$. Then u-exhaustion is used; the substitution of $UP(x)$ for u gives $A[INL(u)/z][UP(x)/u]$, which becomes $A[INL(UP(x))/z]$ and then $A[INLUP(x)/z]$. Similarly v is replaced by $UP(y)$.

There is a similar proof of the other exhaustion rule:

$$\frac{\Gamma \vdash A[\bot/z] \qquad \Gamma \vdash A[INLUP(x)/z] \qquad \Gamma \vdash A[INRUP(y)/z]}{\Gamma \vdash A[t/z]}$$

provided x and y are not free in Γ.

Using this, the exhaustion axiom of the separated sum can be formally derived.

The type *tr*

The exhaustion property and rule for *tr* follows from its construction. Recall that *tr* is equivalent to *void* + *void* with $TT \equiv INLUP()$ and $FF \equiv INRUP()$. One of its exhaustion rules is (type $z : tr$)

$$\frac{\Gamma \vdash A[\bot/z] \qquad \Gamma \vdash A[TT/z] \qquad \Gamma \vdash A[FF/z]}{\Gamma \vdash A[t/z]}$$

which follows directly from those for + and *void*.

Recursive types

What about recursive types? The exhaustion property for lazy lists entails the rule (types $x : \sigma$, $l : \sigma$ *llist*)

$$\frac{\Gamma \vdash A[\bot/l] \qquad \Gamma \vdash A[LNIL/l] \qquad \Gamma \vdash A[LCONS(x)(l)/l]}{\Gamma \vdash A[t/l]}$$

provided x and l are not free in Γ.

Its derivation resembles that for the separated sum.

The exhaustion property for strict lists entails (types $x : \sigma$, $l : \sigma$ *list*)

$$\frac{\Gamma \vdash A[\bot/l] \qquad \Gamma \vdash A[NIL/l] \qquad \Gamma, x \not\equiv \bot, l \not\equiv \bot \vdash A[CONS(x)(l)/l]}{\Gamma \vdash A[t/l]}$$

provided x and l are not free in Γ

and

$$\frac{\Gamma \vdash A[NIL/l] \qquad \Gamma, x \not\equiv \bot, l \not\equiv \bot \vdash A[CONS(x)(l)/l]}{\Gamma, t \not\equiv \bot \vdash A[t/l]}$$

provided x and l are not free in Γ.

Their derivations resemble those for the strict sum.

The exhaustion rules for lazy and strict lists are similar to induction but do not provide an induction hypothesis. They merely allow case analysis on the form of a list. Induction is considered in the following sections.

Exercise 4.35 Derive the exhaustion rule for the type *tr*.

Exercise 4.36 Derive the exhaustion rule for the type *llist*.

4.11 Structural induction over lazy lists

The type *nat llist* of lazy lists contains infinite lists like $[1, 2, 3, \ldots]$ and partial lists like $[2, \bot, \bot, 1]$. At first sight, induction over lazy lists seems to make no sense: induction concerns only finite objects. Yet the following *lazy induction* rule for *llist* is sound even for infinite lists:

$$\frac{\Gamma \vdash A[\bot/l] \qquad \Gamma \vdash A[LNIL/l] \qquad \Gamma, A \vdash A[LCONS(x)(l)/l]}{\Gamma \vdash A[t/l]}$$

provided x and l are not free in Γ *and* $[\![A]\!]_l$ *is chain-complete.*

Note the induction hypothesis, A, in the third premise.

The rule is sound because every lazy list l is the least upper bound of a chain of lists finitely constructed from $\bot$, *LNIL*, and *LCONS*. If l itself is finitely constructed then the chain ends with $l, l, l, \ldots$. These intuitions about lazy lists are reflected in the appropriate inverse limit. The conclusion of the rule holds for finite constructions by a finite number of applications of the $\bot$, *LNIL*, and *LCONS* premises — like in ordinary induction. If t is the least upper bound of the finite constructions $l_0, l_1, l_2, \ldots$, then, by chain-completeness, the conclusion $A[t/l]$ holds because $A[l_0/l]$, $A[l_1/l]$, $A[l_2/l]$, $\ldots$ are all true.

4.11.1 A proof using lazy induction

A proof by structural induction on ordinary lists is valid for lazy lists provided the induction formula is chain-complete and satisfies the $\bot$ premise. It is also necessary that every lemma used in the proof is valid for lazy lists. The $\bot$ premise of induction is usually trivial for ordinary lists, where most functions are strict. Many functions on lazy lists are not strict, so the $\bot$ premise may be false.

Recall the operator *LAPP* for appending lazy lists (Example 4.10). Appending finite lists is obviously associative; what about lazy lists? The append operation

on lazy lists has some unusual properties: it is straightforward to prove in LCF
that if a is an infinite list or ends in $\perp$ then $a\ LAPP\ b \equiv a$. Yet $LAPP$ is associative
for all lazy lists, including infinite ones.

Theorem 4.23 *The operator LAPP is associative:*

$$(a\ LAPP\ b)\ LAPP\ c \ \equiv \ a\ LAPP\ (b\ LAPP\ c)$$

Proof: Lazy induction is admissible because all equations are chain-complete.
Induction over a gives three subgoals. Each can be simplified using the equations
for $LAPP$.

The bottom subgoal is $(\perp\ LAPP\ b)\ LAPP\ c \equiv \perp\ LAPP\ (b\ LAPP\ c)$, which
simplifies to $\perp \equiv \perp$.

The $LNIL$ subgoal is $(LNIL\ LAPP\ b)\ LAPP\ c \equiv LNIL\ LAPP\ (b\ LAPP\ c)$, which
simplifies to $b\ LAPP\ c \equiv b\ LAPP\ c$.

The $LCONS$ subgoal is

$$((LCONS\ x\ l)\ LAPP\ b)\ LAPP\ c \ \equiv \ (LCONS\ x\ l)\ LAPP\ (b\ LAPP\ c)$$

under the induction hypothesis $(l\ LAPP\ b)\ LAPP\ c \equiv l\ LAPP\ (b\ LAPP\ c)$. The
right side of the equation simplifies to $LCONS(x)(l\ LAPP\ (b\ LAPP\ c))$. The left
side simplifies to $(LCONS(x)(l\ LAPP\ b))\ LAPP\ c$, then to $LCONS(x)((l\ LAPP$
$b)\ LAPP\ c)$, and finally, by the induction hypothesis, it becomes identical to the
right side. $\square$

Exercise 4.37 What does $\perp\ LAPP\ b$ become after simplification by the equations
for $LAPP$? What does $(LCONS\ x_1\ \perp)\ LAPP\ b$ become? What does

$$(LCONS\ x_1\ (LCONS\ x_2\ \perp))\ LAPP\ b$$

become? By continuity, what is $[x_1, x_2, x_3, \ldots]\ LAPP\ b$?

Exercise 4.38 Is $LAPP$ strict in its second argument?

4.11.2   Deriving lazy structural induction

Structural induction can be derived from fixed point induction, so PPλ needs no
other induction principle. A theoretical consequence: PPλ contains the theory of
arithmetic and thus is incomplete by Gödel's Incompleteness Theorem.

The formal derivation of the structural induction rule requires assuming a
simple instance of that very rule:

$$\frac{h(\perp) \equiv \perp \qquad h(LNIL) \equiv LNIL \qquad h(LCONS\ x\ l) \equiv LCONS(x)(h(l))}{h(l) \equiv l}$$

This *reachability* rule is intuitively true because the premises imply that the function h simply copies its argument. Observe that structural induction indeed reduces $h(l) \equiv l$ to the premises of this rule. Furthermore $h(l) \equiv l$, like all equations, admits induction.

The LCF formalization makes use of the *copying functional*, *LLIST_FUN*:

$$LLIST\_FUN = \lambda h. \; LLIST\_WHEN(LNIL)(\lambda x l. \; LCONS(x)(hl))$$

Unfolding *LLIST_WHEN* gives the equations

$$
\begin{aligned}
LLIST\_FUN(h)(\bot) &\equiv \bot \\
LLIST\_FUN(h)(LNIL) &\equiv LNIL \\
LLIST\_FUN(h)(LCONS\,x\,l) &\equiv LCONS(x)(hl)
\end{aligned}
$$

The reachability rule gives $FIX(LLIST\_FUN)(l) \equiv l$. In LCF, reachability is assumed by taking this equation as an axiom.

Recall that $FIX(F)$ is the least upper bound, for $n = 0, 1, 2, \ldots$, of $F^n(\bot)$. Clearly $LLIST\_FUN^n(\bot)(l)$ is finitely constructed, containing at most n members. The reachability axiom gives, for an arbitrary list l,

$$l \equiv FIX(LLIST\_FUN)(l) \equiv \bigsqcup_{n=0}^{\infty} LLIST\_FUN^n(\bot)(l)$$

In other words: l is the least upper bound of a chain of finitely constructed lists. Infinite constructions may be approximated to any degree by finite constructions.

The induction rule can now be derived for an arbitrary induction formula. The LCF rule uses quantifiers and implication, but is clearly equivalent to the rule given above.

Theorem 4.24 *The following induction rule can be derived in* PPλ:

$$\frac{\Gamma \vdash A[\bot/l] \qquad \Gamma \vdash A[LNIL/l] \qquad \Gamma \vdash \forall x l. \, A \Longrightarrow A[LCONS(x)(l)/l]}{\Gamma \vdash \forall l. \, A}$$

provided $[\![A]\!]_l$ is chain-complete.

Proof: The PPλ proof tree is too large to present in full, so let us prove that such a tree exists. In keeping with LCF style, the conclusion of the lazy induction rule will be reduced to its premises.

Suppose that A is chain-complete for lazy lists l. By the reachability axiom, to prove $\forall l.A$ it is enough to prove

$$\forall l. \, A[FIX(LLIST\_FUN)(l)/l]$$

Use fixed point induction over the formula $\forall l. \, A[h(l)/l]$, which is chain-complete in h because function application is continuous and the quantifier preserves chain-completeness. Induction gives a $\bot$ goal and a step goal.

The $\bot$ goal is $\forall l . A[\bot(l)/l]$, which reduces to $A[\bot/l]$, which is the $\bot$ premise of the rule being derived.

The step goal is the sequent

$$\forall l . A[h(l)/l] \vdash \forall l . A[LLIST\_FUN(h)(l)/l]$$

Reasoning by exhaustion gives three goals, for l may be $\bot$, $LNIL$, or $LCONS(x)(l')$. In each case, the goal can by simplified by the corresponding equation about $LLIST\_FUN$. The $\bot$ case is $A[LLIST\_FUN(h)(\bot)/l]$, which simplifies to $A[\bot/l]$, which is a premise. Similarly the $LNIL$ case simplifies to the premise $A[LNIL/l]$.

The $LCONS$ case simplifies to

$$\forall l . A[h(l)/l] \vdash A[LCONS(x)(h(l'))/l]$$

To finish, use the cut rule to add the $LCONS$ premise of induction to the hypotheses. Use the rule $\forall$-left and thinning several times, followed by $\Longrightarrow$-left.

$$\frac{\dfrac{A[h(l')/l] \vdash A[h(l')/l] \qquad A[LCONS(x)(h(l'))/l] \vdash A[LCONS(x)(h(l'))/l]}{A[h(l')/l] \Longrightarrow A[LCONS(x)(h(l'))/l], \ A[h(l')/l] \vdash A[LCONS(x)(h(l'))/l]}}{\dfrac{\forall x l. A \Longrightarrow A[LCONS(x)(l)/l], \ A[h(l')/l] \vdash A[LCONS(x)(h(l'))/l]}{\forall x l. A \Longrightarrow A[LCONS(x)(l)/l], \ \forall l. A[h(l)/l] \vdash A[LCONS(x)(h(l'))/l]}}$$

Intuitively, the assumption $\forall l. A[h(l)/l]$ says that A holds of every list of the form $h(l)$, so it holds of $h(l')$. The $LCONS$ premise implies $A[LCONS(x)(h(l'))/l]$ and we are done. $\square$

The universal quantifier in the fixed point induction formula is essential. How did Scott derive structural induction in his quantifier free logic? In his logic, it suffices to derive induction for the formula $t \sqsubseteq u$, and $\forall x . t \sqsubseteq u$ can be expressed without a quantifier as $\lambda x . t \sqsubseteq \lambda x . u$.

LCF does not support the proof of theorem schemes over an arbitrary formula like A. Instead, the induction rule is a function over A and LCF performs the derivation anew for each instance of induction. Fortunately this takes only a few seconds.

Exercise 4.39 Consider the constant FL of type $(\sigma) \, llist \rightarrow tr$, satisfying

$$FL \equiv LLIST\_WHEN(TT)(\lambda x l. \ FL(l))$$

Prove by induction that $FL(a) \equiv \bot$ implies $a \, LAPP \, b \equiv a$. What does $FL(a) \equiv \bot$ say about the structure of l?

4.12 Structural induction over strict lists

The type *list* of strict lists has the structural induction rule

$$\frac{\Gamma \vdash A[\bot/l] \qquad \Gamma \vdash A[NIL/l] \qquad \Gamma, x \not\equiv \bot, l \not\equiv \bot, A \vdash A[CONS(x)(l)/l]}{\Gamma \vdash A[t/l]}$$

provided x and l are not free in Γ *and* $[\![A]\!]_l$ *is chain-complete.*

The third premise has not only an induction hypothesis but assumptions $x \not\equiv \bot$ and $l \not\equiv \bot$, needed because theorems involving $CONS(x)(l)$ apply only if x and l are defined. The proviso that $[\![A]\!]_l$ is chain-complete seems strange. Section 4.12.3, by proving flatness of strict lists, extends structural induction to arbitrary formulae.

4.12.1 A proof using strict induction

Induction on strict lists should be more familiar than for lazy lists, but we must be careful about termination. Consider the associativity of append for strict lists, where the infix *APP* is defined via

$$a \ APP \ b \equiv LIST\_WHEN(b)(\lambda x \ l. \ CONS(x)(l \ APP \ b))(a)$$

For *CONS*, recall that *APP* satisfies

$$x \not\equiv \bot \wedge l \not\equiv \bot \implies (CONS \ x \ l) \ APP \ b \equiv CONS(x)(l \ APP \ b)$$

We set out to prove

$$(a \ APP \ b) \ APP \ c \equiv a \ APP \ (b \ APP \ c)$$

and carry on as for lazy lists. The *CONS* subgoal is

$$((CONS \ x \ l) \ APP \ b) \ APP \ c \equiv (CONS \ x \ l) \ APP \ (b \ APP \ c)$$

under the assumptions

$$x \not\equiv \bot \qquad l \not\equiv \bot \qquad (l \ APP \ b) \ APP \ c \equiv l \ LAPP \ (b \ APP \ c)$$

The right side of the equation simplifies to $CONS(x)(l \ APP \ (b \ APP \ c))$. The left side simplifies to $(CONS(x)(l \ APP \ b)) \ APP \ c$, and we might then expect it to simplify to $CONS(x)((l \ APP \ b) \ APP \ c)$. But here we must pause. There is no way to simplify again before proving that $l \ APP \ b$ is defined. Although the induction rule allows assuming that l is defined, there is no assumption about b. We could use case analysis: if $b \equiv \bot$ then both sides collapse to $\bot$, and the other case can assume $b \not\equiv \bot$. But this collapsing often does not occur in more complex problems.

The general approach is to start over, reformulating the desired theorem with a definedness antecedent:

$$b \not\equiv \bot \implies (a \ APP \ b) \ APP \ c \equiv a \ APP \ (b \ APP \ c)$$

With strict types, it is a good idea to prove that every function you introduce is total. To prove that APP is a total function,

$$a \not\equiv \bot \wedge b \not\equiv \bot \implies a \ APP \ b \not\equiv \bot$$

is a trivial induction on a. Use the definedness properties of the constructors: $NIL \not\equiv \bot$ and $x \not\equiv \bot \wedge l \not\equiv \bot \implies CONS(x)(l) \not\equiv \bot$.

What about functionals? Consider the functional MAP that applies a function to every member of a list:

$$\begin{aligned}
MAP(f)(\bot) &\equiv \bot \\
MAP(f)(NIL) &\equiv NIL \\
x \not\equiv \bot \wedge l \not\equiv \bot \implies MAP(f)(CONS \ x \ l) &\equiv CONS(fx)(MAP \ f \ l)
\end{aligned}$$

This functional preserves totality: if f is a total function, then so is $MAP(f)$, by induction on l:

$$(\forall x . x \not\equiv \bot \implies f(x) \not\equiv \bot) \wedge \forall l . l \not\equiv \bot \implies MAP(f)(l) \not\equiv \bot$$

Of course MAP is not a total function. We can easily find defined f and l such that $MAP(f)(l)$ is undefined. Requiring a function f to be total is much stronger than requiring it to be defined (namely, non-bottom). The function $\lambda x . x \Rightarrow x \mid \bot$ is defined but not total: it maps TT to TT and FF to $\bot$.

Many theorems about strict types hold only when most of the quantifiers are restricted by definedness or totality antecedents. If we are concerned with lists as mathematical objects, then undefined elements are of little interest, and all theorems can be restricted to defined elements. But if we want to justify program transformations then divergent computations are as important as terminating ones. The operator APP is associative even for undefined lists: replacing $(a \ APP \ b) \ APP \ c$ by $a \ APP \ (b \ APP \ c)$ does not affect termination.

4.12.2   Deriving strict structural induction

Structural induction is derived from fixed point induction, as for lazy types.

The copying functional for strict lists is

$$LIST\_FUN = \lambda h. \ LIST\_WHEN(NIL)(\lambda xl. \ CONS(x)(hl))$$

It satisifes

$$\begin{aligned}
LIST\_FUN(h)(\bot) &\equiv \bot \\
LIST\_FUN(h)(NIL) &\equiv NIL \\
x \not\equiv \bot \wedge l \not\equiv \bot \implies LIST\_FUN(h)(CONS \ x \ l) &\equiv CONS(x)(hl)
\end{aligned}$$

The reachability axiom is $FIX(LIST\_FUN)(l) \equiv l$, and is true because every strict list has finite length. The structural induction rule can now be derived.

Theorem 4.25 *The following is a derived rule of* PPλ:

$$\frac{\Gamma \vdash A[\bot/l] \qquad \Gamma \vdash A[NIL/l] \qquad \Gamma \vdash \forall x l \,.\, x \not\equiv \bot \wedge l \not\equiv \bot \wedge A \Longrightarrow A[CONS\,x\,l/l]}{\Gamma \vdash \forall l.\,A}$$

provided $[\![A]\!]_l$ is chain-complete.

Proof: The derivation is exactly like its lazy list counterpart apart from the *CONS* case, which simplifies to the goal

$$x \not\equiv \bot,\ l' \not\equiv \bot,\ \forall l \,.\, A[h(l)/l] \vdash A[CONS(x)(h(l'))/l]$$

Note the hypotheses that x and l' are defined. Because the *CONS* premise is weaker than the lazy *LCONS* premise, the lazy proof does not quite work. Instantiate the *CONS* premise to yield the theorem

$$x \not\equiv \bot \wedge h(l') \not\equiv \bot \wedge A[h(l')/l] \Longrightarrow A[CONS(x)(h(l'))/l]$$

The idea is to prove $A[CONS(x)(h(l'))/l]$ using the *CONS* premise. But that requires proving $h(l') \not\equiv \bot$ from $l' \not\equiv \bot$, which may be false: h could be a partial function. The rule $\Longrightarrow$-left gives an unprovable subgoal:

$$x \not\equiv \bot,\ l' \not\equiv \bot,\ A[h(l')/l] \vdash x \not\equiv \bot \wedge h(l') \not\equiv \bot \wedge A[h(l')/l]$$

The proof requires case analysis on whether or not $h(l')$ is defined. If $h(l') \equiv \bot$ then $A[CONS(x)(h(l'))/l]$ simplifies to $A[CONS(x)(\bot)/l]$ then to $A[\bot/l]$, the bottom premise.

The formal proof uses the rules for classical reasoning from Section 2.14. The rules $\Longrightarrow$ C-left and swap give a sequent with the additional assumption $\neg A[CONS(x)(h(l'))/l]$. Here is the proof tree above that sequent, which reduces it to the premise $A[\bot/l]$. Working backwards, the rules are $\wedge$-right and swap followed by equality reasoning; needless hypotheses are 'thinned' away:

$$\cfrac{x \not\equiv \bot \vdash x \not\equiv \bot \qquad \cfrac{\cfrac{\cfrac{\cfrac{\vdash A[\bot/l]}{h(l') \equiv \bot \vdash A[CONS(x)(\bot)/l]}}{h(l') \equiv \bot \vdash A[CONS(x)(h(l'))/l]}}{\neg A[CONS(x)(h(l'))/l] \vdash h(l') \not\equiv \bot} \qquad A[h(l')/l] \vdash A[h(l')/l]}}{\neg A[CONS(x)(h(l'))/l],\ x \not\equiv \bot,\ l' \not\equiv \bot,\ A[h(l')/l] \vdash x \not\equiv \bot \wedge h(l') \not\equiv \bot \wedge A[h(l')/l]}$$

$\square$

4.12.3   Proving flatness by structural induction

The type operator *list* constructs flat types from flat types. The proof relies on the distinctness and invertibility properties of the constructors. Recall that distinctness is

$$x \not\equiv \bot \wedge l \not\equiv \bot \Longrightarrow \left\{ \begin{array}{c} NIL \not\sqsubseteq CONS(x)(l) \\ CONS(x)(l) \not\sqsubseteq NIL \end{array} \right.$$

and invertibility is

$$NIL \sqsubseteq NIL$$

$$x \not\equiv \bot \wedge a \not\equiv \bot \wedge y \not\equiv \bot \wedge b \not\equiv \bot \Longrightarrow$$
$$(CONS(x)(a) \sqsubseteq_{\sigma \, list} CONS(y)(b) \iff x \sqsubseteq_\sigma y \wedge a \sqsubseteq_{\sigma \, list} b)$$

By distinctness and invertibility, if $a \sqsubseteq b$ in σ *list* then both lists have the same structure of *NIL* and *CONS*, and so $x \sqsubseteq y$ for some x and y in σ. The type (σ) *list* can only be flat if the element type σ is. If $x : \sigma$ were partially defined then so would be $CONS(x)(NIL)$. This argument can be formalized in PPλ.

Theorem 4.26 *The following rule, meaning 'σ is flat implies (σ) list is flat', is derivable in* PPλ:

$$\frac{\forall x \, y : \sigma \, . \, x \sqsubseteq y \Longrightarrow \bot \equiv x \vee x \equiv y}{\forall a \, b : (\sigma) \, list \, . \, a \sqsubseteq b \Longrightarrow \bot \equiv a \vee a \equiv b.}$$

Proof: The proof tree is too big, but we can show that there is a PPλ proof from the premise to the conclusion. Observe that the formula

$$\forall b : (\sigma) \, list \, . \, a \sqsubseteq b \Longrightarrow \bot \equiv a \vee a \equiv b$$

is chain-complete in a, since the only negative occurrence of a is on the left side of an inequivalence. List induction on a produces three subgoals. The $\bot$ goal, namely $\bot \sqsubseteq b \Longrightarrow \bot \equiv \bot \vee \bot \equiv b$, is trivial. The *NIL* goal, namely $NIL \sqsubseteq b \Longrightarrow \bot \equiv NIL \vee NIL \equiv b$, follows by case analysis of b, using definedness and distinctness.
    If $a \equiv CONS(x)(a')$ then similar reasoning provides defined y and b' such that $b \equiv CONS(y)(b')$. The goal is to prove

$$\bot \equiv CONS(x)(a') \vee CONS(x)(a') \equiv CONS(y)(b')$$

from the assumptions

$$\begin{array}{cc} \forall b \, . \, a' \sqsubseteq b \Longrightarrow \bot \equiv a' \vee a' \equiv b & y \not\equiv \bot \\ CONS(x)(a') \sqsubseteq CONS(y)(b') & b' \not\equiv \bot \end{array}$$

Invertibility implies $x \sqsubseteq y$ and $a' \sqsubseteq b'$. The premise (that σ is flat) with $x \sqsubseteq y$ implies $\bot \equiv x$ or $x \equiv y$:

- If $\perp \equiv x$, then strictness implies $\perp \equiv CONS(x)(a')$.

- If $x \equiv y$, then the induction hypothesis implies that $\perp \equiv a'$ or $a' \equiv b'$. Strictness solves the $\perp$ case. If $x \equiv y$ and $a' \equiv b'$, then $CONS(x)(a') \equiv CONS(y)(b')$. $\square$

The derivation of induction requires a chain-complete induction formula, but induction over finitely constructed lists is sound for every formula. If σ is flat, then all chains in (σ) *list* are trivial, so every formula about strict lists is chain-complete. Unrestricted induction is derived in LCF by providing a flatness theorem as an argument to the induction rule (Section 7.3.6).

Plotkin has pointed out a nicer derivation of unrestricted structural induction over a flat type. If τ is flat then for all $x : \tau$

$$x \not\equiv \perp \Longrightarrow A \quad \text{if and only if} \quad x \not\equiv \perp \Longrightarrow \forall y : \tau . x \sqsubseteq y \Longrightarrow A[y/x]$$

The right hand formula is chain-complete in x, for arbitrary A, since x is not free in $A[y/x]$. Structural induction on that formula is valid and yields subgoals that are equivalent to those that would arise from structural induction on $x \not\equiv \perp \Longrightarrow A$. Then prove $A[\perp/x]$ to get $\forall x . A$.

Another reason for proving flatness: unless the type σ is flat, an equality-testing function $(=)$ of type $\sigma \rightarrow \sigma \rightarrow tr$ cannot be total. If σ is not flat then let x and y be distinct, defined elements of σ with $x \sqsubseteq y$. If $(=)$ is a total test for equality then $y = y$ is TT. By monotonicity, $(x = y) \sqsubseteq (y = y)$ and so $x = y$ equals $\perp$ or TT. Yet $x = y$ ought to equal FF.

Figure 4.4 compares the strict and lazy natural numbers. The strict natural numbers, besides $\perp$, are 0, $SUCC\,0$, $SUCC(SUCC\,0)$, $SUCC(SUCC(SUCC\,0))$, ..., or $0, 1, 2, 3, \ldots$ in the usual notation. The lazy natural numbers include the strict ones; furthermore $\perp$, $SUCC\,\perp$, $SUCC(SUCC\,\perp)$, $SUCC(SUCC(SUCC\,\perp))$, ... are distinct. The strict domain is flat while the lazy domain has a complex partial ordering.

Exercise 4.40 Express the function $REV : \sigma\ list \rightarrow \sigma\ list$, to reverse a strict list, in terms of the append operator APP. Prove $REV(a\ APP\ b) \equiv (REV\ b)\ APP$ $(REV\ a)$ by structural induction. Is it necessary to stipulate that a or b is defined?

Exercise 4.41 Use the above result to prove $REV(REV\ l) \equiv l$ by structural induction. Try to prove the corresponding result for lazy lists. Where does the proof break down?

Exercise 4.42 Draw a diagram like Figure 4.4 for the types $tr\ list$, $tr\ sequence$, and $tr\ llist$.

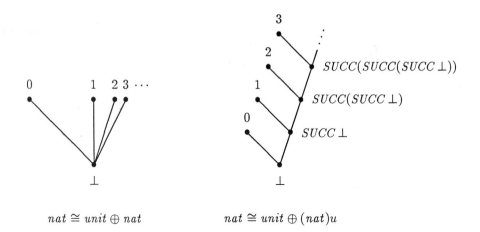

$$nat \cong unit \oplus nat \qquad\qquad nat \cong unit \oplus (nat)u$$

Figure 4.4: Flat and not-so-flat domains of natural numbers

4.13   Automating the derivation of induction

The PPλ formalization of a recursive type follows a regular pattern, at least if the type is like an ML datatype. We have examined lazy and strict lists. For a type having constructor functions, even mixed constructors, you should have little trouble working out the axioms, theorems, and induction rule. The procedure is complicated and regular: ripe for automation.

Robin Milner first took on the challenge of automating the construction of lazy recursive types and the derivation of structural induction. He wrote a structural induction package consisting of a command to construct a data type, the LCF rule for structural induction on the type, and the LCF tactic for backwards proof using the rule. The command, given information about the type, would assert axioms to define the constructor functions and establish the domain isomorphism, prove enough theorems to derive induction, and store them in a regular form on the theory file. The rule and tactic expected a theory constructed by the structural induction command. They would decode the theorems from the theory file to determine the name of the type and its constructors. The package, written in ML for Edinburgh LCF, was used in several parser proofs [21,25,68].

Brian Monahan has extended Milner's package in several ways [71]. He has introduced the strict product in Edinburgh LCF for constructing strict, lazy, and mixed data types. His structural induction command introduces selector and destructor functions as well as constructors, and proves their strictness and definedness properties. His package includes a tactic for proof by case analysis (exhaustion).

Cambridge LCF provides a structural induction package based on Milner's and with ideas from Monahan's. But it does not construct a recursive domain isomorphism; its approach is axiomatic. The necessary properties — exhaustion, strictness, definedness — are simply asserted of the new type. Asserting axioms can be riskier than proving properties of a construction, but gives a simpler implementation: more reliable and also faster. The axioms, like the isomorphisms asserted by the other packages, are justified by domain theory. The exhaustion axiom allows case analysis by the rules of disjunction and existential elimination; this was the original reason for providing ∨ and ∃ in Cambridge LCF.

4.14   Further reading

Scott has written a highly readable description of *information systems*, developing domain theory from elementary notions of logical consequence [91]. The elements of a domain are sets of primitive assertions that hold of the computation. This concrete view of information motivates many of the abstract properties of domains; they can be proved rather than assumed. Scott derives most of the domain constructions presented in this chapter. Larsen and Winskel realize the analogy between recursive functions and recursive domains by defining a partial ordering on information systems and solving domain equations via the Fixed Point Theorem [58].

Scott and Gunter [92] introduce domain theory in more detail than this chapter. They discuss *powerdomains* — domains whose elements are sets — for modeling nondeterminism: a nondeterministic program has a set of possible results. An older paper by Scott [90] describes the representation of domains in $P\omega$, the set of sets of natural numbers.

There are many approaches to solving recursive domain equations:

- by working in $P\omega$, which is a universal domain [90]

- by assuming the existence of a universal domain [92]

- by taking a concrete representation of domains, such as information systems [58,91]

- by the inverse limit construction [2,88]

The standard book on category theory is Mac Lane [61]. It is superbly written but difficult for computer scientists because many of the examples involve abstract algebra or topology. Blyth has written an introductory text [10]. Smyth and Plotkin have written the classic categorical account of recursive domains [93]. Dybjer surveys the role of category theory in programming language semantics [28].

Monahan has written a comprehensive account of LCF data types through category theory [71]. He formalizes lists with concatenation as a free monoid. He defines multisets as equivalence classes of lists, using a computable function to test whether two lists represent the same multiset. He describes resolution tactics, unification, and other operations in Edinburgh LCF, and provides a vast bibliography.

An early paper of mine, despite many flaws, contains an interesting discussion of mutually recursive types and quotient types [77]. Cartwright and Donahue discuss various domains of strict and lazy lists [16].

Plotkin is developing a new domain theory in which a domain need not have a bottom element [82]. His 'bottomless domains' resemble ordinary domain theory with strict type constructors, smashing the bottoms together. Removing the bottoms simplifies matters. Martin-Löf's Constructive Theory of Types is an alternative view of type structure and computable functions [65]. My eliminator functionals resemble operators in the theories of Plotkin and Martin-Löf.

Burstall's classic paper gives many examples of proof by structural induction [14]. He emphasizes data types whose elements are generated from a set of *atoms* by *constructors*. The natural numbers are generated from 0 by *SUCC*; lists are generated from *NIL* by *CONS*. Burge [13] gives examples of programming over lists and trees. He constructs lazy lists like in ML, using λ-abstraction to delay evaluation. Turner [97] gives more examples of lazy lists.

Part II

Cambridge LCF

Syntactic Operations for PPλ

ML, the meta language of LCF, allows computation on expressions of PPλ, the object language. An ML program may use *quotations*, an automatic mechanism for constructing well-typed PPλ expressions. At a lower level there are functions for building and taking apart PPλ expressions: for example, a function that maps $A \wedge B \wedge C$ to the list of formulae A, B, C. The most complicated functions perform substitution or pattern matching.

If you intend to use LCF, now is the time to start. You will find the examples easier to understand if you work them on the computer. Section 5.7 describes how to start and finish a session.

5.1 The syntax of PPλ

PPλ expressions include *types*, *terms*, *formulae*, *goals*, and *theorems*. The corresponding ML data types are *type*, *term*, *form*, *goal*, and *thm*. A function for building formulae might have the type *form* × *form* → *form*.

5.1.1 Syntactic conventions

The *abstract syntax* of a PPλ expression is not a string of symbols but a tree structure. A tree is not only the most convenient representation conceptually, but gives the most efficient implementation in the computer.

Syntax is specified by BNF equations. Alternative syntax phrases are separated by a vertical bar: |. A phrase that can be repeated zero or more times is enclosed in braces: {, }. Syntactic classes like *type-variable* appear in *italics*. Language symbols appear, underlined, in `typewriter font` to emphasize that they are typed and displayed on computer terminals. Symbols are represented in the ASCII character set. The representation of certain symbols is sometimes natural, sometimes strange: $\Longrightarrow$ is `==>`, while $\forall$ is `!`.

PPλ, though implemented on the computer, is a mathematical language of logic and domain theory. So PPλ expressions also appear in the text in standard notation. Syntactic meta variables obey the following conventions, perhaps with primes and subscripts attached:

α, β, γ	type variables for both ML and PPλ types
σ, τ, υ	types (not necessarily type variables!)
x, y, z	variables
p, r, s, t, u	terms
P, Q	predicate symbols
A, B, C	formulae
Γ, Δ, Θ	assumption lists (hypotheses)

5.1.2   Notation for ML functions

Each predefined ML identifier is presented with its name and ML type. The vast majority are functions. Typical arguments of a function may appear under the type. For example, the function *variant* appears as

$$variant : \quad term\ list \quad \rightarrow term \rightarrow term$$
$$[x_1, \ldots, x_n] \qquad y$$

In the description of *variant*, the list $[x_1, \ldots, x_n]$ refers to the value of the first argument while y refers to the value of the second. We need not say 'the value of' since the argument of an ML function is always evaluated.

5.1.3   Types

Every term has a *type* under a polymorphic type system resembling ML's. In the semantics a type denotes a domain, as discussed in the previous chapter. If σ and τ are types, then $\sigma \rightarrow \tau$ is the type of *continuous functions* from σ to τ. The type $\sigma \times \tau$ is the *Cartesian product* of types σ and τ. The type *tr* contains the truth values *TT*, *FF*, and $\bot$.

Types are built using *type constructors*. The standard ones are *void*, *tr*, and the infixes $\times$ and $\rightarrow$. The infixes stand for the 2-place type constructors $(\alpha, \beta)prod$ and $(\alpha, \beta)fun$.[1] A theory may declare additional type constructors, each taking a fixed non-negative number of operands. These are written in *postfix* notation like in ML. Examples: $(\sigma, \tau)tree$ and $\alpha\ list$.

A 0-place type constructor like *tr* is a type constant, and hence a type. The only other atomic types are *type variables*. In ASCII a type variable name consists of an identifier identifier beginning with a quotation mark — exactly like in Standard ML. Examples:

$$\texttt{'a} \qquad \texttt{'b} \qquad \texttt{'elem} \qquad \texttt{'''''x12}$$

---

[1] Edinburgh LCF compatibility: In Cambridge LCF, the type $\alpha + \beta$ abbreviates $(\alpha, \beta)sum$, but there is no standard theory of a sum type. Coalesced and separated sums can be defined using the structural induction commands of Chapter 4, which practically eliminate the need for sum types.

The type variable 'a is sometimes written α and 'b is sometimes written β.

The BNF syntax of types is

type	=	*type-variable*	
	|	*type-constant*	
	|	(*type* {, *type*}) *type-constructor*	
	|	*type* * *type*	the Cartesian product type $\sigma \times \tau$
	|	*type* -> *type*	the function type $\sigma \to \tau$
	|	(*type*)	parentheses for grouping

The precedence of infixes is $\times$ above $\to$; both are right-associative.

Beware of confusing ML types with PPλ types. The ML type *type* ranges over PPλ types. Although both kinds of type have similarities, and both languages are extensions of the λ-calculus, ML and PPλ types are not interchangable.

You may enrich the object language by constructing a *theory* containing new types, constants, infix operators, and predicates. Theories are discussed in Chapter 6.

Example 5.1 Let us enter various types in an LCF. Each type is enclosed by the backquote character ('), forming a *quotation*. General remarks on quotations are given below, but please note the following:

> *A quoted PPλ type always begins with a colon.*

Thus `':tr # (tr->tr)'` is the type $tr \times (tr \to tr)$. If the colon is omitted, LCF tries to parse a term instead of a type.

This is the output of an actual session, slightly edited to save space.

```
! ':tr';
- it = ':tr' : type

! ':((tr,void)prod, (void,tr)prod)fun';
- it = ':tr * void -> void * tr' : type

! ':tr*void->void*tr';
- it = ':tr * void -> void * tr' : type

! ':'a';
- it = ':'a' : type

! ':'b * ('b->'a) -> 'b';
- it = ':'b * ('b -> 'a) -> 'b' : type
```

5.1.4   Terms

Terms come in four syntactic classes: constants, variables, abstractions, and combinations (function applications). Abbreviations are provided for terms involving built-in constants such as the conditional.

Constants

The set of constant symbols is determined by the current theory. A constant symbol has a *generic* type, which is *polymorphic* if it contains type variables. In every occurrence of the constant, its type must be an instance of its generic type. Two constants are equal whenever their names *and types* are the same. For example, the constant $\bot$ can have any type, but $\bot : tr$, $\bot : \beta$, and $\bot : \alpha \times tr$ are three different terms.

The standard constants, with their generic types, are

$\bot : \alpha$	undefined element (<u>UU</u> in ASCII)
$TT : tr$	truth-value 'true'
$FF : tr$	truth-value 'false'
$FIX : (\alpha \to \alpha) \to \alpha$	fixed point operator
$COND : tr \to \alpha \to \alpha \to \alpha$	conditional function
$PAIR : \alpha \to \beta \to (\alpha \times \beta)$	pairing function
$FST : (\alpha \times \beta) \to \alpha$	first projection on a pair
$SND : (\alpha \times \beta) \to \beta$	second projection on a pair
$() : void$	sole element of the type *void* (equals $\bot : void$)

Note that the undefined element, $\bot$, is written <u>UU</u> in ASCII.

Syntax of terms

Here is the BNF syntax of terms in order of decreasing precedence:

term	$=$	*constant*	
	$\mid$	*variable*	
	$\mid$	\ *bound-vars* . *term*	abstraction
	$\mid$	*term term*	combination
	$\mid$	*term* : *type*	type constraint on term
	$\mid$	*term infix term*	infix operator
	$\mid$	*term , term*	ordered pair
	$\mid$	*term* => *term* $\mid$ *term*	conditional
	$\mid$	(*term*)	parentheses for grouping

Note that λ is represented by a backslash in ASCII. The syntax of bound variables allows either a list of variables or a variable with a type constraint, but not both at once:

bound-vars	= *variable* : *type*	type constraint on variable
	| *variable* { *variable* }	several bound variables

Pairs and conditionals are abbreviations for applications of the standard PPλ constants *PAIR* and *COND*. The conditional $p \Rightarrow t \mid u$ abbreviates $COND(p)(t)(u)$. The ordered pair t, u abbreviates $PAIR(t)(u)$. A theory can declare a 2-place function to be an infix operator. Infix status concerns concrete syntax only; the term $t\, f\, u$ stands for either $(ft)u$ or $f(t, u)$.

Parentheses indicate grouping; $t\, u_1 \cdots u_n$ abbreviates $(\cdots(t\, u_1)\cdots u_n)$ and also $\lambda x_1 \cdots x_n.t$ abbreviates $\lambda x_1. \cdots \lambda x_n.t$. Ordered pairs and infixes associate to the right: (x, y, z) is $(x, (y, z))$.

The display of type information

show_types : *bool* $\rightarrow$ *unit*

Calling show_types true commands LCF to print type information when printing terms; calling show_types false suppresses this sometimes verbose output.

Example 5.2 Here is a terminal session in which the terms

$$\lambda p : tr.p$$
$$f(\lambda xyz.x \Rightarrow y \mid z : \alpha) : tr$$
$$\lambda z : \alpha \times \beta. (SND\, z, FST\, z)$$
$$p\, AND\, q \Rightarrow r \mid (x, y)$$

are typed to LCF, enclosed in backquotes. LCF echoes each term, sometimes expanding abbreviations found in the input. The infix symbol AND has been declared prior to the session.

```
! show_types true;
- it = true : bool

! '\p:tr.p';
- it = '\p.p:tr'  : term

! 'f(\x y z. x => y | z:'a): tr';
- it =
'(f:(tr -> 'a -> 'a -> 'a) -> tr)(\x.\y.\z.(x => y | z))'  : term

! '\z:'a*'b .(SND z, FST z)';
- it = '\z.(SND (z:'a * 'b) :'b,FST (z:'a * 'b) :'a)'  : term
```

```
! `p AND q => r | x,y`;
- it = `(p AND q => r | (x:tr,y:'a))` : term

! show_types false;
- it = false : bool

! `\z:'a*'b .(SND z, FST z)`;
- it = `\z.(SND z,FST z)` : term
```

5.1.5 Formulae

Formulae have the usual connectives and quantifiers. The precedence of connectives is $\neg, \wedge, \vee, \Longrightarrow, \Longleftrightarrow$ in decreasing order; the infixes associate to the right. There are six syntactic classes since negation is a special case of implication.

Predicates

A predicate has a *generic* argument type. In every occurrence of the predicate, the type of its one argument must be an instance of the generic type. The type may be a product or *void*, giving the effect of zero or more arguments.

The standard predicates are *TRUTH* and *FALSITY*, of argument type *void*, and *equiv* and *inequiv*, of argument type $\alpha \times \alpha$, taking a pair of arguments of the same type. Note that *TRUTH* is not a formula: we must write *TRUTH*(). Under the typechecking rules, $\equiv$ and $\sqsubseteq$ can be applied to a pair of terms of the same type.

Here is a table:

	TRUTH	tautology ($\Lambda \Longrightarrow \Lambda$, perhaps)
Λ	FALSITY	contradiction
$\equiv$	== or equiv	equivalence
$\sqsubseteq$	<< or inequiv	inequivalence

Syntax of formulae

The BNF syntax of formulae is

formula	=	*predicate term*	
	|	*term* == *term*	equivalence
	|	*term* << *term*	inequivalence
	|	! *bound-vars* . *formula*	universal quantifier
	|	? *bound-vars* . *formula*	existential quantifier
	|	~ *formula*	negation
	|	*formula* /\ *formula*	conjunction

	formula \\/ formula	disjunction
	formula ==> formula	implication
	formula <=> formula	bi-implication (if and only if)
	(formula)	parentheses for grouping

There is no ASCII symbol for 'not equivalent': the formula $x \not\equiv y$ is written
~ x==y.

Example 5.3 Here is a terminal session in which formulae are typed to LCF and
echoed back. The formulae are

$$\forall w : \alpha.\bot(w) \equiv \bot : \beta \to tr \qquad \forall x : tr.x \not\equiv TT \wedge x \sqsubseteq FF \Longrightarrow x \equiv \bot$$

```
! show_types true;
- it = true : bool
```

```
! '!w:'a . UU(w) == UU : 'b->tr';
- it = '!w:'a. UU (w:'a) == UU:'b -> tr' : form
```

```
! '!x:tr. ~(x==TT) /\ x<<FF ==> x==UU';
- it = '!x:tr. ~ x == TT  /\  x << FF  ==>  x == UU:tr' : form
```

Example 5.4 A theory may introduce new predicate symbols and axioms to define them. Predicates often abbreviate more complicated formulae, such as 'f is a
strict function':

$$STRICT\, f \iff f\bot \equiv \bot$$

An axiom can refer to the type of the operand of a predicate. Many predicates
describe properties of types, not of values; you may adopt the convention of writing
$\bot$ as the operand when only its type is relevant. Examples: 'the type α is flat'
would be

$$FLAT(\bot : \alpha) \iff \forall x : \alpha.\, \forall y : \alpha.\, x \sqsubseteq y \Longrightarrow \bot \equiv x \vee x \equiv y$$

'The types α and β are isomorphic' would be

$$ISOMORPHIC(\bot : \alpha, \bot : \beta) \iff \exists fg.(\forall x : \alpha.\, g(fx) \equiv x) \wedge (\forall y : \beta.\, f(gy) \equiv y)$$

5.2 Quotations

The easy way to construct an ML value of type *term*, *form*, or *type* is to write a PPλ
expression enclosed in backquotes. Executing the quotation 'x==TT' constructs
the expression $x \equiv TT$ after performing PPλ typechecking. The *antiquotation*
mechanism constructs an expression from existing PPλ expressions.

The current theory affects the parsing and evaluation of a quotation. A theory's types and constants affect PPλ typechecking; its infix operators and predicates affect parsing. A quotation contained within an ML function is parsed when the function is compiled, and executed when the function is called. A quotation can be executed in a richer theory than the one it was parsed in, which might cause confusing behavior.

PPλ typechecking has a *side effect*! The type assigned to each variable is stored as its *sticky type*, which may affect a later typechecking operation. If the quotation is ill-typed, evaluation fails (raises an exception).

5.2.1   Antiquotation

In a quotation, an *antiquotation* incorporates an existing PPλ expression into the result. Such a quotation is like a template for building PPλ expressions.[2]

An antiquotation may appear within a quotation wherever a term, formula, or type is expected. It begins with a caret character. It has the form $\hat{\ }e$, where e is an *atomic* ML expression: an expression in parentheses or a variable. ML typechecking assigns to e the appropriate ML type (*term*, *form*, or *type*). During evaluation of the quotation, e is evaluated and the result used in building the quoted expression.

Example 5.5 Here is a simple quotation, a quotation containing an antiquotation, and a function definition involving a quotation:

```
! val pr = '(TT,FF)';
- val pr = '(TT,FF)'   : term

! val cond = 'p => ^pr | UU';
- val cond = '(p => (TT,FF) | UU)'   : term

! fun condfun (p,x) = '^p => ^x | ^x';
- val condfun = fn   : ((term * term) -> term)

! condfun ('nn:tr', 'zz:'tyvar->tr');
- it = '(nn => zz | zz)'  : term

! condfun ('nn:tr', cond);
- it = '(nn => (p => (TT,FF) | UU) | (p => (TT,FF) | UU))'  : term
```

---

[2]Lisp's backquote and unquote macros embody the same idea.

5.2.2 PPλ typechecking

PPλ typechecking takes place during run-time as quotations are evaluated. A quotation is well-typed if all these conditions hold:

- The type of every constant is an instance of its generic type.

- Every occurrence of a variable name has the same type. This is true of quotations only; a term can contain variables with the same name and different types!

- In every predicate formula $P(t)$, the type of t is an instance of P's generic type.

- In every combination tu, if t has type $\sigma \to \tau$ and u has type σ then tu has type τ.

- In every abstraction $\lambda x.t$, if x has type σ and t has type τ then $\lambda x.t$ has type $\sigma \to \tau$.

- In every explicit type constraint $t : \sigma$, both t and $t : \sigma$ have type σ.

An expression inserted by antiquotation already has a correct type assignment. It is not checked again; this is essential for efficiency. The type is used for typechecking its context.

The PPλ typechecker resembles the ML one. Milner's algorithm assigns a type to every term and subterm in a quotation [67]. The final type assignment must not contain anonymous type variables: unlike in ML, the typechecker does not invent names. If your term is polymorphic then *you* must name the type variables by writing explicit type constraints. After all, you need to know the names of variables to instantiate them using *inst_term* or *INST_TYPE*.

Example 5.6 Here are examples of quotations that are illegal because the type constraints are not completely determined. Assume that no variable has a sticky type. Sticky types are discussed below.

The quotation 'm3' is illegal; 'm3:'c' is allowed.

```
! 'm3';
exception raised: syntax with "types indeterminate in quotation"
evaluation failed

! 'm3:tr*tr';
- it = 'm3'  : term
```

The quotation '!p. p => UU | UU == UU' is illegal; just a single type constraint is needed.

```
! '!p. p => UU | UU == UU';
exception raised: syntax with "types indeterminate in quotation"
evaluation failed

! '!p. p => UU | UU == UU:   'a->tr';
- it = '!p. (p => UU | UU) == UU' : form
```

The quotation 'f(UU:'d) == UU:void' is legal; removing either type constraint would be illegal.

```
! 'f(UU:'d) == UU:void';
- it = 'f UU == UU' : form

! 'f(UU) == UU:void';
exception raised: syntax with "types indeterminate in quotation"
evaluation failed
```

5.2.3   Sticky types

To reduce the need for type constraints, a variable can have a *sticky type*. Sticky types are assigned during typechecking of a quotation: the type assigned to each variable is stored as its sticky type.

Sticky types are used in the final stage of typechecking. The type assignment of each variable is examined. Any variable with a *completely* unconstrained type is assigned its sticky type, if it has one. For instance, if you evaluate 'w:nat' as a top-level expression, then later you can use just 'w' and type ':nat' is assumed. Sticky types can *never* cause typechecking to fail.[3]

Example 5.7 Atomic sticky types work well; compound ones may not. Consider the function type $\alpha \to \beta$. Evaluating 'f:'a->'b' lets you use the quotation 'f' later, but 'f(UU)' is illegal. Typechecking assigns f the type $\tau_m \to \tau_n$, where τ_m and τ_n are internal type variables. The typechecker does not use the sticky type of f because its type in the quotation is partly constrained.

```
! show_types true;
- it = true : bool

! 'f:'a->'b';
- it = 'f:'a -> 'b' : term

! 'f';
- it = 'f:'a -> 'b' : term
```

---

[3]To achieve this, the conditions for applying sticky types are stricter than in Edinburgh LCF.

```
!  'f(UU)';
exception raised: syntax with "types indeterminate in quotation"
evaluation failed
```

Never write ML code that relies on sticky types. Only in top-level interaction should you omit type constraints. Instead of 'f(UU)' use '(f:'a->'b)(UU)' or 'f(UU:'a):'b'. Better still, define an ML variable and use antiquotation:

```
!  'f(UU:'a)  :  'b';
-  it = '(f:'a -> 'b) UU'  : term

! val f  = 'f:'a->'b';
- val f  = 'f:'a -> 'b'   : term

!  '^f(UU)';
-  it = '(f:'a -> 'b) UU'  : term
```

5.2.4   Error messages

Type errors cause the evaluation of a quotation to fail, raising the exception *syntax* of type *string*. The associated string, an error message, names the cause but not the offending terms or types:

types indeterminate in quotation
  Typechecking, even after using sticky types, did not remove all internal type variables from the type assignment.

types in quotation
  A constant was assigned a type that was not an instance of its generic type, or a variable name was assigned two different types.

mk_comb in quotation
  A combination $t(u)$ was ill-typed: a mismatch between function and argument types.

mk_pred in quotation
  A predicate was applied to a term of the wrong type (not an instance of the predicate's argument type).

mk_equiv in quotation
mk_inequiv in quotation
  In $t \equiv u$ or $t \sqsubseteq u$, the types of t and u did not match.

5.3   Primitive constructors and destructors

LCF provides ML functions to construct, test the form of, and take apart PPλ
types, terms, and formulae. The functions, which define PPλ's abstract syntax,
are the interface between meta language and object language. Quotations are
convenient for most uses, but abstract syntax functions allow a finer level of control
in complicated tactics. The functions obey systematic naming conventions: those
for conjunction are *mk_conj*, *is_conj*, and *dest_conj*.

The *constructors*, one for each syntactic class, have names beginning with
mk. They construct a PPλ expression. While quotations perform type *inference*,
taking instances of types automatically, the constructors perform type *checking*:
mk_const, *mk_comb* and *mk_pred* raise exception *syntax* if their arguments are not
type compatible.

The *discriminators* have names beginning with *is*. They check the top level
form of a PPλ expression for being a conjunction, disjunction, etc. They return
true for every expression made by the corresponding constructor or by a quotation
of the corresponding syntactic class. Only one of the primitive discriminators can
be true of an expression.

The *destructors* have names beginning with *dest*. Each is the inverse of a constructor, breaking an expression into its top-level parts. Unless the corresponding
discriminator is true for the expression, it raises the exception *syntax*, passing its
name.

5.3.1   Types

Type variables

mk_vartype : *string* → *type*
is_vartype : *type* → *bool*
dest_vartype : *type* → *string*

These convert between a type variable and its name.

Type constructors

mk_type : (*string* × *type list*) → *type*
dest_type : *type* → (*string* × *type list*)

These functions operate on compound types: those of the form $(\tau_1, \ldots, \tau_n)tcon$,
where *tcon* is a type constructor. Since the only other types are type variables,
there is no discriminator function. If $is\_vartype(\tau)$ returns *false* then the type τ
is constructed using a type constructor.

The construction $mk\_type(tcon, [\tau_1, \ldots, \tau_n])$ raises exception *syntax* unless *tcon*
is the name of an n-place type constructor in the current theory.

5.3.2 Terms

Warning: A term can contain variables having the same name but different types. Such variables are distinct but print as the same name, which can cause great confusion. For instance, calling mk_pair(`x:tr`, `x:void`) creates a pair (x, x) with different x's. However, a quotation always assigns the same type to all occurrences of a variable: the quotation `(x:tr, x:void)` raises exception *syntax*.

Constants

$mk\_const : (string \times type) \rightarrow term$
$is\_const : term \rightarrow bool$
$dest\_const : term \rightarrow (string \times type)$

The construction $mk\_const(C, \tau)$ raises exception *syntax* unless

- C is the name of a constant of the theory.

- The type τ is an instance of the generic type of C.

Variables

$mk\_var : (string \times type) \rightarrow term$
$is\_var : term \rightarrow bool$
$dest\_var : term \rightarrow (string \times type)$

The construction $mk\_var(x, \tau)$ raises exception *syntax* unless x is an identifier that is not the name of a constant.

Abstractions

$mk\_abs : (term \times term) \rightarrow term$
$is\_abs : term \rightarrow bool$
$dest\_abs : term \rightarrow (term \times term)$

The construction $mk\_abs(t, u)$ raises exception *syntax* unless t is a PPλ variable. (There is no separate type for PPλ variables: they have type *term*.)

Combinations

$mk\_comb : (term \times term) \rightarrow term$
$is\_comb : term \rightarrow bool$
$dest\_comb : term \rightarrow (term \times term)$

The construction $mk\_comb(t, u)$ raises exception *syntax* unless there are types σ and τ such that t has type $\sigma \rightarrow \tau$ and u has type σ.

5.3.3   Formulae

Predicates

$mk\_pred : (string \times term) \rightarrow form$
$is\_pred : form \rightarrow bool$
$dest\_pred : form \rightarrow (string \times term)$

The construction $mk\_pred(P, t)$ raises exception *syntax* unless

- P is the name of a predicate of the theory.

- The type of the term t is an instance of the generic argument type of P.

Conjunction

$mk\_conj : (form \times form) \rightarrow form$
$is\_conj : form \rightarrow bool$
$dest\_conj : form \rightarrow (form \times form)$

Disjunction

$mk\_disj : (form \times form) \rightarrow form$
$is\_disj : form \rightarrow bool$
$dest\_disj : form \rightarrow (form \times form)$

Implication

$mk\_imp : (form \times form) \rightarrow form$
$is\_imp : form \rightarrow bool$
$dest\_imp : form \rightarrow (form \times form)$

Bi-implication (if and only if)

$mk\_iff : (form \times form) \rightarrow form$
$is\_iff : form \rightarrow bool$
$dest\_iff : form \rightarrow (form \times form)$

Universal quantifier

$mk\_forall : (term \times form) \rightarrow form$
$is\_forall : form \rightarrow bool$
$dest\_forall : form \rightarrow (term \times form)$

The construction $mk\_forall(t, A)$ raises exception *syntax* unless t is a PPλ variable.

Existential quantifier

$mk\_exists : (term \times form) \rightarrow form$
$is\_exists : form \rightarrow bool$
$dest\_exists : form \rightarrow (term \times form)$

The construction $mk\_exists(t, A)$ raises exception *syntax* unless t is a PPλ variable.

5.3.4   Theorems

$mk\_fthm : (form\ list \times form) \rightarrow thm$
$dest\_thm : thm \rightarrow (form\ list \times form)$
$hyp : thm \rightarrow form\ list$
$concl : thm \rightarrow form$

No *mk_thm* is available. Constructing a theorem from arbitrary formulae would hardly be sound. The function *mk_fthm* constructs a theorem with arbitrary hypotheses and conclusion, but adds the assumption $FALSITY()$. It facilitates the testing of derived inference rules.

The function *dest_thm* splits $A_1, \ldots, A_n \vdash B$ into the pair $([A_1, \ldots, A_n], B)$, while *hyp* returns the hypothesis (assumptions) $[A_1, \ldots, A_n]$ and *concl* returns the conclusion B of the theorem.

Example 5.8 We often need to form the conjunction of several formulae, or to break such a conjunction into its parts. Many such compound syntax functions are provided; they are listed below.

The constructor function is straightforward, noting that the conjunction $A_1 \wedge \ldots \wedge A_n$ is defined only if $n > 0$. Otherwise exception *syntax* is raised.

```
fun list_mk_conj [A] = A
  | list_mk_conj (A::AS) = mk_conj(A, list_mk_conj AS)
  | list_mk_conj [] = raise syntax with "list_mk_conj";
```

The destructor function, *conjuncts*, splits the conjunction $A \wedge B$ into A and B, then recursively operates on those formulae; if its argument was not a conjunction, the exception handler returns it.

```
fun conjuncts fm =
    (let val (A,B) = dest_conj fm in conjuncts A @ conjuncts B end)
    handle syntax => [fm];
```

Note that *conjuncts* is not strictly the inverse of *list_mk_conj*:

```
! list_mk_conj [ 'UU<<(TT,FF) /\ v==()', 'TT<<FF'];
- it = '(UU << (TT,FF)  /\  v == ())  /\  TT << FF' : form
```

```
! conjuncts it;
- it = ['UU << (TT,FF)','v == ()','TT << FF'] : form list
```

Exercise 5.1 Rewrite the function *conjuncts* to use a discriminator function rather than exception handling.

Exercise 5.2 Explain why *conjuncts* is not the inverse of *list_mk_conj*: how can the problem be corrected?

5.4   Compound constructors and destructors

PPλ's pairs, conditionals, equivalences, and inequivalences are·not primitive but abbreviate the use of standard constants and predicates. The term (x, y) is both a pair and a combination; the discriminators *is_pair* and *is_comb* both return *true* for it. Additional syntax functions handle these abbreviations.

Iterative syntax functions operate on lists of terms and formulae.

Most of these functions are written in ML using the primitive ones. A few are Lisp coded for efficiency — the ML compiler was once very slow. The following functions obtain information from the internal representation:

term_class : *term → string*
 This function maps a term to the name of its syntactic class: one of *const, var, abs, comb*.

form_class : *form → string*
 This function maps a formula to the name of its syntactic class: one of *forall, exists, conj, disj, imp, iff*.

type_of : *term → type*
 This function maps a term to its type.

5.4.1   Ordered pairs and conditionals

mk_pair : (*term × term*) → *term*
is_pair : *term → bool*
dest_pair : *term →* (*term × term*)

mk_cond : (*term × term × term*) → *term*
is_cond : *term → bool*
dest_cond : *term →* (*term × term × term*)

The construction $mk\_cond(p, t, u)$ raises exception *syntax* unless the type of p is *tr* and the types of t and u are the same.

5.4.2   Binary predicates

lhs : *form* → *term*
rhs : *form* → *term*

If the formula has the form $P(t,u)$ for a predicate P, then *lhs* returns t and *rhs* returns u. It raises exception *syntax* for other formulae. Recall that $\equiv$ and $\sqsubseteq$ are predicates, so *lhs* maps

$$t \equiv u \quad \longmapsto \quad t$$

and *rhs* maps

$$t \equiv u \quad \longmapsto \quad u \,.$$

Equivalence

mk_equiv : (*term* × *term*) → *form*
is_equiv : *form* → *bool*
dest_equiv : *form* → (*term* × *term*)

The construction $mk\_equiv(t,u)$ raises exception *syntax* unless the types of t and u are the same.

Inequivalence

mk_inequiv : (*term* × *term*) → *form*
is_inequiv : *form* → *bool*
dest_inequiv : *form* → (*term* × *term*)

The construction $mk\_inequiv(t,u)$ raises exception *syntax* unless the types of t and u are the same.

5.4.3   Iterated constructors and destructors

Each destructor is essentially the inverse of its constructor. Under each constructor/destructor pair there appears a description: *subexpressions* ⟷ *expression*.

list_mk_abs : (*term list* × *term*) → *term*
strip_abs : *term* → (*term list* × *term*)

$$([x_1, \ldots, x_n], t) \quad \longleftrightarrow \quad \lambda x_1 \ldots x_n.t$$

list_mk_comb : (*term* × *term list*) → *term*
strip_comb : *term* → (*term* × *term list*)

$$(t, [u_1, \ldots, u_n]) \quad \longleftrightarrow \quad t u_1 \ldots u_n$$

list_mk_conj : *form list* → *form*

conjuncts : *form* → *form list*

$$[A_1, \ldots, A_n] \quad \longleftrightarrow \quad A_1 \wedge \ldots \wedge A_n \qquad if \ n > 0$$

list_mk_disj : *form list* → *form*
disjuncts : *form* → *form list*

$$[A_1, \ldots, A_n] \quad \longleftrightarrow \quad A_1 \vee \ldots \vee A_n \qquad if \ n > 0$$

list_mk_imp : (*form list* × *form*) → *form*
strip_imp : *form* → (*form list* × *form*)

$$([A_1, \ldots, A_n], B) \quad \longleftrightarrow \quad A_1 \Longrightarrow \cdots \Longrightarrow A_n \Longrightarrow B$$

list_mk_forall : (*term list* × *form*) → *form*
strip_forall : *form* → (*term list* × *form*)

$$([x_1, \ldots, x_n], A) \quad \longleftrightarrow \quad \forall x_1 \ldots x_n.A$$

list_mk_exists : (*term list* × *form*) → *form*
strip_exists : *form* → (*term list* × *form*)

$$([x_1, \ldots, x_n], A) \quad \longleftrightarrow \quad \exists x_1 \ldots x_n.A$$

Note that *list_mk_conj* and *list_mk_disj* require a nonempty list. Failures are propagated from the primitive constructors.

5.5   Functions required for substitution

These functions provide substitution of types and terms in an expression. The implementation requires a library of functions that are available for general use.

5.5.1   Variable handling

During substitution, some of these functions detect that capture of a free variable is possible. Others prevent capture by renaming a bound variable.

Choosing a variant of a variable

variant :   *term list*   → *term* → *term*
         $[x_1, \ldots, x_n]$ y

This function appends zero or more primes to the name of the variable y to make it differ from the names of the variables $x_1, \ldots, x_n$. The variable y could become y', y'', and so on.

It raises exception *syntax* unless each of the x_i is a variable and y is a variable or constant.

Generating a new variable

genvar : *type* → *term*

This function generates a new variable of the given type. Its name is guaranteed to differ from every variable name in use. The name contains special characters; neither quotations nor *mk_var* can construct such variables.

Returning all variables in a PPλ expression

term_vars : *term* → *term list*
form_vars : *form* → *term list*
forml_vars : *form list* → *term list*

These return a list of all the variables occurring (free or bound) in the expression.

Returning the free variables in a PPλ expression

term_frees : *term* → *term list*
form_frees : *form* → *term list*
forml_frees : *form list* → *term list*

These return a list of all the variables occurring *free* in the expression. A variable is free unless it is explicitly bound by an enclosing λ, ∀, or ∃.

Returning the type variables in a PPλ expression

type_tyvars : *type* → *type list*
term_tyvars : *term* → *type list*
form_tyvars : *form* → *type list*
forml_tyvars : *form list* → *type list*

These return a list of all the type variables occurring in the expression. There are no bound type variables in PPλ; every type variable is free.

5.5.2   Occurrence testing

Testing if two expressions are α-convertible

aconv_term : *term* → *term* → *bool*
aconv_form : *form* → *form* → *bool*

These return *true* if the two expressions are α-convertible: identical up to renaming of bound variables.

Testing if a type occurs in an expression

$type\_in\_type : type \rightarrow type \rightarrow bool$
$$\tau$$

$type\_in\_term : type \rightarrow term \rightarrow bool$
$$\tau$$

$type\_in\_form : type \rightarrow form \rightarrow bool$
$$\tau$$

These return *true* if the type τ occurs in the type of a subterm of the second argument.

Testing if an expression occurs free in another

$term\_freein\_term : term \rightarrow term \rightarrow bool$
$term\_freein\_form : term \rightarrow form \rightarrow bool$
$form\_freein\_form : form \rightarrow form \rightarrow bool$

These return *true* if the first expression occurs free as a subexpression of the second. An occurrence of a subexpression is free if none its free variables are bound in the surrounding expression.

5.5.3   Substitution and instantiation

We have previously encountered the substitution of a term for free occurrences of a variable; these functions can substitute a term for free occurrences of another term. It is possible to replace only designated occurrences of a term.

Substitution of types for types is called *instantiation* in LCF, a strange bit of terminology.

Substitution in a term or formula

$subst\_term : \quad (term \times term)\,list \quad \rightarrow term \rightarrow term$
$$[(t_1, u_1), \ldots, (t_n, u_n)]$$

$subst\_form : \quad (term \times term)\,list \quad \rightarrow form \rightarrow form$
$$[(t_1, u_1), \ldots, (t_n, u_n)]$$

$subst\_occs\_term : (int\,list)\,list \rightarrow \quad (term \times term)\,list \quad \rightarrow term \rightarrow term$
$$[o_1, \ldots, o_m] \qquad [(t_1, u_1), \ldots, (t_n, u_n)]$$

$subst\_occs\_form : (int\,list)\,list \rightarrow \quad (term \times term)\,list \quad \rightarrow form \rightarrow form$
$$[o_1, \ldots, o_m] \qquad [(t_1, u_1), \ldots, (t_n, u_n)]$$

These replace every free occurrence of u_i by t_i, a simultaneous substitution for $i = 1, \ldots, n$. Bound variables of the expression are renamed if necessary to prevent capture of free variables of the t_i. Note that the pairs have the form (new term, old term).

The *occs* versions replace just those free occurrences of u_i given in the occurrence list o_i, an increasing list of numbers (1 for first occurrence, etc.).

The substitution functions raise exception *syntax* unless $m = n$ and t_i and u_i have the same type for $i = 1, 2, \ldots, n$.

Instantiation of types in a PPλ expression

$inst\_type :$ $(type \times type)\ list$ $\to type \to type$
              $[(\sigma_1, \tau_1), \ldots, (\sigma_n, \tau_n)]$

$inst\_term :$ $term\ list$ $\to$ $(type \times type)\ list$ $\to term \to term$
              $[x_1, \ldots, x_n]$ $[(\sigma_1, \tau_1), \ldots, (\sigma_n, \tau_n)]$

$inst\_form :$ $term\ list$ $\to$ $(type \times type)\ list$ $\to form \to form$
              $[x_1, \ldots, x_n]$ $[(\sigma_1, \tau_1), \ldots, (\sigma_n, \tau_n)]$

These replace every occurrence of τ_i by σ_i, a simultaneous substitution for $i = 1, \ldots, n$.

Warning: A variable is identified by its type as well as its name: the variables $x : \alpha$ and $x : tr$ are different. Changing the type of a variable amounts to renaming it: replacing α by tr makes the two variables the same. Variable names are changed in the expression to prevent clashes with other variables. The new variable names will be distinct from the variables $x_1, \ldots, x_n$.

5.6   Pattern matching primitives

$term\_match : term \to term \to ((term \times term)list \times (type \times type)\ list)$
               pat exp

$form\_match : form \to form \to ((term \times term)list \times (type \times type)\ list)$
               pat exp

Matching the pattern formula A with the formula B means finding types and terms such that B is obtained from A by substitution. If no type matching takes place, then a successful match finds variables $x_1, \ldots, x_n$ and terms $t_1, \ldots, t_n$ such that t_i has the same type as x_i and $A[t_1/x_1, \ldots, t_n/x_n]$ is the same formula as B, or is at least α-convertible to B.

With matching of types, a match also finds type variables $\alpha_1, \ldots, \alpha_m$ and types $\sigma_1, \ldots, \sigma_m$, such that $A[\sigma_1/\alpha_1, \ldots, \sigma_m/\alpha_m][t_1/x_1, \ldots, t_n/x_n]$ is the same formula as

B. In this case t_i has the same type as $x_i[\sigma_1/\alpha_1, \ldots, \sigma_m/\alpha_m]$, so if x_i has type τ_i then t_i has type $\tau_i[\sigma_1/\alpha_1, \ldots, \sigma_m/\alpha_m]$.

Pattern matching of one term against another is similar.

The functions *term_match* and *form_match* match the expression *exp* against the pattern *pat*. If the expression is an instance of the pattern, then these functions return the appropriate lists of (term, variable) and (type, type variable) pairs. These functions are used in rewriting functions (Chapter 9) and in matching rules like *MATCH_MP*.

They raise exception *general* if *exp* is not an instance of *pat*.

Example 5.9 Here is a session of simple pattern matching.

```
! form_match 'g(p:tr, q:tr) == p'  'FST(TT,TT)==TT';
- it =
([('TT','q'),('TT','p'),('FST','g')],[])
 : ((term * term) list * (type * type) list)


! form_match 'g(p:tr, q:tr) == p'  'FST(TT,q)==p';
exception raised: general with "form_match"
evaluation failed
```

And here is matching of types and terms.

```
! term_match 'f:'a -> 'b'  '\r:tr.r';
- it =
([('\r.r','f')],[(':tr',':'b'),(':tr',':'a')])
 : ((term * term) list * (type * type) list)


! term_match 'p=>x|x:'a' 'f(TT) => (TT,TT) | (TT,TT)';
- it =
([('(TT,TT)','x'),('f TT','p')],[(':tr * tr',':'a')])
 : ((term * term) list * (type * type) list)


! term_match 'p=>x|x:'a' 'q => q | UU';
exception raised: general with "term_match"
evaluation failed
```

5.7 Terminal interaction and system functions

Cambridge LCF has a primitive user interface. You type ML phrases (declarations and commands) at top level; ML parses and evaluates them. If you make an error then you have to type the phrase again, a chore unless your computer provides windows with 'cut and paste' for correcting and re-entering input. On some machines the display editor performs window management: LCF runs in one window while you edit a file in another. Other machines provide window management in the underlying system.

If you have no windows then run LCF and an editor as separate processes. Write each long command onto a file and load it into LCF. If the file contains an error then *suspend* (don't terminate) the LCF session, edit the file, then resume the LCF session to try again. If your operating system does not support multiple processes then order a modern machine and meanwhile log in on two adjacent terminals.

Every time you build an LCF theory that will be needed later, keep a record of the important commands used, including declarations of types and axioms, and proofs of the theorems. When building a hierarchy of theories, mistakes — name clashes, misspelled function symbols, inconsistent axioms — may ruin everything. A proper record of each theory makes rebuilding much easier; you can even make a batch file for building the theory off-line.

5.7.1 Loading an ML source file

load : *string* × *bool* → *unit*
    filename *pflag*

This reads the file *filename.ml* from the user's directory. The file *must* have the extension .ml. Each ML phrase is evaluated as if typed on the terminal. Loading stops if any ML phrase fails. If *pflag* is *true* then results are printed as usual; otherwise a period is printed as each phrase is processed.

Raises exception *general* if

- the *filename* is unacceptable

- the file is not found

- any top-level phrase in the file fails

loadt : *string* → *unit*

Calls *load* with *pflag* = *true*.

loadf : *string* → *unit*

Calls *load* with *pflag* = *false*.

5.7.2   Terminating a session

quit : unit → unit

This terminates the LCF session. Note that you have to type `quit();`.

save :   string   → unit
*   imagename*

This writes a core image as the file *imagename*, then terminates the session. Executing this image resumes the session.

Warning: The image file will occupy around 2 megabytes of disc space. LCF's theory system is a much more efficient way of storing axioms and theorems. The only reasons for saving an image are if you must stop in the middle of a complicated proof, or if the image can be of use to many people.

5.7.3   Timing

timer : bool → unit

This turns the printing of run-time on and off.

5.7.4   Printing

max_print_depth : int → unit

This sets a bound on the printing of ML values: anything nested more deeply is printed as an ampersand (&). It is useful if your work produces enormous formulae. The initial bound is 30.

Chapter 6

Theory Structure

A large proof should be organized as a collection of *theories*. An LCF theory has a *signature*: its type constructors, constants, infixes, predicates. It may have *parent* theories, inheriting all their symbols and axioms. This rich environment may be extended by new axioms. Theorems may be proved and recorded in the theory.

Existing theories may become the *parents* of a new theory if their signatures are disjoint. Names of types, constants, infixes, and predicates cannot be hidden or renamed to avoid clashes. Each theory has separate name spaces for its axioms and theorems. An axiom is designated by the pair (theory name, axiom name), a theorem by (theory name, theorem name).

Theories do not have a tree structure: sharing always occurs. In Figure 6.1, the theory T has parents T_1 and T_2. They both have T_4 as a parent. Both the theories T_3 and T_4 have T_5 as a parent; both T_4 and T_5 have PPλ as a parent. Symbols declared in a common ancestor are shared. If the symbol $+$ is declared in T_4 then it is visible in both T_1 and T_2 and does not cause a clash between the two theories. But if it were declared in both T_2 and T_3 then T_1 and T_2 would clash during the construction of T.

Every theory is ultimately descended from PPλ. A theory is the *child* of its parents. An *ancestor* is a parent or an ancestor of a parent; a *descendant* is a child or or a descendant of a child. The theory T_3 is an ancestor of T, and T_4

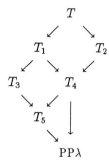

Figure 6.1: A typical theory hierarchy

is a descendant of PPλ directly and via T_5. Make sure a theory is correct before building new theories on it. A serious error, such as an incorrect axiom, requires rebuilding the theory and *all* of its descendants.

LCF theories are stored on disc so that a proof can extend over many terminal sessions. Basic theories, like the natural numbers, may be used in different proofs. A theory named T is stored as the file *T.th* on the current directory. Deleting the file deletes the theory. You should also delete all of the desendants of T; LCF will not do this for you. There is no support for using theory files stored on other directories. Theory files are *not secure*. Editing a theory file or replacing a file by one containing fewer axioms can violate soundness. A hardware error can cause a theory file to become corrupt. Versions of LCF for different operating systems may not be completely compatible — differences in file name syntax mean differences in allowable theory names.

In an LCF session there is always a topmost theory. If T_1 and T_2 are present then so is some theory T descended from both. This *current theory* is part of the *state* of the session, affecting the parsing and typechecking of quotations. Because existing PPλ expressions depend on the current theory, LCF can not leave a theory during a session. It can move deeper into the theory structure: from a theory to one of its children. In the example above, neither of T_1 and T_2 is descended from the other. They must have been created in separate sessions; both existed on disc before T did. In mathematical terminology: the structure of theories on disc is a partially ordered set, while the structure in an LCF session is a lattice.

A theory consists of a signature, axioms, and theorems. Each constant has a generic type, possibly polymorphic, and each predicate has a generic argument type. An infix operator is a constant of a function type; its infix syntax has no logical significance. An LCF session begins in the theory *PPLAMB* (the ASCII name of PPλ). A descendant of the current theory may be loaded, becoming the new current theory. A new theory may be built (or *drafted*) on top of the current theory.

You may enter a new theory or draft at any time. In a single session you can work in a descending chain of theories. Start with *PPLAMB*, move to a descendant T_4, prove some theorems, move to a descendant T_1, and so on. You can build a chain of theories in one session.

You can create a version of LCF specialized for your favorite theory. In a new LCF session, load that theory along with rules and tactics for it. Then save the core image using the command *save*.

6.1   Drafting a new theory

Here are the commands for constructing a theory. Executing *new_theory* enters *draft mode*, allowing new symbols, parents, and axioms to be declared. Executing *close_theory* writes this information to disc and leaves draft mode, preventing further declarations.

A theory command may fail by raising the exception *theory*, of type *string*. The string identifies the failed command and usually contains an error message.

6.1.1 Entering draft mode

new_theory : *string* → *unit*
$$T$$

The current theory is closed if LCF was in draft mode; it becomes a parent of the new theory T. Draft mode begins in T. The other commands in this section may be used to declare new types, constants, predicates, ... in T. The command raises exception *theory* unless

- The theory T does not already exist on the user's directory.

- The name T is suitable for a filename. The operating system may restrict the length of a name or the characters it may contain.

6.1.2 Adding a parent

new_parent : *string* → *unit*
$$T$$

The theory T becomes a parent of the current draft. Information about T and its ancestors is loaded from the disc. No type, constant, infix, or predicate of T may clash with a name already used in the current draft or one of its existing ancestors. The command raises exception *theory* unless

- LCF is in draft mode.

- There is a valid theory file for T on the current directory.

- The signatures do not clash.

6.1.3 Declaring new symbols

New type, constant, infix, and predicate symbols can be declared in a draft. They must not clash with names already used in the draft or its ancestors.

The name of a constant, infix, or predicate may be an alphanumeric identifier, a number, or a symbolic identifier composed from the following characters:

$$\$ \quad \% \quad \& \quad + \quad - \quad / \quad < \quad = \quad > \quad @ \quad | \quad *$$

These are referred to below as *suitable* identifiers.

Declaring a type constructor

$new\_type : int \rightarrow string \rightarrow unit$
$ntcon$

The n-place type constructor *tcon* is declared. The standard type constructors $\rightarrow$ and $\times$ are infix but new infix type constructors cannot be declared. The command raises exception *theory* unless

- LCF is in draft mode.

- The name *tcon* is an identifier, not already a type constructor (of the draft or its ancestors).

- The number of argument places, n, is non-negative.

For example,

```
new_type 0 "nat";
new_type 1 "list";
```

declares the type *nat* and the 1-place type constructor *list*.

Declaring a constant

$new\_constant : string \times type \rightarrow unit$
τ

The constant is declared with generic type τ. The command raises exception *theory* unless

- LCF is in draft mode.

- The name is a suitable identifier, and not already the name of a constant, infix, or predicate.

For example, the commands

```
new_constant ("1", ':nat');
new_constant ("MINUS", ':nat -> nat');
new_constant ("REV", ':'a list -> 'a list');
```

declare a constant 1 of type *nat*, a function *MINUS* of type $nat \rightarrow nat$, and a polymorphic function *REV* on lists.

Declaring an infix operator

$new\_curried\_infix : string \times type \rightarrow unit$
$\sigma \rightarrow (\tau \rightarrow \upsilon)$
$new\_paired\_infix : string \times type \rightarrow unit$
$(\sigma \times \tau) \rightarrow \upsilon$

An infix operator is declared with the given generic type. An infix is a constant that is parsed and printed using infix notation. For a curried function f, write $t\ f\ u$ instead of $(ft)u$. For a paired function f, write $t\ f\ u$ instead of $f(t,u)$. The commands raise exception *theory* unless

- LCF is in draft mode.

- The type is acceptable: a curried function should have type $\sigma \to (\tau \to \upsilon)$, a paired function should have type $(\sigma \times \tau) \to \upsilon$.[1]

- The name is a suitable identifier, and not already the name of a constant, infix, or predicate.

For example,

```
new_curried_infix ("+", ':nat -> nat -> nat');
new_paired_infix  ("-", ':(nat * nat) -> nat');
```

declares the operators $+$ and $-$ on natural numbers.

An infix operator by itself is a term that denotes a function. To stand alone as a term, the operator is written with a prefixed symbol *op*, like in Standard ML. Thus op $+$ denotes the addition function and op $-$ denotes the subtraction function.

Declaring a predicate

new_predicate : *string* × *type* → *unit*
$$\tau$$

The predicate is declared, with generic argument type τ. It may be applied to any argument whose type is an instance of τ. The standard predicates $\equiv$ and $\sqsubseteq$ are infix, but there is no way to declare new infix predicates. The command raises exception *theory* unless

- LCF is in draft mode.

- The name is a suitable identifier, and not already the name of a constant, infix, or predicate.

For example,

```
new_predicate ("SUBLIST", ':('a list) * ('a list)');
new_predicate ("ORDERED", ':int list');
```

declares a binary predicate *SUBLIST* on (polymorphic) lists, and a unary predicate *ORDERED* on lists of natural numbers.

---

[1] A function of type $(\sigma \times \tau) \to (\upsilon_1 \to \upsilon_2)$ could be either curried or paired!

6.1.4   Asserting an axiom

new_axiom : *string × form → thm*
$$A$$
new_closed_axiom : *string × form → thm*
$$A$$

Both of these assert the new axiom A and return a theorem. The function *new_axiom* generalizes A over its free variables: if x and y are the free variables of A then it returns the theorem $\vdash \forall xy.A$. In contrast, *new_closed_axiom* fails unless A is a closed formula: one with no free variables. If you refer to a constant that has not been declared, it is taken for a free variable; *new_closed_axiom* detects this error. The commands raise exception *theory* unless

- LCF is in draft mode.

- The name is not already the name of another axiom of this draft. An ancestor's axiom name may be used: axioms are referred to by the pair of theory and axiom names.

- The formula is closed (*new_closed_axiom* only).

Watch out for inconsistent axioms like $TT \equiv FF$, which implies everything. Less obvious inconsistencies arise from forgetting that functions must be continuous (Example 4.11). Defining an *abbreviation* is safe: an axiom of the form $C \equiv t$, where C is a new constant.

Axioms are retrieved using the function *axiom*, described below. Bind the result of *new_axiom* or *new_closed_axiom* to an ML variable for easy access in the current terminal session.

Example 6.1 Under the previous declaration of + and *MINUS*, the two axiom declarations

```
new_axiom ("MINUS", 'MINUS(m + n) == MINUS(m) + MINUS(n)');
```

```
new_closed_axiom ("MINUS",
      '!m n. MINUS(m + n) == MINUS(m) + MINUS(n)');
```

are equivalent.

On the other hand, *new_closed_axiom* detects the misspelling in

```
new_closed_axiom ("MINUS",
      '!m n. MINUS(m + n) == MINUS(m) + MNUS(n)');
```

The command fails with the message `free variables in axiom:   MINUS`.

This example assumes that m and n have not been declared as constants, infixes, or predicates!

6.1.5 Constructing the theory of a data structure

These commands declare symbols, assert axioms, and prove theorems, to construct the theory of a data structure as described in Chapter 4. LCF must already be in draft mode; the type constructor must already be declared. The more general command is *gen_struct_axm*, which can construct a mixed data structure: partly lazy and partly strict. The simpler *struct_axm* declares a fully lazy or fully strict data structure.

Constructing a mixed data structure

$$gen\_struct\_axm : (type \times (string \times (string \times term) list) list) \rightarrow unit$$
$$\tau \qquad constr_i \qquad mode_{ij} \quad arg_{ij}$$

This is the general function for imposing a data structure on the type τ with strict, lazy, or mixed constructors named $constr_1, \ldots, constr_m$. The type τ must have the form $(\alpha_1, \ldots, \alpha_k)tcon$, where the k-place type constructor $tcon$ has already been declared. In a recursive type, some arguments of constructor functions have the type τ. For each i, its arguments of $constr_i$ are the variables arg_{ij}. The string $mode_{ij}$ specifies whether that argument should be strict or lazy.

The arguments of the constructor functions, arg_{ij}, should be distinct variables for all i and j. Their types collectively specify the type of each constructor function; their names are used by the structural induction tactic for creating goals.

You can declare discriminator or destructor functions, or an eliminator functional; *gen_struct_axm* does not do this for you.

The command raises exception *general*, passing an error message, unless

- The type τ has the form $(\alpha_1, \ldots, \alpha_k)tcon$, where $k \geq 0$ and the $\alpha_1, \ldots, \alpha_k$ are distinct type variables.

- The type of each arg_{ij} either is τ or is built up from other type constructors and the type variables $\alpha_1, \ldots, \alpha_k$.

- Each of the terms arg_{ij} is a variable.

- The constructor and argument names are all distinct.

- No constructor or argument name contains primes. Names generated by *gen_struct_axm* for the theory contain primes, to avoid clashes.

- Every mode flag $mode_{ij}$ is either "strict" or "lazy".

Example 6.2 Consider a 2-place type operator for labelled trees with two kinds of nodes. The *UNIT* nodes have one child and are labelled with an element of type α. The *BRANCH* nodes have two children and are labelled with an element of type β.

```
new_theory "tree_basic";


new_type 2 "tree";


gen_struct_axm
    (':('alpha,'beta)tree',
     [("TIP",[]),
      ("UNIT", [("strict", 'a:'alpha'),
                ("strict", 't:('alpha,'beta)tree')]),
      ("BRANCH", [("strict", 'b:'beta'),
                  ("strict", 't:('alpha,'beta)tree'),
                  ("strict", 't1:('alpha,'beta)tree')])]);
```

The call to *new_theory* creates the theory *tree_basic* and allows the type *tree* to be declared. Each data structure must be put onto a separate theory — otherwise axiom names would clash. Quotations such as 't:('alpha,'beta)tree' refer to the new type in the call to *gen_struct_axm*. Any argument can be made lazy by putting "lazy" in place of "strict" in the corresponding position.

Let us refer back to this example when considering the details of the theory constructed by *gen_struct_axm*.

Constants and axioms

The call to *gen_struct_axm* declares the constants *TIP*, *UNIT*, and *BRANCH*. It also asserts axioms.

The exhaustion axiom, called *CASES*, is

```
!abs'.abs' == UU  \/
       abs' == TIP  \/
       (?a t. abs' == UNIT a t /\ ~ a==UU /\ ~ t==UU)  \/
       (?b t t1. abs' == BRANCH b t t1 /\
                 ~ b==UU /\ ~ t==UU /\ ~ t1==UU)
```

The strictness axioms are represented by a single one, *STRICT*, a conjunction of *m* conjunctions. The conjuncts *TRUTH*() are added to make sure each conjunction has at least one member. Also, each lazy argument has an occurrence of *TRUTH*() in place of the corresponding strictness conjunct. This makes it easy for ML code to locate the strictness axiom for a particular argument of a constructor.

```
TRUTH ()  /\
(!a t. TRUTH ()  /\  UNIT UU t == UU  /\  UNIT a UU == UU)  /\
(!b t t1. TRUTH ()  /\  BRANCH UU t t1 == UU  /\
                   BRANCH b UU t1 == UU  /\  BRANCH b t UU == UU)
```

The definedness axioms are also a conjunction, *DEFINED*. Each conjunct is a nested implication $A_1 \Longrightarrow (\cdots \Longrightarrow (A_n \Longrightarrow B)\cdots)$ rather than $(A_1 \wedge \cdots \wedge A_n) \Longrightarrow B$. Nested implication handles the case $n = 0$ gracefully: no need to use *TRUTH*() as a placeholder.

```
~ TIP==UU  /\
(!a t.  ~ a==UU ==> ~ t==UU ==> ~ UNIT a t == UU)  /\
(!b t t1.  ~ b==UU ==> ~ t==UU ==> ~ t1==UU ==> ~ BRANCH b t t1 ==UU)
```

The axiom *LESS* specifies the partial ordering ($\sqsubseteq$) on the data structure. It is a conjunction of m conjunctions of m formulae, considering all $m \times m$ comparisons of two constructors. Since the type *tree* has three constructors, its axiom *LESS* has nine conjuncts. For different constructors the conjunct asserts distinctness:

```
!b t t1 a t'.  ~ b==UU   ==>   ~ t==UU   ==>   ~ t1==UU   ==>
                  ~ a==UU   ==>   ~ t'==UU   ==>
        ~ BRANCH b t t1 << UNIT a t'
```

For two instances of a single constructor the conjunct asserts invertibility:

```
!a t a' t'.  ~ a==UU   ==>   ~ t==UU   ==>
                ~ a'==UU   ==> ~ t'==UU   ==>
        UNIT a t << UNIT a' t'   ==>
        TRUTH ()  /\   a << a'  /\  t << t'
```

Theorems

Invoking *gen_struct_axm* proves some useful theorems. The theorem *EQ_IFF_ALL* describes the equivalence predicate ($\equiv$) on the data structure. It has the same form as *LESS*: an $m \times m$ conjunction comparing pairs of constructions. Different constructors make distinct elements:

```
!b t t1 a t'.  ~ b==UU   ==> ~ t==UU   ==> ~ t1==UU   ==>
                ~ a==UU   ==> ~ t'==UU   ==>
        (BRANCH b t t1 == UNIT a t'   <=>   FALSITY ())
```

Any single constructor is invertible:

```
!a t a' t'.  ~ a==UU   ==>   ~ t==UU   ==>
                ~ a'==UU   ==> ~ t'==UU   ==>
        (UNIT a t == UNIT a' t'   <=>   TRUTH()  /\   a==a'  /\   t==t')
```

If all constructors are strict then *gen_struct_axm* proves the theorem *FLAT*, by the inductive argument given in Chapter 4. If the types α and β are flat then $(\alpha, \beta)tree$ is flat:

```
(!a a'. a << a'  ==>  UU == a  \/  a == a')  ==>
(!b b'. b << b'  ==>  UU == b  \/  b == b')  ==>
(!abs' abs''. abs' << abs''  ==>  UU == abs'  \/  abs' == abs'')
```

Exercise 6.1 Execute the above call to *gen_struct_axm*. Inspect the theory by calling *print_theory*, which is described below.

Constructing a uniform data structure

$$struct\_axm : (type \times string \times (string \times term \ list) \ list) \rightarrow unit$$
$$\qquad\quad \tau \qquad mode \qquad constr_i \quad arg_{ij}$$

This command handles a common situation: the set of constructors is either uniformly strict or uniformly lazy. It simply calls *gen_struct_axm* passing the single *mode* in every argument position.

For example,

```
struct_axm (':('alpha,'beta)tree',
            "strict",
            [("TIP",[]);
             ("UNIT",  ['a:'alpha',  't:('alpha,'beta)tree']);
             ("BRANCH", ['b:'beta',  't:('alpha,'beta)tree',
                                     't1:('alpha,'beta)tree'])]);
```

is equivalent to

```
gen_struct_axm
    (':('alpha,'beta)tree',
     [("TIP",[]),
      ("UNIT", [("strict", 'a:'alpha'),
                ("strict", 't:('alpha,'beta)tree')]),
      ("BRANCH", [("strict", 'b:'beta'),
                  ("strict", 't:('alpha,'beta)tree'),
                  ("strict", 't1:('alpha,'beta)tree')])]);
```

6.1.6   Closing the current theory

close_theory : unit → unit

Calling *close_theory* terminates draft mode: no additional types, constants, predicates, parents, or axioms may be declared. The theory information is written to disc. The command raises exception *theory* unless LCF is in draft mode.

Warning: the effect of theory declarations may be lost unless they are followed by a call to *close_theory* in the same session.

Example 6.3 A theory of the Boolean operators on type *tr* could be declared as follows.

```
new_theory "tr";

new_constant ("NOT", ':tr -> tr');
new_curried_infix ("AND", ':tr -> tr -> tr');
new_curried_infix ("OR",  ':tr -> tr -> tr');


val NOT_EQN =
new_closed_axiom ("NOT_EQN", '!p. NOT p == p => FF | TT');

val OR_EQN =
new_closed_axiom ("OR_EQN",  '!p q. p OR q == p => TT | q');

val AND_EQN =
new_closed_axiom ("AND_EQN", '!p q. p AND q == p => q | FF');

close_theory();
```

The new theory is named *tr*. It has three constants *NOT*, *AND*, and *OR*, defined by the axioms *NOT_EQN*, *AND_EQN*, and *OR_EQN* respectively. The axioms are stored under those names on the theory file `tr.th` and also assigned to ML variables for use in the current session.

Example 6.4 Here is a theory of the strict sum of Section 4.3.

```
new_theory "ssum";

new_type 2 "ssum";

new_constant ("INL", ':'a-> ('a,'b)ssum');
new_constant ("INR", ':'b-> ('a,'b)ssum');
new_constant ("WHEN", ':('a->'c)->('b->'c)-> ('a,'b)ssum -> 'c');

(*definedness axioms*)
val INL_DEF = new_closed_axiom
        ("INL_DEF", '!x. ~ x==UU ==> ~ INL(x)==UU:('a,'b)ssum');

val INR_DEF = new_closed_axiom
        ("INR_DEF", '!y. ~ y==UU ==> ~ INR(y)==UU:('a,'b)ssum');
```

```
(*strictness axioms*)
val INL_STRICT = new_closed_axiom
      ("INL_STRICT",'INL(UU)==UU:('a,'b)ssum');

val INR_STRICT = new_closed_axiom
      ("INR_STRICT",'INR(UU)==UU:('a,'b)ssum');

(*reduction axioms*)
val WHEN_CLAUSES =
  new_closed_axiom ("WHEN_CLAUSES",
    '!f:'a->'c. !g:'b->'c.
        WHEN f g UU == UU /\
        (!x:'a. ~ x==UU ==> WHEN f g (INL x) == f x) /\
        (!y:'b. ~ y==UU ==> WHEN f g (INR y) == g y)');

val EXHAUSTION =
  new_closed_axiom ("EXHAUSTION",
    '!z: ('a,'b)ssum.
        z==UU  \/
        (?x:'a. ~ x==UU /\ z == INL x) \/
        (?y:'b. ~ y==UU /\ z == INR y)');

close_theory();
```

6.2   Using a theory

You can load a descendant of the current theory and store theorems on it. You can retrieve axioms and theorems of the current theory and its ancestors. To correct a mistake you can delete a stored theorem, or reopen a theory for further declarations.

Many of these functions take a theory name, an ML string, as an argument. They recognize the string "-" (a hyphen) to denote the current draft or theory.

6.2.1   Loading a theory

load_theory : *string* → *unit*
                    T

The theory T, and its ancestors, are loaded into LCF. The current theory becomes T. The command raises exception *theory* unless

- There is a valid theory file for T on the current directory, as defined by the operating system.

- The theory T is a descendant of the current theory.

- Names of constants, types, or predicates do not clash with a name already used in the current theory or its ancestors.

After executing *load_theory* LCF is not in draft mode: the theory may not be extended. Indeed, LCF cannot have been in draft mode at any time before executing *load_theory*, for no theory can be a descendant of a draft.

6.2.2   Fetching an axiom or theorem

$$axiom : string \rightarrow string \rightarrow thm$$
$$ T id$$
$$theorem : string \rightarrow string \rightarrow thm$$
$$ T id$$

The axiom or theorem named *id* is fetched from the theory or draft T. These commands raise exception *theory* unless

- There is a valid theory file for T on the current directory.

- There is an axiom / theorem named *id* on theory T.

Example 6.5 In this session, we fetch the standard axiom *LESS_TRANS* and the standard theorems *EQ_TRANS* and *ETA_EQ*. The third declaration makes *ETAE* shorthand for the standard theorem *ETA_EQ*. Binding an identifier to the result of *axiom* or *theorem* is a good idea; each axiom and theorem of *PPLAMB* is already bound to an ML identifier of the same name.

```
! axiom "PPLAMB" "LESS_TRANS";
- it = |-'!x y z. x << y  /\  y << z   ==>   x << z' : thm

! theorem "PPLAMB" "EQ_TRANS";
- it = |-'!x y z. x == y  /\  y == z   ==>   x == z' : thm

! val ETAE = theorem "-" "ETA_EQ";
- val ETAE = |-'!f. \x.f x == f' : thm
```

6.2.3   Saving a theorem

$$save\_thm : string \times thm \rightarrow thm$$
$$save\_top\_thm : string \rightarrow thm$$

The command *save_thm* writes the given theorem onto the current theory file. Beforehand it discharges all hypotheses and generalizes over all free variables, using the rules *DISCH_ALL* and *GEN_ALL* of Section 7.2. The resulting theorem is returned as the value of *save_thm*.

The command *save_top_thm* is part of the subgoal package (Section 8.6); it saves the topmost theorem on the stack.

They raise exception *theory* if the name is already the name of another theorem of this theory or draft. Names of axioms or of ancestors' theorems may be used.

Example 6.6 If the value of the ML identifier *assocth* is the theorem

$$l_2 \not\equiv \perp, l_3 \not\equiv \perp \vdash l_1 \; APP \; (l_2 \; APP \; l_3) \equiv (l_1 \; APP \; l_2) \; APP \; l_3$$

then

```
let val LIST_ASSOC = save_thm ("ASSOC", assocth);
```

stores the theorem

$$\vdash \forall l_1 \; l_2 \; l_3 . \; l_2 \not\equiv \perp \Longrightarrow l_3 \not\equiv \perp \Longrightarrow l_1 \; APP \; (l_2 \; APP \; l_3) \equiv (l_1 \; APP \; l_2) \; APP \; l_3$$

on the current theory under the name *ASSOC*. The declaration binds the identifier *LIST_ASSOC* to this theorem for easy access later in the session.

The theorem is retrieved by `theorem "-" "ASSOC"`. If the current theory is named *mytheory* then `theorem "mytheory" "ASSOC"` also retrieves the theorem.

6.2.4   Deleting a theorem

$$delete\_thm : \underset{T}{string} \rightarrow \underset{id}{string} \rightarrow thm$$

The theorem named *id* is deleted from the theory or draft *T* and returned as the value of *delete_thm*. This command is useful if a theorem has been stored under the wrong name. There is no command to delete an *axiom*: it would be impossible to locate all theorems depending on the axiom. The command raises exception *theory* unless

- There is a valid theory file for *T* on the current directory.

- There is a theorem named *id* on theory *T*.

6.2.5   Extending a theory

$$extend\_theory : \underset{T}{string} \rightarrow unit$$

Like *load_theory*, this command loads in the theory T, which must be a descendant of the current theory. However it re-enters draft mode, making T the current *draft*. New types, constants, predicates, etc., can then be added to T. Then *close_theory* should be called to write the new declarations to disc and leave draft mode.

Warning: LCF does not check that names of new types, predicates, infixes, and constants, or those brought in by new parents, do not clash with names in descendant theories. It will be impossible to load a descendant theory if such a clash is introduced. The normal way to build upon a theory is to make it the parent of a new theory. You should only use *extend_theory* to correct a mistake when rebuilding the theory hierarchy would involve too much work. The command raises exception *theory* unless

- There is a valid theory file for T on the current directory.

- The theory T is a descendant of the current theory.

- Names of constants, types, and predicates do not clash.

6.3 Inspecting a theory

LCF has a command to print a theory on the terminal, and functions to extract each of the components of a theory. These functions also recognize the "-" shorthand for the current theory. Each raises exception *theory* unless the theory T has been loaded: it must be the current theory or one of its ancestors.

6.3.1 Printing a theory

print_theory : *string* $\rightarrow$ *unit*
$$T$$

This command prints on the terminal the names of the parents and the types, constants, axioms, etc., of the theory T.

6.3.2 Extracting parts of a theory

Each of these functions has one argument, the name of a theory. It returns information from the theory as a list.

parents : *string* $\rightarrow$ *string list*
The names of the parents are returned as a list of strings.

types : *string* $\rightarrow$ (*int* $\times$ *string*) *list*
The type constructors are returned as a list of (arity, name) pairs.

constants : string → term list
The constants are returned as a list of terms.

curried_infixes : string → term list
The curried infixes are returned as a list of terms.

paired_infixes : string → term list
The paired infixes are returned as a list of terms.

predicates : string → (string × type) list
The predicates are returned as a list of (name, type) pairs.

axioms : string → (string × thm) list
The axioms are returned as a list of (name, theorem) pairs.

theorems : string → (string × thm) list
The theorems are returned as a list of (name, theorem) pairs.

Example 6.7 Let us look at the standard theory, PPλ, which is discussed in the
following chapter.

```
! parents "PPLAMB";
- it = [] : string list

! types "PPLAMB";
- it = [(2,"fun"),(2,"prod"),(0,"tr"),(0,"void")]
  : (int * string) list

! constants "PPLAMB";
- it = ['SND','FST','PAIR','COND','FIX','UU','FF','TT','()']
  : term list

! predicates "PPLAMB";
- it =
[("TRUTH",':void'),
 ("FALSITY",':void'),
 ("inequiv",':'a * 'a'),
 ("equiv",':'a * 'a')]
  : (string * type) list

! axioms "PPLAMB";
- it =
[("FIX_EQ",|-'!f. FIX f == f(FIX f)'),
 ("SND_PAIR",|-'!x y. SND(x,y) == y'),
 ("FST_PAIR",|-'!x y. FST(x,y) == x'),
```

```
("MK_PAIR",|-'!x. FST x,SND x == x'),
("VOID_CASES",|-'!x. x == UU'),
("TR_LESS_DISTINCT",
  |-'~ TT << FF  /\  ~ FF << TT  /\  ~ TT << UU  /\  ~ FF << UU'),
("TR_CASES",|-'!p. p == UU  \/  p == TT  \/  p == FF'),
("COND_CLAUSES",
  |-'!x y.
      (UU => x | y) == UU  /\
      (TT => x | y) == x  /\
      (FF => x | y) == y'),
("MINIMAL",|-'!x. UU << x'),
("LESS_EXT",|-'!f g. (!x. f x << g x)  ==>  f << g'),
("MONO",|-'!f g x y. f << g  /\  x << y  ==>  f x << g y'),
("LESS_TRANS",|-'!x y z. x << y  /\  y << z  ==>  x << z'),
("LESS_ANTI_SYM",|-'!x y. x << y  /\  y << x  ==>  x == y'),
("LESS_REFL",|-'!x. x << x'),
("TRUTH",|-'TRUTH ()')]
: (string * thm) list
```

6.4 Limitations of theories

LCF operates with hardly any state. But the current theory is part of the state, making it difficult to move from one theory to another. Hanna and Daeche's theorem prover, *Veritas*, implements a logic using the functional language Miranda in place of ML [43]. Each Veritas term has a theory associated with it. There is no current theory, indeed no state at all.

LCF's theory primitives do not support abstract reasoning. For instance, polynomials have the algebraic structure of a ring. We can develop a theory of rings and a theory of polynomials, but LCF cannot recognize that polynomials form a ring and satisfy theorems about rings. We can construct trees using a theory of lists, but cannot hide the details of construction to produce an abstract theory of trees. The only way to construct a theory is to combine existing theories, adding new symbols and axioms. We must be extremely careful in choosing symbols: if a symbol is used in two different theories then they can never be combined.

Sannella and Burstall point out these limitations [85]. Taking ideas from the specification language CLEAR, they suggest a new set of theory constructors. A *primitive theory* is a set of axioms under a given signature. The *union* of two theories contains the theorems of both under the union of their signatures. The constructor *rename* yields a theory containing the set of theorems obtained by renaming symbols of another theory. The constructor *inverse image* forms the inverse image of a theory under a substitution. Inverse image provides a simple form of abstraction. Sannella and Burstall describe an implementation of their ideas in Edinburgh LCF.

Burstall and Goguen introduce CLEAR through simple examples. They illustrate the problems of structuring a specification, to motivate their approach [15].

Chapter 7

Axioms and Inference Rules

When representing a logic on a computer, how should we treat inference rules? A rule, given appropriate premises, delivers a conclusion, so LCF represents an inference rule by a *function* from theorems to theorems. Theorems of PPλ are represented by the ML data type *thm*. Axioms and rules of PPλ are predefined identifiers. Each axiom is a theorem; applying rules to axioms computes new theorems.

This chapter lists the axioms, inference rules, and predefined theorems of PPλ. The examples include formal proofs from previous chapters, performed in LCF.

7.1 The representation of inference rules

A rule may hold only if its premises have a certain form; otherwise the corresponding ML function fails, raising exception *rule* of type *string* × *thm list*. The exception includes an error message and the offending premises.

In certain inference rules, the premises do not contain enough information to completely determine the conclusion. The corresponding function takes additional arguments, giving parts of the conclusion or even a formula stating the conclusion itself.

To implement quantifier rules, the abstract syntax functions of Chapter 5 perform substitution and enforce the provisos on eigenvariables. If a proviso is violated, the rule fails.

In the sequent $\Gamma \vdash A$, the assumptions Γ are usually regarded as a set. ML represents a set of PPλ formulae as a list without repetitions. The LCF user need not be concerned with the order of the assumptions in the assumption list. When the assumption A is discharged, all assumptions that are α-convertible to A are also discharged. So the implication introduction rule, *DISCH*, can map $\forall x.P(x), \forall y.P(y) \vdash A$ to $\vdash (\forall z.P(z)) \Longrightarrow A$.

It is clumsy to say 'the ML function implementing the rule' instead of simply 'the rule'. To an LCF user, a rule and its ML implementation are the same thing. The names of the ML functions are not systematic. Instead of *IMP_INTRO* and *IMP_ELIM* we must memorize *DISCH* and *MP*.

Here are examples, slightly simplified, of how the inference rules are implemented.

Example 7.1 Recall the conjunction introduction rule, which is

$$\frac{\Gamma \vdash A \qquad \Delta \vdash B}{\Gamma, \Delta \vdash A \wedge B}$$

Here is the code:

```
fun CONJ thA thB =
    mk_thm (union (hyp thA) (hyp thB),
            mk_conj (concl thA, concl thB));
```

Every primitive rule calls the function *mk_thm*, which makes a theorem with the given hypothesis (assumption list) and formula. Ideally, this function should be the constructor of an ML **abstype** declaration of the type *thm*. Instead, *mk_thm* is implemented in Lisp and then redefined, after it is no longer needed, to hide it from the user. The function *union* forms the union of two assumption lists, suppressing repetitions of assumptions. The functions *hyp* and *concl* are destructors for theorems. They are among the syntax functions described in Chapter 5, which is an essential reference for people who are writing inference rules.

It should be clear that *CONJ* forms a theorem asserting the conjunction of the two formulae under the union of their assumption lists.

Example 7.2 The function *disch* is used to discharge assumptions. It removes, from the list of assumptions *asl*, every assumption that is not α-convertible to the formula A:

```
fun disch (A,asl) = filter (fn B => not (aconv_form A B)) asl;
```

Recall the implication introduction rule:

$$\frac{\Gamma, A \vdash B}{\Gamma \vdash A \Longrightarrow B}$$

The corresponding function discharges A from the hypothesis, and forms the implication:

```
fun DISCH A th = mk_thm(disch (A, hyp th), mk_imp(A, concl th));
```

Example 7.3 One of the most complicated rules is existential elimination:

$$\frac{\Gamma \vdash \exists x.A \qquad \Delta, A[y/x] \vdash B}{\Gamma, \Delta \vdash B} \qquad \textit{provided } y \textit{ is not free in } \exists x.A, \Delta, \textit{ or } B$$

The rule could be implemented as follows. The first premise, $\exists x.A$, is broken into x and A. The formula $A[y/x]$ is discharged from the hypothesis of the second premise. The term y is checked to be a variable[1] and the eigenvariable proviso is checked. If all is well then the theorem is created, otherwise exception *rule* is raised.

```
fun CHOOSE (y,thA) thB =
   let val (x,A) = dest_exists (concl thA)
       val bhyp = disch (subst_form [(y,x)] A, hyp thB)
   in
      if not (is_var y)
      orelse exists (term_freein_form y)
            ((concl thA::hyp thA) @ (concl thB::bhyp))
      then raise rule with ("CHOOSE",[thA,thB])
      else mk_thm (union (hyp thA) bhyp, concl thB)
   end handle syntax => raise rule with ("CHOOSE",[thA,thB]);
```

Exercise 7.1 Write an ML implementation of the conjunction elimination and disjunction introduction rules. (Write the code using the function *mk_fthm* if you want to execute it.)

Exercise 7.2 Write an ML implementation of the disjunction elimination rule.

Exercise 7.3 Write an ML implementation of the universal introduction rule.

7.2   First order logic

The primitive rules are those of the sequent calculus presented in Section 2.12. LCF includes some convenient derived rules of first order logic. A few are wired in for efficiency, but most work by executing the primitive inference rules. If a derived rule is used incorrectly, the exception may come from a primitive rule.

7.2.1   General rules

The assumption axiom scheme maps a formula to the corresponding instance of the axiom:

$ASSUME : form \rightarrow thm$
$$A$$
$$A \vdash A$$

The formula $TRUTH()$ is true:

$TRUTH : thm$
$$TRUTH()$$

---

[1]This check was omitted in early releases of LCF, allowing the proof of $TT \equiv FF$.

The *cut rule* is

$CUT : thm \rightarrow thm \rightarrow thm$

$$\frac{\Gamma \vdash A \qquad \Delta, A \vdash B}{\Gamma, \Delta \vdash B}$$

7.2.2   Conjunction

The derived rules allow a theorem to represent a list of theorems.

Introduction

The introduction rule is

$CONJ : thm \rightarrow thm \rightarrow thm$

$$\frac{\Gamma \vdash A \qquad \Delta \vdash B}{\Gamma, \Delta \vdash A \wedge B}$$

A derived rule for conjoining a list of theorems is

$LIST\_CONJ : (thm\ list) \rightarrow thm$

$$\frac{\Gamma_1 \vdash A_1 \qquad \cdots \qquad \Gamma_{n-1} \vdash A_{n-1} \qquad \Gamma_n \vdash A_n}{\Gamma_1, \ldots, \Gamma_n \vdash A_1 \wedge (\ldots (A_{n-1} \wedge A_n) \ldots)} \qquad where\ n > 0$$

The parentheses in the conclusion emphasize that the conjunction can be uniquely decomposed (via *CONJ_LIST*). The list of premises must be non-empty; one way to guarantee this is to include the axiom *TRUTH*.

Elimination

The elimination rules are

$CONJUNCT1 : thm \rightarrow thm$
$CONJUNCT2 : thm \rightarrow thm$

$$\frac{\Gamma \vdash A \wedge B}{\Gamma \vdash A} \qquad\qquad \frac{\Gamma \vdash A \wedge B}{\Gamma \vdash B}$$

They raise exception *rule* unless the premise is a conjunction.

There are two derived rules for splitting a conjunction. One is an inverse of *LIST_CONJ*:

$CONJ\_LIST : int \rightarrow thm \rightarrow (thm\ list)$
$\qquad\qquad\qquad n$

$$\frac{\Gamma \vdash A_1 \wedge (\ldots (A_{n-1} \wedge A_n) \ldots)}{\Gamma_1 \vdash A_1 \qquad \cdots \qquad \Gamma_{n-1} \vdash A_{n-1} \qquad \Gamma_n \vdash A_n} \qquad where\ n > 0$$

The rule appears to have multiple conclusions: it returns a list of theorems. The number n must be given because A_n may be conjunctive. Together with *LIST_CONJ* this provides a list structure for the type *thm*. A list of related theorems can be made into a single theorem; the component theorems can be gotten back *as theorems*. The structural induction commands join related axioms in this way.

The other derived rule splits a theorem into all of its conjuncts, regardless of nesting. It is an inverse to *LIST_CONJ* whenever none of the A_i are conjunctions:

$CONJUNCTS : thm \rightarrow (thm\ list)$

$$\frac{\Gamma \vdash A_1 \wedge \ldots \wedge A_n}{\Gamma \vdash A_1 \quad \ldots \quad \Gamma \vdash A_n} \qquad where\ n > 0$$

7.2.3 Disjunction

Introduction

The introduction rules form the disjunction of the premise with another formula. That formula is passed as an argument to the ML function:

$DISJ1 : thm \rightarrow form \rightarrow thm$
$$B$$
$DISJ2 : form \rightarrow thm \rightarrow thm$
$$A$$

$$\frac{\Gamma \vdash A}{\Gamma \vdash A \vee B} \qquad\qquad \frac{\Gamma \vdash B}{\Gamma \vdash A \vee B}$$

Elimination

The elimination rule is

$DISJ\_CASES : thm \rightarrow thm \rightarrow thm \rightarrow thm$
$$\frac{\Gamma \vdash A \vee B \qquad \Delta, A \vdash C \qquad \Theta, B \vdash C}{\Gamma, \Delta, \Theta \vdash C}$$

It raises exception *rule* unless the first premise is a disjunction.

There are two strange derived rules. The rule *DISJ_IMP* is used for converting a theorem like $q \equiv \bot \vee q \equiv TT \vee q \equiv FF$ to $q \not\equiv \bot \Longrightarrow q \equiv TT \vee q \equiv FF$:

$DISJ\_IMP : thm \rightarrow thm$
$$\frac{\Gamma \vdash A \vee B}{\Gamma \vdash \neg A \Longrightarrow B}$$

$DISJ\_CASES\_UNION : thm \rightarrow thm \rightarrow thm \rightarrow thm$
$$\frac{\Gamma \vdash A \vee B \qquad \Delta, A \vdash C \qquad \Theta, B \vdash D}{\Gamma, \Delta, \Theta \vdash C \vee D}$$

7.2.4   Implication

There are derived rules to turn a hypothetical theorem into an absolute one and vice versa, and there are generalizations of Modus Ponens.

Introduction

The introduction rule is called the *discharge rule* because it discharges an assumption to form an implication. The assumption to be discharged is passed as an argument:

$DISCH : form \rightarrow thm \rightarrow thm$
                  A

$$\frac{\Gamma, A \vdash B}{\Gamma \vdash A \Longrightarrow B}$$

Here is a derived rule to discharge all hypotheses:

$DISCH\_ALL : thm \rightarrow thm$

$$\frac{A_1, \ldots, A_n \vdash B}{\vdash A_n \Longrightarrow \ldots \Longrightarrow A_1 \Longrightarrow B}$$

Elimination

The elimination rule, Modus Ponens, is

$MP : thm \rightarrow thm \rightarrow thm$

$$\frac{\Gamma \vdash A \Longrightarrow B \qquad \Delta \vdash A}{\Gamma, \Delta \vdash B}$$

It raises exception *rule* unless the first premise is an implication whose antecedent is the other premise.

A derived rule, Matching Modus Ponens, instantiates the implication:

$MATCH\_MP : thm \rightarrow thm \rightarrow thm$

$$\frac{\Gamma \vdash \forall x_1 \ldots x_n. A \Longrightarrow B \qquad \Theta \vdash A[\sigma_1/\alpha_1, \ldots, \sigma_m/\alpha_m][t_1/x_1, \ldots, t_n/x_n]}{\Gamma, \Theta \vdash B[\sigma_1/\alpha_1, \ldots, \sigma_m/\alpha_m][t_1/x_1, \ldots, t_n/x_n]}$$

If the second premise is an instance of A, then the conclusion is the corresponding instance of B; otherwise exception *rule* is raised. The types $\sigma_1, \ldots, \sigma_m$ and terms $t_1, \ldots, t_n$ are computed by pattern matching via *form_match*. Unification is not used; the second premise is not instantiated.

A derived rule for repeated Modus Ponens is

LIST_MP : (*thm list*) → *thm* → *thm*

$$\frac{\Gamma_1 \vdash A_1 \quad \cdots \quad \Gamma_n \vdash A_n \qquad \Delta \vdash A_1 \Longrightarrow \cdots \Longrightarrow A_n \Longrightarrow B}{\Gamma_1, \ldots, \Gamma_n, \Delta \vdash B}$$

'Undischarge' means moving the antecedent of an implication to the assumption list. We can undischarge one antecedent or all of them:

UNDISCH : *thm* → *thm*

$$\frac{\Gamma \vdash A \Longrightarrow B}{\Gamma, A \vdash B}$$

UNDISCH_ALL : *thm* → *thm*

$$\frac{\Gamma \vdash A_1 \Longrightarrow \cdots \Longrightarrow A_n \Longrightarrow B}{\Gamma, A_1, \ldots, A_n \vdash B}$$

7.2.5   Negation

The formula $\neg B$ abbreviates $B \Longrightarrow \Lambda$, so negation rules are special cases of implication rules. A practical advantage: ML proof procedures for implication also handle negation. Recall that Λ is written `FALSITY()` in ASCII.

Introduction

Negation introduction is

DISCH : *form* → *thm* → *thm*
        B

$$\frac{\Gamma, B \vdash \Lambda}{\Gamma \vdash \neg B}$$

Elimination

Negation elimination is

MP : *thm* → *thm* → *thm*

$$\frac{\Gamma \vdash \neg B \qquad \Delta \vdash B}{\Gamma, \Delta \vdash \Lambda}$$

A derived rule finds the contrapositive of an implication:

CONTRAPOS : *thm* → *thm*

$$\frac{\Gamma \vdash A \Longrightarrow B}{\Gamma \vdash \neg B \Longrightarrow \neg A}$$

Contradiction

The contradiction rules, from a proof of Λ, conclude an arbitrary formula, passed as an argument. The classical contradiction rule is

$CCONTR : form \rightarrow thm \rightarrow thm$
             B

$$\frac{\Gamma, \neg B \vdash \Lambda}{\Gamma \vdash B}$$

You can hide this rule by redeclaring `val CCONTR = ()` for experiments with intuitionistic deduction. However, PPλ's formalization of domain theory is classical.

The intuitionistic contradiction rule is

$CONTR : form \rightarrow thm \rightarrow thm$
            B

$$\frac{\Gamma \vdash \Lambda}{\Gamma \vdash B}$$

7.2.6   Bi-implication

The formula $A \iff B$ is logically equivalent to $(A \implies B) \land (B \implies A)$. LCF does not unfold it to avoid duplicating A and B. The rules $CONJ\_IFF$ and IFF_CONJ map between the two forms. They are not orthodox natural deduction rules because they refer two different connectives.

The introduction rule is

$CONJ\_IFF : thm \rightarrow thm$

$$\frac{\Gamma \vdash (A \implies B) \land (B \implies A)}{\Gamma \vdash A \iff B}$$

The elimination rule is

$IFF\_CONJ : thm \rightarrow thm$

$$\frac{\Gamma \vdash A \iff B}{\Gamma \vdash (A \implies B) \land (B \implies A)}$$

7.2.7   Universal quantifier

Introduction

The introduction rule *generalizes* its premise over the variable x, an argument of the function:

GEN : *term* → *thm* → *thm*
    x

$$\frac{\Gamma \vdash A}{\Gamma \vdash \forall x.A} \qquad provided\ x\ is\ not\ free\ in\ \Gamma$$

It raises exception *rule* unless the term x is a variable and the proviso is satisfied. The rule scans the assumption list for occurrences of x.

A derived introduction rule generalizes a theorem over all possible variables:

GEN_ALL : *thm* → *thm*

$$\frac{\Gamma \vdash A}{\Gamma \vdash \forall x_1 \ldots x_n.A}$$

The variables $x_1, \ldots, x_n$ all those that are free in A but not in Γ.

Elimination

The elimination rule *specializes* its universal premise to the term t:

SPEC : *term* → *thm* → *thm*
    t

$$\frac{\Gamma \vdash \forall x.A}{\Gamma \vdash A[t/x]}$$

It raises exception *rule* unless

- The premise is universally quantified.

- The type of t equals that of x.

An iterative version, for specialization over a list of terms, is

SPECL : *term list* → *thm* → *thm*
    $[t_1, \ldots, t_n]$

$$\frac{\Gamma \vdash \forall x_1 \ldots x_n.A}{\Gamma \vdash A[t_1/x_1, \ldots, t_n/x_n]}$$

To strip the outer universal quantifiers from a theorem, use the derived rule

SPEC_ALL : *thm* → *thm*

$$\frac{\Gamma \vdash \forall x_1 \ldots x_n.A}{\Gamma \vdash A[x_1'/x_1, \ldots, x_n'/x_n]}$$

For each x_i it chooses a variant x_i' that is not free in Γ. The conclusion is as general as the premise.

7.2.8   Existential quantifier

Introduction

The introduction rule takes an argument stating the conclusion. Not every free occurrence of t in $A[t/x]$ need be replaced by x:

$EXISTS : (form \times term) \rightarrow thm \rightarrow thm$
$\qquad\quad \exists x.A \qquad t$

$$\frac{\Gamma \vdash A[t/x]}{\Gamma \vdash \exists x.A}$$

It raises exception *rule* unless

- The term t has the same type as x.

- If the stated conclusion is $\exists x.A$, then the premise is $A[t/x]$.

Elimination

The elimination rule takes the eigenvariable y as an argument. The name *CHOOSE* suggests choosing a value for which the formula is true.

$CHOOSE : (term \times thm) \rightarrow thm \rightarrow thm$
$\qquad\qquad\quad y$

$$\frac{\Gamma \vdash \exists x.A \qquad \Delta, A[y/x] \vdash B}{\Gamma, \Delta \vdash B} \qquad provided\ y\ is\ not\ free\ in\ \exists x.A,\ \Delta,\ or\ B$$

It raises exception *rule* unless

- y is a variable with the same type as x.

- The proviso is satisfied.

- The first premise is existentially quantified.

Example 7.4 Why does the function *EXISTS* require so much information? The premise $TT \equiv TT$ allows several distinct conclusions, including $p \equiv p$ and $p \equiv TT$. The function *REFL*, the reflexivity axiom scheme, is discussed below.

```
! val thtt = REFL 'TT';
- val thtt = |-'TT == TT' : thm

! EXISTS ('?p. p==p', 'TT') thtt;
- it = |-'?p. p == p' : thm

! EXISTS ('?p. p==TT', 'TT') thtt;
- it = |-'?p. p == TT' : thm
```

Exercise 7.4 What other conclusions follow from $TT \equiv TT$ by existential introduction?

7.2.9 Substitution

Note carefully the specification of each substitution function. The argument order is not systematic. Some take replacement pairs of the form (new, old), others take (old, new).

Simultaneous substitution

A general rule for simultaneous substitution is

$$SUBST : (\;thm \quad \times term)\,list \rightarrow form \rightarrow thm \rightarrow thm$$
$$t_i \equiv u_i \qquad x_i \qquad\qquad A$$

$$\frac{\Gamma_1 \vdash t_1 \equiv u_1 \quad \cdots \quad \Gamma_n \vdash t_n \equiv u_n \quad \Delta \vdash A[t_1/x_1, \ldots, t_n/x_n]}{\Gamma_1, \ldots, \Gamma_n, \Delta \vdash A[u_1/x_1, \ldots, u_n/x_n]}$$

It raises exception *rule* unless the type of x_i equals that of t_i for $i = 1, \ldots, n$. The formula A specifies the substitution; the variables $x_1, \ldots, x_n$ mark the places where substitution should occur. Replacement pairs have the form $old \equiv new$.

Two rules derived from *SUBST* are easier to use:

$$SUBS : (\;thm \quad list) \rightarrow thm \rightarrow thm$$
$$t_i \equiv u_i$$
$$SUBS\_OCCS : ((int\;list) \times \quad thm\;)\,list \rightarrow thm \rightarrow thm$$
$$o_i \qquad\quad t_i \equiv u_i$$

$$\frac{\Gamma_1 \vdash t_1 \equiv u_1 \quad \cdots \quad \Gamma_n \vdash t_n \equiv u_n \quad \Delta \vdash A}{\Gamma_1, \ldots, \Gamma_n, \Delta \vdash A[u_1/t_1, \ldots, u_n/t_n]}$$

SUBS replaces all free occurrences of t_i by u_i. *SUBS_OCCS* replaces just those free occurrences specified in the list o_i, for $i = 1, \ldots, n$. (Section 5.5 describes the ML functions for substitution.)

Substitution rules are efficient but formally redundant. The derived rules *MK_ABS* and *MK_COMB* construct equal abstractions and combinations. Indeed, rewriting is based on those rules rather than substitution.

Instantiation of types

$$INST\_TYPE : (type \times type)\,list \rightarrow thm \rightarrow thm$$
$$\tau_i \qquad\quad \alpha_i$$

$$\frac{\Gamma \vdash A}{\Gamma \vdash A[\tau_1/\alpha_1, \ldots, \tau_n/\alpha_n]} \qquad provided\ no\ \alpha_i\ occurs\ in\ \Gamma$$

It raises exception *rule* unless

- The $\alpha_1, \ldots, \alpha_n$ are type variables,

- The proviso is satisfied.

This rule is necessary in order to make use of polymorphic theorems like *MINIMAL* below. Replacement pairs have the form (new, old).

Instantiation of terms

This rule amounts to universal introduction followed by universal elimination. Replacement pairs have the form (new, old).

$$INST : (term \times term)\, list \rightarrow thm \rightarrow thm$$

$$\begin{array}{cc} t_i & x_i \end{array}$$

$$\dfrac{\Gamma \vdash A}{\Gamma \vdash A[t_1/x_1, \ldots, t_n/x_n]} \qquad provided\ no\ x_i\ occurs\ in\ \Gamma$$

It raises exception *rule* unless

- The terms $x_1, \ldots, x_n$ are variables,

- The proviso is satisfied.

7.2.10   Canonical forms

$$IMP\_CANON : thm \rightarrow thm\ list$$

This function puts a theorem into a canonical form. The conjunction of the resulting list is logically equivalent to the original theorem. The general effect is to strip off outer universal quantifiers, break apart conjunctions, and expand negated disjunctions. Each of these are converted to implications as far as possible: each element of the result list has the form $A_1 \Longrightarrow \cdots \Longrightarrow A_n \Longrightarrow B$. The rewriting functions use *IMP_CANON* to process theorems intended as rewrite rules (Chapter 9).

Here is a precise description. Bear in mind that the argument in a recursive call is *proved* from the original argument.

- For $A \wedge B$ it calls itself on A and B, appending the resulting lists.

- For $(A \wedge B) \Longrightarrow C$ it calls itself on $A \Longrightarrow (B \Longrightarrow C)$.

- For $(A \vee B) \Longrightarrow C$ it calls itself on $A \Longrightarrow C$ and $B \Longrightarrow C$, appending the resulting lists.

- For $(\exists x.A(x)) \Longrightarrow B$ it chooses a variant x' and calls itself on $A(x') \Longrightarrow B$.

- For $\forall x.A(x)$ it chooses a variant x' and calls itself on $A(x')$.

- For other implications $A \Longrightarrow B$, if the canonical form of the theorem $A \vdash B$ is the list $[A \vdash B_1, \ldots, A \vdash B_n]$, then *IMP_CANON* returns $[A \Longrightarrow B_1, \ldots, A \Longrightarrow B_n]$.

- Other formulae are returned unchanged.

FCONV_CANON : $thm \rightarrow thm$

This puts a theorem into a canonical form for formula rewriting (Chapter 9). It implements the rule

$$\frac{\Gamma \vdash A_1 \Longrightarrow \cdots \Longrightarrow A_n \Longrightarrow B}{\Gamma \vdash A_1 \Longrightarrow \cdots \Longrightarrow A_n \Longrightarrow B'}$$

where B' depends upon B as follows:

- If B is $C \Longleftrightarrow D$ then so is B'.

- If B is a predicate $P(t)$ — other than $TRUTH()$, $FALSITY()$, or $t_1 \equiv t_2$ — then B' is $P(t) \Longleftrightarrow TRUTH()$.

- If B is a negated predicate $\neg P(t)$ then B' is $P(t) \Longleftrightarrow FALSITY()$.

- Exception *rule* is raised in other cases.

7.2.11   Construction of equivalent formulae

These derived rules justify the rewriting of formulae. To rewrite $A \vee C$, rewrite A to get B and C to get D. The result is $B \vee D$.

MK_CONJ : $(thm \times thm) \rightarrow thm$

$$\frac{\Gamma \vdash A \Longleftrightarrow B \qquad \Delta, A, B \vdash C \Longleftrightarrow D}{\Gamma, \Delta \vdash (A \wedge C) \Longleftrightarrow (B \wedge D)}$$

To rewrite $A \wedge C$, rewrite A to get B, then assume that these are true when rewriting C to D. The result is $B \wedge D$. The assumptions discharged by *MK_CONJ* (and *MK_IMP*) are the *local assumptions* A and B. In practice, only B is used: it is a simplified form of A.

MK_DISJ : $(thm \times thm) \rightarrow thm$

$$\frac{\Gamma \vdash A \Longleftrightarrow B \qquad \Delta \vdash C \Longleftrightarrow D}{\Gamma, \Delta \vdash (A \vee C) \Longleftrightarrow (B \vee D)}$$

MK_IMP : $(thm \times thm) \rightarrow thm$

$$\frac{\Gamma \vdash A \Longleftrightarrow B \qquad \Delta, A, B \vdash C \Longleftrightarrow D}{\Gamma, \Delta \vdash (A \Longrightarrow C) \Longleftrightarrow (B \Longrightarrow D)}$$

$MK\_IFF : (thm \times thm) \to thm$

$$\frac{\Gamma \vdash A \iff B \qquad \Delta \vdash C \iff D}{\Gamma, \Delta \vdash (A \iff C) \iff (B \iff D)}$$

$MK\_PRED : (string \times thm) \to thm$
$$\qquad\qquad P$$

$$\frac{\Gamma \vdash t \equiv u}{\Gamma \vdash P(t) \iff P(u)}$$

$MK\_FORALL : thm \to thm$

$$\frac{\Gamma \vdash \forall x.\,(A \iff B)}{\Gamma \vdash (\forall x.\,A) \iff (\forall x.\,B)}$$

$MK\_EXISTS : thm \to thm$

$$\frac{\Gamma \vdash \forall x.\,(A \iff B)}{\Gamma \vdash (\exists x.\,A) \iff (\exists x.\,B)}$$

Note that the premise contains a *universal* quantifier. It would be more natural to have an eigenvariable in the premise.

7.3   Domain theory

The formalization of domain theory is based on a set of axioms. The axioms and fundamental theorems are bound to ML identifiers of type *thm*. The same identifier is the name of the axiom or theorem in the standard theory *PPLAMB*.

The theorems, and various rules, are derived from the axioms. Derived rules can be more convenient than axioms: they match terms and instantiate types automatically. In some cases, a single ML function implements several related rules, involving various combinations of $\equiv$ and $\sqsubseteq$. The premises determine which rule to apply.

To emphasize precisely what is assumed, each axiom is marked with an asterisk (*). The theory is developed in Chapters 3 and 4.

7.3.1   Equivalence and inequivalence

The partial ordering $\sqsubseteq$ is reflexive, anti-symmetric, and transitive:

$LESS\_REFL^*$ $\vdash \forall x.\ x \sqsubseteq x$

$LESS\_ANTI\_SYM^*$ $\vdash \forall xy.\ x \sqsubseteq y \land y \sqsubseteq x \implies x \equiv y$

$LESS\_TRANS^*$ $\vdash \forall xyz.\ x \sqsubseteq y \land y \sqsubseteq z \implies x \sqsubseteq z$

The relation of equivalence, $\equiv$, is reflexive, symmetric, and transitive:

EQ_REFL	$\vdash \forall x.\ x \equiv x$
EQ_SYM	$\vdash \forall xy.\ x \equiv y \Longrightarrow y \equiv x$
EQ_TRANS	$\vdash \forall xyz.\ x \equiv y \wedge y \equiv z \Longrightarrow x \equiv z$

The derived rules for the reflexive, symmetric, and transitive properties are

$REFL : term \rightarrow thm$

$$t$$

$$\vdash t \equiv t$$

$SYM : thm \rightarrow thm$

$$\frac{\Gamma \vdash t \equiv u}{\Gamma \vdash u \equiv t}$$

$TRANS : thm \times thm \rightarrow thm$ (infix)

$$\frac{\Gamma \vdash t \sqsubseteq u \qquad \Delta \vdash u \sqsubseteq v}{\Gamma, \Delta \vdash t \sqsubseteq v} \qquad \frac{\Gamma \vdash t \equiv u \qquad \Delta \vdash u \sqsubseteq v}{\Gamma, \Delta \vdash t \sqsubseteq v}$$

$$\frac{\Gamma \vdash t \sqsubseteq u \qquad \Delta \vdash u \equiv v}{\Gamma, \Delta \vdash t \sqsubseteq v} \qquad \frac{\Gamma \vdash t \equiv u \qquad \Delta \vdash u \equiv v}{\Gamma, \Delta \vdash t \equiv v}$$

The formula $t \equiv u$ is equivalent to $t \sqsubseteq u \wedge u \sqsubseteq t$ by the reflexive and anti-symmetric laws. Derived rules for the *analysis* and *synthesis* of an equivalence are

$ANAL : thm \rightarrow thm$

$$\frac{\Gamma \vdash t \equiv u}{\Gamma \vdash t \sqsubseteq u \wedge u \sqsubseteq t}$$

$SYNTH : thm \rightarrow thm$

$$\frac{\Gamma \vdash t \sqsubseteq u \wedge u \sqsubseteq t}{\Gamma \vdash t \equiv u}$$

7.3.2 Extensionality of functions

The axiom for extensionality of functions under $\sqsubseteq$ is

LESS_EXT* $\qquad \vdash \forall fg.\ (\forall x.fx \sqsubseteq gx) \Longrightarrow f \sqsubseteq g$

It has a remarkable number of consequences. The most obvious is extensionality of functions under $\equiv$:

EQ_EXT $\qquad \vdash \forall fg.\ (\forall x.fx \equiv gx) \Longrightarrow f \equiv g$

A derived rule for both $\sqsubseteq$ and $\equiv$ is

$EXT : thm \rightarrow thm$

$$\frac{\Gamma \vdash \forall x.fx \sqsubseteq gx}{\Gamma \vdash f \sqsubseteq g} \qquad \frac{\Gamma \vdash \forall x.fx \equiv gx}{\Gamma \vdash f \equiv g}$$

The completely undefined function is the least element:

MIN_COMB $\vdash \forall x. \perp x \equiv \perp$

MIN_ABS $\vdash \lambda x. \perp \equiv \perp$

Another result is that η-conversion is valid:

ETA_EQ $\vdash \forall f. (\lambda x. fx) \equiv f$

Two derived rules concern the construction of an abstraction:

$MK\_ABS : thm \to thm$

$$\frac{\Gamma \vdash \forall x.\, u \sqsubseteq v}{\Gamma \vdash \lambda x. u \sqsubseteq \lambda x. v} \qquad\qquad \frac{\Gamma \vdash \forall x.\, u \equiv v}{\Gamma \vdash \lambda x. u \equiv \lambda x. v}$$

$HALF\_MK\_ABS : thm \to thm$

$$\frac{\Gamma \vdash \forall x.\, fx \sqsubseteq t}{\Gamma \vdash f \sqsubseteq \lambda x. t} \qquad\qquad \frac{\Gamma \vdash \forall x.\, fx \equiv t}{\Gamma \vdash f \equiv \lambda x. t}$$

7.3.3   Monotonicity of functions

The monotonicity of function application is expressed as follows:

$MONO*$ $\vdash \forall fgxy.\ f \sqsubseteq g \wedge x \sqsubseteq y \implies fx \sqsubseteq gy$

It implies two rules for the construction of combinations. The rules MK_ABS and MK_COMB justify the rewriting of terms.

$MK\_COMB : (thm \times thm) \to thm$

$$\frac{\Gamma \vdash f \equiv g \qquad \Delta \vdash t \equiv u}{\Gamma, \Delta \vdash ft \equiv gu}$$

$LE\_MK\_COMB : (thm \times thm) \to thm$

$$\frac{\Gamma \vdash f \sqsubseteq g \qquad \Delta \vdash t \sqsubseteq u}{\Gamma, \Delta \vdash ft \sqsubseteq gu} \qquad\qquad \frac{\Gamma \vdash f \equiv g \qquad \Delta \vdash t \sqsubseteq u}{\Gamma, \Delta \vdash ft \sqsubseteq gu}$$

$$\frac{\Gamma \vdash f \sqsubseteq g \qquad \Delta \vdash t \equiv u}{\Gamma, \Delta \vdash ft \sqsubseteq gu} \qquad\qquad \frac{\Gamma \vdash f \equiv g \qquad \Delta \vdash t \equiv u}{\Gamma, \Delta \vdash ft \equiv gu}$$

Two related derived rules allow the application of a term to a theorem, and the application of a theorem to a term:

$AP\_TERM : term \to thm \to thm$
$$t$$

$$\frac{\Gamma \vdash u \sqsubseteq v}{\Gamma \vdash tu \sqsubseteq tv} \qquad\qquad \frac{\Gamma \vdash u \equiv v}{\Gamma \vdash tu \equiv tv}$$

$AP\_THM : thm \to term \to thm$
$$t$$

$$\frac{\Gamma \vdash u \sqsubseteq v}{\Gamma \vdash ut \sqsubseteq vt} \qquad\qquad \frac{\Gamma \vdash u \equiv v}{\Gamma \vdash ut \equiv vt}$$

7.3.4 Other properites of functions

The β-conversion axiom scheme is a represented by a function that maps a term to the corresponding instance of the axiom.

$$BETA\_CONV* : \quad term \; \to \; thm$$
$$(\lambda x.t)u$$

$$\vdash (\lambda x.t)u \equiv t[u/x]$$

It raises exception *general* unless the argument has the form $(\lambda x.t)u$.

The axiom scheme for α-conversion is

$$ALPHA\_CONV : term \; \to \quad term \quad \to thm$$
$$x \qquad \lambda y.f(y)$$

$$\vdash \lambda y.f(y) \equiv \lambda x.f(x)$$

7.3.5 Standard types and constants

The axiom asserting the minimality of $\perp$ is

$$MINIMAL* \qquad \vdash \forall x. \perp \sqsubseteq x$$

Two derived rules are *MIN* and *LESS_UU_RULE*:

$$MIN : term \to thm$$
$$t$$

$$\vdash \perp \sqsubseteq t$$

$$LESS\_UU\_RULE : thm \to thm$$

$$\frac{\Gamma \vdash t \sqsubseteq \perp}{\Gamma \vdash t \equiv \perp}$$

Fixed points

The following axiom expresses that $FIX(f)$ is *a* fixed point; induction expresses that it is the *least* one.

$$FIX\_EQ* \qquad \vdash \forall f. \; f(FIX \; f) \equiv FIX \; f$$

Truth values

Every value of type tr is either TT, FF, or $\perp$. The values TT and FF are incomparable and defined.

$$TR\_CASES* \qquad \vdash \forall p : tr. \; p \equiv \perp \quad \vee \quad p \equiv TT \quad \vee \quad p \equiv FF$$

$TR\_LESS\_DISTINCT^* \vdash \neg(TT \sqsubseteq FF) \quad \wedge \quad \neg(FF \sqsubseteq TT) \quad \wedge$
$$\neg(TT \sqsubseteq \bot) \quad \wedge \quad \neg(FF \sqsubseteq \bot)$$

$TR\_EQ\_DISTINCT \quad \vdash \neg(TT \equiv FF) \quad \wedge \quad \neg(FF \equiv TT) \quad \wedge$
$$\neg(TT \equiv \bot) \quad \wedge \quad \neg(\bot \equiv TT) \quad \wedge$$
$$\neg(FF \equiv \bot) \quad \wedge \quad \neg(\bot \equiv FF)$$

Conditional expressions satisfy the equations

$COND\_CLAUSES^* \quad \vdash \forall xy. \ \bot \Rightarrow x \mid y \equiv \bot \quad \wedge$
$$TT \Rightarrow x \mid y \equiv x \quad \wedge$$
$$FF \Rightarrow x \mid y \equiv y$$

Ordered pairs

Every element of a Cartesian product type $\sigma \times \tau$ is a pair (x, y) for unique components x and y. The functions FST and SND return the components. In particular, $(\bot, \bot)$ equals $\bot$ while $(TT, \bot)$ does not equal $\bot$.

$MK\_PAIR^* \qquad\qquad \vdash \forall z : \alpha \times \beta. \ (FST \ z, SND \ z) \equiv z$

$FST\_PAIR^* \qquad\qquad \vdash \forall xy. \ FST(x, y) \equiv x$
$SND\_PAIR^* \qquad\qquad \vdash \forall xy. \ SND(x, y) \equiv y$

The type *void*

The type *void* contains only the element *bot*, so $() \equiv \bot$.

$VOID\_CASES^* \qquad\qquad \vdash \forall x : void. \ x \equiv \bot$

Example 7.5 The axioms are expressed so that they may be easily broken apart using rules like *CONJUNCTS* and *IMP_CANON*.

```
! CONJUNCTS TR_EQ_DISTINCT;
- it =
[|-'~ TT == FF',
 |-'~ FF == TT',
 |-'~ TT == UU',
 |-'~ UU == TT',
 |-'~ FF == UU',
 |-'~ UU == FF'] : thm list


! SPEC_ALL LESS_TRANS;
- it = |-'x << y  /\  y << z   ==>   x << z' : thm


! IMP_CANON COND_CLAUSES;
```

```
- it =
[|-'(UU => x | y) == UU',
 |-'(TT => x | y) == x',
 |-'(FF => x | y) == y']
: thm list
```

7.3.6   Fixed point induction

Fixed point induction on a variable x and formula A is sound if A is *chain-complete* or *admissible* in x, as mentioned in Section 3.6. The induction rule accepts the theorems $B_1, \ldots, B_m$, each stating a property of a type, for use in the admissibility test. For lack of space these additional premises are written above the rule:

$$INDUCT :\quad term\ list\quad \rightarrow\quad thm\ list\quad \rightarrow (thm \times thm) \rightarrow thm$$
$$[f_1, \ldots, f_n]\quad [B_1, \ldots, B_m]$$

$$\frac{\Gamma_1 \vdash B_1 \quad \cdots \quad \Gamma_m \vdash B_m}{\Gamma_1, \ldots, \Gamma_m, \Delta, \Theta \vdash A[\bot/x_1, \ldots, \bot/x_n] \qquad \Theta \vdash \forall x_1 \ldots x_n.\ A \Longrightarrow A[f_1 x_1/x_1, \ldots, f_n x_n/x_n]}{\Gamma_1, \ldots, \Gamma_m, \Delta, \Theta \vdash A[FIX\ f_1/x_1, \ldots, FIX\ f_n/x_n]}$$

It raises exception *rule* unless induction is admissible.

A complete, and technical, description follows; if you prefer to skip it, note that every induction formula is chain-complete that does not involve implication, existential quantification, or user-defined predicates. For every term t and formula A, if A is chain-complete in x then so are

$$t \not\equiv \bot \qquad\qquad t \not\equiv \bot \Longrightarrow A \qquad\qquad t \equiv TT \Longrightarrow A$$

Type properties

A *finite* type is one that has a finite number of elements. A *chain-finite* type is one with no infinite ascending chains, namely distinct elements $a_0 \sqsubseteq a_1 \sqsubseteq a_2 \ldots .$[2] LCF recognizes certain theorems that state that a type is finite or chain-finite. The theorem

$$\vdash \forall x : \sigma.\ x \equiv c_1 \vee \cdots \vee x \equiv c_n$$

where the c_i are constant symbols, states that the type σ is finite and enumerates its elements. The theorem

$$\vdash \forall x_1. \cdots \forall x_n : \sigma.\ x_1 \sqsubseteq x_2 \wedge \cdots \wedge x_{n-1} \sqsubseteq x_n \Longrightarrow \bot \equiv x_1 \vee x_1 \equiv x_2 \vee \cdots \vee x_{n-1} \equiv x_n$$

states that the type σ is chain-finite. When $n = 2$ this is the familiar property of *flatness*:

$$\vdash \forall x.\forall y : \sigma.\ x \sqsubseteq y \Longrightarrow \bot \equiv x \vee x \equiv y$$

---

[2]The Edinburgh LCF manual [41, page 77] calls these *easy* types.

LCF knows that a finite type is also chain-finite, and that certain type constructors preserve these properties. If σ and τ are finite then so are $\sigma \times \tau$ and $\sigma \rightarrow \tau$. If v and v' are chain-finite then so are $v \times v'$ and $\sigma \rightarrow v$.

Chain-complete formulae

LCF recognizes that a formula is chain-complete by its construction from smaller formulae. Sometimes a subformula must be chain-complete, sometimes its negation must be.

The formulae $t \sqsubseteq u$ and $t \equiv u$ are chain-complete in x, as are $t \not\equiv \bot$ and $\bot \not\equiv t$. Furthermore $t \not\sqsubseteq u$ is chain-complete in x if x is not free in u. The formula A is chain-complete in x if x is not free in A or if the type of x is chain-finite.

To see how to construct chain-complete formulae, let A, B, A', B' be formulae where A, B are chain-complete (in x) and $\neg A'$, $\neg B'$ are chain-complete.

Substitution preserves chain-completeness: $A[t/x]$ is chain-complete in each of the free variables of t. For example, $A[f(y)/x]$ is chain-complete in f and y. So

> *The formula A is chain-complete in x if every free occurrence of x is contained within a free occurrence of a term of chain-finite type.*

Several of the connectives preserve chain-completeness: the formulae

$$A \wedge B \qquad\qquad A \vee B \qquad\qquad A' \Longrightarrow B \qquad\qquad \forall y.A$$

are chain-complete. Furthermore $\exists z.A$ is chain-complete in x if z has finite type: the quantification is equivalent to a disjunction.

Also chain-complete in x are the negated formulae

$$\neg(A' \wedge B') \qquad\qquad \neg(A' \vee B') \qquad\qquad \neg(A \Longrightarrow B') \qquad\qquad \neg(\exists y.A')$$

Furthermore $\neg(\forall z.A)$ is chain-complete in x if z has finite type: the quantification is equivalent to a conjunction.

If A, B, $\neg A$, $\neg B$ are chain-complete then so are $A \Longleftrightarrow B$ and $\neg(A \Longleftrightarrow B)$.

7.4   Forwards proof and derived rules

To see how inference works in LCF, let us look again at examples from Chapter 2. Applying rules to axioms, and other rules to the results, yields forwards proof. Abstracting such a proof over some of its types, terms, and formulae yields an ML function: a derived rule. Conversely, an obvious way to understand a derived rule is to apply its steps to particular formulae.

Example 7.6 Recall that conjunction is commutative:

$$\frac{\Gamma \vdash A \wedge B}{\Gamma \vdash B \wedge A}$$

Here is an ML derivation of this rule:

```
fun CC ABth =
    let val Ath = CONJUNCT1 ABth
        and Bth = CONJUNCT2 ABth
    in  CONJ Bth Ath  end;
```

The argument ABth should be the theorem $\Gamma \vdash A \wedge B$. It is split into the two theorems $\Gamma \vdash A$ and $\Gamma \vdash B$, which are then conjoined in reverse order to give $\Gamma \vdash B \wedge A$. To test it we must supply a particular theorem of the form $\Gamma \vdash A \wedge B$. The easiest way is by assumption:

```
- val CC = fn : (thm -> thm)
```

```
! CC (ASSUME 'x==y /\ z==TT');
- it = .|-'z == TT  /\  x == y' : thm
```

Recall that LCF prints a dot for each assumption of a theorem. The above theorem is $z \equiv TT \wedge x \equiv y$ under an unknown assumption. Use the function *hyp* to obtain the assumption list of a theorem:

```
! hyp it;
- it = ['x == y  /\  z == TT'] : form list
```

We can observe the execution of CC by performing each step at top level:

```
! val ABth = ASSUME 'x==y /\ z==TT';
- val ABth = .|-'x == y  /\  z == TT' : thm
```

```
! val Ath = CONJUNCT1 ABth;
- val Ath = .|-'x == y' : thm
```

```
! val Bth = CONJUNCT2 ABth;
- val Bth = .|-'z == TT' : thm
```

```
! CONJ Bth Ath;
- it = .|-'z == TT  /\  x == y' : thm
```

Example 7.7 Part of a distributive law involving $\wedge$ and $\vee$ is the derived rule

$$\frac{\Gamma \vdash (A \wedge B) \vee C}{\Gamma \vdash A \vee C}$$

The ML derivation precisely follows the derivation in Example 2.3. The proof is a nest of function calls, one call for each instance of a rule.

```
fun DIST ABCth =
    let val (AB, C) = dest_disj (concl ABCth);
        val (A, B)  = dest_conj AB
    in  DISJ_CASES ABCth (DISJ1 (CONJUNCT1 (ASSUME AB)) C)
                         (DISJ2 A (ASSUME C))
    end;
```

The formulae AB, C, A, and B are extracted from the premise, $(A \wedge B) \vee C$, for use as arguments of the rules. An ML variable holding a PPλ expression is a meta variable in the same sense that A is a meta variable in this English text. ML is the meta language of LCF while English is the meta language of this book.

Let us test the ML version of the rule.

```
- val DIST = fn : (thm -> thm)
```

```
! DIST (ASSUME '(p == (TT,FF) /\ q==p) \/ FST(p) == SND(q)');
- it = .|-'p == (TT,FF)  \/  FST p == SND q' : thm
```

For a step by step execution we can break up the nest of function calls, evaluating various subexpressions to construct the proof. Recall that the predefined identifier *it* refers to the last value computed at top level:

```
! val ABCth = ASSUME '(p == (TT,FF) /\ q==p) \/ FST(p) == SND(q)';
- val ABCth = .|-'p == (TT,FF) /\ q == p \/ FST p == SND q' : thm
```

```
! val (AB, C) = dest_disj (concl ABCth);
- val AB = 'p == (TT,FF)  /\  q == p' : form
- val C = 'FST p == SND q' : form
```

```
! val (A, B)  = dest_conj AB;
- val A = 'p == (TT,FF)' : form
- val B = 'q == p' : form
```

```
! CONJUNCT1 (ASSUME AB);
- it = .|-'p == (TT,FF)' : thm
```

```
! val th1 = DISJ1 it C;
- val th1 = .|-'p == (TT,FF)  \/  FST p == SND q' : thm
```

```
! ASSUME C;
- it = .|-'FST p == SND q' : thm
```

```
! DISJ2 A it;
```

```
- it = .|-'p == (TT,FF)  \/  FST p == SND q' : thm
```

```
! DISJ_CASES ABCth th1 it;
- it = .|-'p == (TT,FF)  \/  FST p == SND q' : thm
```

Example 7.8 The double negation law is a consequence of classical contradiction:

$$\frac{\Gamma \vdash \neg\neg A}{\Gamma \vdash A}$$

In the code, the formula meta variables are arguments to *CCONTR* and *ASSUME*:

```
fun DOUBLENEG NNAth =
    let val (NA, _) = dest_imp (concl NNAth);
        val (A, _) = dest_imp NA
    in  CCONTR A (MP NNAth (ASSUME NA))
    end;
```

A sample invocation:

```
- val DOUBLENEG = fn : (thm -> thm)
```

```
! DOUBLENEG (ASSUME '~ ~ x==TT');
- it = .|-'x == TT' : thm
```

```
! val NNAth = ASSUME '~ ~ x==TT';
- val NNAth = .|-'~ ~ x == TT' : thm
```

```
! val (NA, _) = dest_imp (concl NNAth);
- val NA = '~ x == TT' : form
```

```
! val (A, _) = dest_imp NA;
- val A = 'x == TT' : form
```

```
! ASSUME NA;
- it = .|-'~ x == TT' : thm
```

```
! MP NNAth it;
- it = ..|-'FALSITY ()' : thm
```

```
! CCONTR A it;
- it = .|-'x == TT' : thm
```

Example 7.9 When reasoning about quantifiers, variable names must be chosen to satisfy the eigenvariable provisos of the rules. Recall Example 2.18, the derivation of the rule

$$\frac{\Gamma \vdash \exists y.\forall x.A}{\Gamma \vdash \forall x.\exists y.A}$$

What if x or y is free in Γ? The rule is still sound — the names of bound variables are immaterial — but x or y may need to be renamed in the proof, when the quantifiers come off.

```
fun QUANTRULE euth =
    let val frees = forml_frees (hyp euth);
        val (y, uA) = dest_exists (concl euth);
        val (x, A) = dest_forall uA;
        val x' = variant frees x
        and y' = variant frees y;
        val A' = subst_form [(y',y), (x',x)] A
    in  GEN x' (CHOOSE (y',euth)
                    (EXISTS (mk_exists(y',A'), y')
                            (SPEC x' (ASSUME (mk_forall(x',A'))))))
    end;
```

The function *variant* renames a variable to be distinct from a given list of variables; the function *forml_frees* returns the list of variables free in the assumptions. The names of the meta variables x', y', and A' emphasize that they contain variants of the values of the meta variables x, y, and A. If the quantified variables are not free in the assumptions, no renaming is necessary. To prevent confusion between meta and object variables, let us use u and v for the variables in the sample formula:

```
- val QUANTRULE = fn : (thm -> thm)

! QUANTRULE (ASSUME '?v:tr. !u:tr. v == f(u)');
- it = .|-'!u. ?v. v == f u' : thm
```

Here is a contrived theorem with the variables free in the assumptions. Observe how it is constructed; such theorems are often needed for testing rules.

```
! val euth = CONJUNCT2 (ASSUME 'u==v:tr /\ ?v:tr. !u:tr. v==f(u)');
- val euth = .|-'?v. !u. v == f u' : thm

! hyp euth;
- it = ['u == v  /\  (?v. !u. v == f u)'] : form list

! QUANTRULE euth;
- it = .|-'!u'. ?v'. v' == f u'' : thm
```

Finally, here is the step by step execution:

```
! val frees = forml_frees (hyp euth);
- val frees = ['u','v','f'] : term list

! val (y, uA) = dest_exists (concl euth);
- val y = 'v' : term
- val uA = '!u. v == f u' : form

! val (x, A) = dest_forall uA;
- val x = 'u' : term
- val A = 'v == f u' : form

! val x' = variant frees x and y' = variant frees y;
- val x' = 'u'' : term
- val y' = 'v'' : term

! val A' = subst_form [(y',y), (x',x)] A;
- val A' = 'v' == f u'' : form

! ASSUME (mk_forall(x',A'));
- it = .|-'!u'. v' == f u'' : thm

! SPEC x' it;
- it = .|-'v' == f u'' : thm

! EXISTS (mk_exists(y',A'), y') it;
- it = .|-'?v'. v' == f u'' : thm

! CHOOSE (y',euth) it;
- it = .|-'?v'. v' == f u'' : thm

! GEN x' it;
- it = .|-'!u'. ?v'. v' == f u'' : thm

! hyp it;
- it = ['u == v  /\  (?v. !u. v == f u)'] : form list
```

Example 7.10 The implementation of the derived rules for PPλ is especially tedious because many of the axioms are polymorphic, and require instantiation of type variables. The simplest rule is *MIN*:

```
fun MIN t = SPEC t (INST_TYPE [(type_of t, ':'a')] MINIMAL);
```

The function *type_of* finds the type of the term t; the rule *INST_TYPE* puts that for the type variable in the axiom. Calling *SPEC* would fail otherwise.

Derived rules often use *MP* and *SPEC*, since axioms often involve universal quantifiers and implication. Derived rules that must run fast use *mk_thm*.

Exercise 7.5 Give an ML derivation of

$$\frac{\Gamma \vdash A \vee B}{\Gamma \vdash B \vee A}$$

Exercise 7.6 Give an ML derivation of

$$\frac{\Gamma \vdash (A \wedge B) \vee C}{\Gamma \vdash (A \vee C) \wedge (B \vee C)}$$

Exercise 7.7 Give an ML derivation of

$$\frac{\Gamma \vdash (A \vee B) \wedge C}{\Gamma \vdash (A \wedge C) \vee (B \wedge C)}$$

Exercise 7.8 Write ML code to derive the rules

$$\frac{\Gamma \vdash \neg(A \vee B)}{\Gamma \vdash \neg A} \qquad\qquad \frac{\Gamma \vdash \neg(A \vee B)}{\Gamma \vdash \neg B}$$

Exercise 7.9 Write an ML function for the excluded middle. Given a formula A it should return the theorem $\vdash A \vee \neg A$. (Recall Example 2.7.)

Exercise 7.10 Write the ML derivation of the rule

$$\frac{\Gamma \vdash \forall x.\, A \Longrightarrow B}{\Gamma \vdash A[x'/x] \Longrightarrow \forall x.B}$$

Your code must choose a variant x, say x', not free in Γ.

Exercise 7.11 Give an ML derivation of

$$\frac{\Gamma \vdash \exists xy.A}{\Gamma \vdash \exists yx.A}$$

Recall Example 2.14.

Exercise 7.12 Give an ML derivation of *SYNTH*.

7.5   Discussion and further reading

Large proofs are typically tackled by backwards reasoning, discussed in the following chapter.

Several LCF-style provers are mainly used for forwards proof. These include the Gothenburg Type Theory system [81] and the Calculus of Constructions system [27]. In describing *Veritas*, Hanna and Daeche [43] claim that using Miranda as meta language allows an extremely compact representation of inference rules: they have implemented a logic in six pages of code.

Representing rules as functions means that derived rules can consist of complicated ML code: slow and difficult to verify. In developing the theorem prover *Isabelle*, I am trying to represent rules as assertions; a derived rule can be verified by inspection [80]. Quantifier rules, with their eigenvariable provisos, are the main difficulty in any representation.

Chapter 8

Tactics and Tacticals

Tactics accomplish backwards proof. You begin with a *goal* — a statement of the desired theorem — and reduce it to simpler subgoals, forming a proof tree. A *tactic* reduces a goal to a list of subgoals such that if every subgoal holds then the goal holds also. If the list of subgoals is empty then the tactic has proved the goal. The standard tactics allow reasoning about logical connectives, substitution, induction, and rewriting. A tactic is a higher order function. It not only reduces a goal to subgoals, but returns a proof function to justify its action.

It is worthwhile to develop tactics specifically for the theory at hand. Operations called *tacticals*, which treat tactics as data, construct sophisticated tactics from simple ones. It is seldom necessary to code a tactic in low-level ML: the standard tactics and tacticals form a language of proofs. Constructing a tactic from simpler ones promotes readability and avoids many kinds of error. The tactic steps of a proof can be composed to form a single tactic, giving a surprisingly readable synopsis of the proof. Tacticals are a prime example of higher order functions in LCF.

The *subgoal package* provides commands for backwards proof. It manages the subgoal tree, presenting the user with unsolved goals. When the last subgoal has been solved, it produces the final theorem.

8.1   The validation of a backwards step

Let Γ be a list of assumptions. A *tactic* is a function that maps a goal $\Gamma \vdash B$ to the pair

$$([\Gamma_1 \vdash B_1, \ldots, \Gamma_n \vdash B_n], \ validation)$$

consisting of a list of subgoals, together with a *validation*. The validation is a function of type *thm list* $\rightarrow$ *thm* that justifies the reduction of the goal to the subgoals. It should map the theorems $\Gamma_1 \vdash B_1$, ..., $\Gamma_n \vdash B_n$ to the theorem $\Gamma \vdash B$. When this obtains, the tactic is said to be *valid*.

First comes a top-down analysis of the goal, then comes a bottom-up synthesis of the theorem. The subgoals are proved using other tactics. Composing the validations reconstructs the proof. Tacticals compose the validations automatically; so do the interactive subgoal commands.

LCF includes the predefined ML type synonyms *proof* (for validations), *goal*, and *tactic*:

```
type proof = thm list -> thm;              (*validation function*)
type goal = form list * form;
type tactic = goal -> (goal list * proof);
type subgoals = goal list * proof;
```

Note that the function *dest_thm* has type *thm → goal*.

Example 8.1 The tactic for conjunction introduction corresponds to the rule

$$\frac{\Gamma \vdash A \qquad \Gamma \vdash B}{\Gamma \vdash A \wedge B}$$

It reduces a goal $\Gamma \vdash A \wedge B$ to the subgoals $\Gamma \vdash A$ and $\Gamma \vdash B$; the validation calls the inference rule *CONJ*. The assumptions Γ are passed on to both subgoals. The tactic fails if the goal is not a conjunction. Tactics fail by raising exception *tactic*, which has type *string × goal list*, giving an error message and a list of goals.

Here is the code, including exception handling. The goal formula $A \wedge B$ is split into the conjuncts A and B. Two subgoals are formed by combining the assumption list *asl* with each conjunct. The validation takes a two-element list and calls *CONJ*. If the goal formula is not a conjunction, *dest_conj* raises exception *syntax*, and then the tactic fails.

```
val CONJ_TAC : tactic =
  fn (asl,C) =>
    let val (A,B) = dest_conj C
    in ( [ (asl,A), (asl,B) ],
         fn [thA,thB] => CONJ thA thB)
    end
    handle syntax => raise tactic with ("CONJ_TAC",[(asl,C)]);
```

Example 8.2 Some rules discharge assumptions from the premises. The typical one is the discharge rule itself:

$$\frac{\Gamma, A \vdash B}{\Gamma \vdash A \Longrightarrow B}$$

The corresponding tactic reduces a goal $\Gamma \vdash A \Longrightarrow B$ to $\Gamma, A \vdash B$. The tactic could be implemented as follows. The goal formula $A \Longrightarrow B$ is split into antecedent A and consequent B. The one subgoal consists of B with the A added to the assumptions. The validation passes A to *DISCH*. For variety, the tactic uses *is_imp* instead of exception handling to test that the goal is an implication.

```
val DISCH_TAC : tactic =
  fn (asl,C) =>
    if is_imp C then
      let val (A,B) = dest_imp C
      in ( [ (A::asl,B) ],
           fn [thB] => DISCH A thB)
      end
    else raise tactic with ("DISCH_TAC",[(asl,C)]);
```

Example 8.3 Recall the rule *GEN* for universal introduction:

$$\frac{\Gamma \vdash A[x'/x]}{\Gamma \vdash \forall x.A} \qquad provided\ x'\ is\ not\ free\ in\ \forall x.A\ or\ \Gamma$$

The tactic, *GEN_TAC*, breaks down the goal $\Gamma \vdash \forall x.A$ to obtain Γ, x, and A. It uses the function *forml_frees* to find the free variables of the goal for choosing a variant of x to be the eigenvariable x'. Then *subst_form* computes $A[x'/x]$. The validation passes x' to the rule *GEN*:

```
fun GEN_TAC (asl,C) =
    let val (x,A) = dest_forall C;
        val x' = variant (forml_frees (C::asl)) x
    in
        ([(asl, subst_form [(x',x)] A)], fn [thA] => GEN x' thA)
    end
    handle syntax => raise tactic with ("GEN_TAC",[(asl,C)]);
```

Exercise 8.1 Write tactics for the rules *DISJ1* and *DISJ2*.

Exercise 8.2 Write a tactic that can solve a goal of the form $\Gamma \vdash A$, where the formula A is a member of the list Γ.

Exercise 8.3 Write a tactic for the rule *EXISTS*.

8.1.1 Valid and conservative tactics

There is *no guarantee* that the validation will prove the goal. LCF cannot prove a false statement, but a validation can raise an exception, run forever, or produce an irrelevant theorem. An invalid tactic is worse than useless: it can lead you down an incorrect path in a proof. The validation fails at the last moment, when the proof seems to be finished. As Milner says [68], 'Such dishonest tactics — those that promise more than can be performed — are to be avoided.'

A tactic is *conservative* provided that it returns an achievable set of subgoals when given an achievable goal.[1] Observe that validity and conservativeness are

---

[1]Compare with the *strongly valid* tactics of Edinburgh LCF [41, page 58].

fundamentally different concepts. To be valid, a tactic must be correctly implemented: the subgoals and validation must be correctly computed, the provisos of the rule checked. To be conservative, the underlying inference rule must be similarly conservative: the conclusion should imply the premises.

A tactic must be valid but need not be conservative. There are classical sequent calculi in which every rule is conservative, but many familiar rules are not:

$$\frac{\Gamma \vdash A}{\Gamma \vdash A \vee B} \qquad \frac{\Gamma \vdash \Lambda}{\Gamma \vdash A} \qquad \frac{\Gamma \vdash \forall x.A}{\Gamma \vdash A[t/x]}$$

The first of these yields a tactic that reduces the goal $A \vee B$ to the subgoal A. It is not conservative because A could be false and B true. On the other hand, the conjunction introduction tactic is conservative: $A \wedge B$ implies both A and B.

A tactic should check the conditions necessary for its validity and reject a goal that violates them. For certain tactics, checking would be inefficient. Instead the necessary conditions are documented and you must make sure they hold. Note particularly the following warning.

Warning: Tactics that take theorem parameters, like *SUBST_TAC* and *CONTR_TAC*, should be supplied with theorems that depend on no assumptions other than those of the goal. Any additional assumptions may appear in the final theorem when the validation is applied.

8.1.2   Functions useful with tactics

These functions are mainly useful with tactics constructed from tacticals, as described later in the chapter.

Proving a theorem using a tactic

TAC_PROOF : (*goal* $\times$ *tactic*) $\rightarrow$ *thm*
prove_thm : (*string* $\times$ *form* $\times$ *tactic*) $\rightarrow$ *thm*

The function *TAC_PROOF* solves the goal by applying the tactic to it, and returns the resulting theorem. The command *prove_thm* similarly proves a theorem and saves it on the current theory file; it can be used in a batch file that creates theories.

Both raise exception *tactic* if

- The tactic fails.

- The tactic's validation fails.

- The tactic returns a non-empty subgoal list (*prove_thm* prints the subgoals).

Testing a validation on dummy theorems

chktac : ((*goal list*) × *proof*) → *thm*

This function 'proves' the subgoals using *mk_fthm*, producing theorems that include the additional assumption Λ. It applies the validation to these theorems. If the tactic is valid, *chktac* returns a theorem stating the goal, but with the additional assumption.

This validity test is fairly reliable. Most validations do not notice the assumption Λ. Use it to debug a new tactic interactively. Invoke your *NEW_TAC* on a test goal, inspect the resulting subgoals, then call *chktac* to test the validation:

```
NEW_TAC test_goal;
chktac it;
```

Now compare the resulting theorem with the test goal.

If the subgoal list is empty then `chktac it;` simply applies the validation to an empty list of theorems. This is useful in actual proof, as will be seen in examples below.

8.2 Tactics for first order logic

A PPλ sequent consists of a list of assumptions and a conclusion: $A_1, \ldots, A_n \vdash B$. The corresponding goal is represented by the ML pair $([A_1, \ldots, A_n], B)$ of type *form list* × *form*. When operating on this goal, a tactic may use theorems that depend on the assumptions $A_1, \ldots, A_n$, notably theorems of the form $A_i \vdash A_i$.

A tactic is described in terms of the inference rule that validates it. Introduction rules yield tactics that break apart the goal formula. Elimination rules yield tactics that break apart the assumptions of the goal. Most basic are the tactics that immediately solve a goal, leaving no subgoals. A theorem can solve a goal in at least two ways: it may equal the goal itself; it may be a contradiction.

$$ACCEPT\_TAC : \quad thm \quad \rightarrow tactic$$
$$\Gamma \vdash A$$

This tactic solves a goal A using the corresponding theorem, and raises exception *tactic* unless the goal has the form $\Gamma \vdash A$ for the same formula A.

See warning in Section 8.1.1.

$ACCEPT\_ASM\_TAC$: *tactic*

This tactic solves a goal $\Gamma \vdash A$ provided that A is a member of the assumption list Γ, and raises exception *tactic* unless the necessary assumption is present.

CONTR_TAC : *thm* → *tactic*
$$\Gamma \vdash \Lambda$$

$$\frac{\Gamma \vdash \Lambda}{\Gamma \vdash B}$$

This is the intuitionistic contradiction tactic. It solves a goal that has the assumptions Γ using the theorem that those assumptions are contradictory. Recall that Λ is written `FALSITY()` in LCF.

CONTR_TAC raises exception *tactic* unless the theorem has the form $\Gamma \vdash \Lambda$. See warning in Section 8.1.1.

CUT_TAC : *form* → *tactic*
$$A$$

$$\frac{\Gamma \vdash A \qquad \Gamma, A \vdash B}{\Gamma \vdash B}$$

This tactic implements the cut rule, allowing a lemma A to be introduced into the backwards proof. The first subgoal is to prove A; the second is to prove B under the assumption A.

CUT_THM_TAC : *thm* → *tactic*
$$A$$

$$\frac{\Gamma, A \vdash B}{\Gamma \vdash B}$$

This tactic, which works via the cut rule, adds a theorem to the assumption list. It is useful with tactics that operate on the assumptions, including the resolution and rewriting tactics described below. Another use is to 'freeze' the free variables of A. The assumption A corresponds to the theorem $A \vdash A$, so type variables and free variables in A can not be instantiated. If A is a rewrite rule, freezing some of its variables controls its behavior (Chapter 9).

See warning in Section 8.1.1.

CHECK_THM_TAC : *thm* → *tactic*

This tactic tries to solve the goal using *ACCEPT_TAC* and *CONTR_TAC*. If these fail, and the theorem is not already in the assumptions, then *CUT_THM_TAC* is called to put it there.

See warning in Section 8.1.1.

8.2.1 Conjunction

The tactic for conjunction introduction breaks a conjunctive goal in two:

CONJ_TAC : *tactic*

$$\frac{\Gamma \vdash A \qquad \Gamma \vdash B}{\Gamma \vdash A \wedge B}$$

It is often invoked via *STRIP_TAC*. It raises exception *tactic* unless the goal is a conjunction.

The tactic for conjunction elimination implements the ∧-left sequent calculus rule:

CONJ_LEFT_TAC : *tactic*

$$\frac{\Gamma, A, B \vdash C}{\Gamma, A \wedge B \vdash C}$$

It produces a subgoal in which the conjunctive assumption $A \wedge B$ has been replaced by the two assumptions A and B. Conjunction elimination is also available via *STRIP_THM_TAC*, described below.

8.2.2 Disjunction

The tactics for disjunction introduction choose one of the disjuncts:

DISJ1_TAC : *tactic*
DISJ2_TAC : *tactic*

$$\frac{\Gamma \vdash A}{\Gamma \vdash A \vee B} \qquad\qquad \frac{\Gamma \vdash B}{\Gamma \vdash A \vee B}$$

They raise exception *tactic* unless the goal is a disjunction.

The tactic for disjunction elimination implements the ∨-left rule:

DISJ_LEFT_TAC : *tactic*

$$\frac{\Gamma, A \vdash C \qquad \Gamma, B \vdash C}{\Gamma, A \vee B \vdash C}$$

It produces two subgoals in which the disjunctive assumption $A \vee B$ has been replaced by the assumption A or B. Disjunction elimination is also available via *STRIP_THM_TAC*.

8.2.3 Implication and negation

The tactic for implication introduction moves the antecedent to the assumption list:

DISCH_TAC : *tactic*

$$\frac{\Gamma, A \vdash B}{\Gamma \vdash A \Longrightarrow B}$$

It is often invoked via *STRIP_TAC*. It raises exception *tactic* unless the goal is an implication.

A tactic for implication elimination implements the intuitionistic sequent calculus rule, $\Longrightarrow$-left:

IMP_LEFT_TAC : *tactic*

$$\frac{\Gamma, A \Longrightarrow B \vdash A \qquad \Gamma, B \vdash C}{\Gamma, A \Longrightarrow B \vdash C}$$

It finds an assumption of the form $A \Longrightarrow B$ and produces two subgoals: to prove A, and to prove C assuming B.

Another implication elimination tactic is

MP_TAC :   *thm* $\rightarrow$ *tactic*

$$\frac{\Gamma \vdash A \qquad \Gamma \vdash A \Longrightarrow B}{\Gamma \vdash B}$$

This peculiar tactic is useful in case analysis. If A has the form $A_1 \vee A_2$ then the subgoal is $(A_1 \vee A_2) \Longrightarrow B$. Calling *REWRITE_TAC* converts this to the subgoal $(A_1 \Longrightarrow B) \wedge (A_2 \Longrightarrow B)$, essentially simplifying $A_1 \Longrightarrow B$ and $A_2 \Longrightarrow B$ separately.

See warning in Section 8.1.1.

Resolution tactics, described below, also work by implication elimination.

8.2.4   Bi-implication

The tactic for implication introduction proves a bi-implication by considering both directions:

IFF_TAC : *tactic*

$$\frac{(A \Longrightarrow B) \wedge (B \Longrightarrow A)}{A \Longleftrightarrow B}$$

It raises exception *tactic* unless the goal is a bi-implication.

8.2.5   Universal quantifier

Introduction

The $\forall$-introduction rule yields two tactics: one for top-level use, one for programming.

GEN_TAC : *tactic*

$$\frac{\Gamma \vdash A[x'/x]}{\Gamma \vdash \forall x.A} \qquad \text{provided } x' \text{ is not free in } \forall x.A \text{ or } \Gamma$$

The tactic chooses a new variable x' as a variant of x not free in Γ. *GEN_TAC* is often invoked via *STRIP_TAC*.

It raises exception *tactic* unless the goal is universally quantified.

$X\_GEN\_TAC : term \to tactic$
$$\qquad\qquad y$$

$$\frac{\Gamma \vdash A[y/x]}{\Gamma \vdash \forall x.A} \qquad provided\ y\ is\ not\ free\ in\ \forall x.A\ or\ \Gamma$$

This tactic takes an explicit variable y as an argument. It is only valid if y is not free in Γ. It is used to write tactics where the programmer needs to choose the variable name.

It raises exception *tactic* unless the goal is universally quantified and y is a variable.

Elimination

There are also two different $\forall$-elimination tactics: one operates on the right of the $\vdash$, one on the left.

$SPEC\_TAC : (term \times term) \to tactic$
$$\qquad\qquad t \qquad x$$

$$\frac{\Gamma \vdash \forall x.A}{\Gamma \vdash A[t/x]}$$

This tactic substitutes x for t in the goal. It is only valid if the goal formula is $A[t/x]$: every free occurrence of x must be contained within t itself.

It raises exception *tactic* unless x is a variable of the same type as t.

The tactic *SPEC_TAC* embodies Boyer and Moore's notion of *generalizing* a goal, though without their heuristics [12]. If t is irrelevant in $A[t/x]$ then $\forall x.A$ is simpler to prove. The tactic is called *SPEC_TAC* because generalizing the goal requires specializing the resulting theorem. The terminology is confusing because a tactic uses an inference rule backwards.

$FORALL\_LEFT\_TAC : term \times term \to tactic$
$$\qquad\qquad\qquad\quad t \qquad x$$

$$\frac{\Gamma, \forall x.A, A[t/x] \vdash B}{\Gamma, \forall x.A \vdash B}$$

The tactic *FORALL_LEFT_TAC* implements the sequent rule $\forall$-left. Given a variable x and a goal, it searches for an assumption of the form $\forall x.A$ for the same x. It makes a new assumption $A[t/x]$.

8.2.6   Existential quantifier

The introduction tactic takes a term, the *witness*, as an argument.

$EXISTS\_TAC : term \rightarrow tactic$
t

$$\frac{\Gamma \vdash A[t/x]}{\Gamma \vdash \exists x.A}$$

It raises exception *tactic* unless the goal is existentially quantified.

$EXISTS\_LEFT\_TAC : tactic$

$$\frac{\Gamma, A[x'/x] \vdash B}{\Gamma, \exists x.A \vdash B} \qquad provided \; x' \; is \; not \; free \; in \; \exists x.A, \; \Gamma, \; or \; B$$

The tactic *EXISTS_LEFT_TAC* implements the sequent rule $\exists$-left. It searches for an assumption of the form $\exists x.A$ and replaces it by $A[x'/x]$, where x' is a variant of x satisfying the proviso. Exists elimination is also provided via *STRIP_THM_TAC*.

8.2.7   Substitution

There are tactics for substitution in the goal, in selected occurrences in the goal, and in the assumptions. But rewriting is often preferable to substitution.

Substitution in the goal

$SUBST\_TAC : (\; thm \quad list) \rightarrow tactic$
$t_i \equiv u_i$

$SUBST\_OCCS\_TAC : ((int \; list) \times \quad thm \;) \; list \rightarrow tactic$
$o_i \qquad t_i \equiv u_i$

$$\frac{\Gamma \vdash A[u_1/t_1, \ldots, u_n/t_n]}{\Gamma \vdash A}$$

The arguments include a theorem list $[\vdash t_1 \equiv u_1, \ldots, \vdash t_n \equiv u_n]$. *SUBST_TAC* replaces every free occurrence of t_i in the goal by u_i. *SUBST_OCCS_TAC* is also given an occurrence list for each theorem, stating which free occurrences of t_i to substitute. (Section 5.5 describes substitution.) These tactics are validated by the rule *SUBST*, *not* by the rules *SUBS* and *SUBS_OCCS*. These tactics substitute in the goal while those rules substitute in the premise.

They raise exception *tactic* unless the theorems are equivalences. See warning in Section 8.1.1.

Simple substitution

SUBST1_TAC : *thm* → *tactic*

$$t \equiv u$$

$$\frac{\Gamma \vdash A[u/t]}{\Gamma \vdash A}$$

SUBST1_TAC calls *SUBST_TAC* with one theorem. It is easy to use with tacticals like *FIRST_ASSUM*.

It raises exception *tactic* unless the theorem is an equivalence. See warning in Section 8.1.1.

Substitution in the goal and its assumptions

SUBST_ALL_TAC : *thm* → *tactic*

$$t \equiv u$$

$$\frac{\Gamma[u/t] \vdash A[u/t]}{\Gamma \vdash A}$$

SUBST_ALL_TAC replaces every free occurrence of t by u throughout the goal, including the assumptions Γ.

It raises exception *tactic* unless the theorem is an equivalence. See warning in Section 8.1.1.

8.3   Domain theory

In Cambridge LCF, domain-theoretic reasoning takes place in first order logic. The theorems of PPλ include many equalities and implications that can be given to rewriting and resolution tactics. Very few tactics are specific to domain theory.

8.3.1   Fixed point induction

The tactic for fixed point induction is

INDUCT_TAC :   *thm list*   →   *(term × term) list*   → *tactic*

$$[B_1, \ldots, B_m]   [(f_1, x_1), \ldots, (f_n, x_n)]$$

$$\frac{TR\_CASES \ \ \Gamma_1 \vdash B_1 \ \ \cdots \ \ \Gamma_m \vdash B_m \qquad \Delta \vdash A[\bot/x_1, \ldots, \bot/x_n] \qquad \Theta \vdash \forall x_1 \ldots x_n.\ A \Longrightarrow A[f_1 x_1/x_1, \ldots, f_n x_n/x_n]}{\Gamma_1, \ldots, \Gamma_m, \Delta, \Theta \vdash A[FIX \ f_1/x_1, \ldots, FIX \ f_n/x_n]}$$

Conditions of validity: The tactic makes subgoals by substituting for *FIX* f_i; there should be no free occurrences of the x_i in the goal formula. The theorems $[B_1, \ldots, B_m]$ should assert properties of types for testing chain-completeness (Section 7.3.6). The axiom *TR_CASES* is included: the type *tr* is finite.

See warning in Section 8.1.1.

8.3.2   Case split on a conditional expression

COND_CASES_TAC : *tactic*

$$\frac{\Gamma, p \equiv \perp \vdash A[\perp/x] \qquad \Gamma, p \equiv TT \vdash A[t/x] \qquad \Gamma, p \equiv FF \vdash A[u/x]}{\Gamma \vdash A[(p \Rightarrow t \mid u)/x]}$$

This tactic searches in A for a free conditional expression $p \Rightarrow t \mid u$, where p is not a constant. It reasons by exhaustion over *tr*, a case analysis: p is either $\perp$, *TT*, or *FF*.

COND_CASES_TAC raises exception *tactic* unless the goal contains such a conditional expression.

8.4   Simple backwards proof

Normally, tacticals and the subgoal commands keep track of subgoal lists and validations. Proving a theorem using tactics alone is tedious but reveals the basic mechanisms.

Example 8.4 In backwards proof, the commutative law for conjunction is best expressed as the sequent $A \wedge B \vdash B \wedge A$. The steps of the proof are as follows. Break apart the assumption, leaving $A, B \vdash B \wedge A$. Break apart the goal, leaving $A, B \vdash B$ and $A, B \vdash A$. These subgoals follow by the assumption axiom. Compare with the forwards proof, Example 7.6.

The LCF session begins by stating the goal to be proved. With tacticals we could construct a tactic for solving any goal of the form $A \wedge B \vdash B \wedge A$. But this example is a step by step proof, where specific formulae must be given for A and B. Observe the use of antiquotation in g.

```
! val A = 'f(x:tr)==()';
- val A = 'f x == ()' : form

! val B = '!q. UU<<q : tr';
- val B = '!q. UU << q' : form

! val g = (['^A /\ ^B'], '^B /\ ^A');
- val g =
```

```
(['f x == () /\ (!q. UU << q)'],'(!q. UU << q) /\ f x == ()')
 : goal
```

The tactic *CONJ_LEFT_TAC* finds a conjunctive assumption and splits it in two. The one subgoal and the validation are bound to new identifiers g1 and prf1 using pattern matching and the special variable *it*.

```
! CONJ_LEFT_TAC g;
- it =
([(['f x == ()','!q. UU << q'], '(!q. UU << q) /\ f x == ()')], fn)
 : subgoals

! val ([g1],prf1) = it;
- val g1 =
(['f x == ()','!q. UU << q'],'(!q. UU << q) /\ f x == ()')
 : goal
- val prf1 = fn : proof
```

The tactic *CONJ_TAC* splits the goal in two. The two subgoals are named g21 and g22; the validation is named prf2.

```
! CONJ_TAC g1;
- it =
([(['f x == ()','!q. UU << q'],'!q. UU << q'),
  (['f x == ()','!q. UU << q'],'f x == ()')],
 fn) : subgoals

! val ([g21,g22],prf2) = it;
- val g21 = (['f x == ()','!q. UU << q'],'!q. UU << q') : goal
- val g22 = (['f x == ()','!q. UU << q'],'f x == ()') : goal
- val prf2 = fn : proof
```

The tactic *ACCEPT_ASM_TAC* solves a goal by assumption. It solves both subgoals, producing no new ones. The validations are bound to the variables prf31 and prf32.

```
! val (g31,prf31) = ACCEPT_ASM_TAC g21;
- val g31 = [] : 'b list
- val prf31 = fn : ('c list -> thm)

! val (g32,prf32) = ACCEPT_ASM_TAC g22;
- val g32 = [] : 'b list
- val prf32 = fn : ('c list -> thm)
```

No subgoals remain. Let us apply the validations and combine the results.

```
! prf31[];
- it = .|-'!q. UU << q'  : thm


! prf32[];
- it = .|-'f x == ()'  : thm


! prf2[prf31[],prf32[]];
- it = ..|-'(!q. UU << q)  /\  f x == ()'  : thm


! prf1[it];
- it = .|-'(!q. UU << q)  /\  f x == ()'  : thm
```

All the validations can be combined in a single expression.

```
! prf1[prf2[prf31[],prf32[]]];
- it = .|-'(!q. UU << q)  /\  f x == ()'  : thm


! hyp it;
- it = ['f x == ()  /\  (!q. UU << q)']  : form list
```

Example 8.5 Proving $\exists x.\forall y.A \vdash \forall y.\exists x.A$ requires all of the quantifier rules. Here the proof from Example 2.18 is performed using tactics.

For A let us use the formula $f(x,y) \equiv TT$. The obvious first step is *GEN_TAC*, for stripping off the universal quantifier.

```
! val g = ([ '?x:tr. !y:tr. f(x,y)==TT' ],
            '!y:tr. ?x:tr. f(x,y)==TT');
- val g = (['?x. !y. f(x,y) == TT'],'!y. ?x. f(x,y) == TT')  : goal


! val ([g1],prf1) = GEN_TAC g;
- val g1 = (['?x. !y. f(x,y) == TT'],'?x. f(x,y) == TT')  : goal
- val prf1 = fn  : proof
```

Now an existential rule must be used, either $\exists$-left or $\exists$-right. Is the choice arbitrary? Let us invoke $\exists$-right first.

```
! val ([g2],prf2) = EXISTS_TAC 'x:tr'  g1;
- val g2 = (['?x. !y. f(x,y) == TT'],'f(x,y) == TT')  : goal
- val prf2 = fn  : proof


! val ([g3],prf3) = EXISTS_LEFT_TAC g2;
- val g3 = (['!y. f(x',y) == TT'],'f(x,y) == TT')  : goal
- val prf3 = fn  : proof
```

Problems! The tactic *EXISTS_LEFT_TAC* has chosen x' for the eigenvariable because x is free in the goal formula. The subgoal $\forall y.f(x',y) \equiv TT \vdash f(x,y) \equiv TT$ is not true because x and x' may have different values. We should have remembered the advice on quantifier rules from the end of Chapter 2. Let us abandon this branch, and get a new g2 and prf2 by applying *EXISTS_LEFT_TAC* to g1. Observe that x is not free in that goal.

```
! val ([g2],prf2) = EXISTS_LEFT_TAC g1;
- val g2 = (['!y. f(x,y) == TT'],'?x. f(x,y) == TT') : goal
- val prf2 = fn : proof
```

Now either ∀-left or ∃-right must be performed. Chapter 2 recommends postponing both rules, but nothing else can be done. An arbitrary choice is to perform ∃-right then ∀-left.

```
! val ([g3],prf3) = EXISTS_TAC 'x:tr' g2;
- val g3 = (['!y. f(x,y) == TT'],'f(x,y) == TT') : goal
- val prf3 = fn : proof
```

```
! val ([g4],prf4) = FORALL_LEFT_TAC ('y:tr','y') g3;
- val g4 = (['f(x,y)==TT','!y. f(x,y)==TT'], 'f(x,y)==TT') : goal
- val prf4 = fn : proof
```

The new assumption is equal to the goal formula, so *ACCEPT_ASM_TAC* completes the proof. The validations can be applied to obtain the desired theorem.

```
! val (gl5,prf5) = ACCEPT_ASM_TAC g4;
- val gl5 = [] : goal list
- val prf5 = fn : proof
```

```
! val QUANT_THM = prf1[prf2[prf3[prf4[prf5[]]]]];
- val QUANT_THM = .|-'!y. ?x. f(x,y) == TT' : thm
```

The function *hyp* reveals the theorem's hypothesis. The command *save_thm* saves it on the theory file after discharging the hypothesis and generalizing over the variable f.

```
! hyp QUANT_THM;
- it = ['?x. !y. f(x,y) == TT'] : form list
```

```
! save_thm("QUANT_TH",QUANT_THM);
- it = |-'!f. (?x. !y. f(x,y)==TT) ==> (!y. ?x. f(x,y)==TT)' : thm
```

Exercise 8.4 Using tactics, try to prove a goal of the form $\exists x.A \vdash \forall x.A$. What can go wrong? What condition on the formula A allows the proofs to succeed?

Exercise 8.5 Prove a goal of the form $\exists xy.A \vdash \exists yx.A$.

Exercise 8.6 Prove a goal of the form $\forall xy.A \vdash \forall u.A[f(u)/x, g(u)/y]$.

8.5   Complex tactics

The following tactics are implemented using tools discussed later: tacticals, theorem continuations, rewriting functions. Tactics that perform several or hundreds of inferences can be called proof *strategies*.

8.5.1   Breaking up a goal or theorem

STRIP_TAC : *tactic*

The tactic *STRIP_TAC* removes the outermost connective from the goal using the introduction tactics *CONJ_TAC*, *DISCH_TAC*, or *GEN_TAC*. If the goal is an implication $A \implies B$, it applies *DISCH_TAC*. Then *STRIP_THM_TAC*, described below, breaks up the antecedent A. The tactic is implemented via *theorem continuations*, described below. It is normally used with the tactical *REPEAT* to strip off as many connectives as possible. It does not use the introduction rules for $\vee$ and $\exists$: these require direction from the user.

The tactic fails, raising exception *tactic*, unless the goal's outer connective is $\forall$, $\wedge$, or $\implies$.

STRIP_THM_TAC : *thm* $\rightarrow$ *tactic*

The tactic *STRIP_THM_TAC* uses elimination rules to break a theorem apart, stripping off certain outer connectives. It adds a conjunction as separate conjuncts, validated by the inference rules *CONJUNCT1* and *CONJUNCT2*. It causes a case split given a disjunction, validated by the rule *DISJ_CASES*. It eliminates an existential quantifier by choosing an arbitrary variable, validated by the rule *CHOOSE*. Finally, it puts the resulting pieces through *CHECK_THM_TAC* to detect theorems that satisfy the goal.

The tactic is particularly useful for reasoning by exhaustion of the elements of a type, as described in Section 4.10.

Like *STRIP_TAC* it is implemented using theorem continuations. Its effect is like repeatedly using *CONJ_LEFT_TAC*, *DISJ_LEFT_TAC*, and *EXISTS_LEFT_TAC*, for the sequent calculus rules of Section 2.13. However, new assumptions cause recursive calls to *STRIP_THM_TAC* whenever possible; the tactic does not add contradictions, conjunctions, disjunctions, or existentials to the assumption list.

The theorem $A \wedge B$ is split into A and B:

$$\frac{\Gamma, A, B \vdash C}{\Gamma, A \wedge B \vdash C}$$

The theorem $A \lor B$ splits the goal in two:

$$\frac{\Gamma, A \vdash C \qquad \Gamma, B \vdash C}{\Gamma, A \lor B \vdash C}$$

The theorem $\exists x.A$ becomes $A[x'/x]$, where x' is a variant of the variable x:

$$\frac{\Gamma, A[x'/x] \vdash B}{\Gamma, \exists x.A \vdash B} \qquad \text{provided } x' \text{ is not free in } \exists x.A, \Gamma, \text{ or } B$$

8.5.2 Rewriting tactics

$REWRITE\_TAC$: *thm list* $\to$ *tactic*
$ASM\_REWRITE\_TAC$: *thm list* $\to$ *tactic*

These tactics are real workhorses: an entire chapter (the next) is devoted to them. $REWRITE\_TAC$ simplifies the goal using the given list of theorems as rewrite rules. $ASM\_REWRITE\_TAC$ adds the assumptions to the input list of theorems.

See warning in Section 8.1.1.

8.5.3 Structural induction tactics

The structural induction tactics implement the derivation given in Chapter 4 through a complex combination of tactics and tacticals. No structural induction *rule* is provided, but a rule can be obtained from the validation by calling the tactic. The tactic has two forms. For interactive proof use $STRUCT\_TAC$. For implementing derived induction tactics, use $BASIC\_STRUCT\_TAC$ together with other tactics and tacticals.

Both tactics are curried functions. The first argument, T, is the name of a theory that was built using the structural induction commands *gen_struct_axm* or *struct_axm*. Building the tactic involves reading the theory file, an expensive operation, so bind the resulting tactic to an ML identifier. The next argument is a list (often empty) of theorems $[B_1, \ldots, B_m]$ asserting properties of types for chain-completeness.

Exception *tactic* is raised unless

- The goal admits induction (is chain-complete).

- The goal is universally quantified over a variable of the type formalized in the theory T.

If T was not built by structural induction commands, exception *theory* is raised.

See warning in Section 8.1.1. The theorems B_i undergo processing that could turn antecedents of implications into unwanted assumptions. Each theorem may be an implication, giving conditions under which the type property holds. For instance, the type α *list* is flat provided that α is:

$$(\forall xy.\, x \sqsubseteq (y : \alpha) \implies \bot \equiv x \lor x \equiv y) \implies (\forall ab.\, a \sqsubseteq (b : \alpha\ list) \implies \bot \equiv a \lor a \equiv b)$$

The tactic instantiates the type variables in each B_i as they are instantiated in the goal. Then it 'undischarges' all antecedents to become assumptions, to put the theorem into the proper form for the rule *INDUCT*. Since the validation will use these assumptions, the tactic is *invalid* unless they are already assumed in the goal. If the goal concerns a *tr list* then α is replaced by *tr*, giving the theorem

$$\forall xy.\, x \sqsubseteq (y : tr) \implies \bot \equiv x \lor x \equiv y \vdash \forall ab.\, a \sqsubseteq (b : tr\ list) \implies \bot \equiv a \lor a \equiv b$$

$STRUCT\_TAC : string \rightarrow thm\ list \rightarrow term \rightarrow tactic$
$$\quad\quad\quad\quad\quad T \quad\quad B_i \quad\quad\quad\quad x$$

This is the structural induction tactic for interactive use. It splits up the goal by calling *STRIP_TAC* zero or more times until it finds a universal quantification over the variable x. Then it calls *BASIC_STRUCT_TAC* for induction on the subformula $\forall x.A$. Then it puts the subgoals into a convenient form. Recall the type contructor (α, β)*tree* from Example 6.2. The validation of the tactic, ignoring the effect of *STRIP_TAC*, is

$$\dfrac{\begin{array}{rcl} \Gamma &\vdash& A[\bot/x] \\ \Gamma &\vdash& A[\mathit{TIP}\,/x] \\ \Gamma, a \not\equiv \bot, t \not\equiv \bot, A[t/x] &\vdash& A[(\mathit{UNIT}\,a\,t)/x] \\ \Gamma, b \not\equiv \bot, t \not\equiv \bot, t_1 \not\equiv \bot, A[t/x], A[t_1/x] &\vdash& A[(\mathit{BRANCH}\,b\,t\,t_1)/x] \end{array}}{\Gamma \vdash \forall x : (\alpha, \beta)tree.A}$$

$BASIC\_STRUCT\_TAC : string \rightarrow thm\ list \rightarrow tactic$
$$\quad\quad\quad\quad\quad\quad T \quad\quad B_i$$

This is primitive structural induction, useful for implementing derived induction tactics. The tactic for the type *tree* corresponds to the rule

$$\dfrac{\begin{array}{l} \Gamma \vdash \mathit{TRUTH}() \implies \mathit{TRUTH}() \implies A[\bot/x] \\ \Gamma \vdash \mathit{TRUTH}() \implies \mathit{TRUTH}() \implies A[\mathit{TIP}\,/x] \\ \Gamma \vdash \forall at.\,(\mathit{TRUTH}() \land a \not\equiv \bot \land t \not\equiv \bot) \implies \\ \quad\quad (\mathit{TRUTH}() \land A[t/x]) \implies A[(\mathit{UNIT}\,a\,t)/x] \\ \Gamma \vdash \forall btt_1.\,(\mathit{TRUTH}() \land b \not\equiv \bot \land t \not\equiv \bot \land t_1 \not\equiv \bot) \implies \\ \quad\quad (\mathit{TRUTH}() \land A[t/x] \land A[t_1/x]) \implies A[(\mathit{BRANCH}\,b\,t\,t_1)/x] \end{array}}{\Gamma \vdash \forall x.\,A}$$

The subgoals look ugly but have a systematic form for further processing. Other tactics can easily locate components of the subgoals:

$$(universal\ quantifiers)\ (definedness\ antecedents) \implies$$
$$(induction\ hypotheses) \implies A[constr_i/x]$$

8.5.4 Simple resolution tactics

Cambridge LCF provides weak resolution tactics, sometimes helpful for detecting contradictions or generating rewrite rules. Take a list of theorems $[A_1, \ldots, A_m]$ and an implicative theorem $\forall xy \ldots . B_1 \implies \cdots \implies B_n \implies C$. Resolution consists of matching the antecedents $B_1, \ldots, B_n$ against the theorems $A_1, \ldots, A_m$, instantiating type variables and fluid variables, to prove instances of C by Modus Ponens. The resulting theorems, which may still have unproven B's as antecedents, are added to the assumption list. Resolution uses matching, not unification: it instantiates variables in the implication, not in $A_1, \ldots, A_m$.

IMP_RES_TAC : *thm* $\rightarrow$ *tactic*

The tactic *IMP_RES_TAC impth* resolves a theorem against the assumptions. The theorem is transformed by *IMP_CANON* into a list of implications. *IMP_RES_TAC* adds the results to the assumption list using *STRIP_THM_TAC*. In particular, it solves the goal if it finds a contradiction. See warning in Section 8.1.1.

RES_TAC : *tactic*

RES_TAC calls *IMP_RES_TAC* for every implication in the assumptions, accumulating the results in the assumptions. Recall that the free variables and type variables of an assumption are 'frozen': they cannot be instantiated.

IMP_CHAIN_TAC : *thm* $\rightarrow$ *tactic*

The tactic *IMP_CHAIN_TAC impth* provides the opposite kind of resolution: backwards chaining. If the theorem is $\forall xy \ldots . B_1 \implies \cdots \implies B_n \implies C$, then the tactic corresponds to the rule

$$\frac{B_1 \quad \cdots \quad B_n}{C}$$

The goal is matched against C, which instantiates variables in the implication, producing instances of $B_1, \ldots, B_n$ as subgoals. When n is zero, *IMP_CHAIN_TAC* is like a version of *ACCEPT_TAC* using pattern matching.

It raises exception *tactic* unless the goal matches C. See warning in Section 8.1.1.

8.6   The subgoal package

A tactical proof consists of the analysis of a goal followed by the synthesis of the
corresponding theorem. A tactic reduces the goal to a list of subgoals, and this
process is repeated until every goal is solved. To obtain the desired theorem, the
validations returned from each call of a tactic must be composed in the correct
order — a difficult and tedious task for large proofs. It is easier to let the *subgoal package* manage tactical proofs. It maintains a tree of subgoals, stores the
validations on a stack, and applies them, when possible, as the proof proceeds.

The package offers a simple framework for interactive proof. You create and
traverse the proof tree in a top-down, depth-first order. Using a tactic, you expand
the current goal into subgoals and validation, which are pushed onto the goal stack.
You can consider the new subgoals in any order, but cannot jump to an arbitrary
subgoal in the tree. If the tactic returns an empty subgoal list, that goal is solved:
the package proceeds to the next goal in the tree.

The goal stack contains the current proof state in layers. Each layer is a
(subgoals, validation) pair returned by a tactic. Commands of the subgoal package
change the state. Several preceding states are saved: you can back up to a saved
state to undo a mistake. Bear in mind that LCF is largely applicative (stateless)
apart from the subgoal commands and the theory commands. The inference rules,
tactics, rewriting functions, and so forth are pure functions.

8.6.1   Basic commands

set_goal : goal → unit

A new proof begins with the given goal. The previous proof state is saved for
backup.

expandf : tactic → unit

The tactic is applied to expand the goal. The new subgoal list is pushed, as a single
layer, onto the stack. The resulting subgoals are printed. If there are none, the
validations of each completed proof layer are composed. The resulting theorems
are printed. The previous proof state is saved for backup.

expand : tactic → unit
        tac

This command is equivalent to *expandf(VALID(tac))*: slightly slower but safer.
An invalid tactic gives an unpleasant surprise. But recall that *VALID* is not 100%
reliable.

print_state : *int* → *unit*
                  n

This command prints *n* layers of the stack.

save_top_thm : *string* → *thm*
                      id

The theorem on top of the stack is saved as *id* on the current theory, via *save_thm*.
Recall that *save_thm* discharges hypotheses and generalizes over free variables.

8.6.2   Other commands

rotate : *int* → *unit*
              n

The subgoals on the top layer of the stack are rotated by *n* steps. This allows
choosing which of those goals to tackle next, but goals below the top of the stack
cannot be brought to the top. The previous proof state is saved for backup.

backup : *unit* → *unit*

This command backs up from the last state change. It discards the present proof
state, replacing it by the most recent state on the backup list. It may be invoked
repeatedly until the list is exhausted. The backup list grows no longer than the
value (initially 12) of the reference variable *backup_min*.

get_state : *unit* → *goalstack*

The current proof state is returned as a value of the abstract type *goalstack*.

set_state : *goalstack* → *unit*

The proof state is set to the given value of type *goalstack*. The previous proof
state is saved for backup.

  You can use *get_state* to save the current proof in an ML variable, use the
subgoal package to prove a lemma, and return to the main proof via *set_state*.
This style of work indicates poor planning.

top_thm : *unit* → *thm*

The theorem on top of the stack is returned (if there is one).

top_goal : *unit* → *goal*

The first subgoal on top of the stack is returned.

Example 8.6 Let us return yet again to the distributive law for conjunction and disjunction:

$$(A \wedge B) \vee C \Longrightarrow (A \vee C) \wedge (B \vee C)$$

The proof involves disjunction-right, disjunction-left, conjuction-left, and assumption. Example 7.7 gives a forwards proof; here is a backwards proof.[2]

State the goal and break up the disjunctive hypothesis.

```
! val A = 'p==TT' and B = 'q==TT' and C = 'r==TT';
- val A = 'p == TT' : form
- val B = 'q == TT' : form
- val C = 'r == TT' : form

! set_goal ([' (^A /\ ^B) \/ ^C'], '(^A \/ ^C) /\ (^B \/ ^C)');
1 subgoal
'(p == TT  \/  r == TT)  /\  (q == TT  \/  r == TT)'
   ['p == TT  /\  q == TT  \/  r == TT']

! expand DISJ_LEFT_TAC;
2 subgoals
'(p == TT  \/  r == TT)  /\  (q == TT  \/  r == TT)'
   ['r == TT']

'(p == TT  \/  r == TT)  /\  (q == TT  \/  r == TT)'
   ['p == TT  /\  q == TT']
```

The last goal printed is the current one. It has a conjunctive hypothesis: eliminate it. Then we shall break up the conjunction and disjunctions in the goal.

```
! expand CONJ_LEFT_TAC;
1 subgoal
'(p == TT  \/  r == TT)  /\  (q == TT  \/  r == TT)'
   ['q == TT']
   ['p == TT']

! expand CONJ_TAC;
2 subgoals
'q == TT  \/  r == TT'
   ['q == TT']
```

---

[2]To save space, the sessions in this book have been slightly edited: by adding or deleting spaces and newlines, and deleting uninteresting responses. No drastic reformatting has been necessary: Cambridge LCF has a pretty printer.

```
['p == TT']
```

```
'p == TT  \/  r == TT'
  ['q == TT']
  ['p == TT']
```

```
! expand DISJ1_TAC;
1 subgoal
'p == TT'
  ['q == TT']
  ['p == TT']
```

This goal will hold trivially by assumption. To see where we are in the proof tree, let us print the four most recent levels:

```
! print_state 4;
2 subgoals
'(p == TT  \/  r == TT)  /\  (q == TT  \/  r == TT)'
  ['r == TT']
```

```
'(p == TT  \/  r == TT)  /\  (q == TT  \/  r == TT)'
  ['p == TT  /\  q == TT']
```

```
1 subgoal
'(p == TT  \/  r == TT)  /\  (q == TT  \/  r == TT)'
  ['q == TT']
  ['p == TT']
```

```
2 subgoals
'q == TT  \/  r == TT'
  ['q == TT']
  ['p == TT']
```

```
'p == TT  \/  r == TT'
  ['q == TT']
  ['p == TT']
```

```
1 subgoal
'p == TT'
  ['q == TT']
```

```
! expand ACCEPT_ASM_TAC;
```

```
goal proved
.|-'p == TT'
.|-'p == TT  \/  r == TT'

previous subproof:
1 subgoal
'q == TT  \/  r == TT'
  ['q == TT']
  ['p == TT']
```

The subgoal package has automatically moved to the next unsolved goal.

```
! expand DISJ1_TAC;
1 subgoal
'q == TT'
  ['q == TT']
  ['p == TT']


! expand ACCEPT_ASM_TAC;
goal proved
.|-'q == TT'
.|-'q == TT  \/  r == TT'
..|-'(p == TT  \/  r == TT)  /\  (q == TT  \/  r == TT)'
.|-'(p == TT  \/  r == TT)  /\  (q == TT  \/  r == TT)'

1 subgoal
'(p == TT  \/  r == TT)  /\  (q == TT  \/  r == TT)'
  ['r == TT']
```

We have gone up many levels in the tree, and are tackling the other branch of the
original case analysis: the second subgoal from the first step of the proof.

```
! expand CONJ_TAC;
2 subgoals
'q == TT  \/  r == TT'
  ['r == TT']

'p == TT  \/  r == TT'
  ['r == TT']


! expand DISJ1_TAC;
1 subgoal
'p == TT'
```

```
['r == TT']
```

```
! expand ACCEPT_ASM_TAC;
exception raised: tactic with
                        ("ACCEPT_ASM_TAC",[(['r == TT'],'p == TT')])
```

The last call to *DISJ1_TAC* was a mistake. Fortunately we can undo that step and continue.

```
! backup();
2 subgoals
'q == TT  \/  r == TT'
  ['r == TT']
```

```
'p == TT  \/  r == TT'
  ['r == TT']
```

```
! expand DISJ2_TAC;
1 subgoal
'r == TT'
  ['r == TT']
```

```
! expand ACCEPT_ASM_TAC;
goal proved
.|-'r == TT'
.|-'p == TT  \/  r == TT'
```

```
previous subproof:
1 subgoal
'q == TT  \/  r == TT'
  ['r == TT']
```

```
! expand DISJ2_TAC;
1 subgoal
'r == TT'
  ['r == TT']
```

```
! expand ACCEPT_ASM_TAC;
goal proved
.|-'r == TT'
.|-'q == TT  \/  r == TT'
.|-'(p == TT  \/  r == TT)  /\  (q == TT  \/  r == TT)'
```

```
.|-'(p == TT  \/  r == TT)  /\  (q == TT  \/  r == TT)'

previous subproof:
goal proved
! save_top_thm "distributive";
- it =
|-'!p q r.
    p == TT  /\  q == TT  \/  r == TT  ==>
    (p == TT \/  r == TT)  /\  (q == TT  \/  r == TT)'
  : thm
```

There was a lot of repetition. We shall see how to build, using tacticals, a tactic
that solves the goal at once.

Exercise 8.7 Prove a goal of the form $(A \lor B) \land C \Longrightarrow (A \land C) \lor (B \land C)$ using
the subgoal commands.

Exercise 8.8 Prove $(A \Longrightarrow B \land C) \Longrightarrow (A \Longrightarrow B) \land (A \Longrightarrow C)$ using the subgoal
commands.

Exercise 8.9 Perform the proof of $\exists y.\forall x.A \vdash \forall x.\exists y.A$ using the subgoal commands.

8.7   Tacticals

Tactics are combined using tacticals. The basic tacticals apply tactics in sequence
or as alternatives. Theorem continuations provide a powerful means of letting
intermediate theorems direct the course of inference. List tacticals operate on lists
of tactics or on the assumption list of the goal.

8.7.1   Basic tacticals

The tacticals *THEN*, *ORELSE*, and *REPEAT* provide sequential, alternative, and
repetitive invocation of tactics. Their polymorphic types are complex: they apply in the general case where goals need not involve formulas, the subgoals may
have a different type than the goal, and validations may have various types. The
Edinburgh LCF manual gives an example of using tactics to factor numbers into
primes [41, page 58]. When the general type is complicated, the instance of the
type for PPλ tactics is given first.

Sequencing

THEN: tactic × tactic → tactic   (infix)

$THEN$: $(\alpha \rightarrow (\beta \; list \times (\beta' \; list \rightarrow \alpha'))) \times$
$\qquad (\beta \rightarrow (\gamma \; list \times (\gamma' \; list \rightarrow \beta'))) \rightarrow$
$\qquad (\alpha \rightarrow (\gamma \; list \times (\gamma' \; list \rightarrow \alpha')))$

The tactic tac_1 *THEN* tac_2 applies two tactics in succession. It applies tac_1 to the goal, then applies tac_2 to the resulting subgoals, and returns a flattened list of the subgoals of the subgoals. Its validation composes tac_1's validation with those returned by tac_2 for each of the subgoals. If tac_1 returns an empty subgoal list, then tac_2 is never invoked.

The resulting tactic fails, raising exception *tactic*, if tac_1 or tac_2 does.

$THENL$: $tactic \times tactic \; list \rightarrow tactic$ (infix)
$THENL$: $(\alpha \rightarrow (\beta \; list \times (\beta' \; list \rightarrow \alpha'))) \times$
$\qquad\quad (\beta \rightarrow (\gamma \; list \times (\gamma' \; list \rightarrow \beta'))) \; list \rightarrow$
$\qquad\quad (\alpha \rightarrow (\gamma \; list \times (\gamma' \; list \rightarrow \alpha')))$

The tactical *THENL* is like *THEN* but applies a different tactic to each subgoal. The tactic tac_1 *THENL* $[tac_{21}, \ldots, tac_{2k}]$ applies tac_1 to the goal, producing subgoals $g_1, \ldots, g_k$; it then applies tac_{21} to $g_1, \ldots$, and tac_{2k} to $g_k, \ldots$. Useful when you know the exact number and kind of subgoals that tac_1 will produce, and want to handle each goal specially. Typically tac_1 is *CONJ_TAC*, *STRUCT_TAC*, or *COND_CASES_TAC*.

The resulting tactic fails if

- tac_1 or any of the tac_{2i} does

- tac_1 does not return exactly k subgoals

Alternation

$ORELSE$: $tactic \times tactic \rightarrow tactic$ (infix)
$ORELSE$: $(\alpha \rightarrow \beta) \times (\alpha \rightarrow \beta) \rightarrow (\alpha \rightarrow \beta)$

The tactic tac_1 *ORELSE* tac_2 applies either of two tactics: the first tactic that succeeds. It applies tac_1 to the goal, returning the subgoals and validation. If tac_1 fails then the tactic calls tac_2.

The resulting tactic fails if both tac_1 and tac_2 do.

TRY : $tactic \rightarrow tactic$
TRY : $(\alpha \rightarrow (\alpha \; list \times (\beta \; list \rightarrow \beta))) \rightarrow (\alpha \rightarrow (\alpha \; list \times (\beta \; list \rightarrow \beta)))$

The tactic *TRY tac* applies *tac* to the goal. If *tac* fails then the tactic returns its goal unchanged.

Identity elements for tacticals

These tactics, though trivial, are useful building blocks.

$ALL\_TAC : tactic$
$ALL\_TAC : \alpha \rightarrow (\alpha\ list \times (\beta\ list \rightarrow \beta))$

This tactic accepts all goals, passing the goal unchanged. It is an identity element for the tactical *THEN*.

$NO\_TAC : tactic$
$NO\_TAC : \alpha \rightarrow \beta$

This tactic accepts no goals: it always fails. It is an identity element for the tactical *ORELSE*.

$FAIL\_TAC : string \rightarrow tactic$
$FAIL\_TAC : string \rightarrow \alpha \rightarrow \beta$

This tactic is like *NO_TAC* but takes its failure string as an argument. It can produce error messages:

```
MY_TAC  THEN  FAIL_TAC "MY_TAC left unsolved subgoals!"
```

If *MY_TAC* returns the empty list of subgoals then *FAIL_TAC* is never called.

Repetition

$REPEAT : tactic \rightarrow tactic$
$REPEAT : (\alpha \rightarrow (\alpha\ list \times (\beta\ list \rightarrow \beta))) \rightarrow (\alpha \rightarrow (\alpha\ list \times (\beta\ list \rightarrow \beta)))$

The tactic *REPEAT tac* applies *tac* to the goal, and to all resulting subgoals. The tactic can never fail: it returns all subgoals for which *tac* fails. The tactic can easily diverge. In order to terminate, *tac* should produce a proof tree where every branch terminates either by failing or by having no subgoals.

The tactical is implemented using recursion and simple primitives. The actual code is

```
fun REPEAT tac g =
    ((tac THEN REPEAT tac) ORELSE ALL_TAC) g;
```

Observe the similarity to the treatment of repetition in syntax rules. The argument *g* must be mentioned; if it were omitted from both sides, the definition would contain an infinite recursion in REPEAT tac.

Making a tactic valid

VALID : *tactic* → *tactic*
    tac

The tactical *VALID* constructs (usually) valid tactics. It applies *tac* to the goal, then tests the resulting validation on dummy theorems. If the resulting theorem differs from the goal, or contains additional assumptions, then *VALID* fails; otherwise it returns the goal list and validation. *VALID* uses *chktac*, which is imperfect but fairly reliable.

Example 8.7 The tactical *REPEAT* applied to the tactics *CONJ_TAC*, *CONJ_LEFT_TAC*, and *DISCH_TAC* yields a tactic that can prove many theorems about conjunction and implication.

```
! val A = 'p==TT' and B = 'q==TT' and C = 'r==TT';
- val A = 'p == TT' : form
- val B = 'q == TT' : form
- val C = 'r == TT' : form

! val g = ([], '^A /\ ^B /\ ^C ==> ^C /\ ^B /\ ^A');
- val g =
([],
 'p == TT  /\  q == TT  /\  r == TT  ==>
  r == TT  /\  q == TT  /\  p == TT')
 : ('a list * form)
```

First, try *CONJ_TAC* and *DISCH_TAC*. It is easy to see that three subgoals will be produced.

```
! val ([g11,g12,g13],prf1) = REPEAT (DISCH_TAC ORELSE CONJ_TAC) g;
- val g11 = (['p == TT /\ q == TT /\ r == TT'], 'r == TT') : goal
- val g12 = (['p == TT /\ q == TT /\ r == TT'], 'q == TT') : goal
- val g13 = (['p == TT /\ q == TT /\ r == TT'], 'p == TT') : goal
- val prf1 = fn : proof
```

Working on the goal g11, clearly the tactic *CONJ_LEFT_TAC* should be called repeatedly to break up the conjunctive assumption. The alternative is to call *ACCEPT_ASM_TAC* to check if the goal has been proved. The tactical *ORELSE* combines these into a tactic to solve the goal.

```
! REPEAT (CONJ_LEFT_TAC ORELSE ACCEPT_ASM_TAC) g11;
- it = ([],fn) : subgoals

! chktac it;
- it = .|-'r == TT' : thm
```

Observe the use of *chktac* to apply the validation. Since the other goals can probably be solved in the same way, why not join the two calls to *REPEAT* into a big tactic, and apply it to the original goal?

```
! val REP_CONJ_TAC =
>       REPEAT (DISCH_TAC ORELSE CONJ_TAC) THEN
>       REPEAT (CONJ_LEFT_TAC ORELSE ACCEPT_ASM_TAC);
- val REP_CONJ_TAC = fn : tactic

! REP_CONJ_TAC g;
- it = ([],fn) : subgoals

! chktac it;
- it =
|-'p == TT  /\  q == TT  /\  r == TT  ==>
   r == TT  /\  q == TT  /\  p == TT' : thm
```

The tactic *STRIP_TAC* uses most of the rules for the connectives, solving the goal more easily. It can remove all the connectives from the original goal.

```
! REPEAT STRIP_TAC g;
- it =
([(['r == TT','q == TT','p == TT'],'r == TT'),
  (['r == TT','q == TT','p == TT'],'q == TT'),
  (['r == TT','q == TT','p == TT'],'p == TT')],
 fn) : subgoals
```

By including *ACCEPT_ASM_TAC* in the repetition, the goal is solved in a single step.

```
! REPEAT (STRIP_TAC ORELSE ACCEPT_ASM_TAC) g;
- it = ([],fn) : subgoals

! chktac it;
- it =
|-'p == TT  /\  q == TT  /\  r == TT  ==>
   r == TT  /\  q == TT  /\  p == TT' : thm
```

Example 8.8 As promised, we shall now see Example 8.6 proved in a few steps. Let the goal be as in that example, and *REPEAT*edly apply tactics to break it apart:

```
! set_goal (['(^A /\ ^B) \/ ^C'], '(^A \/ ^C) /\ (^B \/ ^C)');
1 subgoal
'(p == TT  \/  r == TT)  /\  (q == TT  \/  r == TT)'
```

```
['p == TT  /\  q == TT  \/  r == TT']
```

```
! expand (REPEAT (DISJ_LEFT_TAC  ORELSE
>                 CONJ_LEFT_TAC  ORELSE  CONJ_TAC));
4 subgoals
'q == TT  \/  r == TT'
  ['r == TT']

'p == TT  \/  r == TT'
  ['r == TT']

'q == TT  \/  r == TT'
  ['q == TT']
  ['p == TT']

'p == TT  \/  r == TT'
  ['q == TT']
```

Each of these four subgoals can be solved by either *DISJ1_TAC* or *DISJ1_TAC*, followed by *ACCEPT_ASM_TAC*. But observe that the tactic

```
                DISJ1_TAC  ORELSE  DISJ2_TAC
```

cannot help us: it always performs *DISJ1_TAC*. The problem is to choose the disjunction tactic that makes the next step, *ACCEPT_ASM_TAC*, succeed. Recall that *THEN* applies one tactic after another, and fails if either does. Let us try such a composite tactic:

```
! expand (DISJ2_TAC THEN ACCEPT_ASM_TAC);
exception raised: tactic with
      ("ACCEPT_ASM_TAC",[(['p == TT','q == TT'],'r == TT')])
```

A tactic to choose a disjunction tactic *and* perform the next step is

```
      (DISJ1_TAC THEN ACCEPT_ASM_TAC)  ORELSE
      (DISJ2_TAC THEN ACCEPT_ASM_TAC)
```

This tactic should be included in the big *REPEAT* that attacks the original goal. We return to that goal and try it; it solves the goal at once.

```
! backup();
1 subgoal
'(p == TT  \/  r == TT)  /\  (q == TT  \/  r == TT)'
  ['p == TT  /\  q == TT  \/  r == TT']
```

```
! expand (REPEAT (DISJ_LEFT_TAC   ORELSE
>                 CONJ_LEFT_TAC   ORELSE CONJ_TAC   ORELSE
>                 (DISJ1_TAC THEN ACCEPT_ASM_TAC)   ORELSE
>                 (DISJ2_TAC THEN ACCEPT_ASM_TAC)));
goal proved
. |-'(p == TT  \/  r == TT)  /\  (q == TT  \/  r == TT)'

previous subproof:
goal proved

! save_top_thm"distributive";
- it =
|-'!p q r.
    p == TT  /\  q == TT  \/  r == TT  ==>
    (p == TT  \/  r == TT)  /\  (q == TT  \/  r == TT)'  : thm
```

8.7.2   Theorem continuations

Elimination rules break apart theorems and assumptions. *Theorem continuations,* which are functions of type *thm → tactic,* control the proof using theorems generated as intermediate results. For example, breaking up the theorem $A \land B \land C$ yields A and $B \land C$; the latter result is not made visible but broken into B and C. The three theorems A, B, and C are then put through the process again. The word *continuation* is used with the same meaning as in denotational semantics [96]: a function describing what to do with any theorems that are generated. Here a theorem is turned into a tactic for continuing the proof.

A tactical of type *(thm → tactic) → (thm → tactic)* transforms one continuation into another. The transformation may consist of composing instances of the continuations using the tactical *THEN.* Another possible transformation is composing an inference rule with the continuation, so that it handles theorems of a different form.

If Cambridge LCF has a theme, it is higher order functions. Higher order functions appear again in the following chapter, on rewriting. Theorem continuations may seem pointless: the rules of the sequent calculus perform the same deductions with greater clarity. Higher order functions can be difficult to understand, but provide more control and probably greater efficiency. To be honest, I developed theorem continuations before I appreciated the sequent calculus.

Notation: When a theorem appears in an ML program, as in $\langle \Gamma \vdash A \rangle$, it stands for ML code whose value is that theorem. For example, the ML expression $ACCEPT\_TAC\langle A \vdash A \rangle$ stands for $ACCEPT\_TAC(ASSUME(A)))$. When the proof involves a complicated combination of inference rules, writing the theorem itself is more readable. This notation is only for exposition, of course: it cannot be used in a real program.

Conjunction elimination

$$CONJUNCTS\_THEN : \underset{c}{(thm \rightarrow tactic)} \rightarrow (\underset{A \wedge B}{thm} \rightarrow tactic)$$

$$\frac{\Gamma, A, B \vdash C}{\Gamma, A \wedge B \vdash C}$$

The resulting continuation handles the theorem $A \wedge B$ by calling its input continuation c with the theorems A and B, giving the tactic

$$c\langle \vdash A \rangle \; THEN \; c\langle \vdash B \rangle$$

Disjunction elimination

$$DISJ\_CASES\_THEN : (thm \rightarrow tactic) \rightarrow (\underset{A \vee B}{thm} \rightarrow tactic)$$

$$\frac{\Gamma, A \vdash C \qquad \Gamma, B \vdash C}{\Gamma, A \vee B \vdash C}$$

The resulting continuation handles the assumption $A \vee B$ by calling its input continuation with the assumptions A and B. This produces a tactic tac_A using the implicit assumption $A \vdash A$, and likewise a tactic tac_B for B. These are combined; the resulting tactic performs the case split $A \vee B$ goal by applying both tac_A and tac_B to the given goal, appending the subgoal lists for A and B.

Implication introduction

$$DISCH\_THEN : (thm \rightarrow tactic) \rightarrow tactic$$

$$\frac{\Gamma, A \vdash B}{\Gamma \vdash A \Longrightarrow B}$$

The resulting tactic handles a goal $A \Longrightarrow B$ by calling the continuation on the assumption A.

Bi-implication elimination

$$IFF\_THEN : (thm \rightarrow tactic) \rightarrow (\underset{A \Longleftrightarrow B}{thm} \rightarrow tactic)$$

$$\frac{\Gamma \vdash A \Longleftrightarrow B}{\Gamma \vdash (A \Longrightarrow B) \wedge (B \Longrightarrow A)}$$

The resulting continuation handles the theorem $A \iff B$ by calling its input
continuation c with the theorems $A \implies B$ and $B \implies A$, giving the tactic

$$c\langle\vdash A \implies B\rangle \; THEN \; c\langle\vdash B \implies A\rangle$$

Exists elimination

$$CHOOSE\_THEN : (thm \rightarrow tactic) \rightarrow (\; thm \; \rightarrow tactic)$$
$$\exists x. A(x)$$

$$\frac{\Gamma, A[x'/x] \vdash B}{\Gamma, \exists x. A \vdash B} \qquad provided \; x' \; is \; not \; free \; in \; \exists x.A, \; \Gamma, \; or \; B$$

The resulting continuation handles the assumption $\exists x. A(x)$ by choosing a variant
x' of x and calling its input continuation with the assumption $A(x')$.

Stripping connectives from a theorem

$$STRIP\_THM\_THEN : (thm \rightarrow tactic) \rightarrow (thm \rightarrow tactic)$$

This uses the continuation transformer determined by the input theorem: it handles conjunctions with $CONJUNCTS\_THEN$, disjunctions with $DISJ\_CASES\_THEN$,
and existentials with $CHOOSE\_THEN$. The tactic $STRIP\_THM\_TAC$ works by repeatedly invoking $STRIP\_THM\_THEN$ with $CHECK\_THM\_TAC$ as the final continuation.

Stripping connectives from a goal

$$STRIP\_GOAL\_THEN : (thm \rightarrow tactic) \rightarrow tactic$$

This tries one of GEN_TAC, $CONJ\_TAC$, or $DISCH\_THEN$ with the given continuation. It is used to implement $STRIP\_TAC$.

8.7.3   List tacticals

List tacticals operate on lists, notably the goal's assumption list. The tactical
$ASSUM\_LIST$ gives access to the assumptions; other tacticals are elaborations of
the 2-place tacticals $THEN$ and $ORELSE$. Their n-place versions, $EVERY$ and
$FIRST$, operate on lists of tactics. They express compound tactics concisely:

```
EVERY [GEN_TAC, CONJ_TAC, EXISTS_LEFT_TAC]
```

is tidier than

```
GEN_TAC  THEN  CONJ_TAC  THEN  EXISTS_LEFT_TAC
```

Given a tactic-valued function — a tactic having additional arguments — *MAP_EVERY* and *MAP_FIRST* map that function over a list. Examples are *X_GEN_TAC* and *EXISTS_TAC*, which have type *term → tactic*. These tacticals provide a concise notation for iteration. Try

```
MAP_EVERY  EXISTS_TAC  [t,u,v]
```

instead of

```
(EXISTS_TAC t)  THEN  (EXISTS_TAC u)  THEN  (EXISTS_TAC v)
```

EVERY_ASSUM and *FIRST_ASSUM* map a function of type *thm → tactic* over the goal's assumption list, typically using *CONTR_TAC* or *SUBST1_TAC*. They produce tactics that search the assumption list, like Cohn's [22]. For instance, the tactic

```
FIRST_ASSUM (fn asm=> (CONTR_TAC asm)  ORELSE  (ACCEPT_TAC asm))
```

searches the assumptions for either a contradiction or the desired conclusion. The abstraction is a theorem continuation: it describes what to do with each assumption.

Applying a tactic to the assumption list

ASSUM_LIST : (*thm list → tactic*) → *tactic*

This maps the rule *ASSUME* over the assumptions, and supplies them to the tactic function *thltac* of type *thm list → tactic*. The tactic *ASSUM_LIST thltac*, applied to the goal $A_1, \ldots, A_n \vdash B$, is equivalent to the tactic

$$thltac[\langle A_1 \vdash A_1 \rangle, \ldots, \langle A_n \vdash A_n \rangle]$$

applied to the same goal.

Applying every tactic in sequence

EVERY : *tactic list → tactic*

The tactical *EVERY* is an n-place version of *THEN*: it maps

$$[tac_1, \ldots, tac_n] \quad \longmapsto \quad tac_1 \ THEN \ \ldots \ THEN \ tac_n \ THEN \ ALL\_TAC$$

MAP_EVERY : (α → *tactic*) → (α *list*) → *tactic*

This tactical maps its two arguments to a tactic:

$$tacf \ [x_1, \ldots, x_n] \quad \longmapsto \quad EVERY[tacf(x_1), \ldots, tacf(x_n)]$$

$EVERY\_ASSUM : (thm \rightarrow tactic) \rightarrow tactic$

The tactic $EVERY\_ASSUM\ thtac$, applied to the goal $A_1, \ldots, A_n \vdash B$, is equivalent to the tactic

$$EVERY\,[thtac\langle A_1 \vdash A_1 \rangle, \ldots, thtac\langle A_n \vdash A_n \rangle]$$

applied to the same goal.

Applying the first successful tactic

$FIRST : tactic\ list \rightarrow tactic$

The tactical $FIRST$ is an n-place version of $ORELSE$: it maps

$$[tac_1, \ldots, tac_n] \quad \longmapsto \quad tac_1\ ORELSE\ \ldots\ ORELSE\ tac_n\ ORELSE\ NO\_TAC$$

$MAP\_FIRST : (\alpha \rightarrow tactic) \rightarrow (\alpha\ list) \rightarrow tactic$

This tactical maps its two arguments to a tactic:

$$tacf\,[x_1, \ldots, x_n] \quad \longmapsto \quad FIRST\,[tacf(x_1), \ldots, tacf(x_n)]$$

$FIRST\_ASSUM : (thm \rightarrow tactic) \rightarrow tactic$

The tactic $FIRST\_ASSUM\ thtac$, applied to the goal $A_1, \ldots, A_n \vdash B$, is equivalent to the tactic

$$FIRST\,[thtac\langle A_1 \vdash A_1 \rangle, \ldots, thtac\langle A_n \vdash A_n \rangle]$$

applied to the same goal.

8.8   Discussion and further reading

Schmidt formally develops tactics and tacticals from natural deduction rules [87]. Gordon presents the implementation of inference rules, tactics, and tacticals for a propositional logic in the ML dialect of Edinburgh LCF [31]. Milner discusses the concepts of validation and achievement of a goal, and presents tactics; a parser correctness proof is expressed as a composite tactic [68]. Cohn's paper on her semantic equivalence proof describes the tactics she developed, including one of the first resolution tactics [22].

The tactics involving quantifiers, including the resolution tactics, are weak because Cambridge LCF does not support unification. Unification is easy [17], but allowing a tactic to unify against the goal is hard: goals and tactics must maintain an environment of variable bindings. Using Edinburgh LCF, Sokołowski implemented such a system [94]. He then developed tactics for his problem area, Hoare logic, and developed powerful proof procedures [95].

Chapter 9

Rewriting and Simplification

The axioms defining a function often consist of equations for patterns of input. For instance, the conditional operator is defined by the axiom $COND\_CLAUSES$:

$$\forall x : \alpha. \forall y : \alpha. (\bot \Rightarrow x \mid y) \equiv \bot \wedge (TT \Rightarrow x \mid y) \equiv x \wedge (FF \Rightarrow x \mid y) \equiv y$$

The three equations are called *rewrite rules*, or just *rewrites*. In a theory of lists with strict $CONS$, the axiom

$$\forall b : (\alpha)\, list. \; \bot \; APP \; b \equiv \bot \; \wedge$$
$$NIL \; APP \; b \equiv NIL \; \wedge$$
$$\forall x l. \, x \not\equiv \bot \Longrightarrow l \not\equiv \bot \Longrightarrow (CONS \; x \; l) \; APP \; b \equiv CONS \; x(l \; APP \; b)$$

defines the infix operator APP for appending two lists. This conjunction contains three rewrite rules. The third is an *implicative* rewrite: the equation holds only when the antecedents $x \not\equiv \bot$ and $l \not\equiv \bot$ hold.

A proof often requires the simplification of expressions containing symbols like $COND$ and APP. LCF's rewriting functions are designed to perform this symbolic execution. Substitution, using an equivalence $t_1 \equiv t_2$, can only replace free occurrences of t_1 by t_2. Rewriting is much more powerful. It accepts rewrite rules that contain variables, say $\forall x y. \, t_1 \equiv t_2$. Instances of the left hand side, say $t_1[u/x, v/y]$, are replaced by the corresponding instance $t_2[u/x, v/y]$. Rewriting traverses the formula recursively, replacing instances of t_1 at whatever depth they occur. Tautologies are reduced: $TRUTH() \wedge A$ becomes A. Rewriting continues until no further simplifications are possible.

An implicative rewrite $\forall x y. \, A \Longrightarrow t_1 \equiv t_2$ causes replacement of $t_1[u/x, v/y]$ by $t_2[u/x, v/y]$ only if the antecedent $A[u/x, v/y]$ can be proved. In the general case there can be any number of variables and antecedents. Moreover, a rewrite can be polymorphic: type variables are also instantiated. The rewrite rules for the conditional operator and for APP are both polymorphic. A *formula* rewrite rule might be $\forall x y. \, B_1 \Longleftrightarrow B_2$, and can be implicative and polymorphic. Formula rewriting replaces instances of a formula by an equivalent formula.

Rewriting continues as long as a rewrite rule matches a part of the expression being rewritten. If a term t gets rewritten — in one or more steps — to a term containing an instance of t, then rewriting runs forever. Certain rewrites are obviously dangerous. The commutative law $x + y \equiv y + x$ rewrites $t + u$ to $u + t$ to $t + u$ and so on. The axiom $\forall x : void \,.\, x \equiv \bot$ rewrites t to $\bot$ to $\bot$ and so on. An implicative rewrite $A \Longrightarrow t \equiv u$ causes nontermination if t occurs in A: the rule may be chosen to rewrite its own antecedent. An example is $p(t) \Longrightarrow t \equiv u$. Rewriting t via the rule causes rewriting of the formula $p(t)$; then the rule is chosen to rewrite t, and so on to infinity.

Rewriting can express all computable functions. So it is undecidable whether rewriting with a set of rewrite rules will terminate. In practice, interactions between rules can be devilishly tricky, especially with implicative rewrites. A policy of 'wait and see' is tedious: successful rewriting can take several minutes to terminate.

The primary purpose of rewriting is to simplify goals. Terms, formulae, and theorems can also be simplified. LCF's rewriting operators, which are similar in spirit to tactics and tacticals, can implement various rewriting strategies [75]. The standard rewriting strategy should be sufficient for most users.

9.1 The extraction of rewrite rules

The first step of rewriting is to extract the rewrite rules from the list of theorems. The derived rule *IMP_CANON* returns a list of theorems in canonical form (Section 7.2.10):

$$A_1 \Longrightarrow \cdots \Longrightarrow A_n \Longrightarrow B$$

This can be taken as an implicative rewrite using *FCONV_CANON*, depending on the form of B:

- The formula $t_1 \equiv t_2$ yields a term rewrite.

- The formula $B_1 \Longleftrightarrow B_2$ yields a formula rewrite.

- A predicate $P(t)$ yields the formula rewrite $P(t) \Longleftrightarrow TRUTH()$, unless the predicate is *FALSITY*() or $t_1 \equiv t_2$.

- A negated predicate $\neg P(t)$ yields the formula rewrite $P(t) \Longleftrightarrow FALSITY()$, even if the predicate is $t_1 \equiv t_2$ or $t_1 \sqsubseteq t_2$.

- Other formulae are rejected.

A rewrite whose right side is an instance of the left, which would obviously cause nontermination, is rejected. Rewriting proceeds using the acceptable rewrite rules. The rejection of rewrites produces *no* error message. The functions *used_rewrites* and *asm_used_rewrites* reveal what rewrites are extracted from a list of theorems.

The *fluid* variables are those that can be instantiated in a rewrite rule. For a theorem in canonical form, these are variables that are free in the conclusion but

not free in the hypotheses. All others are *frozen*: they cannot be instantiated.[1]
Type variables of polymorphic rewrite rules are also instantiated, such as α in
COND_CLAUSES. All type variables appearing in the hypothesis of a rewrite rule
are frozen because PPλ type variables cannot be bound.

The freezing effect of assumptions can help to control rewriting. Although
the assumption $\forall xy.\ x + y \equiv y + x$ causes rewriting to diverge, the assumption
$x + y \equiv y + x$ does not because x and y are frozen. The tactic *CUT_THM_TAC*
puts a theorem into the assumption list; it can be used to freeze the theorem's
variables.

Example 9.1 Suppose f, g, and h are function constants. The fluid variables of
the rewrite rule

$$\vdash \forall xy.\ f(x,y) \equiv g(h(x),y)$$

are x and y. This rewrite rule matches any term of the form $f(t,u)$ for arbitrary
terms t and u. Since *IMP_CANON* strips off quantifiers, the theorem

$$\vdash f(x,y) \equiv g(h(x),y)$$

is equivalent. The fluid variables are also x and y in the implicative rewrite

$$\vdash x \not\equiv \perp \Longrightarrow f(x,y) \equiv g(h(x),y)$$

However in

$$x \not\equiv \perp \vdash f(x,y) \equiv g(h(x),y)$$

only y is a fluid variable; the rewrite only matches terms of the form $f(x,t)$. The
variable x is frozen because it appears free in the hypothesis.

If A is an assumption of a goal then the theorem $A \vdash A$ may be used in proving
the goal. In such theorems *all* free variables are frozen: only bound variables can
be fluid. For instance, the assumption $f(x,y) \equiv g(h(x),y)$ corresponds to the
theorem

$$f(x,y) \equiv g(h(x),y) \vdash f(x,y) \equiv g(h(x),y)$$

where both x and y are frozen. The assumption $\forall x.\ f(x,y) \equiv g(h(x),y)$ corresponds to the theorem

$$\forall x.\ f(x,y) \equiv g(h(x),y) \vdash \forall x.\ f(x,y) \equiv g(h(x),y)$$

where only y is frozen.

---

[1]See the inference rules *INST* and *INST_TYPE*, Section 7.2.9.

9.2   The standard rewriting strategy

The extraction process produces a list of term rewrites of the form

$$A_1 \Longrightarrow \cdots \Longrightarrow A_n \Longrightarrow t_1 \equiv t_2$$

and formula rewrites of the form

$$A_1 \Longrightarrow \cdots \Longrightarrow A_n \Longrightarrow (B_1 \Longleftrightarrow B_2) \,.$$

A rewriting step replaces a term or formula. An instance of the term t_1 causes a recursive call of rewriting on the corresponding instances of the antecedents $A_1, \ldots, A_n$. If they are all rewritten to $TRUTH()$, then the instance of t_1 is replaced t_2. Formula rewriting is similar. An instance of the formula B_1 is replaced by the corresponding instance of B_2 provided the antecedents can be rewritten to $TRUTH()$.

The standard rewriting strategy accumulates *local assumptions*. For a conjunction $A \wedge C$ or implication $A \Longrightarrow C$, it rewrites A to B, then extracts new rules from B for rewriting C to D. The derived rule *MK_IMP* discharges the local assumptions:

$$\frac{\Gamma \vdash A \Longleftrightarrow B \qquad \Delta, A, B \vdash C \Longleftrightarrow D}{\Gamma, \Delta \vdash (A \Longrightarrow C) \Longleftrightarrow (B \Longrightarrow D)}$$

The rule for conjunction is similar.

Tautologous formulae such as $A \wedge TRUTH()$ are simplified. Beta-conversion occurs whenever possible. Disjunctions are expanded wherever they appear as conjuncts or antedecents:

$$
\begin{aligned}
(A \vee B) \wedge C &\longmapsto & (A \wedge C) \vee (B \wedge C) \\
C \wedge (A \vee B) &\longmapsto & (C \wedge A) \vee (C \wedge B) \\
(A \vee B) \Longrightarrow C &\longmapsto & (A \Longrightarrow C) \wedge (B \Longrightarrow C)
\end{aligned}
$$

The last gives case analysis on whether A or B is true; C is simplified twice. Local assumptions in A and B may rewrite the two occurrences of C to different results.

Existential formulae are similarly expanded. The bound variable x may be renamed to x' to avoid its capture by the surrounding formula:

$$
\begin{aligned}
(\exists x.A) \wedge B &\longmapsto & \exists x'. \, A[x'/x] \wedge B \\
B \wedge (\exists x.A) &\longmapsto & \exists x'. \, B \wedge A[x'/x] \\
(\exists x.A) \Longrightarrow B &\longmapsto & \forall x'. \, A[x'/x] \Longrightarrow B
\end{aligned}
$$

Subexpressions are repeatedly rewritten until no transformations are applicable.

9.3   Top-level rewriting tools

Rewriting tactics apply the standard rewriting strategy to goals. LCF also provides functions for rewriting theorems, terms, and formulae. Each function takes two arguments: a list of theorems and the expression to rewrite. It extracts rewrite rules from the list of theorems, then rewrites the expression. It returns justification that the rewritten expression is equivalent to the original expression. The form of justification depends on the kind of expression being rewritten, but always involves a PPλ theorem.

9.3.1   The rewriting of goals

REWRITE_TAC : *thm list* $\rightarrow$ *tactic*
ASM_REWRITE_TAC : *thm list* $\rightarrow$ *tactic*

REWRITE_TAC extracts rewrite rules from the given list of theorems and uses them to simplify the goal. If it simplifies the goal to *TRUTH*() then it returns the empty list of subgoals; otherwise it returns the simplified goal. *ASM_REWRITE_TAC* is similar but adds the goal's assumptions to the given list of theorems. The tactics return a validation to justify the rewriting.

Only the right side formula of the goal is simplified: *not* the assumptions.

Example 9.2 Here is the justification of an elementary program transformation. If f is a strict function then it commutes with the conditional operator, namely $f(p \Rightarrow x \mid y)$ equals $p \Rightarrow f(x) \mid f(y)$. The proof is by case analysis on p followed by rewriting.

Start by constructing the goal

$$f(\bot) \equiv \bot \vdash f(p \Rightarrow x \mid y) \equiv (p \Rightarrow f(x) \mid f(y))$$

The meta variable f contains the polymorphic object variable $f : \alpha \rightarrow \beta$. Inserting f by antiquotation makes types unambiguous in the goal.

```
! val f = 'f : 'a -> 'b';
- val f = 'f' : term

! val g = (['^f(UU)==UU'],  '^f(p=>x|y)  == (p => ^f x | ^f y)');
- val g = (['f UU == UU'],'f(p => x | y) == (p => f x | f y)')
      : goal
```

The axiom *TR_CASES* gives case analysis over type *tr*. The logical rules are ∨-elimination and ∀-elimination, which can be used via *DISJ_LEFT_TAC* and *FORALL_LEFT_TAC*, or by *STRIP_THM_TAC* and the rule *SPEC*.

```
! STRIP_THM_TAC (SPEC 'p:tr' TR_CASES) g;
- it =
([(['p == UU','f UU == UU'],'f(p => x | y) == (p => f x | f y)'),
  (['p == TT','f UU == UU'],'f(p => x | y) == (p => f x | f y)'),
  (['p == FF','f UU == UU'],'f(p => x | y) == (p => f x | f y)')],
 fn) : subgoals
```

Clearly *ASM_REWRITE_TAC* can simplify each of these goals. The easiest way to apply the tactic to all three goals is to apply a compound tactic — built from *STRIP_THM_TAC* and *ASM_REWRITE_TAC* via *THEN* — to the original goal.

```
! (STRIP_THM_TAC (SPEC 'p:tr' TR_CASES) THEN
>   ASM_REWRITE_TAC []) g;
- it =
([(['p == UU','f UU == UU'],'f(UU=> x | y) == (UU => f x | f y)'),
  (['p == TT','f UU == UU'],'f(TT=> x | y) == (TT => f x | f y)'),
  (['p == FF','f UU == UU'],'f(FF=> x | y) == (FF => f x | f y)')],
 fn) : subgoals
```

The rewriting tactic has substituted for *p* in each subgoal. The conditional expressions can be simplified using the axiom *COND_CLAUSES*. Again, it is simplest to go back to the original goal. The tactic leaves no subgoals; applying the validation gives the desired theorem.

```
! (STRIP_THM_TAC (SPEC 'p:tr' TR_CASES) THEN
>   ASM_REWRITE_TAC [COND_CLAUSES]) g;
- it = ([],fn) : subgoals

! chktac it;
- it = .|-'f(p => x | y) == (p => f x | f y)' : thm

! hyp it;
- it = ['f UU == UU'] : form list
```

Example 9.3 Recall the isomorphism that justifies the currying of functions:

$$(\sigma \times \tau) \to \upsilon \; \cong \; \sigma \to (\tau \to \upsilon)$$

It was discussed but not proved in Example 4.3. When trying to prove that two types are isomorphic, guessing the isomorphism functions is interesting but verifying that they satisfy the equations is a tedious exercise of rewriting.

First we construct the goal: that there are isomorphism functions ϕ and ψ between the types.

```
! val h = 'h : ('a * 'b) -> 'c';
```

```
- val h = 'h' : term

! val k = 'k: 'a -> ('b -> 'c) ';
- val k = 'k' : term

! set_goal ([], '?phi psi. (!^h. phi(psi ^h) == ^h) /\
>                           (!^k. psi(phi ^k) == ^k)');
1 subgoal
'?phi psi. (!h. phi(psi h) == h)  /\  (!k. psi(phi k) == k)'
```

Now we supply terms for the functions in question:

```
! expand (EXISTS_TAC '\^k z. ^k(FST z)(SND z)');
1 subgoal
'?psi.
  (!h. (\k.\z.k(FST z)(SND z))(psi h) == h)  /\
  (!k. psi((\k.\z.k(FST z)(SND z))k) == k)'

! expand (EXISTS_TAC '\^h x y.  ^h(x,y)');
1 subgoal
'(!h. (\k.\z.k(FST z)(SND z))((\h.\x.\y.h(x,y))h) == h)  /\
 (!k. (\h.\x.\y.h(x,y))((\k.\z.k(FST z)(SND z))k) == k)'
```

Rewriting appears to be necessary, but break down the goal first.

```
! expand (REPEAT STRIP_TAC);
2 subgoals
'(\h.\x.\y.h(x,y))((\k.\z.k(FST z)(SND z))k) == k'

'(\k.\z.k(FST z)(SND z))((\h.\x.\y.h(x,y))h) == h'

! expand (REWRITE_TAC []);
1 subgoal
'\z.h(FST z,SND z) == h'
```

Standard facts about pairing and extensionality of functions solve this goal.

```
! expand (REWRITE_TAC [MK_PAIR,ETA_EQ]);
goal proved
|-'\z.h(FST z,SND z) == h'
|-'(\k.\z.k(FST z)(SND z))((\h.\x.\y.h(x,y))h) == h'

previous subproof:
1 subgoal
'(\h.\x.\y.h(x,y))((\k.\z.k(FST z)(SND z))k) == k'
```

This obviously requires rewriting, using facts about *FST* and *SND*. The resulting
subgoal again involves extensionality.

```
! expand (REWRITE_TAC [FST_PAIR,SND_PAIR]);
1 subgoal
'\x.\y.k x y == k'

! expand (REWRITE_TAC [ETA_EQ]);
goal proved
|-'\x.\y.k x y == k'
|-'(\h.\x.\y.h(x,y))((\k.\z.k(FST z)(SND z))k) == k'
|-'(!h. (\k.\z.k(FST z)(SND z))((\h.\x.\y.h(x,y))h) == h)  /\
    (!k. (\h.\x.\y.h(x,y))((\k.\z.k(FST z)(SND z))k) == k)'
|-'?psi.
    (!h. (\k.\z.k(FST z)(SND z))(psi h) == h)  /\
    (!k. psi((\k.\z.k(FST z)(SND z))k) == k)'
|-'?phi psi. (!h. phi(psi h) == h)  /\  (!k. psi(phi k) == k)'

! top_thm();
- it =
|-'?phi psi. (!h. phi(psi h) == h) /\ (!k. psi(phi k) == k)'  : thm
```

Actually, rewriting can finish the proof after the two calls to *EXISTS_TAC*. A
tactic to solve the original goal is

```
        EXISTS_TAC '\^k z. ^k(FST z)(SND z)'    THEN
        EXISTS_TAC '\^h x y.   ^h(x,y)'         THEN
        REWRITE_TAC [MK_PAIR, FST_PAIR, SND_PAIR, ETA_EQ]
```

9.3.2   The rewriting of terms and formulae

rewrite_term : *thm list* → *term* → *thm*
rewrite_form : *thm list* → *form* → *thm*

These functions rewrite a term or formula. The result is a *theorem*, not a term
or formula! If a term t is simplified to u then the result is $t \equiv u$; if a formula A
is simplified to B then the result is $A \iff B$. The theorem is justification that
the rewritten expression is equivalent to the orginal one. Its assumptions are the
assumptions of the rewrite rules used. The simplified expression is obtained from
the theorem using the functions *rhs* or *dest_iff*.

Example 9.4 Let us look at the rewriting of terms. The meta variable tm holds
a term containing a conditional expression and the function *SND*.

```
! val tm = 'f((TT=>r|UU : tr), SND(t:tr, r)) : tr';
- val tm = 'f((TT => r | UU),SND(t,r))' : term
```

Calling *rewrite_term* with no rewrite rules, not surprisingly, has no effect on the
term. Including the axiom *COND_CLAUSES* simplifies the conditional, and including *SND_PAIR* simplifies the term completely.

```
! rewrite_term [] tm;
- it =
|-'f((TT => r | UU),SND(t,r)) == f((TT => r | UU),SND(t,r))' : thm
```

```
! rewrite_term [COND_CLAUSES] tm;
- it = |-'f((TT => r | UU),SND(t,r)) == f(r,SND(t,r))' : thm
```

```
! rewrite_term [COND_CLAUSES,SND_PAIR] tm;
- it = |-'f((TT => r | UU),SND(t,r)) == f(r,r)' : thm
```

A more complicated example requires β-reduction and the simplification of
FST. The β-reduction is always performed, even if no theorems are supplied to
rewrite_term.

```
! rewrite_term [] 'FST((\p. p => (c,TT) | (FF,d))(TT))';
- it =
|-'FST((\p.(p=> (c,TT) | (FF,d)))TT) == FST(TT=> (c,TT) | (FF,d))'
    : thm
```

```
! rewrite_term [COND_CLAUSES,FST_PAIR]
>                         'FST((\p. p => (c,TT) | (FF,d))(TT))';
- it = |-'FST((\p.(p => (c,TT) | (FF,d)))TT) == c' : thm
```

Example 9.5 The rewriting of formulae is similar, but here is an opportunity
to understand frozen and fluid variables. Start with a formula that simplifies to
$f(q,q) \equiv f(r,r)$ by removing occurrences of *SND*.

```
! val f = 'f:tr*tr -> tr';
- val f = 'f' : term
```

```
! val fm = '^f(q, SND(FF,q)) == ^f(SND(TT,r), r)';
- val fm = 'f(q,SND(FF,q)) == f(SND(TT,r),r)' : form
```

```
! rewrite_form [SND_PAIR] fm;
- it = |-'f(q,SND(FF,q)) == f(SND(TT,r),r)  <=>  f(q,q) == f(r,r)'
    : thm
```

In the rewrite rule

$$f(q, q) \equiv g(q) \vdash f(q, q) \equiv g(q)$$

the variable q is frozen because it is free in the hypothesis, so the formula simplifies to $g(q) \equiv f(r, r)$. In

$$\forall q.\, f(q, q) \equiv g(q) \vdash \forall q.\, f(q, q) \equiv g(q)$$

the variable q is fluid, and the formula simplifies to $g(q) \equiv g(r)$.

The resulting theorem depends on the hypotheses of the rewrite rules.

```
! rewrite_form [SND_PAIR, ASSUME      '^f(q,q) == g(q)'] fm;
- it = .|-'f(q,SND(FF,q)) == f(SND(TT,r),r)   <=>   g q == f(r,r)'
    : thm


! hyp it;
- it = ['f(q,q) == g q'] : form list


! rewrite_form [SND_PAIR, ASSUME '!q. ^f(q,q) == g(q)'] fm;
- it = .|-'f(q,SND(FF,q)) == f(SND(TT,r),r)   <=>   g q == g r' : thm


! hyp it;
- it = ['!q. f(q,q) == g q'] : form list
```

Example 9.6 Formula rewrites are less often used than term rewrites, but are occasionally valuable. The formula rewrite $h(x) \equiv \bot \Longleftrightarrow x \equiv \bot$ expresses that the function h is both strict and total. In the session below, the subformula $h(h(hn)) \equiv \bot$ is rewritten to $h(hn) \equiv \bot$, to $hn \equiv \bot$, and finally to $n \equiv \bot$. The subformula $h(\bot) \equiv \bot$ is rewritten to $\bot \equiv \bot$ and then to $TRUTH()$, which is cancelled by tautology reasoning.

The first declaration defines a meta variable for antiquotation. The second declares the formula rewrite rule as an assumption. The third uses that rewrite on the formula $(\exists n. h(h(hn)) \equiv \bot) \wedge \forall z. g(hz) \equiv z \wedge h(\bot) \equiv \bot$.

```
! val h = 'h:tr -> tr';
- val h = 'h' : term


! val frew = ASSUME '!x. ^h(x)==UU <=> x==UU';
- val frew = .|-'!x. h x == UU   <=>   x == UU' : thm


! rewrite_form [frew] '(?n. ^h(^h(^h n))==UU) /\
>                       !z. g(^h z)==z /\ ^h(UU)==UU';
- it =
```

```
.|-'(?n. h(h(h n)) == UU) /\ (!z. g(h z) == z /\ h UU == UU)  <=>
    (?n. n == UU /\ (!z. g(h z) == z))' : thm


! hyp it;
- it = ['!x. h x == UU  <=>  x == UU'] : form list
```

9.3.3   The rewriting of theorems

REWRITE_RULE : *thm list → thm → thm*
ASM_REWRITE_RULE : *thm list → thm → thm*

These derived inference rules rewrite the premise to yield a simplified conclusion. *REWRITE_RULE* extracts rewrite rules from the given list of theorems and
uses them to simplify the premise. *ASM_REWRITE_RULE* is similar but adds the
premise's assumptions to the list of theorems. The assumptions of the rewrite rules
may become assumptions of the conclusion. The rewriting needs no justification
since its result is a theorem.

Example 9.7 It is rarely useful to rewrite a theorem, and hard to find a convincing example. Here, the meta variable h, from a previous example, is used to
construct a term not in simplest form. The specialization rule produces a theorem
containing that term.

```
! SPEC 'FST(^h(v),^h(w))' TR_CASES;
- it =
|-'FST(h v,h w) == UU \/ FST(h v,h w) == TT \/ FST(h v,h w) == FF'
  : thm


! REWRITE_RULE [FST_PAIR] it;
- it = |-'h v == UU \/ h v == TT \/ h v == FF' : thm
```

9.3.4   Useful functions

The following functions are intended for use with rewriting.

REV_REWRITE : *thm → thm*

The orientation of a term or formula rewrite rule is reversed. The argument
should be a theorem that concludes $t \equiv u$ or $A \Longleftrightarrow B$, possibly with quantifiers
and antecedents in front. *REV_REWRITE* returns a logically equivalent theorem
that concludes $u \equiv t$ or $B \Longleftrightarrow A$.

used_rewrites : *thm list → (thm list × thm list)*
asm_used_rewrites : *thm list → goal → (thm list × thm list)*

These functions extract rewrite rules from a list of theorems, in the standard
way, for predicting the outcome of *REWRITE_TAC* and *ASM_REWRITE_TAC*. The
function *used_rewrites* puts the theorems into canonical form and classifies them as
term rewrites, formula rewrites, or unsuitable for rewriting. The output consists
of a pair (term rewrites, formula rewrites). Similar is *asm_used_rewrites*. Its
argument is a goal; it extracts rewrites from the goal's assumptions as well as the
theorems.

Example 9.8 These functions welcome experimentation at the terminal. The axiom *COND_CLAUSES* contains only term rewrites, *TR_LESS_DISTINCT* only formula rewrites.

```
! REV_REWRITE FST_PAIR;
- it = |-'x == FST(x,y)' : thm


! REV_REWRITE (ASSUME '!x. ^h(x)==UU <=> x==UU');
- it = .|-'x == UU  <=>  h x == UU' : thm


! REV_REWRITE (ASSUME '!y. ~ y==UU /\ x<<y ==>
>                                ^f(x, ^h y) == ^f(^h x, y)');
- it = .|-'~ y == UU  ==>  x << y  ==>  f(h x,y) == f(x,h y)' : thm
```

In the last example above, the theorem has been put into canonical form with
stripping of quantifiers and 'currying' of implications. It is also the only example
in which we might actually want to reverse the rewrite rule.

```
! used_rewrites [COND_CLAUSES];
- it =
([|-'(UU => x | y) == UU',
  |-'(TT => x | y) == x',
  |-'(FF => x | y) == y'],
 []) : (thm list * thm list)


! used_rewrites [TR_LESS_DISTINCT];
- it =
([],
 [|-'TT << FF  <=>  FALSITY ()',
  |-'FF << TT  <=>  FALSITY ()',
  |-'TT << UU  <=>  FALSITY ()',
  |-'FF << UU  <=>  FALSITY ()']) : (thm list * thm list)
```

Observe how negated predicates are treated as formula rewrites to *FALSITY*().

9.4   Conversions

Functions that map terms t to theorems $t \equiv u$ are called *term conversions*; they play a fundamental role in rewriting. Functions that map formulae A to theorems $A \Longleftrightarrow B$ are called *formula conversions*. Rewriting is implemented through conversions and operators (conversionals?) for constructing conversions from smaller ones. Conversions fail by raising exception *general* of type *string*.

LCF defines type abbreviations for conversions and formula conversions:

```
type conv = term -> thm;
type fconv = form -> thm;
```

The top-level rewriting functions create conversions. Note their types:

$$rewrite\_term : thm\ list \rightarrow conv$$

$$rewrite\_form : thm\ list \rightarrow fconv$$

9.4.1   Basic conversions

The basic conversions accept just a few different inputs, failing on all others. Nonetheless they are the building blocks of all LCF simplification. They are β-conversion, replacement of a term, and replacement of a formula.

First of all, observe that the axiom scheme *BETA_CONV* is indeed a conversion in the present sense, giving the map

$$(\lambda x.t)u \quad \longmapsto \quad \vdash (\lambda x.t)u \equiv t[u/x]$$

REWRITE_CONV : *thm* $\rightarrow$ *conv*

This regards an equality theorem $\Gamma \vdash \forall x_1 \ldots x_n . t_1 \equiv t_2$ as a term rewrite rule. The resulting term conversion maps an instance of t_1 to the corresponding instance of t_2. The fluid variables include $x_1 \ldots x_n$ and all variables and type variables that are free in t_1 and not free in the assumptions Γ. Let $[\cdots]$ be a substitution for the fluid variables; note that it does *not* affect Γ. The effect is

$$t_1[\cdots] \quad \longmapsto \quad \Gamma \vdash t_1[\cdots] \equiv t_2[\cdots] \, .$$

It raises exception *general* unless its input is an instance of t_1.

REWRITE_FCONV : *thm* $\rightarrow$ *fconv*

This regards the bi-implication $\Gamma \vdash \forall x_1 \ldots x_n . B_1 \Longleftrightarrow B_2$ as a formula rewrite rule. The resulting formula conversion maps

$$B_1[\cdots] \quad \longmapsto \quad \Gamma \vdash B_1[\cdots] \Longleftrightarrow B_2[\cdots] \, .$$

It raises exception *general* unless its input is an instance of B_1. Again, the substitution does not affect Γ.

9.4.2   Conversion operators

Conversions are constructed using operators related to the tacticals *THEN* and *ORELSE*.

Sequencing

$$THENC : conv \times conv \to conv \qquad\qquad\qquad\qquad\qquad \text{(infix)}$$
$$THENFC : fconv \times fconv \to fconv \qquad\qquad\qquad\qquad \text{(infix)}$$

The conversion c_1 *THENC* c_2 performs two conversions in succession on a term. It converts a term t as follows. Using c_1 it converts

$$t \quad \longmapsto \quad \Gamma_1 \vdash t \equiv t_1$$

Using c_2 it converts

$$t_1 \quad \longmapsto \quad \Gamma_2 \vdash t_1 \equiv t_2$$

Via transitivity, the overall effect is

$$t \quad \longmapsto \quad \Gamma_1, \Gamma_2 \vdash t \equiv t_2$$

It fails if c_1 or c_2 does.

The analogous operator for formula conversions is *THENFC*.

Alternation

$$ORELSEC : conv \times conv \to conv \qquad\qquad\qquad\qquad\quad \text{(infix)}$$
$$ORELSEFC : fconv \times fconv \to fconv \qquad\qquad\qquad\quad \text{(infix)}$$

The conversion c_1 *ORELSEC* c_2 performs either of two conversions on a term, the first conversion that succeeds. It converts a term t as follows. Using c_1 it converts

$$t \quad \longmapsto \quad \Gamma \vdash t \equiv t_1$$

If c_1 fails then using c_2 it converts

$$t \quad \longmapsto \quad \Gamma \vdash t \equiv t_2$$

It fails if both c_1 and c_2 do.

The analogous operator for formula conversions is *ORELSEFC*.

Identity elements

ALL_CONV : *conv*
NO_CONV : *conv*
ALL_FCONV : *fconv*
NO_FCONV : *fconv*

The conversion *ALL_CONV* converts all terms, mapping

$$t \quad \longmapsto \quad \vdash t \equiv t$$

by reflexivity. It is an identity for the operator *THENC*. The tactic *NO_CONV* converts no term — it always raises exception *general* — and is an identity for the operator *ORELSEC*.

   ALL_FCONV and *NO_FCONV* are the analogous identities as formula conversions.

Repetition

REPEATC : *conv* → *conv*
REPEATFC : *fconv* → *fconv*

The conversion *REPEATC c* applies a conversion repeatedly to a term until failure. It converts a term t by deriving successively

$$t \quad \longmapsto \quad \Gamma_1 \vdash t \equiv t_1$$
$$t_1 \quad \longmapsto \quad \Gamma_2 \vdash t_1 \equiv t_2$$
$$\cdot$$
$$\cdot$$
$$\cdot$$
$$t_{n-1} \quad \longmapsto \quad \Gamma_n \vdash t_{n-1} \equiv t_n$$

Note that *REPEATC* does not convert subterms of t. Operators for recursive traversal are described below. *REPEATC* never fails; it continues until the conversion c fails. It is implemented similarly to the tactical *REPEAT*:

```
fun REPEATC conv t =
    ((conv THENC (REPEATC conv)) ORELSEC ALL_CONV) t;
```

   Similarly, *REPEATFC* performs repetition of formula conversions.

List conversion operators

LCF provides n-place conversion operators as it does for tacticals.

EVERY_CONV : *conv list* → *conv*
EVERY_FCONV : *fconv list* → *fconv*

The function *EVERY_CONV* is an n-place version of *THENC*:

$$EVERY\_CONV[c_1,\ldots,c_n] \quad \text{is like} \quad c_1 \; THENC \; \ldots \; THENC \; c_n$$

Likewise *EVERY_FCONV* is an n-place version of *THENFC*.

FIRST_CONV : conv list → conv
FIRST_FCONV : fconv list → fconv

The function *FIRST_CONV* is an n-place version of *ORELSEC*:

$$FIRST\_CONV[c_1,\ldots,c_n] \quad \text{is like} \quad c_1 \; ORELSEC \; \ldots \; ORELSEC \; c_n$$

Likewise *FIRST_FCONV* is an n-place version of *ORELSEFC*.

9.4.3   Rewriting of subexpressions

Conversions can be constructed with operators for rewriting subexpressions. Recursive conversions so constructed can rewrite subexpressions of arbitrary depth, which is essential for simplification.

Rewriting of subterms

SUB_CONV : conv → conv

The function *SUB_CONV* applies a conversion to the *immediate* subterms of a term. The conversion *SUB_CONV c* converts

x	$\longmapsto$	$\vdash x \equiv x$	(constants and variables)
$\lambda x.t$	$\longmapsto$	$\Gamma \vdash \lambda x.t \equiv \lambda x'.u$	(abstractions)
$t(u)$	$\longmapsto$	$\Gamma, \Delta \vdash t(r) \equiv u(s)$	(combinations)

It uses c to convert t to $\Gamma \vdash t \equiv u$ and r to $\Delta \vdash r \equiv s$. The bound variable may be renamed. The resulting theorem is proved via the derived inference rules *REFL*, *MK_ABS*, and *MK_COMB*.

DEPTH_CONV : conv → conv

The function *DEPTH_CONV* applies a conversion to all subterms. Its traversal order is bottom-up: it decomposes the term to constants and variables, then rebuilds it while applying the conversion c as it reconstructs the term. Like *REPEATC*, it loops unless c eventually fails. It does not re-traverse the result of such a conversion, so its final result may *not be in simplest form*: there may be subterms where the conversion c could be applied. When this is acceptable, *DEPTH_CONV* is more efficient than *TOP_DEPTH_CONV*.

    The ML definition is

```
fun DEPTH_CONV conv t =
   (SUB_CONV (DEPTH_CONV conv) THENC (REPEATC conv)) t;
```

TOP_DEPTH_CONV : *conv* → *conv*

The function *TOP_DEPTH_CONV* implements the standard rewriting strategy for terms. Unlike *DEPTH_CONV*, it applies the conversion in both the top-down and bottom-up phases. Moreover, it calls itself recursively so that its final result is in simplest form.

A ML definition, slightly less efficient than that actually used, is

```
fun TOP_DEPTH_CONV conv t =
   (REPEATC conv THENC
         SUB_CONV (TOP_DEPTH_CONV conv) THENC
             ((conv THENC TOP_DEPTH_CONV conv) ORELSEC ALL_CONV)) t;
```

Rewriting of subformulae

SUB_FCONV : *conv* → *fconv* → *fconv*

The function *SUB_FCONV* applies a formula conversion to the *immediate* subformulae of a subformula. One of its arguments is a term conversion, for converting predicates. It converts $P(t)$ by converting t as $\Gamma \vdash t \equiv u$, proving

$$P(t) \quad \longmapsto \quad \Gamma \vdash P(t) \Longleftrightarrow P(u).$$

The conversion of other formulae is analogous to *SUB_CONV*. It converts conjunctions $A \wedge C$ to $A \wedge C \Longleftrightarrow B \wedge D$, quantifications $\forall x.A$ to $\forall x.A \Longleftrightarrow \forall x'.B$, and so on.

DEPTH_FCONV : *conv* → *fconv* → *fconv*

The resulting formula conversion applies a formula conversion to all subformulae using a bottom-up traversal. The term conversion is applied to arguments of predicates. *DEPTH_FCONV* is typically called with a term conversion built from *DEPTH_CONV*, to apply the same traversal order to the terms.

The ML definition is

```
fun DEPTH_FCONV conv fconv fm =
   (SUB_FCONV conv (DEPTH_FCONV conv fconv) THENFC
    (REPEATFC fconv)) fm;
```

TOP_DEPTH_FCONV : *conv* → *fconv* → *fconv*

The resulting formula conversion applies a formula conversion using top-down and bottom-up traversals. The term conversion is applied to arguments of predicates. *TOP_DEPTH_FCONV* is typically called with a term conversion built from *TOP_DEPTH_CONV*.

9.5   Implementing new rewriting strategies

The standard rewriting tools involve more concepts than there is space to discuss:

- *tautology conversions* for simplifying tautologous formulae

- conversions for expanding disjunctions and existential quantifiers

- a version of *SUB_FCONV* that handles *local assumptions*

- *discrimination nets* for fast searching through a large number of conversions

- a version of *REWRITE_CONV* that handles *implicative rewrites*

Local assumptions and implicative rewrites call rewriting recursively through complicated recursive functionals. Few users need a completely new rewriting strategy. Minor adjustments to the standard strategy should require only minor (obvious?) changes to the source code.

Are the tautology conversions needed? It would be annoying to wait ten minutes for rewriting to finish, only to receive the subgoal $TRUTH() \land A \lor FALSITY()$. Yet this subgoal is trivially reduced to A by the rules of first order logic. It might be better to have tactics for first order reasoning, powerful enough to simplify tautologies. Cambridge LCF packs almost all of its power into rewriting instead of providing separate tools for separate reasoning methods.

Discrimination nets cause the most complication. Each conversion is paired with an indexing pattern, a term or formula. The patterns for the set of conversions are compiled into a network for fast matching of all the patterns simultaneously. The speedup is about 30%; is it worth it?

Example 9.9 Let us examine the difference between a single step of rewriting, repeated rewriting, and depth rewriting. The term

$$SND(TT, SND(TT, SND(TT, FF)))$$

can be simplified by top-level rewriting. It reduces to *FF* in three rewriting steps. Calling *REWRITE_CONV* alone performs only one step. Applying *REPEATC* to that conversion performs all three, as does *DEPTH_CONV*.

```
! REWRITE_CONV SND_PAIR 'SND(TT, SND(TT, SND(TT,FF)))';
- it = |-'SND(TT,SND(TT,SND(TT,FF))) == SND(TT,SND(TT,FF))' : thm


! REPEATC (REWRITE_CONV SND_PAIR)
>                        'SND(TT, SND(TT, SND(TT,FF)))';
- it = |-'SND(TT,SND(TT,SND(TT,FF))) == FF' : thm


! DEPTH_CONV (REWRITE_CONV SND_PAIR)
```

```
>                         'SND(TT, SND(TT, SND(TT,FF)))';
- it = |-'SND(TT,SND(TT,SND(TT,FF))) == FF' : thm
```

A conversion of the form *REPEATC(c THENC c)* performs the conversion *c* an even number of times. It performs only two of the three possible steps below.

```
! REPEATC (REWRITE_CONV SND_PAIR  THENC  REWRITE_CONV SND_PAIR)
>    'SND(TT, SND(TT, SND(TT,FF)))';
- it = |-'SND(TT,SND(TT,SND(TT,FF))) == SND(TT,FF)' : thm
```

In contrast, the term

$$SND(SND(SND(TT,(TT,(TT,FF)))))$$

requires depth rewriting. The innermost occurrence of *SND* must be simplified first. Calling *REWRITE_CONV* alone results in an exception. Nor does *REPEATC* have any effect on the term. Only through *DEPTH_CONV* can the conversion affect the subterm.

```
! REWRITE_CONV SND_PAIR 'SND(SND(SND(TT,(TT,(TT,FF)))))';
exception raised: general with "term_match"
evaluation failed

! REPEATC (REWRITE_CONV SND_PAIR)
>                         'SND(SND(SND(TT,(TT,(TT,FF)))))';
- it =
|-'SND(SND(SND(TT,TT,TT,FF))) == SND(SND(SND(TT,TT,TT,FF)))' : thm

! DEPTH_CONV (REWRITE_CONV SND_PAIR)
>                         'SND(SND(SND(TT,(TT,(TT,FF)))))';
- it = |-'SND(SND(SND(TT,TT,TT,FF))) == FF' : thm
```

9.6   Further reading

Boyer and Moore describe their rewriting techniques, many adopted in LCF, down to the minutest detail [12]. Charniak et al. discuss discrimination nets, pattern matching, and their applications to artificial intelligence research [17]. I have written a thorough account of rewriting in Cambridge LCF, developing layer upon layer of conversions and operators [75].

Huet and Oppen survey rewriting and other methods of reasoning with equations, such as unification in an equational theory [51]. They discuss how to prove the termination of rewriting for a set of rewrite rules. Elsewhere Huet discusses *confluence*, another fundamental property of a set of rewrites [50]. In a confluent set, if a term can be reduced by two different rewrites, the choice is arbitrary: the fully rewritten term will be the same in either case. The *Knuth-Bendix completion procedure* can sometimes be used to extend a set of rewrite rules to a confluent set. Then, rewriting is guaranteed to reduce equal terms to the same canonical form, yielding a decision procedure for equality.

The Knuth-Bendix procedure operates on a set of theorems, producing new theorems. Given the goal $\Gamma \vdash A$, rewriting tactics are good at simplifying the goal formula A but terrible at simplifying or discovering contradictions among the hypotheses Γ. The main purpose of *MP_TAC* is to move a hypothesis into the goal formula, where it can be simplified. A better approach is required.

Term rewriting is a thriving field with its own international conference [56]. Much current research is limited to equational logic; the next step is to extend these results to first order logic.

Chapter 10

Sample Proofs

Now it is time to join the separate strands together. This chapter presents several examples: the natural numbers, fixed point induction, infinite sequences. For each it presents an annotated LCF session, edited to save space. The sessions include a few errors and their correction. Finally, some projects are suggested.

10.1 Addition of natural numbers

This section develops a theory of the natural numbers, proving the associativity of addition. Though these proofs may seem elementary, they resemble many parts of my unification proof [76].

Start up LCF and open a theory *nat* for the natural numbers, with a type *nat*.[1] The structural induction command declares the constructors $0 : nat$ and $SUCC : nat \rightarrow nat$.

```
# Cambridge LCF (RAL 1.3) #

! new_theory "nat";

! new_type 0 "nat";

! struct_axm (':nat', "strict",
>               [ ("0",      []),
>                 ("SUCC",  [ 'n: nat' ])]);
```

The structural induction command does not provide an eliminator functional, so let us declare one. We also declare the infix operator +.

```
! new_constant("NAT_WHEN", ':'a -> (nat -> 'a) -> (nat -> 'a)');

! new_paired_infix ("+", ':nat*nat -> nat');
```

---

[1]It does not matter that the type and theory have the same name.

The eliminator functional, *NAT_WHEN*, gives computation on the natural numbers by cases: whether its argument is 0 or a successor number. If the argument is ⊥, then so is the result. (Recall the examples in Chapter 4.) Here we introduce the axioms for *NAT_WHEN* and +, binding them to ML variables.

```
! val NAT_WHEN_CLAUSES = new_closed_axiom ("NAT_WHEN_CLAUSES",
>        '!x:'a. !f. NAT_WHEN x f UU == UU  /\
>                    NAT_WHEN x f 0 == x  /\
>        (!m. ~ m==UU  ==>  NAT_WHEN x f (SUCC m) == f(m))');
- val NAT_WHEN_CLAUSES =
|-'!x f.
    NAT_WHEN x f UU == UU  /\
    NAT_WHEN x f 0 == x  /\
    (!m. ~ m == UU  ==>  NAT_WHEN x f(SUCC m) == f m)'
  : thm
```

```
! val PLUS = new_closed_axiom
>        ("PLUS", '!m n. m+n == NAT_WHEN n (\k.SUCC(k+n)) m');
- val PLUS = |-'!m n. m + n == NAT_WHEN n(\k.SUCC(k + n))m' : thm
```

10.1.1   The recursion equations for addition

The axiom for addition may look strange, but it implies the usual recursion equations. Once you know what you are doing, it is all right to take such equations as axioms.

```
! set_goal([], '!n.    UU + n == UU    /\    0 + n == n  /\
>        (!m. ~ m==UU  ==>    (SUCC m) + n == SUCC (m + n))');
1 subgoal
'!n. UU + n == UU  /\
     0 + n == n  /\
     (!m. ~ m == UU  ==>  (SUCC m) + n == SUCC(m + n))'
```

The obvious tactic is rewriting with the axioms for + and *NAT_WHEN*. But the axiom for + is recursive and rewriting would diverge. A solution here is to specialize the axiom so that it applies only when + is applied to the term ⊥, 0, or $SUCC(k)$.

```
! val PLUS_UU = SPEC 'UU:nat' PLUS;
- val PLUS_UU = |-'!n. UU + n == NAT_WHEN n(\k.SUCC(k + n))UU'
  : thm
```

```
! val PLUS_0 = SPEC '0' PLUS;
- val PLUS_0 = |-'!n. 0 + n == NAT_WHEN n(\k.SUCC(k + n))0' : thm
```

```
! val PLUS_SUCC = SPEC 'SUCC k' PLUS;
- val PLUS_SUCC =
|-'!n. (SUCC k) + n == NAT_WHEN n(\k.SUCC(k + n))(SUCC k)' : thm
```

Rewriting with these three theorems and the axiom for *NAT_WHEN* solves
the goal. Applying *REWRITE_RULE* with *NAT_WHEN_CLAUSES* to the three
theorems would give a similar result using forwards proof.

```
! expand (REWRITE_TAC [NAT_WHEN_CLAUSES,PLUS_UU,PLUS_0,PLUS_SUCC]);
goal proved
```

```
! val PLUS_CLAUSES = save_top_thm "PLUS_CLAUSES";
- val PLUS_CLAUSES =
|-'!n. UU + n == UU  /\
      0 + n == n  /\
      (!m. ~ m == UU  ==>  (SUCC m) + n == SUCC(m + n))' : thm
```

10.1.2   The termination of addition

Here is the goal that + is a total function.

```
! set_goal([], '!i j. ~ i==UU  ==>  ~ j == UU  ==>  ~ i+j == UU');
1 subgoal
'!i j. ~ i == UU  ==>  ~ j == UU  ==>  ~ i + j == UU'
```

The termination of addition is proved by induction on the natural numbers.
Typically the induction scheme should correspond to the recursive calls: this sug-
gests induction on i. First, bind the structural induction tactic to the variable
NAT_TAC.

```
! val NAT_TAC = STRUCT_TAC "nat" [];
- val NAT_TAC = fn : (term -> tactic)
```

```
! expand  (NAT_TAC 'i');
3 subgoals
'!j. ~ SUCC n == UU  ==>  ~ j == UU  ==>  ~ (SUCC n) + j == UU'
   ['~ n == UU']
   ['!j. ~ n == UU  ==>  ~ j == UU  ==>  ~ n + j == UU']

'!j. ~ 0 == UU  ==>  ~ j == UU  ==>  ~ 0 + j == UU'

'!j. ~ UU == UU  ==>  ~ j == UU  ==>  ~ UU + j == UU'
```

Three subgoals. The subgoal package shows subgoals in reverse order — the last shown is the next one to attack — because the first shown may have scrolled off the screen. The current subgoal has the contradictory antecedent $\bot \neq \bot$, so *REWRITE_TAC* can solve it.

```
! expand (REWRITE_TAC []);
goal proved
|-'!j. ~ UU == UU  ==>  ~ j == UU  ==>  ~ UU + j == UU'

previous subproof:
2 subgoals
'!j. ~ SUCC n == UU  ==>  ~ j == UU  ==>  ~ (SUCC n) + j == UU'
   ['~ n == UU']
   ['!j. ~ n == UU  ==>  ~ j == UU  ==>  ~ n + j == UU']


'!j. ~ 0 == UU  ==>  ~ j == UU  ==>  ~ 0 + j == UU'
```

The next subgoal follows by the definition by +. A general strategy for recursive functions: after induction, simplify the subgoals using the function's recursion equations, here *PLUS_CLAUSES*.

```
! expand  (ASM_REWRITE_TAC [PLUS_CLAUSES]);
goal proved
|-'!j. ~ 0 == UU  ==>  ~ j == UU  ==>  ~ 0 + j == UU'

previous subproof:
1 subgoal
'!j. ~ SUCC n == UU  ==>  ~ j == UU  ==>  ~ (SUCC n) + j == UU'
   ['~ n == UU']
   ['!j. ~ n == UU  ==>  ~ j == UU  ==>  ~ n + j == UU']
```

The final subgoal is the induction step. It has the induction hypothesis that $n + j$ is defined for all defined j and for some fixed, defined n. Rewriting ought to help. Here *ASM_REWRITE_TAC* allows the induction hypothesis to take part in the rewriting. I often use *ASM_REWRITE_TAC* out of habit, even when the subgoal has no assumptions.

```
! expand (ASM_REWRITE_TAC [PLUS_CLAUSES]);
1 subgoal
'!j. ~ SUCC n == UU  ==>  ~ j == UU  ==>  ~ SUCC(n + j) == UU'
   ['~ n == UU']
   ['!j. ~ n == UU  ==>  ~ j == UU  ==>  ~ n + j == UU']
```

The goal is unchanged! I forgot to include the axiom that *SUCC* is total, though the goal involves proving that $SUCC(n + j)$ is defined. This axiom, called *DEFINED*, was automatically asserted when *struct_axm* built the theory of *nat*. Let us load *DEFINED* and another axiom, strictness.

```
! val NAT_DEFINED = axiom "nat" "DEFINED";
- val NAT_DEFINED =
|-`~ 0 == UU  /\  (!n. ~ n == UU  ==>  ~ SUCC n == UU)` : thm

! val NAT_STRICT = axiom "nat" "STRICT";
- val NAT_STRICT =
|-`TRUTH ()  /\  (!n. TRUTH ()  /\  SUCC UU == UU)` : thm
```

Invoke rewriting again, supplying the necessary axioms. Many special features of rewriting come into play: implicative rewrites, local assumptions, and formula rewrite rules.

```
! expand (ASM_REWRITE_TAC [PLUS_CLAUSES, NAT_DEFINED]);
goal proved
..|-`!j. ~ SUCC n == UU  ==>  ~ j == UU  ==>  ~ SUCC(n + j) == UU`
..|-`!j. ~ SUCC n == UU  ==>  ~ j == UU  ==>  ~ (SUCC n) + j == UU`
|-`!i j. ~ i == UU  ==>  ~ j == UU  ==>  ~ i + j == UU`
```

The subgoal package has printed three theorems, from intermediate nodes in the goal tree. There is no *previous subproof* so the proof is finished. We can save the theorem and simultaneously bind it to an ML variable.

```
! val PLUS_TOTAL = save_top_thm "PLUS_TOTAL";
- val PLUS_TOTAL =
|-`!i j. ~ i == UU  ==>  ~ j == UU  ==>  ~ i + j == UU` : thm
```

It is a good idea to make a file of LCF commands that can rebuild the theory in a batch job, for recovery from disasters — like discovering inconsistent axioms in some parent theory. Although subgoal package commands could be used in a batch job, it seems tidier to package the proof as a single tactic. For this proof the batch command could be

```
val PLUS_TOTAL = prove_thm ("PLUS_TOTAL",
   `!i j. ~ i==UU  ==>  ~ j == UU  ==>  ~ i + j == UU`,
   NAT_TAC `i` THEN  ASM_REWRITE_TAC [PLUS_CLAUSES, NAT_DEFINED]);
```

The file of batch commands also constitutes a concise description of the theory.

Exercise 10.1 What rewrite rules are extracted from the axiom *NAT_DEFINED*?

Exercise 10.2 Where does rewriting make use of local assumptions? What tactic could be inserted into the proof to make local assumptions unnecessary?

10.1.3   The associativity of addition

The associativity of addition is another easy induction proof. The goal is stated
with an antecedent that one of the variables is defined, thereby avoiding a problem
with the definedness antecedents in *PLUS_CLAUSES* (like in Section 4.12).

```
! set_goal([], '!i j k. ˜ j==UU  ==>    (i+j)+k == i+(j+k)');
1 subgoal
'!i j k. ˜ j == UU  ==>  (i + j) + k == i + (j + k)'
```

How do we choose an induction variable when the recursive function (here +)
occurs four times? Induction on i unfolds two of these occurrences; j unfolds one
and k unfolds none. So i is indicated; often the choice requires trial and error.
The Boyer/Moore theorem prover uses sophisticated induction heuristics [12].

   After induction, rewrite with the clauses for +.

```
! expand  (NAT_TAC 'i'  THEN  ASM_REWRITE_TAC [PLUS_CLAUSES]);
1 subgoal
'!j k. ˜ j == UU  ==>  (SUCC(n + j)) + k == SUCC(n + (j + k))'
  ['˜ n == UU']
  ['!j k. ˜ j == UU  ==>  (n + j) + k == n + (j + k)']
```

The *SUCC* subgoal remains. The proof follows from

$$SUCC(n + j) + k \equiv SUCC((n + j) + k),$$

which holds because $n + j$ is defined: because n and j are defined and + is
total. (Refer to *PLUS_CLAUSES*.) This calls for more rewriting using the previous
theorem, *PLUS_TOTAL*.

```
! expand  (ASM_REWRITE_TAC [PLUS_CLAUSES, PLUS_TOTAL]);
goal proved
..|-'!j k. ˜ j == UU  ==>  (SUCC(n + j)) + k == SUCC(n + (j + k))'
|-'!i j k. ˜ j == UU  ==>  (i + j) + k == i + (j + k)'
```

We are finished and save the theorem.

```
! val PLUS_ASSOC = save_top_thm "PLUS_ASSOC";
- val PLUS_ASSOC =
|-'!i j k. ˜ j == UU  ==>  (i + j) + k == i + (j + k)' : thm
```

This associativity proof can be summarized, giving a batch file command.

```
val PLUS_ASSOC = prove_thm ("PLUS_ASSOC",
       '!i j k. ˜ j==UU  ==>   (i + j) + k ==  i + (j + k)',
   NAT_TAC 'i'  THEN  ASM_REWRITE_TAC [PLUS_CLAUSES, PLUS_TOTAL]);
```

10.2 Commutativity of addition

This section continues the previous session, proving that + is commutative. The proof requires three lemmas, one for each of the subgoals in the induction. Each concerns the value of $i + j$ when j has the form $\perp$, 0, or $SUCC(n)$, showing that + satisfies the same equations in the right operand as in the left. The proof of each lemma is routine: induction then rewriting. The only decision we must make is which rewrite rules to supply.

To try this example in a fresh session, use *load_theory* to re-enter the theory and *axiom* and *theorem* to re-bind the ML identifiers to the theorems.

```
load_theory "nat";
val PLUS_CLAUSES = theorem "nat" "PLUS_CLAUSES";
```

10.2.1 The right strictness lemma

Addition is strict in its right operand because *SUCC* is strict.

```
! set_goal([],   ʻ!n. n + UU == UUʼ);
1 subgoal
ʻ!n. n + UU == UUʼ


! expand (NAT_TAC ʻnʼ  THEN
>          ASM_REWRITE_TAC [PLUS_CLAUSES, NAT_STRICT]);
goal proved
|-ʻ!n. n + UU == UUʼ


! val PLUS_RIGHT_UU = save_top_thm "PLUS_RIGHT_UU";
- val PLUS_RIGHT_UU = |-ʻ!n. n + UU == UUʼ : thm
```

10.2.2 The right identity lemma

Proving $n + 0 \equiv n$ by induction on n is one of the simplest examples of induction.

```
! set_goal([],   ʻ!n. n + 0 == nʼ);
1 subgoal
ʻ!n. n + 0 == nʼ


! expand (NAT_TAC ʻnʼ  THEN  ASM_REWRITE_TAC [PLUS_CLAUSES]);
goal proved


! val PLUS_RIGHT_ZERO = save_top_thm "PLUS_RIGHT_ZERO";
- val PLUS_RIGHT_ZERO = |-ʻ!n. n + 0 == nʼ : thm
```

10.2.3   The right successor lemma

This proof should also be simple, but $\bot$ complicates matters.

```
! set_goal([],    '!i j. i + (SUCC j) == SUCC (i + j)');
1 subgoal
'!i j. i + (SUCC j) == SUCC(i + j)'


! expand (NAT_TAC 'i'   THEN  ASM_REWRITE_TAC [PLUS_CLAUSES]);
1 subgoal
'!j. UU == SUCC UU'
```

Somehow strictness is involved. This subgoal is spurious in that it would not arise
in the traditional treatment of addition. It could be suppressed by restricting
the initial goal to defined i, but the present approach will give a commutativity
theorem free of definedness conditions.

```
! expand (REWRITE_TAC [NAT_STRICT]);
goal proved
|-'!j. UU == SUCC UU'
|-'!i j. i + (SUCC j) == SUCC(i + j)'


! val PLUS_SUCC = save_top_thm "PLUS_RIGHT_SUCC";
- val PLUS_SUCC = |-'!i j. i + (SUCC j) == SUCC(i + j)'  : thm
```

10.2.4   The main result: commutativity

The theorem $\forall ij.\, i+j \equiv j+i$ is proved by induction on i. The induction hypothesis
will involve commutativity, so rewriting could diverge. So let us not rewrite using
the assumptions: use *REWRITE_TAC*, not *ASM_REWRITE_TAC*. The lemmas solve
the $\bot$ and 0 subgoals.

```
! set_goal([],    '!i j. i+j == j+i');
1 subgoal
'!i j. i + j == j + i'


! expand (NAT_TAC 'i'   THEN
>        REWRITE_TAC [PLUS_CLAUSES, PLUS_RIGHT_ZERO, PLUS_RIGHT_UU]);
1 subgoal
'!j. (SUCC n) + j == j + (SUCC n)'
  ['~ n == UU']
  ['!j. n + j == j + n']
```

The induction hypothesis looks safe for rewriting because the variable n is
frozen. Rewriting of $n+n$ would run forever, but $n+n$ does not occur in the goal.

```
! expand (ASM_REWRITE_TAC [PLUS_CLAUSES, PLUS_RIGHT_SUCC]);
goal proved
..|-'!j. (SUCC n) + j == j + (SUCC n)'
|-'!i j. i + j == j + i'

! val PLUS_COMMUTE = save_top_thm "PLUS_COMMUTE";
- val PLUS_COMMUTE = |-'!i j. i + j == j + i' : thm
```

A batch command could be

```
val PLUS_COMMUTE = prove_thm ("PLUS_COMMUTE",  '!i j. i+j == j+i',
    NAT_TAC 'i'  THEN
    ASM_REWRITE_TAC [PLUS_CLAUSES, PLUS_RIGHT_ZERO,
                     PLUS_RIGHT_UU, PLUS_RIGHT_SUCC]);
```

Exercise 10.3 Explain why one of the subgoals from *NAT_TAC* contains the variable n. What do you think would happen if n occurred in the input goal? Try it and see.

10.3   Equality on the natural numbers

The theory *EQ* of the equality function = is built on top of the previous theory, *nat*. This session continues the previous one, so the axioms and theorems are still bound to ML variables and *nat* is automatically a parent.

```
! new_theory "EQ";

! new_parent "nat";
Theory nat loaded
```

The *new_parent* declaration would be essential if we were starting a fresh LCF session, and must appear in the batch file: a new version of the theory *EQ* can be built on an earlier version of the theory *nat*.

Now declare the infix truth-valued function =, the equality test. The computation of $m = n$ tests, in turn, whether m and n are zero. If m is $SUCC(i)$ and n is $SUCC(j)$ then it recursively tests $i = j$.

```
! new_paired_infix ("=", ': nat*nat -> tr');

! val EQ = new_closed_axiom ("EQ",
>       '!m n. m=n == NAT_WHEN (NAT_WHEN TT (\j.FF) n)
>                             (\i. NAT_WHEN FF (\j. i=j) n)
>                             m');
```

```
- val EQ =
|-'!m n. m = n ==
     NAT_WHEN(NAT_WHEN TT(\j.FF)n)(\i.NAT_WHEN FF(\j.i = j)n)m'
  : thm
```

10.3.1   The recursion equations for the equality function

Like for +, the definition using *NAT_WHEN* is concise but hard to work with. Let
us derive nicer recursion equations for =.

```
! set_goal([], '(!n.  UU=n == UU) /\ (!m. m=UU == UU) /\
>        0=0 == TT  /\
>        (!n. ~ n==UU ==>  0=(SUCC n) ==  FF) /\
>        (!m. ~ m==UU ==>  (SUCC m)=0 ==  FF) /\
>        (!m n. ~ m==UU ==> ~ n==UU ==>  (SUCC m)=(SUCC n) == m=n)');
1 subgoal
'(!n. UU = n == UU)  /\
 (!m. m = UU == UU)  /\
 0 = 0 == TT  /\
 (!n. ~ n == UU  ==>  0 = (SUCC n) == FF)  /\
 (!m. ~ m == UU  ==>  (SUCC m) = 0 == FF)  /\
 (!m n.   ~ m == UU  ==>  ~ n == UU  ==>
                 (SUCC m) = (SUCC n) == m = n)'
```

Rewriting with the axiom *EQ* would infinitely unfold any term of the form
$t = u$, so specialize the axiom to cover each of the six equations. Only four
specialized versions are necessary.

```
! val EQ_UU = SPEC 'UU:nat' EQ;
- val EQ_UU =
|-'!n. UU = n ==
     NAT_WHEN(NAT_WHEN TT(\j.FF)n)(\i.NAT_WHEN FF(\j.i = j)n)UU'
  : thm

! val EQ_RIGHT_UU = SPECL ['m', 'UU:nat'] EQ;
- val EQ_RIGHT_UU =
|-'m = UU ==
     NAT_WHEN(NAT_WHEN TT(\j.FF)UU)(\i.NAT_WHEN FF(\j.i = j)UU)m'
  : thm

! val EQ_0 = SPEC '0' EQ;
- val EQ_0 =
|-'!n. 0 = n ==
```

```
        NAT_WHEN(NAT_WHEN TT(\j.FF)n)(\i.NAT_WHEN FF(\j.i = j)n)0'
   : thm
```

```
! val EQ_SUCC = SPEC 'SUCC k' EQ;
- val EQ_SUCC =
|-'!n.   (SUCC k) = n ==
     NAT_WHEN
       (NAT_WHEN TT(\j.FF)n)
       (\i.NAT_WHEN FF(\j.i = j)n)
       (SUCC k)'    : thm
```

Rewriting with these four theorems should do the trick.

```
! expand (REWRITE_TAC [NAT_WHEN_CLAUSES, EQ_UU, EQ_RIGHT_UU,
>                      EQ_0, EQ_SUCC]);
```

```
1 subgoal
'!m. NAT_WHEN UU(\i.UU)m == UU'
```

Not quite: we need to argue by exhaustion on *nat*. Induction on *m*, followed by simplification, accomplishes this.

```
! expand (NAT_TAC 'm' THEN  ASM_REWRITE_TAC [NAT_WHEN_CLAUSES]);
goal proved
|-'!m. NAT_WHEN UU(\i.UU)m == UU'
|-'(!n.  UU = n == UU)  /\
   (!m.  m = UU == UU)  /\
   0 = 0 == TT  /\
   (!n. ~ n == UU  ==>  0 = (SUCC n) == FF)  /\
   (!m. ~ m == UU  ==>  (SUCC m) = 0 == FF)  /\
   (!m n.  ~ m == UU  ==>  ~ n == UU  ==>
                    (SUCC m) = (SUCC n) == m = n)'
```

```
! val EQ_CLAUSES = save_top_thm "EQ_CLAUSES";
- val EQ_CLAUSES = |-'...'  : thm
```

10.3.2 Partial correctness of the equality function

The function call $i = j$ is a computable equality test on i and j. If correct it should return *TT* precisely when defined numbers i and j are equal. It would then follow that = was reflexive, symmetric, and transitive.

```
! set_goal ([],
>              '!i j. ~ i==UU ==> ~ j==UU ==> (i=j == TT <=> i==j)');
```

```
1 subgoal
'!i j. ~ i == UU  ==>  ~ j == UU  ==>  (i = j == TT  <=>  i == j)'
```

Since $i = j$ is recursive in both operands, this proof will probably require induction on both i and j.

```
! expand (NAT_TAC 'i');
exception: tactic with ("INDUCT_TAC: does not admit induction",...)
```

This error message is dreaded: admissibility is complicated even to experienced users. Fortunately structural induction is possible because *nat* is flat. We need only fetch the theorem *FLAT*, which *struct_axm* proved automatically, and supply it to *STRUCT_TAC*.

```
! val NAT_FLAT = theorem "nat" "FLAT";
- val NAT_FLAT =
|-'!abs' abs''. abs' << abs''  ==>  UU == abs'  \/  abs' == abs'''
  : thm

! val NAT_TAC = STRUCT_TAC "nat" [NAT_FLAT];
- val NAT_TAC = fn : (term -> tactic)

! expand (NAT_TAC 'i');
3 subgoals
'!j. ~ SUCC n == UU  ==>  ~ j == UU  ==>
                    ((SUCC n)=j == TT  <=>  SUCC n == j)'
  ['~ n == UU']
  ['!j. ~ n==UU  ==>  ~ j==UU  ==>  (n=j == TT  <=>  n==j)']

'!j. ~ 0==UU  ==>  ~ j==UU  ==>  (0=j == TT  <=>  0==j)'

'!j. ~ UU==UU  ==>  ~ j==UU  ==>  (UU=j == TT  <=>  UU==j)'
```

The $\perp$ subgoal is vacuous:

```
! expand (REWRITE_TAC []);
goal proved

previous subproof:
2 subgoals
'!j. ~ SUCC n == UU  ==>  ~ j == UU  ==>
                    ((SUCC n)=j == TT  <=>  SUCC n == j)'
  ['~ n == UU']
  ['!j. ~ n==UU  ==>  ~ j==UU  ==>  (n=j == TT  <=>  n==j)']
```

`'!j. ~ 0==UU  ==>  ~ j==UU  ==>  (0=j == TT  <=>  0==j)'`

The remaining subgoals require reasoning about equality of natural numbers. The structural induction package provides the necessary axioms and theorems. Here *EQ_IFF_ALL* is appropriate, for it concerns equalities between various forms of number.

```
! val EQ_IFF_ALL = theorem "nat" "EQ_IFF_ALL";
- val EQ_IFF_ALL =
|-'((0 == 0  <=>  TRUTH ()) /\
   (!n. ~ n == UU  ==>  (0 == SUCC n  <=>  FALSITY ())))) /\
   (!n. ~ n == UU  ==>  (SUCC n == 0  <=>  FALSITY ())) /\
   (!n n'. ~ n == UU  ==>  ~ n' == UU  ==>
       (SUCC n == SUCC n'  <=>  TRUTH () /\  n == n'))'
 : thm
```

The proof requires case analysis (induction) on *n*, followed by simplification. This compares all possible pairs of ⊥, 0, or successor.

```
! expand (NAT_TAC 'j' THEN ASM_REWRITE_TAC[EQ_CLAUSES,EQ_IFF_ALL]);
goal proved
```

```
previous subproof:
'!j.  ~ SUCC n == UU  ==>  ~ j == UU  ==>
                    ((SUCC n)=j == TT  <=>  SUCC n == j)'
  ['~ n == UU']
  ['!j.  ~ n==UU  ==>  ~ j==UU  ==>  (n=j == TT  <=>  n==j)']
```

The same tactic should work for this last goal.

```
! expand (NAT_TAC 'j' THEN ASM_REWRITE_TAC[EQ_CLAUSES,EQ_IFF_ALL]);
goal proved
..|-'!j.  ~ SUCC n == UU  ==>  ~ j == UU  ==>
            ((SUCC n) = j == TT  <=>  SUCC n == j)'
```

```
! val EQUAL_IFF_EQ = save_top_thm "EQUAL_IFF_EQ";
- val EQUAL_IFF_EQ =
|-'!i j.  ~ i==UU  ==>  ~ j==UU  ==>  (i=j == TT  <=>  i==j)' : thm
```

Exercise 10.4 Explain why the induction formula above is not admissible.

Exercise 10.5 How would you prove that = is a total function?

10.4   A simple fixed point induction

Each of the examples of fixed point induction in Section 3.5 is easily performed in
LCF. Here we consider the example from page 71.

Create the theory *FUNCS* and declare P, G, H, and K as polymorphic constants.

```
! new_theory "FUNCS";
! new_constant ("P", ‘:’a->tr‘);
! new_constant ("G", ‘:’a->’a‘);
! new_constant ("H", ‘:’a->’a‘);
! new_constant ("K", ‘:(’a->’a) -> (’a->’a)‘);
```

The assumption that P is strict, and the definitions of K and H, correspond to
axioms in an obvious manner. Observe that H is expressed as the fixed point of the
functional K: this allows fixed point induction. Instead of declaring the functional
as a constant we could bind its body to an ML variable and use antiquotation.

```
! val P_STRICT = new_closed_axiom ("P_STRICT", ‘P(UU:’a) == UU‘);
- val P_STRICT = |-‘P UU == UU‘ : thm

! val K = new_closed_axiom("K", ‘K == \h x. P x => x | h(h(G x))‘);
- val K = |-‘K == \h.\x.(P x => x | h(h(G x)))‘ : thm

! val H = new_closed_axiom ("H", ‘H == FIX K :’a->’a‘);
- val H = |-‘H == FIX K‘ : thm
```

10.4.1   An unfolding lemma

The following lemma, which is trivially proved by rewriting, allows the controlled
unfolding of H to KH. Obviously rewriting with $H \equiv KH$ would never stop; the
lemma will be used with *SUBST_TAC*.

```
! set_goal([], ‘H == K H :’a->’a‘);
1 subgoal
‘H == K H‘

! expand (REWRITE_TAC [H, FIX_EQ]);
goal proved
|-‘H == K H‘

! val H_UNFOLD = save_top_thm "H_UNFOLD";
- val H_UNFOLD = |-‘H == K H‘ : thm
```

10.4.2   The strictness of H

The strictness of H follows from that of P and the conditional. The first step is to unfold H.

```
! set_goal([], 'H UU == UU : 'a');
1 subgoal
'H UU == UU'


! expand (SUBST_TAC [H_UNFOLD]);
1 subgoal
'K H UU == UU'


! expand (REWRITE_TAC [K, P_STRICT, COND_CLAUSES]);
goal proved
|-'K H UU == UU'
|-'H UU == UU'


! val H_STRICT = save_top_thm "H_STRICT";
- val H_STRICT = |-'H UU == UU' : thm
```

10.4.3   The idempotence of H

Here is the main theorem: $H \circ H \equiv H$. Compare the LCF proof with the proof in Section 3.5, particularly the use of rewriting. First we must perform fixed point induction on the second and third occurrences of H. Observe how *SUBST_OCCS_TAC* replaces selected occurrences of H by *FIX K*, which then undergo induction. The induction variable, h, is passed to *INDUCT_TAC*.

```
! set_goal([], '!x. H(H x) == H x');
1 subgoal
'!x. H(H x) == H x'


! expand (SUBST_OCCS_TAC [ ([2,3], H) ]);
1 subgoal
'!x. H(FIX K x) == FIX K x'


! expand (INDUCT_TAC [] [ ('K: ('a->'a) -> ('a->'a)', 'h') ]);
2 subgoals
'!h. (!x. H(h x) == h x)  ==>  (!x. H(K h x) == K h x)'


'!x. H(UU x) == UU x'
```

The ⊥ subgoal holds because *H* is strict and because ⊥ is the completely undefined function.

```
! expand (REWRITE_TAC [H_STRICT, MIN_COMB]);
goal proved
|-'!x. H(UU x) == UU x'
```

```
previous subproof:
1 subgoal
'!h. (!x. H(h x) == h x)  ==>  (!x. H(K h x) == K h x)'
```

The inductive step is expressed as an implication; *STRIP_TAC* puts the induction hypothesis into the assumptions. Then *REWRITE_TAC* opens the definition of *K* and simplifies.

```
! expand (REPEAT STRIP_TAC);
1 subgoal
'H(K h x) == K h x'
   ['!x. H(h x) == h x']
```

```
! expand (REWRITE_TAC [K]);
1 subgoal
'H(P x => x | h(h(G x))) == (P x => x | h(h(G x)))'
   ['!x. H(h x) == h x']
```

Calling *COND_CASES_TAC* performs case analysis on $P(x)$. Rewriting solves two of the cases; for $P(x) \equiv TT$ we must unfold *H* again.

```
! expand (COND_CASES_TAC  THEN  ASM_REWRITE_TAC [H_STRICT]);
1 subgoal
'H x == x'
   ['!x. H(h x) == h x']
   ['P x == TT']
```

```
! expand (SUBST_TAC [H_UNFOLD]);
1 subgoal
'K H x == x'
   ['!x. H(h x) == h x']
   ['P x == TT']
```

```
! expand (ASM_REWRITE_TAC [K, COND_CLAUSES]);
goal proved
.|-'K H x == x'
.|-'H x == x'
```

```
.|-'H(P x => x | h(h(G x))) == (P x => x | h(h(G x)))'
.|-'H(K h x) == K h x'
|-'!h. (!x. H(h x) == h x)  ==>  (!x. H(K h x) == K h x)'
|-'!x. H(FIX K x) == FIX K x'
|-'!x. H(H x) == H x'
```

```
! val H_IDEM = save_top_thm "H_IDEM";
- val H_IDEM = |-'!x. H(H x) == H x' : thm
```

Exercise 10.6 Perform the proof in Example 3.8 in LCF.

10.5 A mapping functional for infinite sequences

LCF can be used to study lazy evaluation. This section constructs a type of infinite sequences and a functional to apply a function to every member of a sequence, and proves a theorem by structural induction on infinite sequences. A descendant theory contains a functional for generating a sequence, and a proof by fixed point induction.

The type $(\sigma)seq$ resembles (σ) *llist*, the type of lazy lists over σ, which was discussed in Section 4.8. But $(\sigma)seq$ has no constructor for the empty list, and hence no finite, total lists. Write $[x_0, x_1, \ldots]$ for the least upper bound of the increasing chain

$$\bot \sqsubseteq SCONS(x_0)(\bot) \sqsubseteq SCONS(x_0)(SCONS(x_1)(\bot)) \sqsubseteq \cdots$$

In a new LCF session we start the theory *sequences* and declare the 1-place type operator *seq*. Calling *struct_axm* makes *seq* into the type of infinite sequences with one constructor, *SCONS*.

```
# Cambridge LCF (RAL 1.3) #
```

```
! new_theory "sequences";
```

```
! new_type 1 "seq";
```

```
! struct_axm (':'a seq', "lazy",
>                 [("SCONS", [ 'x: 'a', 's: 'a seq' ])]);
```

Here are the constant declarations. The eliminator functional *SEQ_WHEN* takes a function h and returns the function that maps $SCONS(x)(s)$ to $h(x)(s)$. The mapping functional *MAPS* takes a function f and returns the function that maps $[x_0, x_1, \ldots]$ to $[f(x_0), f(x_1), \ldots]$. The infix operator o is the usual function composition.

```
! new_constant("SEQ_WHEN",
>                 ':('a -> 'a seq -> 'b) -> ('a seq -> 'b)');

! new_constant("MAPS", ':('a -> 'b) -> ('a seq -> 'b seq)');

! new_paired_infix ("o", ': ('b->'c) * ('a->'b) -> ('a->'c)');
```

Here are the corresponding axioms.

```
! val SEQ_WHEN_CLAUSES = new_closed_axiom ("SEQ_WHEN_CLAUSES",
>        '!h. SEQ_WHEN h UU == UU : 'b  /\
>          (!x:'a. !s. SEQ_WHEN h (SCONS x s) == h x s)');
- val SEQ_WHEN_CLAUSES =
|-'!h. SEQ_WHEN h UU == UU  /\
        (!x s. SEQ_WHEN h (SCONS x s) == h x s)' : thm


! val MAPS = new_closed_axiom ("MAPS",
>        '!s. !f: 'a->'b. MAPS f s ==
>                SEQ_WHEN (\x t. SCONS (f x) (MAPS f t)) s');
- val MAPS =
|-'!s f. MAPS f s == SEQ_WHEN(\x.\t.SCONS(f x)(MAPS f t))s' : thm


! val COMPOSE = new_closed_axiom ("COMPOSE",
>        '!f:'b->'c. !g: 'a->'b. f o g == \x.f(g x)');
- val COMPOSE = |-'!f g. f o g == \x.f(g x)' : thm
```

10.5.1   The recursion equations for the mapping functional

As we have seen before, the recursion equations for *MAPS* are derived from its axiom by applying the specialization rule.

```
! val MAPS_UU = SPEC 'UU:'a seq' MAPS;
- val MAPS_UU =
|-'!f. MAPS f UU == SEQ_WHEN(\x.\t.SCONS(f x)(MAPS f t))UU' : thm


! val MAPS_SCONS = SPEC 'SCONS x s' MAPS;
- val MAPS_SCONS =
|-'!f. MAPS f(SCONS x s) ==
        SEQ_WHEN(\x'.\t.SCONS(f x')(MAPS f t))(SCONS x s)'     : thm
```

We state and prove the desired recursion equations, thereby verifying that the axiom in terms of *SEQ_WHEN* is appropriate.

```
! set_goal([], '!f: 'a->'b.  MAPS f UU == UU  /\
```

```
>       (!x s. MAPS f(SCONS x s) == SCONS (f x) (MAPS f s))`);
1 subgoal
`!f. MAPS f UU == UU  /\
     (!x s. MAPS f(SCONS x s) == SCONS(f x)(MAPS f s))`

! expand (REWRITE_TAC [SEQ_WHEN_CLAUSES, MAPS_UU, MAPS_SCONS]);
goal proved

! val MAPS_CLAUSES = save_top_thm "MAPS_CLAUSES";
- val MAPS_CLAUSES = |-`!f. ...` : thm
```

10.5.2   Mapping preserves function composition

We now prove

$$MAPS(f \circ g) \equiv (MAPS\ f) \circ (MAPS\ g)\,,$$

an interesting result that can be regarded as part of the proof that *seq* is a functor
on the category of domains. Let *SEQ_TAC* be the structural induction tactic for
sequences; set the initial goal; strip its quantifiers using *GEN_TAC*.

```
! val SEQ_TAC = STRUCT_TAC "sequences" [];
- val SEQ_TAC = fn : (term -> tactic)

! set_goal([],
>    `!f:'b->'c. !g: 'a->'b. MAPS (f o g) == (MAPS f) o (MAPS g)`);
1 subgoal
`!f g. MAPS(f o g) == (MAPS f) o (MAPS g)`

! expand (REPEAT GEN_TAC);
1 subgoal
`MAPS(f o g) == (MAPS f) o (MAPS g)`
```

The proof will use structural induction. But first we must have a variable of
sequence type. By extensionality of functions, it is enough to prove

$$\forall s.\ MAPS(f \circ g)s \equiv (MAPS\ f) \circ (MAPS\ g)s$$

Applying *IMP_CHAIN_TAC* to the standard theorem *EQ_EXT* gives a tactic for extensionality. We must be careful here: the subgoal contains the variable $x : (\alpha)seq$;
elsewhere we have used the variable $x : \alpha$. These are distinct — variables are dis-
tinguished by type as well as by name — but are printed alike. Now invoke
structural induction on $x : (\alpha)seq$.

```
! expand (IMP_CHAIN_TAC EQ_EXT);
1 subgoal
'!x. MAPS(f o g)x == ((MAPS f) o (MAPS g))x'

! expand (SEQ_TAC 'x: 'a seq');
2 subgoals
'MAPS(f o g)(SCONS x' s) == ((MAPS f) o (MAPS g))(SCONS x' s)'
  ['MAPS(f o g)s == ((MAPS f) o (MAPS g))s']

'MAPS(f o g)UU == ((MAPS f) o (MAPS g))UU'
```

The induction formula is admissible. The two subgoals yield easily to rewriting, by the properties of *MAPS* and composition.

```
! expand (REWRITE_TAC [MAPS_CLAUSES, COMPOSE]);
goal proved
|-'MAPS(f o g)UU == ((MAPS f) o (MAPS g))UU'

previous subproof:
1 subgoal
'MAPS(f o g)(SCONS x' s) == ((MAPS f) o (MAPS g))(SCONS x' s)'
  ['MAPS(f o g)s == ((MAPS f) o (MAPS g))s']

! expand (ASM_REWRITE_TAC [MAPS_CLAUSES, COMPOSE]);
goal proved
.|-'MAPS(f o g)(SCONS x' s) == ((MAPS f) o (MAPS g))(SCONS x' s)'
|-'!x. MAPS(f o g)x == ((MAPS f) o (MAPS g))x'
|-'MAPS(f o g) == (MAPS f) o (MAPS g)'
|-'!f g. MAPS(f o g) == (MAPS f) o (MAPS g)'

! val MAPS_COMPOSE = save_top_thm "MAPS_COMPOSE";
- val MAPS_COMPOSE =
|-'!f g. MAPS(f o g) == (MAPS f) o (MAPS g)' : thm
```

Exercise 10.7 Explain precisely the pattern matching involved in the use of *IMP_CHAIN_TAC* above.

Exercise 10.8 Prove, informally or in LCF, that *MAPS* preserves the identity function: $MAPS(ID_\sigma) \equiv ID_{\sigma\,seq}$.

10.5.3   Generating an infinite sequence

This section introduces the functional *SEQ_OF*, which, given f and x, generates the sequence $[x, f(x), f(f(x)), \ldots]$. For example, *SEQ_OF(SUCC)*(1) generates

$[1, 2, 3, \dots]$.

We build the theory in a new session but could have continued the previous session since *sequences* is a parent theory.

```
# Cambridge LCF (RAL 1.3) #

! new_theory "SEQ_OF";

! new_parent "sequences";
Theory sequences loaded
```

Now *SEQ_OF* could be expressed by the recursion equation

$$SEQ\_OF(f)(x) \equiv SCONS(x)(SEQ\_OF(f)(fx))$$

but instead it is expressed as the fixed point of the functional *SEQ_OF_FUN*, since we will need fixed point induction. The type of *SEQ_OF* is bound to the ML variable *seq_of_ty*, which is used via antiquotation. Otherwise we would have to write complicated types.

```
! val seq_of_ty = ':('a->'a) -> 'a -> 'a seq';
- val seq_of_ty = ':('a -> 'a) -> ('a -> ('a)seq)' : type

! new_constant("SEQ_OF_FUN", ':^seq_of_ty -> ^seq_of_ty');

! new_constant("SEQ_OF", ':^seq_of_ty');

! val SEQ_OF_FUN = new_closed_axiom ("SEQ_OF_FUN",
>      'SEQ_OF_FUN == \sf:^seq_of_ty. \f x. SCONS x (sf f (f x))');
- val SEQ_OF_FUN = |-'SEQ_OF_FUN == \sf.\f.\x.SCONS x(sf f(f x))'
: thm

! val SEQ_OF = new_closed_axiom ("SEQ_OF",
>                'SEQ_OF : ^seq_of_ty == FIX SEQ_OF_FUN');
- val SEQ_OF = |-'SEQ_OF == FIX SEQ_OF_FUN' : thm
```

We prove and store the usual unfolding lemma.

```
! set_goal([], 'SEQ_OF == SEQ_OF_FUN SEQ_OF :^seq_of_ty');
1 subgoal
'SEQ_OF == SEQ_OF_FUN SEQ_OF'

! expand (REWRITE_TAC [SEQ_OF, FIX_EQ]);
goal proved
```

```
|-'SEQ_OF == SEQ_OF_FUN SEQ_OF'

! val SEQ_OF_UNFOLD = save_top_thm "SEQ_OF_UNFOLD";
- val SEQ_OF_UNFOLD = |-'SEQ_OF == SEQ_OF_FUN SEQ_OF' : thm
```

10.5.4   A theorem about *SEQ_OF* and *MAPS*

Informally, the theorem

$$SEQ\_OF(f)(f(x)) \equiv MAPS(f)(SEQ\_OF \ f \ x)$$

is true because both sides are equal to $[f(x), f(f(x)), f(f(f(x))), \ldots]$, but that is
no proof. A formal proof involves the recursive calls of *SEQ_OF*, which calls for
fixed point induction.

We enter the goal and substitute for *SEQ_OF*, so that induction takes place on
each occurrence of that function.

```
! set_goal([], '!f. !x:'a. SEQ_OF f (f x) == MAPS f (SEQ_OF f x)');
1 subgoal
'!f x. SEQ_OF f(f x) == MAPS f(SEQ_OF f x)'

! expand (SUBST_TAC [SEQ_OF]);
1 subgoal
'!f x. FIX SEQ_OF_FUN f(f x) == MAPS f(FIX SEQ_OF_FUN f x)'

! expand (INDUCT_TAC []
>            [ ('SEQ_OF_FUN:^seq_of_ty -> ^seq_of_ty', 'sf') ]);
2 subgoals
'!sf. (!f x. sf f(f x) == MAPS f(sf f x))  ==>
         (!f x. SEQ_OF_FUN sf f(f x) == MAPS f(SEQ_OF_FUN sf f x))'

'!f x. UU f(f x) == MAPS f(UU f x)'
```

The $\perp$ subgoal is provable by rewriting since *MAPS* is strict. The relevant
theorem is taken from the theory file.

```
! val MAPS_CLAUSES = theorem "sequences" "MAPS_CLAUSES";
- val MAPS_CLAUSES =
|-'!f. MAPS f UU == UU  /\
        (!x s. MAPS f(SCONS x s) == SCONS(f x)(MAPS f s))' : thm

! expand (REWRITE_TAC [MAPS_CLAUSES, MIN_COMB]);
goal proved
|-'!f x. UU f(f x) == MAPS f(UU f x)'
```

previous subproof:
1 subgoal
'!sf. (!f x. sf f(f x) == MAPS f(sf f x)) ==>
      (!f x. SEQ_OF_FUN sf f(f x) == MAPS f(SEQ_OF_FUN sf f x))'

The inductive subgoal needs rewriting: occurrences of *SEQ_OF_FUN* should be replaced by their bodies, then *MAPS* can be simplified. All this will take place in the consequent of the implication, so *STRIP_TAC* is used to strip quantifiers and move the antecedent into the assumptions.

! expand (REPEAT STRIP_TAC);
1 subgoal
'SEQ_OF_FUN sf f(f x) == MAPS f(SEQ_OF_FUN sf f x)'
  ['!f x. sf f(f x) == MAPS f(sf f x)']

! expand (ASM_REWRITE_TAC [SEQ_OF_FUN, MAPS_CLAUSES]);
goal proved
.|-'SEQ_OF_FUN sf f(f x) == MAPS f(SEQ_OF_FUN sf f x)'
|-'!sf. (!f x. sf f(f x) == MAPS f(sf f x)) ==>
        (!f x. SEQ_OF_FUN sf f(f x) == MAPS f(SEQ_OF_FUN sf f x))'
|-'!f x. FIX SEQ_OF_FUN f(f x) == MAPS f(FIX SEQ_OF_FUN f x)'
|-'!f x. SEQ_OF f(f x) == MAPS f(SEQ_OF f x)'

! val MAPS_SEQ_OF = save_top_thm "MAPS_SEQ_OF";
- val MAPS_SEQ_OF = |-'!f x. SEQ_OF f(f x) == MAPS f(SEQ_OF f x)'
: thm

Exercise 10.9 Prove this theorem by hand, giving a detailed description of the rewriting in the inductive step.

10.6   Project suggestions

These examples do not cover LCF in its full generality. The papers mentioned in the first chapter show the range of projects you can undertake.

In the theory of natural numbers, try introducing multiplication, subtraction, and division. Prove that multiplication is commutative, enjoys a distributive law, and is associative. Manna and Waldinger [64] describe theories of numbers, lists, trees, and so forth: try formalizing these in LCF.

Functional programs, whether they use strict or lazy evaluation, are easily expressed in PPλ. Burstall [14] demonstrates how to reason about programs using structural induction. Research on functional program development suggests LCF projects; for instance, see Bird [5,6] and Wand [99].

The abstract syntax of a simple programming language can be formalized using the structural induction commands. Its denotational semantics is a function over abstract syntax trees. It is now possible to prove the validity of program transformations. A harder project is to prove the correctness of a translator from one language to another.

Bibliography

Note: LNCS is Springer Lecture Notes in Computer Science.

[1] L. Aiello, M. Aiello, R. Weyhrauch, Pascal in LCF: semantics and examples of proof, *Theoretical Computer Science* **5** (1977), pages 135–177.

[2] H. P. Barendregt, *The Lambda Calculus: Its Syntax and Semantics* (North-Holland, 1984).

[3] J. Barwise, editor, *Handbook of Mathematical Logic* (North-Holland, 1977).

[4] J. Barwise, An introduction to first-order logic, *in*: Barwise [3], pages 5–46.

[5] R. S. Bird, The promotion and accumulation strategies in transformational programming, *ACM Transactions on Programming Languages and Systems* **6** (1984), pages 487–504. Addendum, *ACM Transactions on Programming Languages and Systems* **7** (1985), pages 490–492.

[6] R. S. Bird, Using circular programs to eliminate multiple traversals of data, *Acta Informatica* **21** (1984), pages 239–250.

[7] G. Birtwistle, J. Joyce, B. Liblong, T. Melham, R. Schediwy, Specification and VLSI design, *in*: G. J. Milne, P. A. Subrahmanyam, editors, *Formal Aspects of VLSI Design* (North Holland, 1986), pages 83–97.

[8] G. Birtwistle, P. A. Subrahmanyam, editors, *VLSI Specification, Verification and Synthesis* (Kluwer Academic Publishers, 1988).

[9] W. W. Bledsoe, D. W. Loveland, editors, *Automated Theorem Proving: After 25 Years* (American Mathematical Society, 1984).

[10] T. S. Blyth, *Categories* (Longman, 1986).

[11] G. Boolos, R. Jeffrey, *Computability and Logic* (Cambridge University Press, 1974).

[12] R. S. Boyer, J S. Moore, *A Computational Logic* (Academic Press, 1979).

[13] W. H. Burge, *Recursive Programming Techniques* (Addison-Wesley, 1975).

[14] R. M. Burstall, Proving properties of programs by structural induction, *Computer Journal* **12** (1969), pages 41–48.

[15] R. M. Burstall, J. A. Goguen, An informal introduction to specifications using Clear, *in*: R. S. Boyer, J S. Moore, *The Correctness Problem in Computer Science* (Academic Press, 1981), pages 185–213.

[16] R. Cartwright, J. Donahue, The semantics of lazy (and industrious) evaluation, *ACM Symposium on Lisp and Functional Programming* (1982), pages 253–264.

[17] E. Charniak, C. K. Riesbeck, D. V. McDermott, *Artificial Intelligence Programming* (Lawrence Erlbaum Associates, Hillsdale, New Jersey, 1980).

[18] P. Chisholm, Derivation of a parsing algorithm in Martin-Löf's theory of types, *Science of Computer Programming* 8 (1987), pages 1–42.

[19] A. J. Cohn, High level proof in LCF, *in*: W. H. Joyner, Jr., editor, *Fourth Workshop on Automated Deduction* (University of Texas at Austin, 1979), pages 73–80.

[20] A. J. Cohn, *Machine Assisted Proofs of Recursion Implementation*, Report CST-6-79, PhD Thesis, University of Edinburgh (1980).

[21] A. J. Cohn, The correctness of a precedence parsing algorithm in LCF, Report 21, Computer Laboratory, University of Cambridge (1982).

[22] A. J. Cohn, The equivalence of two semantic definitions: a case study in LCF, *SIAM Journal of Computing* 12 (1983), pages 267–285.

[23] A. J. Cohn, A proof of correctness of the Viper microprocessor: the first level, *in*: Birtwistle and Subrahmanyam [8]. Also Report 104, Computer Laboratory, University of Cambridge (1987).

[24] A. J. Cohn, M. J. C. Gordon, A mechanized proof of correctness of a simple counter, Report 94, Computer Laboratory, University of Cambridge (1986).

[25] A. J. Cohn, R. Milner, On using Edinburgh LCF to prove the correctness of a parsing algorithm, Report CSR-113-82, Department of Computer Science, University of Edinburgh (1982).

[26] R. L. Constable, S. F. Allen, H. M. Bromley, W. R. Cleaveland, J. F. Cremer, R. W. Harper, D. J. Howe, T. B. Knoblock, N. P. Mendler, P. Panagaden, J. T. Sasaki, S. F. Smith, *Implementing Mathematics with the Nuprl Proof Development System* (Prentice-Hall, 1986).

[27] Th. Coquand, G. Huet, Constructions: a higher order proof system for mechanizing mathematics, *in*: B. Buchberger, editor, *EUROCAL '85: European Conference on Computer Algebra*, Volume 1: *Invited lectures*, (Springer LNCS 203, 1985), pages 151–184.

[28] P. Dybjer, Category theory and programming language sematnics: an overview, *in*: D. Pitt, S. Abramsky, A. Poigné, and D. Rydeheard, editors, *Category Theory and Computer Programming* (Springer LNCS 240, 1986), pages 165–181.

[29] M. Dummett, *Elements of Intuitionism* (Oxford University Press, 1977).

[30] J. H. Gallier, *Logic for Computer Science: Foundations of Automatic Theorem Proving* (Harper & Row, 1986).

[31] M. J. C. Gordon, Representing a logic in the LCF metalanguage, *in*: D. Néel, editor, *Tools and Notions for Program Construction*, (Cambridge University Press, 1982), pages 163–185.

[32] M. J. C. Gordon, LCF_LSM: A system for specifying and verifying hardware, Report 41, Computer Laboratory, University of Cambridge (1983).

[33] M. J. C. Gordon, Proving a computer correct with the LCF_LSM hardware verification system, Report 42, Computer Laboratory, University of Cambridge (1983).

[34] M. J. C. Gordon, HOL: A machine oriented formulation of Higher Order Logic, Report 68, Computer Laboratory, University of Cambridge (1985).

[35] M. J. C. Gordon, Hardware verification by formal proof, *Silicon Design* **2** No. 9 (1985). Also Report 74, Computer Laboratory, University of Cambridge.

[36] M. J. C. Gordon, Why higher-order logic is a good formalism for specifying and verifying hardware, *in*: G. J. Milne, P. A. Subrahmanyam, editors, *Formal Aspects of VLSI Design* (North Holland, 1986), pages 153–177.

[37] M. J. C. Gordon, HOL: A proof generating system for higher-order logic, *in*: Birtwistle and Subrahmanyam [8]. Also Report 103, Computer Laboratory, University of Cambridge (1987).

[38] M. J. C. Gordon, A. J. Camilleri, T. F. Melham, Hardware verification using higher-order logic, *From H. D. L. Descriptions to Guaranteed Correct Circuit Designs* (Proceedings, IFIP, 1986). Also Report 91, Computer Laboratory, University of Cambridge.

[39] M. J. C. Gordon, J. M. J. Herbert, Formal hardware verification methodology and its application to a network interface chip, *IEE Proceedings* **133** (1986), pages 255–269.

[40] M. J. C. Gordon, J. Joyce, G. Birtwistle, Proving a computer correct in higher-order logic, Report 100, Computer Laboratory, University of Cambridge (1986).

[41] M. J. C. Gordon, R. Milner, C. P. Wadsworth, *Edinburgh LCF: A Mechanised Logic of Computation* (Springer LNCS 78, 1979).

[42] P. R. Halmos, *Naive Set Theory* (Van Nostrand, 1960).

[43] F. K. Hanna, N. Daeche, Purely functional implementation of a logic, *in*: J. H. Siekmann, editor, *8th International Conference on Automated Deduction* (Springer LNCS 230, 1986), pages 598–607.

[44] R. Harper, Introduction to Standard ML, Report ECS-LFCS-86-14, Laboratory for Foundations of Computer Science, University of Edinburgh (1986).

[45] R. Harper, D. B. MacQueen, R. Milner, Standard ML, Report ECS-LFCS-86-2, Laboratory for Foundations of Computer Science, University of Edinburgh (1986).

[46] J. M. J. Herbert, The application of formal specification and verification to a hardware design, *in*: C. J. Koomen, T. Moto-oka, editors, *Seventh International Conference on Computer Hardware Description Languages and their Applications* (North-Holland, 1985), pages 434–451.

[47] J. R. Hindley, J. P. Seldin, *Introduction to Combinators and λ-calculus* (Cambridge University Press, 1986).

[48] C. A. R. Hoare, J. C. Shepherdson, editors, *Mathematical Logic and Programming Languages* (Prentice-Hall, 1985).

[49] S. Holmström, Experiments and experiences with Edinburgh LCF, Report LPM-6, Department of Computer Sciences, Chalmers University, Göteborg, Sweden (1981).

[50] G. Huet, Confluent reductions: abstract properties and applications to term rewriting systems, *Journal of the Association for Computing Machinery* **27** (1980), pages 797–821.

[51] G. Huet, D. C. Oppen, Equations and rewrite rules: a survey, *in*: R. Book, editor, *Formal Language Theory: Perspectives and Open Problems* (Academic Press, 1980), pages 349–406.

[52] S. Igarashi, Admissibility of fixed-point induction in first-order logic of type theories, Report STAN-CS-72-287, Computer Science Department, Stanford University (1972). (Presented at *Symposium on Theoretical Programming*, Novosibirsk).

[53] F. V. Jensen, Inductive inference in reflexive domains, Report CSR-86-81, Department of Computer Science, University of Edinburgh (1981).

[54] F. V. Jensen, An LCF-system for automatic creation of theories for 1-constructible data types, Report CSR-87-81, Department of Computer Science, University of Edinburgh (1981).

[55] F. V. Jensen, K. G. Larsen, Recursively defined domains and their induction principles, Report CSR-176-84, Department of Computer Science, University of Edinburgh (1984).

[56] J.-P. Jouannaud, editor, *Rewriting Techniques and Applications* (Springer LNCS 202, 1985).

[57] G. Kahn, D. B. MacQueen, G. Plotkin, editors, *Semantics of Data Types* (Springer LNCS 173, 1984).

[58] K. G. Larsen, G. Winskel, Using information systems to solve recursive domain equations effectively, *in*: Kahn et al. [57], pages 109–129.

[59] J. Leszczyłowski, An experiment with 'Edinburgh LCF', *in*: W. Bibel, R. Kowalski, editors, *Fifth Conference on Automated Deduction*, (Springer LNCS 87, 1980), pages 170–181.

[60] J. Leszczyłowski, Theory of FP systems in Edinburgh LCF, *in*: J. Diaz, I. Ramos, editors, *Formalization of Programming Concepts*, (Springer LNCS 107, 1981), pages 374–386.

[61] S. Mac Lane, *Categories for the Working Mathematician* (Springer, 1971).

[62] Z. Manna, *Mathematical Theory of Computation* (McGraw-Hill, 1974).

[63] Z. Manna, R. Waldinger, Deductive synthesis of the unification algorithm, *Science of Computer Programming* **1** (1981), pages 5–48.

[64] Z. Manna, R. Waldinger, *The Logical Basis for Computer Programming: Volume I: Deductive Reasoning* (Addison-Wesley, 1985).

[65] P. Martin-Löf, Constructive mathematics and computer programming, *in*: Hoare and Shepherdson [48], pages 167–184.

[66] R. Milner, Implementation and applications of Scott's logic of continuous functions, *Conference on Proving Assertions About Programs, SIGPLAN* **1** (1972), pages 1–6.

[67] R. Milner, A theory of type polymorphism in programming, *Journal of Computer and System Sciences* **17** (1978), pages 348–375.

[68] R. Milner, The use of machines to assist in rigorous proof, *in*: Hoare and Shepherdson [48], pages 77–88.

[69] R. Milner, L. Morris, M. Newey, A logic for computable functions with reflexive and polymorphic types, *IRIA Conference on Proving and Improving Programs* (1975), pages 371–394.

[70] R. Milner, R. Weyhrauch, Proving compiler correctness in a mechanized logic, *in*: B. Meltzer, D. Michie, editors, *Machine Intelligence 7* (Wiley, 1972), pages 51–70.

[71] B. Q. Monahan, *Data Type Proofs using Edinburgh LCF*, PhD Thesis, University of Edinburgh (1984).

[72] K. Mulmuley, The mechanization of existence proofs of recursive predicates, *in*: R. E. Shostak, editor, *Seventh Conference on Automated Deduction* (Springer LNCS 170, 1984), pages 460–475.

[73] K. Mulmuley, *Full Abstraction and Semantic Equivalence*, Report CMU-CS-85-148, PhD thesis, Carnegie-Mellon University (1984).

[74] B. Nordström, J. Smith, Propositions and specifications of programs in Martin-Löf's type theory, *BIT* **24** (1984), pages 288–301.

[75] L. C. Paulson, A higher-order implementation of rewriting, *Science of Computer Programming* **3** (1983), pages 119–149.

[76] L. C. Paulson, Verifying the unification algorithm in LCF, *Science of Computer Programming* **5** (1985), pages 143–170.

[77] L. C. Paulson, Deriving structural induction in LCF, *in*: Kahn et al. [57], pages 197–214.

[78] L. C. Paulson, Lessons learned from LCF: a survey of natural deduction proofs, *Computer Journal* **28** (1985), pages 474–479.

[79] L. C. Paulson, Proving termination of normalization functions for conditional expressions, *Journal of Automated Reasoning* **2** (1986), pages 63–74.

[80] L. C. Paulson, Natural deduction as higher-order resolution, *Journal of Logic Programming* **3** (1986), pages 237–258.

[81] K. Petersson, A programming system for type theory, Report 21, Department of Computer Sciences, Chalmers University, Göteborg, Sweden (1982).

[82] G. D. Plotkin, Types and partial functions, Handwritten notes, Department of Computer Science, University of Edinburgh (1986).

[83] D. Prawitz, *Natural Deduction: A Proof-theoretical Study* (Almquist and Wiksell, 1965).

[84] J. C. Reynolds, Mathematical semantics, *in*: B. W. Arden, editor, *What Can Be Automated? The Computer Science and Engineering Research Study* (MIT Press, 1980), pages 261–288.

[85] D. Sannella, R. M. Burstall, Structured theories in LCF, *in*: G. Ausiello, M. Protasi, editors, *CAAP '83: Eighth Colloquium on Trees in Algebra and Programming* (Springer LNCS 159, 1983), pages 377–391.

[86] D. A. Schmidt, Natural deduction theorem proving in set theory, Report CSR-142-83, Department of Computer Science, University of Edinburgh (1983).

[87] D. A. Schmidt, A programming notation for tactical reasoning, *in*: R. E. Shostak, editor, *Seventh Conference on Automated Deduction* (Springer LNCS 170, 1984), pages 445–459.

[88] D. A. Schmidt, *Denotational Semantics: A Methodology for Language Development* (Allyn and Bacon, 1986).

[89] D. S. Scott, A type-theoretic alternative to CUCH, ISWIM, OWHY, Typed notes, Oxford (1969).

[90] D. S. Scott, Data types as lattices, *SIAM Journal of Computing* **5** (1976), pages 522–587.

[91] D. S. Scott, Domains for denotational semantics, *in*: M. Nielsen, E. M. Schmidt, *Automata, Languages and Programming* (Springer LNCS 140, 1982), pages 577–613.

[92] D. S. Scott, C. A. Gunter, Semantic domains, *in*: J. van Leeuwen, editor, *Handbook of Theoretical Computer Science* (North-Holland, in press).

[93] M. B. Smyth, G. D. Plotkin, The category-theoretic solution to recursive domain equations, *SIAM Journal of Computing* **11** (1982), pages 761–783.

[94] S. Sokołowski, A note on tactics in LCF, Report CSR-140-83, Department of Computer Science, University of Edinburgh (1983).

[95] S. Sokołowski, Soundness of Hoare's logic: an automatic proof using LCF, *ACM Transactions on Programming Languages and Systems* **9** (1987), pages 100–120.

[96] J. E. Stoy, *Denotational Semantics: The Scott-Strachey Approach to Programming Language Theory* (MIT Press, 1977).

[97] D. A. Turner, Functional programs as executable specifications, *in*: Hoare and Shepherdson [48], pages 29–54.

[98] D. A. Turner, Miranda: A non-strict functional language with polymorphic types, *in*: J.-P. Jouannaud, editor, *Functional Programming Languages and Computer Architecture* (Springer LNCS 201, 1985), pages 1–16.

[99] M. Wand, Continuation-based program transformation strategies, *Journal of the Association for Computing Machinery* **27** (1980), pages 164–180.

[100] Å. Wikström, *Functional Programming using ML* (Prentice-Hall, 1987).

Index